Teresa de la Parra

Teresa de la Parra:
A Literary Life

By

RoseAnna Mueller

For Teresa,
The works of another Teresa
who understood the importance
of women in history.
con cariño
RoseAnn

CAMBRIDGE
SCHOLARS

P U B L I S H I N G

Teresa de la Parra:
A Literary Life ,
by RoseAnna Mueller

This book first published 2012

Cambridge Scholars Publishing

12 Back Chapman Street, Newcastle upon Tyne, NE6 2XX, UK

British Library Cataloguing in Publication Data
A catalogue record for this book is available from the British Library

ISBN (10): 1-4438-3799-7, ISBN (13): 978-1-4438-3799-6

TABLE OF CONTENTS

ACKNOWLEDGEMENTS

This book was years in the making and would not have been possible without the help of several institutions and helpful and generous people. I am indebted to the Fulbright Association for the Teaching/Research Grant that got me interested in Teresa de la Parra when I taught Latin American Women's Literature at the University of the Andes, Instituto de Investigaciones Literarias "Gonzalo Picón Febres", Mérida, Venezuela, 2002-2003. Gregory Zambrano and the students I met there inspired me to continue with my study of one of their outstanding authors.

Friends and colleagues in Mérida supported and encouraged the idea of writing a book about one of their favorite authors in English. Special thanks to Maen Puerta, who brought me what I needed just at the right time. Laura Febres shared her enthusiasm for de la Parra and took me on a personal tour of Caracas. We visited the Panteón Nacional searching for de la Parra's tomb, and to our dismay, we found the author's headstone under the carpet. Douglas Bohórquez gave me his book, which suggested the next step. He suggested that what remained to be done was to tie the author's life to her work, her texts to her biography, and to join the fragmentary criticism about de la Parra together. He saw the need to link her relationships to her fiction. Her letters were incomplete; her family had censored some and burned others. He wondered what had happened to the notes for the unwritten novel about Bolívar. De la Parra's work rejected conventional forms and constantly searched for ways to renew and create a new kind of writing, from the intimate and personal, to the collective and the oral, but that she had yet to be assimilated into literary tradition. That is the challenge I took up in writing this book.

In Mérida I was assisted by Andrés Seijas, University of the Andes, who helped with the translation of the *Three Colombian Lectures*. Thanks, Andrés. Michele Lee, at Centro Venezolano Americano deserves special thanks for smoothing the way on many occasions.

I extend my thanks to Karen Osborne, who first looked over the proposal and helped to strengthen it, to Jeanne Petrolle for her encouragement, and to Clark Hulse, who helped to send the manuscript on its way. Thanks to Olympia Gonzalez for her help translating a particularly difficult stanza of Amarilis' poetry.

The Undergraduate Research Mentorship Initiative, sponsored by Dean Deborah Holdstein, the School of Liberal Arts and Sciences at Columbia College Chicago, provided me with the opportunity to work with my former student Samantha Blattner, who helped me to research and organize the materials. For your many hours of work, gracias, Sam.

Lisa Brock, Chair, Humanities, History and Social Sciences, Columbia College Chicago, supported a sabbatical leave, spring 2011, and steered me in the right direction.

A grant from The Center for Teaching Excellence, along with the sabbatical allowed me to return to Mérida, Venezuela, spring 2011.

The staff at Columbia College Library was always helpful in obtaining materials. My special thanks to Roland Hansen and Maryam Foukuri.

Boris Isakov provided his technical know-how and was a tremendous help with the illustrations.

Thanks to my son, Chris, who always reminds me to strike a balance.

Everlasting gratitude and thanks to Bob, my faithful travelling companion of many years who shares in and enriches our adventures. What's next?

PREFACE

FOUND IN TRANSLATION

I read Bertie Acker's excellent translation of Teresa de la Parra's *Ifigenia: diario de una señorita que escribió porque se fastidiaba, (Iphigenia: The diary of a young lady who wrote because she was bored) (1924)* while designing a syllabus for a graduate course on Latin American Women Writers I was to teach at the Universidad de los Andes, Mérida, Venezuela during a Fulbright Teaching/Research Grant in 2002-2003. When I arrived in Mérida, I realized that the course I planned to teach would be a new experience for the students. The course was "Representative Hispanic American Women," the name the director of the Instituto de Investigaciones Gonzalo Picón Febres gave it. I wanted to include a Venezuelan woman writer. I happened on *Iphigenia,* read it and found it amusing and entertaining. I fell in love with the author's style, and it was a good story. I included the book in the syllabus. As soon as I got to Mérida, I bought de la Parra's complete works, read the novel in Spanish and enjoyed it all over again. I read de la Parra's second novel, *Mama Blanca's Memoirs,* a collection of sketches, and loved that, too. De la Parra became the subject of my research for the grant. I wanted to learn more about this versatile author. To better prepare for the course I was teaching, I read de la Parra's *Tres conferencias,* the talks she delivered in Bogotá in 1930. Since most of the students in my class had read *Ifigenia,* I had to find a way to teach it from a new perspective, especially since several of the students had read the book in high school and some wanted to make *Ifigenia* the focus of their term papers. The *Tres conferencias* worked their way into our class discussions since they lent themselves to women's roles in Latin American society, and de la Parra mentions several women writers, pausing to make her audience appreciate the literary works of Sor Juana Inés de la Cruz, Madre Castillo and the anonymous poet known as Amarilis.

De la Parra's works have begun to attract more attention and appreciation, and several Venezuelan critics call her a national treasure. I was lucky to meet with some of these critics, and they have contributed to my understanding of this complex woman. Then I discovered that Iván

Feo had turned *Ifigenia* into a film in 1986, which was being shown on Venezuelan television while I was there.

When I began this study, I thought the closest writer in the English language to compare Teresa de la Parra with would be Virginia Woolf, but as I re-read de la Parra's first novel I found that the Venezuelan writer had more in common with Jane Austen, Edith Wharton and Katherine Mansfield. Like Austen, de la Parra wrote about polite society and its preoccupation with class, manners and making good matches for its daughters. Both authors use gentle humor to poke fun at contemporary manners, and both are not above showing their heroines as less than perfect, naïve at first, and unable to see their imperfections. Ultimately, they learn how to get on in their societies, and Austen's heroines learn about themselves and often make happy matches. Unfortunately, as the title of de la Parra's novel implies, her heroine will have to make sacrifices as she herself becomes one.

De la Parra's literary contributions can be approached in several ways: her contribution to her own national Venezuelan literature, to Latin American literature, and to women's literature. In this study I hope to provide an overview of a writer whose novels were widely read and have been translated into many languages. Because English translations of *Ifigenia* and *Las memorias de Mamá Blanca* exist, the aim of this work is to make some of the criticism written in Spanish available to an English-speaking audience and to translate some of de la Parra's writings unavailable in English. This includes some of her letters, especially the ones that contextualize her work by shedding light on her published works and her plans for her future work. Her short stories were experimental works-in-progress, and only one has been translated into English. The lectures she delivered in Colombia and Cuba are more than a survey of Latin American women's contributions to the formation of Latin America, and have not been translated in their entirety into English. These were very popular lectures that she delivered several times due to public demand. Her associations and relationships with various members of the intelligentsia of her generation made her one of the first female public intellectuals. De la Parra was way ahead of her time in several ways which I hope this book will demonstrate.

CHAPTER ONE

A HEROINE IN THE NOVEL OF HER OWN LIFE

"You and I—all of us who, moving through the world, have some talents and some sorrows—are heroes and heroines in the novels of our own lives, which is nicer and a thousand times better than written novels" (*Iphigenia* 10).

There are two biographies about Teresa de la Parra: *Between Flight and Longing: The Journey of Teresa de la Parra* by Louis Antoine Lemaître, and María Fernanda Palacios's *Teresa de la Parra*. Perhaps the best introduction to the author is in the letter she wrote to García Prada[1] when he asked for her permission to publish her second novel, *Mama Blanca's Memoirs* (1929), for educational purposes. Despite the fact that she mistakenly stated in the letter that she was born in Venezuela, it gives a succinct summary of her life. Carlos García Prada, an assistant professor of Spanish at the University of Washington, was taken with both of de la Parra's novels and wanted to use *Ifigenia, diario de una señorita que escribió porque se fastidiaba* (1924), as a model of good literature for his Spanish students. De la Parra wrote this letter:

To Señor García Prada
Paris, May 5, 1931
Washington

I was born in Venezuela to a large family of six children. I spent most of my early childhood on a sugar plantation in Caracas. Many of the memories from my early childhood are contained in *Mama Blanca's Memoirs*. My father died when I was eight years old and my mother moved our family to a province in Spain to live near our maternal grandmother to be educated. Both my grandmother and mother belonged, in their outlook and in their customs, to the established colonial society of Caracas. Therefore, in my late childhood and adolescence I had a strict Catholic upbringing. Corpus Christi processions, Holy Week, Marian feast days, and other holy feast days of the Catholic Church, along with walks in the country, were my only celebrations and social outlets. I returned to Venezuela when I was eighteen years old. I spent a lot of time in the countryside reading as much as possible. It was in Caracas that I first came into contact with the world and society. I observed the continual conflict of the new mentality of young women who traveled and read, but who lived bound to old assumptions and to the customs of an earlier age. They were ruled by the old values but did not believe in them and longed, in their hearts, for an independent life and ideas, until they married, gave them up, and reverted to the old ideas, thanks to motherhood. This eternal female conflict with its end in renunciation gave me the idea for *Iphigenia.* Because the novel was critical of men and was opposed to established ideas, it was not well received in my country. Conservative Catholics in Venezuela and Colombia deemed the novel to be dangerous to young girls, since they enjoyed seeing themselves portrayed by the heroine with her aspirations and her limitations and sided with her. The novel was attacked and defended by both sides, which contributed to its readership. In 1923 I moved to Paris, and I have lived here since. In 1928 I wrote my second book, *Mama Blanca's Memoirs,* which, unlike *Iphigenia,* was very well received by the traditionalists but disappointed the female readers of *Iphigenia,* who missed María Eugenia Alonso, the heroine sacrificed to custom. I am currently studying colonial Latin American history, which I would like to write about some day *(Obra* 599-510).[2]

Ana Teresa Parra Sanojo, who took the pen name Teresa de la Parra, was born on October 5, 1889 in Paris to a Venezuelan couple.[3] She was the first daughter born to Rafael Parra Hernaíz and Isabel Sanojo Ezpelosin de Parra. She lived much of her life in Europe, but always considered herself to be Venezuelan, and such was her identification with Venezuela that in the letter to García Prada, she erroneously claimed that she was born in Venezuela, whereas her birth certificate states that she was born in Paris. Today she is considered one of the most distinguished Venezuelan authors, and her works are based on her time spent in Caracas *(Iphigenia,* 1924), and her childhood on a hacienda near Caracas *(Mama Blanca's Memoirs,* 1929). She described her upbringing and her experiences in Venezuela in a new style free of the criollismo or picturesque style in vogue at the time.

De la Parra was born in Paris because her father, Rafael Parra Hernaíz, was posted as the Venezuelan consul to Berlin, but the family lived in Paris at Avenue Wagram Number 7 bis. On February 1 she was baptized in the Church of the Madeleine, Paris, and her uncle Antonio (the inspiration for Tio Pancho in *Iphigenia)* was her godfather. Her older brothers were Luis Felipe and Miguel. Her younger sisters were Isabelita, Elia, and María del Pilar. In the family records her father wrote, "We returned on the 25th of August, 1890. We went to 'Tazón' on the 22nd of September the same year and settled in Caracas the first of September,

1891." Ana Teresa was two at the time, and she spent her early childhood in Tazon, the family hacienda, which she used as the source for her second novel. Her sister María described the young Ana Teresa as a daydreamer with green cat's eyes.

Casa Teresa de la Parra, Caracas. Photo by the author.

From 1890 to 1897 the family lived in Tazón, the inspiration for Piedra Azul in *Mama Blanca's Memoirs*. Her father's death on December 24, 1898 from a serious intestinal infection brought an end to her idyllic life on the hacienda and began what her biographer Lemaître calls her journey of longing and nostalgia. Her uncle, Rafael's brother Miguel, died two days later. Following the death of her father, de la Parra, her mother moved the family to Godella, near Valencia, Spain, where Teresa was educated in a religious school administered by nuns, the Colegio de las Damas del Sagrado Corazón. There she received an education appropriate to a young woman of her station. She also read contemporary authors Guy de Maupassant and Valle Inclán, who would influence her writing. De la Parra owed much to her Catholic education. It instilled in her a love of language and literature, fed her rich imagination, and introduced her to contemplation and submission, which led to her search for an ideal inner life. In her school days she was immersed in the writings of Cervantes and the mystical writings of Santa Teresa of Avila. She learned to speak fluent and unaccented French. The life of retreats, prayer, and spiritual exercises she experienced during her Catholic school education never left her. She was an excellent student, and in 1904 she was awarded highest honors and a green ribbon. In 1908 she won the first prize for her poem commemorating the day of the beatification of the Venerable Mother Magdalena Sophia Barat, and the poem was published in the *Bulletin of the Sacred Heart.*

Following her return from Spain in 1910, de la Parra lived an uneventful life in Caracas, until 1922. Her Venezuelan biographer María Fernanda Palacios calls this a prolonged period of adolescence while *Iphigenia* was incubating. Her life, like those of most young women at the time, could be summarized as waiting for death or matrimony. There was tension between high society, the descendants of the original founders of the city, and the members of a new society whose wealth and status depended on the political connections of the Gómez regime and the booming oil industry. There was a preference for all things French. Paris lent a sophisticated tone to Caracas society. Mercedes Galindo, a young married woman in *Iphigenia,* serves as the model for rich caraqueños who traveled back and forth from France, acquired Parisian art and furnishings, and spoke French at their soirees. Venezuelans considered France to be their spiritual home, and there are references to French products—wines, perfumes, cosmetics and fashionable clothing—in *Iphigenia* that were coveted at the time.

Palacios can only speculate on how de la Parra spent her time between the ages of eighteen and thirty-three. Life for women in Caracas in the 1910s revolved around public holidays, attending Sunday mass, private celebrations and endless rounds of social calls. De la Parra attended dances, watched films at the Cine Rialto, attended charity functions, went to the opera at the Opera Municipal, attended mass at the Caracas Cathedral or at the nearby Church of Las Mercedes, and generally grew bored. By the time she was twenty-six she was still keeping up her societal obligations, but was spending more time reading in her room. She read French novels *pour jeunes filles*, and she makes fun of these poorly written, sentimental novels in *Iphigenia*. Her literary influences were Gustave Flaubert, Marie-Henri Beyle (Stendhal), Guy de Maupassant, and contemporary authors Pierre Loti, Maurice Maeterlink, Alphonse Daudet, Anatole France, and the French women writers Gyp, Marcelle Tynaire, Sidonie-Gabrielle Colette and Anne de Noailles. She was especially fond of the novel *Juan Cristobal* by Romain Rolland, and she was profoundly influenced by Rolland's works.

After the family returned from Spain, de la Parra's sisters married, but she did not, which became a source of worry for her conservative mother. De la Parra was a beautiful woman, but according to Palacios she was too educated, and too outspoken on some issues, despite her beauty. Juan Liscano recalls, "Fragments of biographical anecdotes related to me by my mother set her in motion, dressed as she was ten years ago, wearing a wide-brim hat, her green eyes flashing in its shadow" ("Testimony" in *Mama Blanca's Memoirs* 121). He continues his recollection, "The image of Teresa is that of a modern woman from the twenties. She is smoking with a cigarette holder, she is wearing pajamas; she is elegant" (125). Mariano Picón Salas described de la Parra as "so beautiful a woman, who could be seen at all parties with her splendid eyes and her bearing of a young Spanish marquise who dressed in Paris and could tell us about episodes and anecdotes that dated back a century, because she had heard them from grandmothers and old servants.[4]

After graduating, she traveled to Paris in 1915 before returning to Venezuela. There she wrote some short stories under the pen name Fru-Fru. Supposedly this was the sound of silk swishing against silk, but the name also suggests frivolousness. Later on, her first short stories were published in *El Universal* and in other Parisian magazines. Articles published at this time include: "An Indian Gospel: Buddha and the Leper" and "Lotus Flower: a Japanese Legend." Her imaginative and fantastical stories "The Hermit in the Clock," "The Genie of the Letter Scale," and the "Story of Miss Dust-Mote, Sun Dancer," were published together for the first time in *Obra* (1982), edited by Velia Bosch. It was these magazine articles and short stories that paved the way for writing *Iphigenia*. Like María Eugenia's long letter and diary in *Iphigenia,* Lemaître suggested that de la Parra's writing was prompted by her boredom, and he believes her pen name, Fru-Fru, reflected an under-appreciation of her own work.

Her friendship with Emilia Ibarra, Guzman Blanco's sister-in-law, began in 1913.[5] Emilia Ibarra (the inspiration for Mercedes Galindo in *Iphigenia*), twenty years her senior, became her patron and de la Parra lived with her for eight years. Ibarra's household was not as strict as de la Parra's family's, and Ibarra frequently hosted salons and tertulias, literary gatherings that helped to spark de la Parra's literary career. Ibarra was widowed in 1916. She died childless and left her entire inheritance to de la Parra after her death in 1924. This guaranteed that de la Parra could live as she liked and wherever she chose. The relationship between the two was one of friendship, devotion, protection and tenderness, and de la Parra referred to Ibarra as "her second mother." She would continue to grieve Ibarra's death for the rest of her life. Inheriting Ibarra's fortune, however, would allow her to live an independent life.

In 1920 she published *Diario de una caraqueña por el lejano oriente,* or *The Diary of a Woman from Caracas through the Far East* based on the letters her sister María, the real traveler, was mailing to her, in *Actualidades,* the literary magazine edited by Rómulo Gallegos. Her sister María married Marc Bunimovich, who worked for City Bank in New York. In 1919 the couple travelled to Japan, China and Manchuria. As Teresa received her sister's letters, aware that oriental themes were popular with the French Symbolists, she rewrote María's letters in the form of a travelogue. De la Parra also wrote for the weekly *La lectura semanal,* whose editor was José Rafael Pocaterra.

She made her first public speaking appearance in 1921 when the Prince of Bourbon visited Venezuela. That year was the centenary celebration of the 1821 Battle of Carabobo,[6] and *El Nuevo Diario* asked her to write an address for King Alfonso XII of Spain's visit to Venezuela. She was declared a "very distinguished writer" (Lemaître 62), and she wrote the introductory greeting "La Madre España" or "Mother Spain" for this occasion. The Infanta Doña Paz de Bourbon had written a greeting to Venezuelan women, to which de la Parra was invited to respond. (De la Parra was happy to report later that the Infanta found *Iphigenia* so funny she laughed loudly enough to summon her maid.) After delivering this speech, de la Parra was praised for her charming prose and her profound thinking.

In 1922 she won the Outstanding Prize in the National Short Story contest sponsored by *El Luchador,* Ciudad Bolívar, for her short story, "Mama X," later integrated into *Iphigenia.* Her experience on her return to Caracas provided the raw material for the novel which she started writing in 1922 in Macuto, a popular beach community about thirty kilometers from Caracas. She describes how she wrote the novel in a letter to Vicente

Lecuna, April, 1932. She read parts of the novel aloud to Ibarra and to her friends, Rafael Carias and Carmen Helena de la Casas. Later in life, she recalled 1922 as her ideal year. Parts of the novel were published on July 4, 1922 in *La lectura semanal* #12, edited by José Rafael Pocaterra as *Diario de una señorita que se fastidia,* or *The Diary of a Young Lady Who is Bored,*[7] and for the first time she signed her work as Teresa de la Parra.

De la Parra traveled to Paris in 1923 to enter her novel in a contest in which 70 entries had been submitted. While there, she struck up friendships with Latin-American diplomats and writers like Simón Barceló, Zérega Fombona, Ventura García Calderón and Gonzalo Zaldumbide, among others. Her life now revolved around various diplomatic circles and social events. At the time, many of the diplomats were intellectuals and embassies were worlds frequented by translators, newspaper writers, and editors of literary journals such as *Les Nouvelles Litteraraires.* It was within this milieu that she met writers such as Miguel de Unamuno, Alfonso Reyes, Gómez de la Serna, and her future translator Francis de Miomandre. She later translated his short stories but despaired that they lost a lot in translation.

Unfortunately, Emilia Ibarra, de la Parra's friend, mentor and patron, died in Paris in 1924, just a few months before the publication of *Iphigenia* in its entirety. The devastated author dedicated the novel to her: "To you, dear absent one, in whose shadow this book flowered little by little. To that clear light from your eyes that always lit the writing with hope, and also to the white, cold peace of your two crossed hands that will never turn its pages, I dedicate this book."

As an independent woman living in Paris, she dedicated herself to seeing the typical tourist sites. She took classes in elocution and diction and attended art lectures at the Louvre and literary lectures and readings at the Societé des Annales, where she heard the writers she had read in her youth. She took long walks in the Luxembourg Gardens and the Tuileries, and her afternoons ended with her taking tea with other Venezuelans (Palacios 65).

A year before *Iphigenia's* publication in 1924, de la Parra wrote a long letter to Venezuelan dictator Juan Vicente Gómez asking for financial assistance to publish the novel.[8] She received no reply. She would later be taken to task for writing this letter. She managed to get her novel published without the help of the dictator, and the first edition in Spanish of *Ifigenia* was published in 1924. The 6,000 copies printed sold out on the first day and the manuscript of the novel circulated among her friends. At thirty-four, de la Parra found herself at the brink of fame and independence, thanks to her heroine María Eugenia, who, as Palacios points out, achieved neither. She was awarded 10,000 francs for the novel as a prize sponsored by Casa Editora Franco-Ibero-Americana de Paris.

After Ibarra's death de la Parra travelled to Geneva. It was a summer of mourning, and she tried to distract herself by taking car trips. This was also the year of her secret engagement to Gonzalo Zaldumbide. In October, she returned to Caracas to settle the estate Ibarra left her. Her inheritance included Ibarra's house on Las Mercedes and six other rental properties, and stocks in the Banco de Venezuela. She claimed after writing *Iphigenia,* inheriting this estate was the most important thing that had happened in her life (Palacios 67).

Statue of Teresa de la Parra by Carmen Cecilia Caballero de Blanch, Parque los Caobos, Caracas. Photo by Veronidae.

When she returned to Venezuela for a brief time to settle her inheritance in 1925, she wrote to Gonzalo Zaldumbide, with whom she had an intimate amorous relationship. Her correspondence with Zaldumbide describes their relationship as it progressed from an infatuation, to love, to a lasting friendship. Twenty years after her death, Zaldumbide confessed to Díaz Sanchez that de la Parra was the only woman he ever loved (Palacios 75). They first met in 1923 through Zaldumbide's friend, Alfonso Reyes. Zaldumbide was forty and single and de la Parra was thirty-five. Following the custom of the times, de la Parra was always escorted when she attended lectures, went to cafes or visited friends in their homes. When she travelled to Geneva that June (1925) to attend a meeting of the Society of Nations, she wrote him flirty, seductive letters: "I have to go to Paris to get dressed (don't be alarmed, I'm not undressed, merely badly dressed)." By August she had dropped the Ud.

(the formal form of address in Spanish) and began calling him Lillo. They began their romantic relationship in his apartment. She wrote in a letter that she feared "what the butler saw." There followed a six-day-long romantic escapade, a car trip through Bordeaux, Garrone, Bayonne, and Guéthery, a little town outside San Juan de Luz, where María and her mother were living. Zaldumbide discreetly stayed at a hotel in Biarritz. In September, before she left for Venezuela, she ripped out a page from a book and scribbled, "As always, I am thinking of you: Guéthery, then Bayonne, all those dear little towns of love and car trips, how happy I am we are seeing each other, without it I would have embarked with sad thoughts." Zaldumbide had given her his ring to seal the commitment, de la Parra later returned it through her sister María, and in Caracas Lola Ibarra gave it back to her (Palacios 78). In total, she wrote him at least five letters from Venezuela. Her letter to Zaldumbide on November 16, 1933 shows that they kept up their loving correspondence.

After settling Emilia Ibarra's estate, she returned to Paris and she and Zaldumbide met again and continued to share their intimate, family and financial details. Palacios believes that Zaldumbide took the place of Ibarra in de la Parra's heart; he replaced her and became the man in her life (79). Gossip about them circulated in Caracas, which de la Parra denied. On March 18, 1926 Zaldumbide married Isabel Rosales Pareja, the daughter of an Ecuadorian diplomat. He later claimed it was a marriage of laziness, and that de la Parra had run away from him. They met again a few months later, and he claimed he loved her more than ever. There were more secret meetings and many letters and the affair lasted four more years.

In 1926, de la Parra began writing her second novel, *Mama Blanca's Memoirs,* in Vevey, Switzerland, at her sister Isabelita's house. She also became president of a literary society in Paris. The next year she prepared the second edition of *Iphigenia* (Bendelac 1928) with additions and corrections. As a participant in the Latin Press Conference, she traveled to Cuba for the first time in 1927 and delivered a series of lectures on Simón Bolívar. These talks inspired her to write an alternative biography of The Liberator, and she threw herself into the study of colonial Latin American history and began her correspondence with Vicente Lecuna, a noted historian. De la Parra hoped that her biography of Bolívar would inspire a spiritual regeneration in Venezuela, and felt that writing this novel from a woman's point of view would further the cause. She also identified with Bolívar, with whom she would share the same fate, since he died of tuberculosis at forty-seven, and she would die of the same disease at the same age. In a letter written on May 18, 1930 to Don Vicente Lecuna, de la Parra wrote that she thought many women had inspired and animated Bolívar. "From his black nursemaid Matea to Manuelita Saenz, his last love, Bolívar could not live without the image of a woman to inspire him, to console him during his periods of melancholy, and to see through their eyes and look within to see his own genius" (*Obra* 514).

While in Cuba to deliver her lectures, de la Parra began her friendship with the Cuban folklorist Lydia Cabrera.[9] The two women first met in 1924 when de la Parra was on board the *Macoris,* on her way to Venezuela and France by way of Havana. Lydia Cabrera, a Cuban anthropologist, was writing a manuscript on Afro-Cuban folklore. The research later led to Cabrera's preservation of the African influence in Cuba through her collection of *Cuentos Negros de Cuba,* which she would dedicate to de la Parra. After completing her secondary studies Cabrera left for Paris in 1922 to study painting, art and Oriental culture.

When de la Parra and Cabrera first met, the former was thirty-four and Lydia was ten years her junior. They became lifelong friends and collaborated on literary and other projects from 1927 onward. Cabrera was with de la Parra when she died of tuberculosis in 1936. Teresa considered Lydia her younger sister, and they shared many interests and traveled together. "Lydia, the wizened younger sister, smoothed out as much of the obstructive and the treacherous from Teresa's physical path as she could, and their shared interests were many" (Lemaître 198). In a letter to Rafael Carias, de la Parra describes her travels in Italy with Cabrera, whom she described as "intelligent, a good artist, whom I love and with whom I share the same tastes." When de la Parra wanted to return to Venezuela to get some background for her novel about Bolívar, she patiently waited until Cabrera recovered from an illness. Palacios describes the relationship between Cabrera and de la Parra like that of a mother or an older sister (89). Perhaps de la Parra assumed the role Ibarra played in her own life in her relationship with Cabrera.

The reticence of family and friends on the nature of the relationship between de la Parra and Cabrera, and the absence of a marriage or an acknowledged relationship with a man has left many questions concerning de la Parra's sexuality unanswered.[10] In an interview with Laura Febres, a leading de la Parra critic in Caracas, in 2003, Febres dismissed the idea that Lydia and Teresa had a lesbian relationship.[11] She attributes the silence about any romantic attachments on the part of de la Parra to the fact that she was in love with Zaldumbide. Cabrera herself claimed that de la Parra preferred platonic relationships. She resisted both her family's pressure to marry as well as pressure to be more militantly feminist. At the time of her death, Febres claims that de la Parra's family burned letters and other documents that would have clarified the matter of her sexuality. In 1988 Febres interviewed Cabrera when the Cuban anthropologist visited Venezuela.[12] Febres recounted how Cabrera pointed out to her that the dead can continue to influence us. Cabrera wanted to dispel the false image of de la Parra as a frivolous woman. On the contrary, the author read and thought and was concerned with philosophy and spiritual knowledge. Cabrera was with de la Parra when the author came down with tuberculosis, but Cabrera was not afraid of being infected with TB because she thought she had been exposed to the disease as a child and therefore had acquired immunity to it. Febres pointed out that being infected with tuberculosis was like having AIDS in those days. Febres quoted Cabrera as saying "You did not deserve her" meaning that Venezuelans did not appreciate Teresa de la Parra as a writer. But that, according to Febres, seems to be the fate of Venezuelans, Simón Rodríquez, Andrés Bello, and Simón Bolívar, were all exiled if not geographically, then in the minds of their countrymen, and suffered at the hands of their contemporaries. These outstanding Venezuelans had to suffer before they could be appreciated by their fellow countrymen. De la Parra was aware of this situation and attacked the conditions that allowed it to occur. She was upset by the narrow-mindedness, hypocrisy and the rampant machismo of her time.

In her letters to "Cabrita", which is how de la Parra referred to Lydia Cabrera, she confided her suffering to her friend, telling her about the morphine and opium she had to take to alleviate her pain and how she was preparing herself for death. Lydia appreciated her friend because she recognized de la Parra's greatness and accompanied her when she was alone, and she was with her when she died in Madrid in 1936.

In 1927, de la Parra went to Spain with her sister Isabelita and was introduced to the court of the Infanta Paz, one of her devoted readers. She also travelled to Veresnes and was invited to the Castle of Pelabon by Baron Fouquie to hunt, That same year she traveled to Italy with Lydia Cabrera and met Romain Rolland, a writer whom she greatly admired.[13] Still sensitive to the negative criticism leveled at *Iphigenia,* she vowed to write a nostalgic novel, and in 1927 she wrote to a friend that she was working on the novel *Mama Blanca,* and she assured her friend that it would be "the most criollo of criollo literature" (*Epistolario Íntimo* 70). This novel, according to Palacios, is not the naive, sentimental, inoffensive book some critics make it out to be. It is an anachronistic parody and shows the distrust of power in all its forms, a song to natural incoherence that abandons all logic (95).

In 1928, the third year of their relationship, Zaldumbide began to look for a way to dissolve his marriage. That year she was invited to attend the

VII International Interamerican Press Conference as the foreign correspondent for *El Universal* and spent time with the French delegation on board the ship. Perhaps she flirted with Maurice de Waleffe, who presided over the delegation, and he may have proposed to her. Years later, months before her death, she received a romantic postcard from him. After attending this conference, she travelled to Cuba, and there were rumors that President Machado was also in love with her, had proposed marriage, and would not allow her to leave Cuba (Palacios 83). She delivered her talk, "The Hidden Influence of Women on the Independence of the Continent and in the Life of Simón Bolívar." This is the talk that she eventually expanded into the *Three Colombian Lectures* in 1930. This lecture also inspired her to write a historical novel about Bolívar.

In Cuba, de la Parra stayed as a guest of the Cabrera family for a few days. She observed women's life in Cuba and wrote her reactions to it in her *Three Colombian Lectures*. Cabrera claimed she was "infected" by Zaldumbide at the time. According to Palacios, Cabrera and de la Parra never lived together. Each lived her separate and independent life. De la Parra wrote that she sometimes felt invaded by Lydia, and they had their disagreements, as she wrote in her *Bellevue- Madrid- Fuenfría Diary,* even months before she died. According to both Palacios and Cabrera, de la Parra was never a passionate woman. Her relationship with Zaldumbide frightened her. Her first love affair caught her off-guard. In a letter to him she compared falling in love to the brutality of the bullfights on Sundays. She was afraid of being swept away, afraid of losing control. Her relationship to others was based on social ties, and she was never part of an inner circle, as some critics suggest. She was not interested in politics or greater social or political problems (Palacios 101). Rather than being reactionary or conservative or indifferent to politics, she viewed politics as dirty business, to wit, her humorous line in the first of the *Three Columbian Lectures* in which she compared politics to coal mining and doesn't want women to get their hands dirty. Since she was aware of what went on in diplomatic circles, she witnessed first- hand the hatred, exaggeration, and the falsehoods that took place at political goings-on (Palacios 105).

She returned to Caracas on April 12, 1928, from Cuba. She also traveled to Spain and Switzerland, and to Munich, to attend the Wagner Festival. Back in Paris, she was busy editing her second novel. In Vevey, on the shores of Lake Laman, she accompanied her ailing mother, and she wrote to her friends in Caracas that she was living like a hermit and reading.

On April 1, 1928 the *Diario de la Marina* in Cuba published an interview of de la Parra by Armando Maribona.[14] She was taken to task for it by Venezuelans who were bitterly opposed to the Gómez dictatorship. When she passed through Caracas, the city was swarming with popular and student demonstrations. As a result, Gómez's police shot the demonstrators down with machine guns, closed the universities, and sentenced the young people of the 'Generation of 28' to hard labor on the roads and the rest to prison or exile. The writer wrote to Gómez on April 12, 1928, and enclosed a clipping of the Havana interview. According to Palacios, however, this interview was given in innocence, it was untimely, and de la Parra really had no idea of the political climate in Venezuela, or the importance of the student protests in February, which she downplayed in the interview. She was unaware of the seriousness of the situation and the increased state of repression (101). When she agreed to the interview, she was expecting to have a caricature of herself made, like the famous Messaguer caricature that today graces the covers of books and articles about her. She was caught off-guard. Later that year de la Parra returned to Venezuela, but her stay was cut short when she was diagnosed with tuberculosis. She returned to a sanatorium in Madrid. Doctors suggested a hot, dry climate would help her.

Mémoirs de Maman Blanche, with a prologue by Miomandre was published in *Le Cabinet Cosmopolite* in 1929. Editorial Le Livre Libre published *Las Memorias de Mamá Blanca.* De la Parra and Cabrera travelled through Italy. In 1930 she returned to Havana. The years 1930 and 1931 were spent in Neuilly. She wrote letters to Carias and to Lecuna as a historian-apprentice for her novel on Bolivar and to Zea-Uribe as a friend and disciple. This began a period of striving for inner perfection. She read about and followed the disciplines and healing techniques popular in the 1920s. During this period she also corresponded with Gabriela Mistral, the Chilean poet, and Lydia Cabrera.

In 1930 she delivered three lectures on the *The Influence of Women in the Formation of the American Soul: Conquest, Colony, Independence,* in Bogota, Colombia, to great acclaim and standing-room-only crowd. These lectures were not published until 1961.[15]

She referred to 1931 as her "año en blanco." This is the year she began experiencing symptoms of her illness. She became more withdrawn, more unsociable, seeing her life as blank and empty. She read Ortega y Gasset, Proust, Rainier María Rilke and the German Romantics, Nietzsche, and Freud. After reading Freud's theories, she tried to analyze her dreams. She wrote about having a dream in which Ibarra's ghost visited her. She read Tolstoy's autobiography and the *Life of Gandhi,* which fed into her spirit of renunciation and sacrifice. She spent August in Bauliuie in the Hotel Metropole with Lydia, and read about nature and philosophy. She wrote the first pages of her *Bellevue, Fuenfría, Madrid Diary*, published for the first time in *Obra* and translated for the first time in this book.

Bust of Teresa de la Parra by M. de la Fujite, 1998, south lawn of the Organization of American States Building, Washington. Photo by Judith Guy.

On her return to Europe in 1931 she began writing a sentimental biography of Simón Bolívar. After preparing to give the *Three Colombian Lectures,* what Palacios calls a "dangerous fantasy" to write a novelized biography of Bolívar materialized, an illness almost as bad as the illness that would take her life (110).

Doctors discovered a lesion on her lung in 1932. This year marks the beginning of the search for a cure for T.B. and striving for internal perfection. She became reflective and wrote painful letters to her family and friends scattered throughout the world. In February she consulted with Dr. Jacquerod, who sent her to Leysin, a sanatorium in the Swiss Alps. After she entered the sanitarium searching for a cure for her tuberculosis, she began to read about occult disciplines. Her correspondence with Dr. Luis Zea Uribe attests to their mutual interest in alternative spiritual practices. Her early short stories had also shown an interest in the supernatural, the occult and Eastern religion. Her letters reveal a deep spiritual need for faith, and she studied the lives of mystics and saints. "Outside her novels, Parra had difficulty building a permanent bridge between her opposing self-images of ultramodern woman and Christian mystic" (Lemâitre 14). In her metaphysical exchanges with Zea Uribe, the Colombian who wrote *Mirando al Misterio* and who shared her belief in visions, transports and telepathic communication, she wrote how she tried to visualize Emilia Ibarra in her meditations.

De la Parra began practicing Coué, repeating the words the French psychotherapist suggested, while she tried to visualize her friend and patron. She notes in her diary that she practiced Coué, a self-help method and philosophy designed to bring inner peace and happiness. She explained the method to Zea Uribe in a letter in 1933. In her diary she described the practice as a form of meditation that included the mechanical repetition of words, banishing all negative thoughts and concentrating on positive ones. She practiced Coué along with visualization for five minutes every morning and then prayed for Ibarra's soul. The "cure" began to agree with her, and she started putting on weight. She was allowed to go to Lausanne and spend the fall in Vevey, in 1932 with her mother, who still did not know about her illness.

The year 1933 began badly and ended worse. She became more ill, the bolivar was devalued, and she began to worry about being able to afford living in the Grand Hotel in Leysin. She moved to the Richmond Clinic, which was less costly. That fall the money crisis worsened and she moved to Hotel Montblanc, which cost half as much. She was hoping for a quick recovery and received an optimistic diagnosis. In September, however, she underwent a pneumothorax, an invasive procedure designed to collapse the lung to allow it to heal. This therapy went on weekly for two years. Antibiotics would not be discovered until ten years later. During this time she started to write about her "mysticism without faith" and she abandoned dogma and formed her own credos. She renounced Catholicism in a letter to Lydia, claiming it was counterproductive and materialistic. She continued to read about other religions. After she rejected Catholicism, she became an atheist, then started reading about Buddhism and eventually saw all religions as "possibilities." She rejected the idea of both Hell and Nirvana. But months before her death, when she thought she had a "visitation" from Ibarra, she promised to have masses said for her soul and vowed to attend all of them.

On October 1933 she wrote to Cabrera that she was in a receptive period, ideas were incubating, and she hoped that someday the writing would flow so quickly that Lydia would have to stem the flow of words. In September she lost more money, 2,000 Swiss Francs, when the bank she kept her money in failed. During 1934 she wrote how she "took trips around her bed." The therapy no longer worked, and she left the sanatorium at her own risk, against the advice of her doctors. She declared herself cured and headed back to Paris, despite suffering from attacks of bronchitis and asthma. Her letter to Zaldumbide, on November 16, 1933 demonstrates that the two kept up a loving correspondence, and she wrote him that she wanted to go to Caracas for the remainder of her cure. The pneumothorax therapy proved to be useless. In 1934 she left Leysin and travelled to Paris, Barcelona and Madrid. The most painful period of her life began in 1934, when she began to record more about her suffering in her diary.

By 1935 she was growing weary of her restless, rootless lifestyle. While living in hotels freed her from everyday chores and the hotel staff took care of her daily needs, she never had a home of her own. She had always lived as a guest, either in hotels, or in her mother's or sisters' households. Palacios claims she was a perpetual guest of not only places, but of time (68). Her life was provisional; she was always coming or going from Switzerland to Paris, to spas in Brittany, the Costa Azul, or staying at various hotels in Paris. While she attended several salons, she never held one of her own. She returned to Paris to consult with Dr. Valery-Radot that year, accompanied by her youngest sister María, hoping to learn more about the mysteries of tuberculosis, its causes, and the best climate for its cure. She sadly realized there was no ideal climate. The disease caused her to put herself into a kind of voluntary exile, living in various sanatoriums. In a strange way, her illness forced her to live the only kind of life in which she felt at home with herself. She lived life on her own terms from 1930-1935. She observed life in Leysin, learned more about her disease, and wrote she felt at times having the disease was like riding a train. In her writing during this period she reflected on Macuto and the tropical sun. She wrote only in her diary.

In February of 1935, she travelled to Barcelona with Lydia to consult with Dr. Sayé, another specialist, but her condition worsened and she was sent to Fuenfría, a sanatorium near Madrid in the Sierra de Cercedilla. She was still corresponding with Zaldumbide and in a letter she described to him how miserable she was, how much she suffered, and how the disease was making her life unbearable. She lived her life in agony, taking pain pills, sedatives and sleeping pills. When she awoke, the "demon in her chest" took over once again the moment she opened her eyes. She longed for death to relieve her suffering. On June 15, 1935 Dr. Sayé travelled to Madrid to perform another pneumothorax, increasing the pressure. She girded her loins during the painful treatment and promised to be cold-blooded, though she fainted from the procedure. Despite her asthma, Dr. Tapia allowed her to travel through Spain and to Paris with her sister María and a Belgian friend, who was perhaps the last of her admirers, Baron de Tarwagne. During seven days they drove through Avila, Segovia, Valladolid, Burgos, San Sebastian, Bordeaux, Poiters, Tours, Chartres, Rambouillet, Versailles and Suresnes, where María lived. Her health worsened and she sought medical advice from Dr. Valery-Radot, Louis Pasteur's grandson.[16] She returned to spend the Christmas holidays at Fuenfría.

In a letter to Zaldumbide in 1935 she wrote of her nostalgia for Leysin. The longing for it was like an illness. She found it hard to adjust to the real world after living at the sanatorium. In her final days in Madrid, the blue skies and the bright Spanish sun cheered her up at first, but in the long run only made things worse and contributed to her sadness. Surrounded by friends who were concerned for her health, she grew sick of their advice, of cures, and the things that were prohibited to her. Palacios writes that contrary to what has been written, or what people believe about her, or would like to believe about her, de la Parra did not live an intense intellectual life in Madrid. Among her acquaintances were exiled Venezuelans, Cabrera's Cuban friends and Spaniards who were friends of friends. She referred to her contradictory moods as a symptom of "neurasthenia." She was hopeful about the house in Madrid she and Cabrera had rented and the kind of life she would lead there, but her hopes were soon dashed. She found it difficult to put up with the vulgar and trivial goings-on in the rented house, and she felt subjected to the tyranny of visits that encroached on her time. She complained that her time was being wasted, and longed for solitude. She recalled how her stay in Leysin shielded her from being bothered by people, and how in the sanatorium she could live "outside time," retreat from real life, feeling above it all, literally and figuratively, high up in the Swiss Alps. She missed the life of seclusion in Leysin in the Grand Hotel and fondly looked back on it as a time of enchantment and endless possibilities. In Madrid she unpacked her memories, family photos and letters, sorting and keeping some and destroying others. She learned of Gómez's death on December 18, 1935 in the newspapers. This news awakened a sense of patria, and a longing for her homeland.

The year 1936 marks the end of her anguished search for a cure. Palacios writes that the author's final days can be summed up with a list of drugs she took: sanocrisina, neurinase (Barbitol and Valerian), pantapón, sedebol, efedrina, creosote, carybendrina, adalina, spasmalgine and geneatropine. With her mother, her sister María and her friend Lydia Cabrera at her side, de la Parra died in Madrid on April 23, 1936, during the beginning of the Spanish Civil War, a world war and the transformation of Venezuela into an oil producing nation. The morning of her death, Cabrera offered her a cup of coffee, to which she replied, "I will eat a little earth." According to her doctors, the official cause of death was a lack of oxygen to the heart, since tuberculosis attacks and weakens internal organs. When Gabriela Mistral was informed of her death, she recalled how much she loved her, "I've never met a woman more pure, well-formed and proper." De la Parra was buried in the Almudama Cemetery in Madrid. Her remains were brought to the Cementerio General del Sur, in the Parra Sanojo family crypt in Caracas in 1947. On the centennial of her birth, in 1989, her remains were brought to the National Pantheon in Caracas.

Innovation and Legacy

De la Parra's published work consists of two novels, some short stories, her correspondence, fragments of a diary and the *Three Colombian Lectures: Women's Influence in the Formation of the American Soul,* which she was invited to deliver in Bogotá and Cuba in 1930. She eschewed modernism, which, as she reported in her letters, left her cold, though her short stories hint at experimentation with this contemporary mode of writing. Both of her novels are detailed character studies with well-drawn characters, and de la Parra's gift for describing defects and prejudices in Venezuelan society, all the while employing tongue-in-cheek humor and subtle irony, make her an outstanding social critic. She is considered a model of Latin American feminist literature. Audacious, convincing and sincere in its outlook, *Iphigenia* is a reference point for understanding the feminine world of a young girl who struggles to fit in her society, questions its values, but succumbs to its demands. De la Parra's works penetrated into the deepest reaches of feminine identity and the search for women's universal worth. She wrote about women—how they view the world and their domestic lives, using letters, diaries, vignettes and lively dialog: "Instead of lamentation in Teresa's writing there is confession; instead of rage, irony" (Liscano in *Mama Blanca's Memoirs* 125).

Part of de la Parra's charm and vitality lies in how she accepted her vocation, and how she fell into the role of a writer. She was not very driven, and discovered late in life that inspiration was not enough, that she had to have discipline. She realized first hand when she lived in the sanatorium that inspiration without discipline led to lost opportunities. A case in point was the novel about Bolívar that never got written. She was aware of her limitations and never became a professional novelist. According to Palacios, "She heard the call of ancestral voices" (60). De la Parra was aware of her heritage and mined the information she received from her female relatives and acquaintances. She was proud of her ancestral line, and she could trace her family to one of the first conquistadors of Venezuela.

She considered Venezuela her homeland. She traced her roots there and it was the source of her material. Caracas and the hacienda where she grew up became mythical places, and her experiences there served as the basis of her fiction. Her family's hacienda, Tazón, was a timeless place where she could recall her childhood memories. At the time it was still a typical colonial hacienda, and one had to travel there by horse and cart (Palacios 25). This colonial time also formed part of her inner geography and provides a key to who she was, as she later explained in the *Three Colombian Lectures*. "All of her aristocratic virtue, her criollo humor, her respect for hierarchy, that unique unwillingness or inner distance that made her impermeable to fashionable influences, all of them have their origin in the colonial homeland of her childhood (Palacios 28)."

"If there is truly something worth telling in Teresa de la Parra's life, it lies in her personality, to whose independent flowering she first sacrificed social respectability and which, in the end and with vengeance, she sacrificed to the mystical ideal" (Lemaître 213). This critic focuses on the prevailing theme of de la Parra's novels, which concerns the stratification of Venezuelan society and the concerns of criollos, who were trying to increase their financial standing and preserve their racial purity. There was in increased awareness of the role of women in Venezuelan society, and de la Parra's novels bridged both the criollo and European cultures she was intimately familiar with.

During Juan Vicente Gómez's dictatorship (1857-1935), a time of repression and social upheaval, Venezuela emerged into the 20th century. His rule coincided with the discovery of oil in Venezuela in the 1910s. His regime was aided by this discovery, and he was able to stabilize the country. By the late 1920s Venezuela was the world's largest exporter of oil and the country was able to pay off its foreign debt. It was on its way to economic recovery, but this was not true for the country's poor, who continued to live in poverty. The economic changes and progress brought about by the petroleum boom did not show up in the mentality or the modernization of the country. Women's lives were restricted and they continued to be treated as though they lived in the previous century. After having lived in Paris during a time when it was the intellectual capital of the world, the stark contrast of life in Caracas during the Gómez dictatorship surprised de la Parra, and her literary output as well as her personal correspondence reflects the two worlds. *Mama Blanca's Memoirs* captured the author's longing for her bucolic upbringing on the family hacienda. This novel is set a postcolonial period. In *Iphigenia* she wrote beyond the anecdotal and nostalgic mode to create a new work that both chronicled and criticized the society she was currently living in. De la Parra wrote a letter to Gómez in 1931, petitioning to reinstate her pension. According to Lemaître, she was forced to defend Gómez because she had relatives working in high places in his government (128). Later critics, however, condemned her for corresponding with the dictator, and for an interview she granted in Cuba, in which she commented favorably on Venezuela's progress during Gómez's rule.

De la Parra chronicled the many changes taking place in her homeland from a woman's point of view. Her work was groundbreaking insofar as her fiction created a space for women, and she refused to write in the dominant styles of the period. The author's limited body of work showcases her diversity and her depth. *Iphigenia* is a coming-of-age novel and a love story. *Mama Blanca's Memoirs* evoke a happy childhood and a dying way of life. Her lectures reveal her concern for the status of women in modern society as she summarized their influence and their roles in all Latin-American societies across the centuries. Her extant correspondence records her personal concerns, sheds light on her writing process, outlines her literary ambitions, attests to her friendships, and in the last years, chronicles her painful life as a tuberculosis patient in a sanatorium. Her *Bellevue-Madrid- Fuenfría Diary* is a chronicle of her illness and the last unhappy months before her death in Madrid. But up to the end, living in a cold, substandard house, surrounded by ugly furniture, missing the mementos that were bequeathed to her by her beloved patron Emilia Ibarra, she continued to read philosophy, history, and current literary criticism. Her energy lagging and her tuberculosis progressing, she recalled the pleasant days when she had the time and inspiration to write for hours, without shallow and frivolous people coming to encroach on her time.

For Venezuelan literary critics, de la Parra is the founder of a new school of fiction. She focused on contemporary society rather than on nature. She wrote about her contemporary world in ways that opened her up to criticism. Her second novel, *Mama Blanca's Memoirs,* was set in an idealized past on an imaginary plantation not too far from Caracas. Using the sugar hacienda Piedra Azul as the setting, she described the idiosyncratic characters that inhabited the plantation, a small world unto itself. The premise of this novel relies on the memoirs of Blanca Nieves, one of the six daughters who live on the hacienda. Blanca Nieves grows up to become Mama Blanca. She turns over her unedited manuscript to a young woman who had befriended her. In this way de la Parra inaugurated a narrative tradition in Venezuela. She took a big risk when she wrote about the seemingly insignificant events in young women's lives at a time when José Rafael Pocaterra and Rómulo Gallegos were writing "great novels" of nation-building. Instead, de la Parra told stories about human foibles narrated by perceptive young women who lived in interesting times.

Most criticism of de la Parra concerns her two novels. While her letters, diaries and lectures are occasionally referred to in critical studies, they all deserve more attention. The critical work on the novels tends to focus on the autobiographical content of her fiction and do not take into account her unprecedented writing style and her finely wrought sense of irony. Her work could not be placed within the literary movements in her time or the contemporary literary styles popular in Venezuela. While the themes of her novels deal with life on a Venezuelan plantation and the dilemma of a young woman rebelling against the bourgeois mores of turn-of-the century Caracas, her European education and her perspective imbued her writing with a breezy, cosmopolitan tone. Her real gift, much underestimated and under-appreciated, is her subtle irony and her good-natured humor. She was misunderstood in her own day and was frustrated at having to defend her work, and had to explain what she had written about in *Iphigenia.* She defended herself in the press and in her letters, sometimes relishing the task. The subject matter of the second book, however, did not stir as much controversy.

Panteón Nacional, Caracas, burial site of Teresa de la Parra. Photo by the author.

In all works of art and above all, in novels, it is often hard to separate fiction from autobiography. De la Parra faced accusations that her novels were disguised autobiographies that also exposed her family. The author spent her childhood years on a sugar plantation very similar to the setting of Piedra Azul in her second novel, *Mama Blanca's Memoirs.* And while some critics claimed that *Iphigenia* was autobiographical, María Eugenia Alonso was not Teresa de la Parra. Lydia Cabrera claimed that while *Iphigenia* contains little autobiographical information, de la Parra's second novel is indeed based on the author's personal experiences. It would be easy to assume that the author and her heroine had much in common. But the author was an educated and celebrated public speaker, while María Eugenia Alonso spouted the first thing that came into her head, prompting her grandmother to accuse her of having a head full of cockroaches. María Eugenia, despite her multilingualism, is often at a loss for the right words, so any words will do. Nevertheless, de la Parra's lover, Gonzalo Zaldumbide, observed, "Woman that she is, she'll never manage to create anything different from herself. Instead of telling stories, women write confessions; there is no disguise that doesn't reveal them" (Sommer, *Mama Blanca's Memoirs*, xvi).

In an addendum to de la Parra's biographical letter to García Prada, she asked him to respect her privacy. She was wary of the criticism she received after *Iphigenia's* publication in which critics confused the rebellious and outspoken narrator with the book's author. Erroneously claiming that she was born in Venezuela at the beginning of the letter shows that she considered it to be her true home. She traced her roots to Venezuela, and considered herself a daughter of the place. Venezuela was her homeland and the source of her writing material. De la Parra wanted to write about her Caracas roots, but she did not want to live there. Caracas and the hacienda where she grew up became mythical places and her experiences there served as the basis of her fiction. Her family's hacienda, Tazón, was a timeless place where she could recall her childhood memories. This colonial time also formed part of her inner geography and provides a key to who she was, as she later explained in the *Three Colombian Lectures*.

She could trace her ancestry through long lines of powerful and influential Venezuelan women. Lemaître describes this connection in his biography.

> Parra's ancestral names—Soublette, de Tovar, Ezpelosin, Olmedo, Sanojo, and de la Parra—were all once synonymous with great wealth, military courage, and progressive social concern. Like Mercedes Ezpelosin, her progenitors were long-lived and their wartime experiences still fresh and it was in the eyewitness accounts of the women in the family that these experiences came to life in de la Parra's imagination. Often sorrowful, always obscure, these storytellers were wives, daughters, and mothers of illustrious men. Of all their tales of admonishment, of praise, or of lament, Parra took most to heart those limning the private struggles of the women, to which, in her lectures of 1930, she assigned the value of having formed the roots of her feminism.... If the stories of the lives of her female ancestors imparted a sense of social injustice, the brilliance of the men inspired her to feel a rightful heir to their more universal concerns (Lemaître 15).

In both her works of fiction, de la Parra established a tone that invites the reader to become the narrator's friend. For Venezuelan critics, the characters in de la Parra's novels serve as touchstones and icons. Readers worldwide were attracted to the exotic nature and local color of the works, which is why the novels were so popular in Paris. While de la Parra's characters are not entirely stereotypes, they do represent certain types of people, and each is a character (in both senses of the word) in his or her own right. The characters are unforgettable creations. Mention the name of Vicente Cochocho from *Mama Blanca's Memoirs,* or Gregoria from *Iphigenia,* and a knowing smile and an appreciative nod follows. It's as though simply naming the character assures a universal understanding and creates a common bond among readers.

With the renewed interest in women writers in general, North American critics have joined in the praise for the two novels. The excellent translations of de la Parra's novels should increase her readership, and she needs to be taken out of the confines of Venezuelan criticism and recognized seriously as a major writer in the literary canon that includes women writers worldwide. De la Parra stands out for coming up with a new organizational scheme for narratives which would have repercussions not only in Venezuelan letters of its day, but for the literature that would follow. She was a pioneer. Her works included letters, diaries, and memoirs, genres usually associated with traditional women's writing. The inclusion of these styles in fiction inspired contemporary Venezuelan women novelists such as Laura Antillano, Ana Teresa Torres and Milagros Mata Gil, just to name a few.

Understanding de la Parra's irony and wit is a fundamental key in appreciating her works. She expressed her vision for women's roles in society directly in her lectures and indirectly in *Iphigenia,* where she did not feel free to express her real thoughts. Some critical studies point to the contradictions between her published works, especially her novels, and the opinions she expresses in her letters and her journal. The fact that her two novels are so different in scope, tone and subject matter also holds a key to de la Parra's thoughts on women's roles and her other overarching theme, the arrival of modernity in Venezuela. Women could not keep living the sheltered, dependent lives society dictated. Nor could life on the plantations continue to be benevolent dictatorships. De la Parra wrote to amuse and entertain, while exposing a changing country and a hypocritical society halfway between the colonial age and a rapidly encroaching modern age. According to Velia Bosch, "Teresa's work was produced at the most difficult moment in Venezuela's history, with no democratic tradition, with associations, unions and political parties being founded, that only much later, would allow intellectuals the possibility of political debate" (*Mama Blanca's Memoirs* 134).

Iphigenia takes place in a Caracas that is undergoing transition, but it is still a city that seems backward to someone raised and educated in Spain and someone who had traveled to Paris. In *Iphigenia*, the penniless heroine has returned to a strict and proper criollo household and her maiden aunt and grandmother want her to make a good match. The novel is a criticism of arranged marriages of convenience, which, according to the author, amounted to a sacrifice on the part of the bride. De la Parra denounced this unjust situation to the point that some critics saw *Iphigenia* as a protest novel. On the other hand, in *Mama Blanca's Memoirs,* the hacienda is lyrically invoked and reconstructed so that family life in Piedra Azul is presented as a lost paradise. Or so it would seem to be on the surface.

De la Parra had to walk a fine line. She was a member of a conservative family. Her family belonged to the "Godos" (Goths), the name of the political party for conservative criollos. She felt nostalgia for the old hacienda way of life although she clearly recognized that this way of living was outmoded. She was aware that women had to struggle to attain a better position for themselves in Venezuelan society. In *Iphigenia* and in her lectures, she criticized the current society and its values and mores, hoping for a future in which women would be educated, gainfully employed, and free to marry whomever they pleased, rather than to have the choice made by their family members or based on financial need.

At the time de la Parra was writing, the prevailing literary modes were unsuitable for the themes she wanted to examine in her novels. She created a new, unique, graceful and intimate style, which according to some critics approached the style used by Proust. She was adored and admired by contemporary writers including Romain Rolland, Miguel de Unamuno, Juan Ramón Jiménez and Francis de Miomandre. On the other hand, she was frustrated when she picked up Thomas Mann's Nobel Prize winning *The Magic Mountain.* Ironically, she was in the sanitarium "taking the cure" like the novel's protagonist, Hans Castorp. In a letter to Carias (October 12, 1932) she explained that she tried to read the novel, but that she could not get past the first volume, claiming that it contained page after page of the common, the ordinary, and that it was all on the surface. "Sometimes so much can be said in one word, one silent glance...." (*Obra* 617).

She challenged social hypocrisy. Because of her family's economic situation and the generosity of her patroness, she was able to live the life of a writer, traveling and participating in literary groups and giving talks on women's history and the need for their emancipation. She suffered because her work was misunderstood. Her writing served as a forum for women's rights. She was a precursor for the achievement of cultural

androgyny and had hoped to provide role models for the future by
promoting the lives of women who led worthy and notable lives in the
past. Her examples and conclusions in the *Three Colombian Lectures*
offered a sweeping view of women's roles in Latin American history,
which amounted to consciousness-raising.

Teresa de la Parra's grave marker in the floor of the Pantheón Nacional, Caracas.
Photo by the author.

In their anthology about Venezuelan women writers, *El hilo de la voz,*
critics Yolanda Pantin and Teresa Torres point out that both Teresa de la
Parra and the poet Enriqueta Arvelo Larriva (1886-1961) stand out for the
quality of their work and for their awareness of being authors. "They do
not write to cultivate *belles lettres,* nor for didactic ends; they write
because they wanted to" (53).The extended title of de la Parra's novel is
ironic because it expressed the futility attributed to the gesture of writing,
the gratuitousness of a young lady dedicating herself to frivolous novel
writing, when other more important tasks necessary for the national
morality were waiting to be fulfilled, according to these critics. Both de la
Parra and Arvelo Larriva decided to construct their own systems of
writing, aware that a hostile world surrounded them. They wrote aware
that they were entering *la barbarie*—that is, going into the wild zone. De
la Parra inaugurated a narrative tradition. *Las Memorias de Mamá Blanca*
was published the same year as *Doña Barbara,* 1929, which won the
Nobel Prize and would gain fame as Venezuela's "official" novel, the
"national" novel of Venezuela, while both of de la Parra's novels would
continue to take second place. De la Parra succeeded, however, in her
depiction of women, not as stereotypical representations, but as flesh-and-

blood characters who speak for themselves. Her talent was recognized immediately, and her works were widely read and praised.

Palacios considers de la Parra's own life as the writer's third novel, calling it the story an adventure of a beautiful, talented woman who devoted herself to writing letters in the last few years of her life. Her longing for inner perfection did not lend itself to writing another novel, and her last adventure was the story of her soul striving to be in tune with her life. In the understated and ironic tone her subject would appreciate, de la Parra's biographer writes, "She did not invent anything, or found anything, did not break with anything and did not even write much—her legacy leaves little material for a biography, one must read between the lines, imagine, hint at and guess" (10). She spent years traveling to and from Paris without writing anything publishable. She never wrote another book. Instead, she wrote a series of outstanding letters to friends and detractors, such as Dr. Ignacio Vetancourt Aristeguieta, attached to the embassy in Peru, who circulated spiteful comments about her novel *Iphigenia* under the pseudonym Carlos Villera. In her letters, according to Palacios, the author became her own spectator. They reveal her disappointment in not being able to pursue formal studies, which would not have been an option for her. Throughout her life she compensated for her lack of university study by making up reading lists, attending lectures at the Sorbonne, corresponding with historians and other intellectuals, moving in Latin American diplomatic circles and traveling extensively. According to Palacios, her letters are an unbound book, available for the reader who wants to bind it. The letters were witty and spontaneous, and in her remaining few years they represented her last adventure: her description of her time spent in sanitariums, her striving for inner perfection and her correspondence with intellectuals, friends and family members.

Venezuelan literary critic Mariano Picón Salas' opinion about de la Parra in *Estudios de literatura venezolana*) and quoted on the back cover of *Obra,* sums up the purity of de la Parra's language, her originality and her important role in Venezuelan letters and culture, while sadly commenting on her relative obscurity:

> Teresa de la Parra died quietly at a time when Venezuelans didn't stop to think how important she was to the pure cultural tradition of this country. Going beyond the times and fashions, Teresa is distinguished as one of our classic writers. In a very proper Spanish, with the perfect natural tone of a good conversation, she collected the most interesting and nostalgic part of the Venezuelan soul. If we had more taste and less pedantry in our

educational system, Teresa would be read everywhere, to teach us the language we should all want to speak.

Notes

[1] García Prada eventually edited *Las memorias de Mamá Blanca,* The Macmillan Company, 1932 and *Obras Completas,* Editorial Arte, 1982.

[2] All translations from *Obra* are mine.

[3] She chose Teresa partly to pay tribute to her great-grandmother Teresa Jerez de Aristeguieta. She claimed she never liked the name Ana, and she preferred a last name that was more "antique." She added "de la" because she thought it sounded better, giving the examples Sor Juana Inés de la Cruz and Teresa de Cepeda. She had always been fond of the writings of St. Teresa de Avila. She needed a literary name and wanted that name to create a distinctive voice and a separate identity. (Palacios 56).

[4] *Estudios de literatura venezolana,* Madrid: Ediciones Edime, 1961, pp.166-67).

[5] Guzman Blanco was the president of Venezuela between 1870 and 1880.

[6] The Battle of Carabobo was the victorious battle fought by the leaders of the independence movement. It was led by Bolívar against Royalist forces and resulted in Venezuela's independence.

[7] The novel was supposed to have been called *El Diario de una señorita que se aburre.* De la Parra sent a chapter of *Ifigenia* to José Pocaterra to be published in *La lectura semanal* and that is when the accidental title change occurred. Her first choice was to use the word aburre which conveys the meaning of bored, annoyed, or disgusted. But fastidia was used instead.

[8] Juan Vicente Gómez (1857-1935) was the de-facto ruler of Venezuela between 1867-1935).As far as her ties to Gómez, his tyrannical reign began the year she returned to Venezuela, and he died a few months before she did. Her letters to him are in the Archive in Miraflores. In examining the rhetoric of the letter she wrote to him in June 18, 1923, Palacios sees nothing out of the ordinary: de la Parra petitioned him for financial help to publish her novel. In 1924 she had been a guest at his house in Maracay, "Las Delicias" with her sister Isabelita. She recalled flirting with Gómez's younger son, which reminded her of María Eugenia's flirtation with Perucho in *Iphigenia.* She also petitioned to get her 200 bolivar pension which had been cancelled when she inherited Ibarra's bequest. She did not get it back, and in a letter to Carias she wrote that since her pension was not reinstated, she felt free from obligations. However, the bolivar would be devalued in 1933 while she was in the sanatorium which added stress to her financial situation.

[9] After completing her secondary studies, Cabrera left for Paris in 1922 to study painting, art and Oriental culture where she became acquainted with significant artists of that time, among them Teresa de la Parra, with whom she shared a friendship for several years. Cabrera's collection of stories and legends was first published in 1940 and features the Yoruba pantheon of Obaogó, Oshún, Ochosí and other African deities. The renowned anthropologist Fernando Ortiz calls the

stories the African counterparts of Aesop's fables and the African-American version of the tales of Uncle Remus. The collection is a rich tribute to Cuba's Yoruba roots and an important contribution to Cuban culture.

[10] In her notes in the critical edition of *Mama Blanca's Memoirs,* Sylvia Molloy, however, affirms that de la Parra had an intimate relationship with Lydia Cabrera and with Gabriela Mistral, the Chilean poet who won the Nobel Prize for literature in 1945 (Mama Blanca's Memoirs, xii). See Molloy's essay, "Disappearing Acts: Reading Lesbian in Teresa de la Parra Entiendes? Queer Readings, Hispanic Writings, ed. Emilie L. Bergmann and Paul Julian Smith, Duke University Press, Durham, 1995. 230-256.

[11] When I mentioned to Febres that American feminist critics assumed the de la Parra was gay and that she and Lydia Cabrera had a lesbian relationship, Febres was very surprised. She questioned this assumption, pointing out de la Parra's frustrated relationship with the Ecuadorian Gonzalo Zaldumbide and the extant letters that describe her romance with this man. She also believes that de la Parra's family destroyed or suppressed additional letters between them. In any event, Febres claims that Cabrera denied a romantic relationship with de la Parra. Personal interview with Laura Febres, October 30, 2003, in Caracas, during the XXIX Simposio de docentes e investigadores de la literatura venezolana.

[12] The interview appeared in *Suplemento Cultural de Últimas Noticias,* Caracas, October 8, 1989, p. 40.

[13] Romain Rolland (1866-1944) was a French writer who was awarded the Nobel Prize for Literature in 1915. De la Parra was fond of his multi-volume novel *Jean-Christophe*, 1904-1912 which she claimed had influenced her own writing.

[14] Interview by Armando Maribona in Havana's *Diario de La Marina,* April 1, 1928 Section 1, pp.1 and 16 in which de la Parra unwittingly defended the Gómez regime. Refer to my translation of this interview in chapter 11.

[15] Refer to the analysis and introduction to the *Three Colombian Lectures* in chapter 5 and my translation of the lectures in Chapter 8,9 and 10.

[16] Louis Pasteur (1822-1895) was a microbiologist known for discovering the pasteurization process of milk.

CHAPTER TWO

IPHIGENIA:
THE DIARY OF A YOUNG LADY
WHO WROTE BECAUSE SHE WAS BORED

A Very Long Letter, a Diary, and More

De la Parra's first novel, *Iphigenia: the diary of a young lady who wrote because she was bored* was published in 1924 and won the Ibero-Americana Company Publishing prize, a writing contest directed by the Peruvian Ventura García Calderón. The novel created a sensation and achieved instant popularity. The book is "a novel whose five hundred manuscript pages were begun in 1922 and completed in less than a year. As de la Parra finished chapters, they appeared serialized in both Spanish and French-language literary magazines (*Obra* x)[1]." The novel was different from anything else that had been written to that point. It was an intimate novel, psychologically penetrating, where time and details are important and all revolves around the family drama of a young bourgeois woman. While its feminist stance had nothing to do with 19th century women's movements, the writer focused on the condition of being a woman and demonstrated the need for women to live their own lives. De la Parra is the founder of a new school of fiction. While other novelists situated their plots in other centuries and other countries, de la Parra took the bold step of presenting the psychological analysis of a contemporary young woman and revealed her limited options through her first-person narration.

For de la Parra literature was an act of accusation, reflexion and questioning (Febres7)[2]. She wrote with grace, subtlety and irony. These three ingredients are very important in good literature but were sadly lacking in tropical writers, according to Ramón Díaz Sánchez[3] (104). The author never shouted or gesticulated, she simply told. She knew how to write about the contemporary urban scene in Venezuela and held it up to a mirror, reflecting a predicament many Latin American women found themselves in. Like Agamemnon's and Clytemnestra's daughter, María

Eugenia/Iphigenia had to be sacrificed for the greater good of the status quo. In an interview the author granted to Edmundo Chispa, she explained "I'm writing a book about female psychology written in the form of a diary. At the least I want it to be literary, the simplest, and the most ingenuous in the world, and it will contain within it... a bit of making fun, irony, and fine laughter." In this interview she also explained where she got her pen name after she stopped using the pseudonym Fru-Fru, explaining that Teresa de la Parra was the person who wrote the novels[4].

The opening words of Jane Austen's *Pride and Prejudice* state, "It is a truth universally acknowledged that a single man in possession of a good fortune, must be in want of a wife." These sentiments also apply to *Iphigenia*. In this novel, de la Parra wrote about an upper class young woman who was financially pressed and who needed to make a good match. The crass, rich and well-connected César Leal needed a wife who could lend her spotless reputation and her good name to his newly acquired money and his growing political career. The woman who can fulfill this need turns out to be the once rebellious María Eugenia Alonso, a witty and observant young lady and the author of a very long letter to her best friend and a diary written during her "entombment" in her Abuela's house.

By the time she sat down to write her first novel in a beachside house in the resort town of Macuto, de la Parra had published short stories under her pseudonym Fru-Fru. The whimsical short stories appeared in *El Universal* in 1915[5]. One of those stories, "Mama X," garnered a prize for the writer; she was becoming more confident in her approach to fiction writing. "Mama X" was later included in *Iphigenia* as Chapter 6.

In 1922 de la Parra vacationed with Emilia Ibarra de Barros and Rafael Carias in Macuto, a seaside resort near Caracas. This is where she wrote most of *Iphigenia*. In a letter to Vicente Lecuna, she described how she shut herself up daily to write in the dilapidated house invaded by rats and lizards. It was only partially roofed; she swept the floor, and wrote on a pine table she set up near the window, writing while she overheard the passersby's conversation. In the afternoons she bathed in the river and rejoined her friends and have them read what she had written. She later recalled this year as the best in her life.

Her conservative mother did not approve of her writing, and feeling misunderstood, in the dedication page of the first edition of *Iphigenia* that de la Parra gave her mother, she asked her not to judge her too harshly:

> Mother,
> To you I dedicate this book which belongs to you, since it was from you that I learned to admire the spirit of sacrifice above all things. In its pages

you will see yourself, Abuela, Old Tia, and Don Ramón himself, with all the attendant discussions against rebellious speech.

Learn from it how great a distance lies between what is said and what is done, so that you may never fear the arguments of revolutionaries, if they bear within their souls the mirror of example and the roots of tradition.

Close your eyes now to one or another case of nudity; remember that you gave birth to all of us with very little clothing on; you dressed us. Dress these pages too with the white skirts of indulgence.

I embrace you with all my heart, Ana Teresa

Paris, July, 1925

Later, in 1928 she confessed to her friend Elena Maderos Gonzales that writing *Iphigenia* was therapeutic and it kept her from "screaming from every street corner (Lemaître 89)."[6] Disgusted with the current values and mores in Caracas, she launched into writing the novel that gave her an outlet for her "moderately feminist" views.[7] The novel was supposed to have been called *El Diario de una señorita que se fastidiaba*. De la Parra sent a chapter of *Ifigenia* to José Pocaterra to be published in *La lectura semanal* and that is when the accidental title change occurred. Her first choice was to use the word *aburre* which conveys the meaning of bored, annoyed, or disgusted. But *fastidia* was used instead. This is the more general term for boredom in Castilian, but without the connotations of disgust and loathing (Lemaître 64). Miguel de Unamuno, who was in Paris after having left the University of Salamanca read the novel de la Parra presented to him at a social gathering and later questioned her choice of wording for the title, to which de la Parra responded in a letter, "The original title of my novel was *Iphigenia* and the subtitle was *The Diary of a Young Lady Who is Bored*. Before I finished the book, fragments of it were published under this subtitle. But by mistake the editors wrote *se fastidia* and I didn't correct it, partially through inertia and because substituting *fastidia* was more spontaneous and natural in Venezuelan speech. I never expected my novel to be read outside Venezuela (*Obra* 563)." De la Parra's defense of more colloquial Venezuelan speech sets her aside from the other writers of her time who were either conforming to more high-blown polished language (the kind César Leal is guilty of and de la Parra makes fun of in *Iphigenia*) or the continued use of rustic speech All 6,000 copies of *Lectura Semanal* in which an excerpt of *Iphigenia* appeared were sold out on the first day, and this became a point of pride for the author. The story exposed social realities and demonstrated that an independent spirit in a young woman was a barrier to marriage. Readers read de la Parra's work as autobiographical, but the author insisted that the work was meant to be "a disinterested revolutionary protest."[8] In *Iphigenia* there are pretensions to tragedy, but María Eugenia's fate is not a tragedy itself. Furthermore, the heroine's identification with her sacrificial end could be read as an overstatement and a satire. De la Parra succeeded in exposing centuries-old prejudices and outdated values. She described how the criollos were living in the past and how the practice of educating young women for domestic ends would curtail their lives and keep them dependent on men. She was disappointed by the fact that some of the readers of *Iphigenia,* especially men, failed to understand the subtleties of her novel.

Iphigenia was immediately successful because it was readable and entertaining. It dared to attack the lives of the upper class and the values to which they insisted on clinging to. Through her heroine, de la Parra spoke the unspoken, and said what needed to be said. The heroine's decision to marry Leal had been brought about by a network of women who protected and coddled their men, allowed them to spend their money, and who had in one way or another sacrificed themselves to men. Society in general and women in particular were continuing to enforce this form of sacrifice on their daughters.

The novel is structured in four main parts. The "First Part' of *Iphigenia* begins with María Eugenia's return to Caracas from her months of freedom and shopping in Paris. She brings packages of gifts to her family. She learns that her inheritance, the hacienda San Nicolás has been appropriated by her Tío Eduardo. She never asks why or how this came about. Since she spent the last of her money in Paris, she is at the mercy of her family's financial support. We learn that her father was a spendthrift during the time they lived in Paris. Profligacy seems to run in the paternal side of the family. The novel is a depiction of criollo culture and family relationships, according to María Fernanda Palacios, who writes psychological essays based on the characters in the novel. María Eugenia reacts to the news that she is poor by exclaiming "Oh, how hot it is (46)."[9] The heroine's inability to confront reality is a typical Venezuelan reaction, according to Palacios. "As always there's the heat that settles everything and gets us out of embarrassing situations (2)."[10] Palacios interprets the reaction as repressive behavior, and María Eugenia's rage as misdirected and ill-timed. She does not know the rituals of the criollo household, does not understand the reactions of her Abuela, cannot interpret the meaningful silences, and Tío Pancho's cryptic and smiling leave-takings. Realizing the impossibility of a resolution through argumentation, Tío Pancho always finds an easy exit. María Eugenia analyzes those around her but ultimately, despite her introspection, she does not analyze herself very well. As a member of her social class de la Parra was able to get beyond it, and explain its imperfections, but the naïve heroine of *Iphigenia* must suffer and learn, and learn to acquiesce.

When we arrive in Caracas with María Eugenia, who summarizes her adventures in a letter to her best friend Cristina during the past three months, we read that letter, too. During the course of the novel, the protagonist turns to writing to either relieve her boredom, to describe her hermetic world, to gain self-knowledge, and ultimately to describe the changes that allow her to accept her fate and enter into a marriage of convenience. María Eugenia's mother had died, and following this, the young girl lived a cosmopolitan life with her spendthrift father in Paris. On his death, she is forced to return to her paternal Abuela's house in Caracas. Due to societal expectations, she is confined to the house and undergoes a two-year period of strict mourning. She cannot speak freely, leave the house on her own, and her hopes of living an adventurous and independent life are dashed when she learns her unscrupulous Tio has taken over her inheritance, the Hacienda San Nicolás.

The narrative is driven by the protagonist's motivation for writing, which accounts for the different genres within the novel. "The First Part" is a long[11] letter to her friend Cristina, entitled, "A Very Long Letter Wherein Things are Told as They Are in Novels," that covers a period of four months. Only the mention of Cristina's name from time to time reminds us that the letter in not meant for us. After sending the letter, María Eugenia is in the habit of writing. Two years later she begins a diary. This "Second Part" titled "Juliet's Balcony" begins with Chapter 1. The motivation to begin the diary is boredom. Once we have been introduced to the relatives who live in the house with her, María Eugenia slowly begins to describe the other characters she will meet and will influence her life in Caracas. In Chapter 1 she introduces "the genteel" Mercedes Galindo, a young married woman. Mercedes represents everything Eastern and exotic, and María Eugenia refers to her as "Semiramis."[12] The writing in the diary is much more self-conscious and self-referential. María Eugenia begins the diary protesting its very form, declaring that she will write her diary despite the fact that she considers diary-writing old-fashioned, foolish, romantic and cheap. Yet writing relieves her monotony.

For women, writing letters was one way to escape domestic boredom and stay in touch with the outside world. Dissecting the role of women trapped in convention, witnessing the testimony of these women and how difficult it was to escape from societal restrictions began a new tradition in feminine letters, allowing the interior voice of women to speak for themselves. De la Parra avoided photographic reproductions of place and a naturalistic style of writing and introduced psychological insights into feminine writing. The narrator's tone shifts from gushy and girlish to the introspection of an intimate feminine world. We read the heroine's reactions through her point of view, a first person account shared with the reader. Her observations are spontaneous, and they reflect her world. But we also get the point of view of the characters who surround her and influence her thinking and shape her world and her experiences. The author succeeded in writing a witty and entertaining narrative based on the life of an orphaned upper-class adolescent who succumbs to societal pressure and caves in to her family's demands to marry a man she doesn't love. Her "entombment" takes place in a house in Caracas that is peopled with interesting and amusing characters. To escape boredom, and because she misses Cristina, María Eugenia takes in every detail, every conversation, and every event in the staid household and writes about it to the friend she left behind in Paris. She doesn't hesitate to say whatever comes into her head, as her Abuela often reminds her. The success of the novel is due to the freshness of its language, de la Parra's use of irony, her sharp observation of the social scene, and her ability to both report on it and parody it.

In Chapter 2 María Eugenia introduces Gabriel, with whom she falls in love. Later in Chapter 6 she writes a letter to Gabriel, which she never sends, and writes a sonnet to distill the feelings she had written about in the letter. After a long wait, an abrupt letter from Cristina arrives. "Cristina has barely answered my long letter that was so intimate, that held so much of myself. She scribbled a few phrases alluding to my conflicts and hurts, joking phrases in the worst possible taste. And finally, in a few short words she ends by telling me of her marriage. She boasts of joy, of happiness, of mutual love, in the braggart tone of a newly rich person trying to dazzle everyone with ostentatious luxury (183)." Her reaction to Cristina's letter and her lack of understanding has parallels to the critics' reactions to *Iphigenia*. "Because of all possible repentance, the most perfect and absolute, the one that incites the greatest desire to reform is this repentance, this great regret for having made a sincere, intimate confession that was not understood (*Obra* 183)." María Eugenia's disappointment with Cristina's letter is also a de la Parra's pronouncement on the sorry state of letters in Venezuela and a rispote to her critics. "Writers, who are very honest about their convictions, are in the habit of considering most delightful all the works that come from their pen. For the same reason, with no less honesty, they are in the habit of condemning as imbeciles and cretins all readers who do not judge their works delightful (*Obra* 212)."

The space for self-reflection and personal growth occurs in María Eugenia's room, during the afternoon get-togethers with Mercedes, the enforced stay on the hacienda that was rightfully hers, where nature plays an important role, and in the patio of the ancestral home in Caracas where she interacts with the black laundress Gregoria. The enforced stay at the hacienda provides the heroine's archetypal fusion with nature, and introduces the heroine's relationship with the green world and her reflection on a lost paradise (Pratt 9). Her hopes and illusions gradually give way to self-annihilation when the much awaited letter from Gabriel fails to arrive. After María Antonia's brusque announcement of Gabriel's marriage to María Monasterios, the heroine can no longer escape into daydreams or an imagined future with her beloved. She is on her way to accepting reality.

By Chapter 3 Maria Eugenia has been living in her Abuela's house for four months and her Abuela begins to shape her to her will. Her Tia Clara also criticizes her. Maria Eugenia meets Mercedes Galindo. Abuela considers her to be a bad influence, and to keep her out of Caracas, the heroine is banished to the hacienda which is rightfully hers in Chapter 4. This chapter provides a pastoral interlude in which the narrator communes with nature.

Chapter 5 continues the bucolic interlude and the heroine's deepening of her love for Gabriel. She writes a long letter to Gabriel that she eventually turns into a love sonnet.[13]

Chapter 6 contains the "Mama X" story. This story lays the foundation for María Eugenia and Cristina's close friendship, their mutual admiration, and a shared secret. The story of Cristina and the narrator's friendship, however, serves to reinforce the reason María Eugenia dedicates such a long letter, a piece of her own self, to her best friend. Cristina and the narrator's friendship is based on a secret, the fact that Cristina is a "natural child." This secret binds the two girls. Back in Caracas, living a confined life with her fussy and conservative relatives, Cristina represents María Eugenia's only lifeline to her more carefree schoolgirl days. Writing to Cristina affords her with an opportunity to describe her current unhappy, restricted and bored condition. When, months later, María Eugenia receives Cristina's terse and abrupt reply to her own long outpouring, she is heartbroken. "This morning I received a letter from Cristina Iturbide. It is her grudging and late reply to my poor mammoth letter (183)." Regretting that she poured out her soul to her friend, María Eugenia exclaims, "Oh! What a betrayal of oneself; what an irreparable indiscretion; what a feeling of shame before the nakedness of one's soul! "(183). With these words María Eugenia recalls the secret that cemented the girls' friendship and segues into the story of "Mama X." The touching story is the search for the secret of Cristina's illegitimate birth and the identity of her unknown mother, who may be a famous opera singer.

In Chapter 7, "Supremum Vale" or "The Last Farewell" the protagonist learns that Gabriel Olmedo married Maria Monasterios, whose father has connections to the oil industry.

The "Third Part" of the novel, "Toward the Port of Aulis" consists of two chapters that allow the conflict and drama to develop as María Eugenia adopts the coping mechanisms that will eventually make her accept her role in society. Chapter 1 of this part is written two years after Maria Eugenia began keeping a diary. She is aware of her situation but deals with it indirectly and evasively. She abandons the bourgeois archetypes of romantic love, the myth of an ideal marriage. She looks for a way out of her economic, emotional, social and intellectual situation. She recognizes the futility of this situation, being fully aware of it. She describes all the changes she has gone through in the past two years, admitting "Yes. In these two years I have learned a great many things" (213).

The "Fourth Part, Iphigenia" consists of nine short chapters that span the week before Maria Eugenia's wedding. These later chapters in the novel are much briefer and build up to the crescendo of Maria Eugenia's capitulation and acceptance of her situation. The reader witnesses María Eugenia's physical change. She uses a different, toned-down lipstick, and adopts a different way of dressing. There are linguistic changes. She no longer expresses herself using foreign words and she immerses herself in domestic chores, cooking, sewing, taking charge of the laundry. She rubs Elliman's ointment (whose smell she once detested) on her Abuela, gives her injections, and prays the rosary with Tia Clara. She is now aware of the passage of time; it's been two years since she's written in her diary. Instead of presenting large chunks of time, time is minutely broken down in the fourth part of the novel, giving us a blow-by-blow account of the action. Tio Pancho's death serves to reunite the lovers.

Chapter 8 contains Gabriel's long letter (319-327) urging María Eugenia to elope with him. Tio Pancho's illness has brought the two lovers into contact for the first time in two years, and María Eugenia realizes that she is in love with Gabriel. After kissing Gabriel twice, her former negative opinion about kissing changes. Unlike Leal's unwelcome kisses, Gabriel's kisses are sought after. Gabriel has confessed that his marriage is a sham and warns María Eugenia that her impeding marriage to Cesar Leal means sacrificing the rest of her life.

The structure and rhetoric of Gabriel's letter bears a second look. Its rhetoric is high blown, overwrought and melodramatic. He structures his arguments in a number of ways: he implores, beseeches, begs, makes promises, threats, and cajoles his beloved. All of his arguments, however, ultimately point to the machismo that ruled Venezuelan society. Yet Gabriel's letter reveals the author's own idea of a fairy tale life; her love of travel, her interest in Eastern religions, and her fascination with the Orient. Parts of the letter reiterate Tio Pancho's philosophic outlook on life and his revelations to María Eugenia regarding her economic condition. It's as though with Tio Pancho's passing, a bit of him has been left behind in Gabriel.

The letter proves to be a convincing one and María Eugenia prepares for her elopement with Gabriel. These preparations are outlined in Chapter 9, the concluding chapter of the novel. She takes great pains to appear well-dressed and very pretty and is enchanted by her own vision, much as she was on shipboard from Paris to Caracas two years earlier. But both fear and materialism have her in their grip. She wastes time deciding what things to take with her. She can't bear to leave her silk trousseau behind. She is aware that she had sold the emerald earrings, her Abuela's only article of value, to buy the silk trousseau, and searching for a larger suitcase to hold it, she knocks over a vase. The noise awakens Tia Clara. At that point María Eugenia loses her nerve. Too much time has elapsed, and she can't make her escape.

When she next sees Leal, she realizes she feels an immense aversion to him. At this point, she has become her Abuela inwardly, and she realizes that she now physically resembles her Tia Clara, who was described in her youth as being a beautiful and precious flower at fifteen, but a mere shadow of herself at twenty five after her lover jilted her.

María Eugenia asks that the wedding be postponed, but Leal will not allow it. She reminds herself that she can't be disloyal to the man who in "one week was going to give me a luxuriously appointed home, filled with everything I needed, and his name and support, and a position in society, and a secure future sheltered from want and humiliating dependency" (348).

She replies to Gabriel's letter. She writes two brief letters, but discards the first one because she becomes aware that even mentioning her fiancé's name sounds pompous and out of place. Both letters are full of lies. In the second and briefer letter, she writes to Gabriel that Cesar is there to defend her, that she will marry him within a week and that she considers her fiancé "vastly superior to you from every point of view" (348). This letter is sent to Gabriel via Gregoria.

In the last two pages of the novel, María Eugenia is in her room, staring at her wedding dress. She picks up her pen and resumes the lyrical writing and philosophical ruminations that makes this novel such an entertaining read. When her Tia Clara asks her to try on the wedding dress, María Eugenia refuses. Instead she sets her dress against a chair: "The chair seems like a sadistic lover embracing a dead woman (353). In the last two pages of the novel she becomes the bride of sacrifice. She welcomes the spirit of sacrifice as her lover. The novel ends with these insights, so we see what María Eugenia has been thinking about in the "part not written" of her diary. Readers must imagine her trudging to the altar, but that part, too, is left unwritten by de la Parra.

The Absent Aphrodite

The heroine's inconclusive relationships begin with her initial dislike and eventual falling in love with Gabriel, her teasing flirtation with her much younger cousin Perucho in order to annoy her hateful Tia, and her courtship with César Leal, whom she refuses to kiss before they are married. Her refusal to kiss her husband-to-be repeats her refusal to kiss the unknown Colombian poet she met onboard the ship who unsuccessfully tried to kiss her. María Eugenia has no real amorous experience, and experiences no sexual awakening. As Palacios points out in her mythological and archetypal analysis of the novel, the goddess Aphrodite as the goddess of sexuality is lacking, not only in *Iphigenia's* world, but that of the author as well[14]. María Eugenia panics when men approach her and want to kiss her; they are both daughters of Artemis (247). After reading de la Parra's long letter to Colombian critic Eduardo Gúzman Esponda, June 1926, in which the author defended her heroine and her actions, Palacios concludes that it is clear that María Eugenia wants to be admired, she wants to captivate and fascinate, but she lacks passion (249).

The heroine's relationship with men is never brought to maturation. It begins with her flirtation with the Colombian poet on the ship bringing her to Caracas, one of the first humorous incidents in the novel. As she moves away to escape his kiss, she manages to knock his glasses off. "He was very myopic, and therefore at that critical moment, to the pain of defeat and the pain of scorn was added the dark pain of blindness" (20). The role of kisses in the novel begin a new phase for the heroine that ranges from comic to catastrophic. The incident with the Colombian poet was comical. Gabriel's kisses are sinful and sacrilegious. Just thinking about kissing her future husband repulses her. Kisses provoke either ridicule, panic, guilt or hatred and repugnance. She continues to flee from all erotic encounters.

María Eugenia at first makes fun of the pretentious Leal and in doing so she attacks all men of his class. She realizes, however, that she has to abandon her belligerent stance and become submissive. At the point in the novel where she becomes Iphigenia, the Greek heroine about to be sacrificed to society, the die is cast and María Eugenia begins her process of self-erasure. Her personality does an about face, and she denies knowing what she knows. At this point, a new pact has to be established with her audience. Before she can convince her readers that these changes are necessary, the heroine has to convince herself. In Chapter 2 of "The Third Part" she comes to the realization that she is a fine object and sits in front of the window grille shouting "I'm for sale. Who will buy me? (218)" She recognizes that she is a commodity, and that her capital is her beauty, her virtue and her family name. She is a perfect match for Leal, who has money but lacks class. She fulfills the fate her family has been planning for her: to be above reproach until a man is seduced by her nothingness.

Ifigenia is not concerned with mother/daughter relationships, which become more evident in de *Mama Blanca's Memoirs*. María Eugenia never mentions her dead mother, and sadly, she lacks healthy female role models. It is her illegitimate friend Cristina who is burdened with the search for her mother's identity.

A Multi-Vocal Novel

De la Parra's fiction is richly detailed in characters, situations, and settings. It is precisely this combination of observed, felt and recorded living detail that lends her novels their powerful emotional charge. Her material was taken from memory, personal experience, keen observation, and bolstered by the kind of classical education that was available to women of her class at the time. María Eugenia is a character who spots the contradictions and the shams this society perpetuates. She sees and protests, but ultimately accepts and succumbs, but only after having moved to self-awareness about her limitations. Her style is a rare combination of subtlety and insight.

María Eugenia is already well aware of the social realities which make women slaves, victims and pariahs. She now appreciates the suffragettes and wished she had listened more attentively to Pankhurst, an early English feminist, when she lectured in Paris about the rights of women. But as she wrote to her friend Cristina, she was not receptive to

Pankhurst's message and could not listen at the time because the fashion-conscious heroine was appalled by thick stockings the speaker wore (81). But now that the heroine has matured and is aware of women's inequality in her patriarchal society, she is more concerned about women's status in Venezuelan society than in her own good looks.

De la Parra pushed the boundaries of Venezuelan society by questioning marriage as a legal contract and motherhood as the basis for sacrifice. The marriages in the novel are examples of relationships based on economics, class expectations and appearances. They provide a scathing criticism of middle class matrimonial practices. The elegant Mercedes Galindo has sacrificed herself to a marriage of convenience that keeps her loveless and unhappy, but from which she cannot escape. She serves as a preview and a foreshadowing of what will happen to the heroine if she marries Leal, who can provide her with security in return for her family name and good reputation. Gabriel Olmedo has entered into a marriage of convenience with a woman he doesn't love, but whose family has good ties to the current regime. The novel offers these examples of unhappy marriages, all lacking love but fulfilling a social obligation. The only person who is happy in love, a free and independent spirit is Gregoria, the black laundress, the unmarried mother of four who is proud to answer only to herself.

According to Maríano Picón Salas, many Hispanic-American women, still imprisoned in the most trivial routines and conventions, were waiting for such a message. And *Ifigenia,* unique for its grace and adolescent malice… conquered the entire Hispanic world. It was read simultaneously in Mexico, Bogota, Montevideo, in Santiago de Chile. I knew an elderly Chilean philosophy professor who confessed to me, like on who has committed a delightful sin, that he devoted to the small and fantastic María Eugenia Alonso a moment he had stolen from Kant (*The Male Critic* 186). According to Lydia Cabrera, these women were ready to hear de la Parra's message especially because Caracas society was machista. In Cuba, argued Cabrera, women were not as submissive as they were in Venezuela. While it was suggested that good Catholics should not read the novel, it did not keep them from buying it (Hiriart 119).

P. Dorame-Holoviak examines this novel as a literary labyrinth. The protagonist sets up the characters in the book into two teams. There is the team of her supporters (Tio Pancho, Gregoria, Mercedes Galindo, and Gabriel Olmedo), and the team of her adversaries (Abuela, Tia Clara, Tio Eduardo and his wife María Antonia.) The former team is comprised of characters who have found a way to survive the ideology of the times and offer this possibility, through their examples, to María Eugenia. They are gifted speakers, masters of speech and argumentation. The latter group maintains and supports a conventional and rigid social order: thievery, lies, ideological posing, and ingeniousness that borders on stupidity, conventionalism, and the dissolution of the individual (27).

Maria Eugenia starts out wanting to be a free and rebellious spirit, and her Tio Pancho takes her under his wing. As the other rebellious and free spirit, he is aware of the social injustice his niece is subjected to. Pancho Alonso is treated lovingly, but he is a sad character; a once promising youth who grows up and becomes a skeptical public servant. Through it all he maintains his aristocratic spirit and his ironic vision. He dies a poor man and at times he is the mouthpiece for de la Parra's ideology, if one compares Pancho's outbursts with what the author wrote in her letters. Pancho provides a discordant note at gatherings, but his character loses force as the novel proceeds. María Eugenia manages to bring some happiness into his life and he encourages her not to "hold things up to the light". Pancho Alonso is the only member of the family who opposed María Eugenia's marriage to Leal. When Pancho becomes seriously ill, the lovers are reunited at his bedside when Gabriel becomes his doctor and María Eugenia acts as his nurse. Pancho is the last of the Alonsos. When Pancho dies, something in Maria Eugenia also dies, and she loses her sense of humor.

Gregoria is the black laundress who is lovingly depicted by de la Parra. The outspoken and wise Gregoria, who knew the heroine from the time she was born, becomes María Eugenia's confidante, tells her family secrets, and borrows books from the circulating library which the protagonist devours in her room[15]. Gregoria's darkness, repeatedly described by Maria Eugenia in terms of its "brilliance" and "purity," transforms her into a symbol of the Venezuelan elite's longing for a stable, unmixed racial order (Russ 741). The black servant Gregoria is treated lovingly and is María Eugenia's spiritual refuge. It is Gregoria who reveals the family history to María Eugenia. This history includes Tia Clara's failed engagement and facts about María Eugenia's mother. Gregoria borrows books for María Eugenia from the circulating library and acts as letter carrier and go-between with Gabriel. She also warns María Eugenia about guarding her reputation.

While Leal has a fortune and searches for a good wife, there is a parallel story about a woman with a fortune in search of a good husband. The newly rich María Monasterios marries the heroine's true love, Gabriel Olmedo. Through Tio Pancho we get a description of Gabriel: he is thirty, elegant, slim and distinguished. He graduated with degrees in both medicine and law, has lived ten years in Europe, and has a doctorate in

Philosophy and Political Science. Gabriel has lectured at universities in Spain and France and was writing a book on sociology and American history. His only drawback is that he doesn't have money. He is pro-government and must align himself with someone who has money and connections. He disappears from María Eugenia's life while she is at the hacienda San Nicolas. After the lovers are reunited at Pancho's bedside, Gabriel writes María Eugenia a long letter asking her to elope with him. Palacios describes him as a criollo Romeo trapped by his ambition, who would turn Maria Eugenia into another Mercedes (385). This critic points out that the repetition of Gabriel's name in the letter Maria Eugenia writes to him renders him unreal and magical, as though it is not so much the man but the man's name that fascinates her. Gabriel, named for an archangel is the heraldic messenger who awakens what little sensuality there is to awaken in María Eugenia, the archangel who becomes the white knight in her eyes (170).

Leal represents the *nouveaux riches*. He is pedantic and his speech is a pastiche and a parody of political oratory. With the exception of Gabriel's letter urging Maria Eugenia to elope with him, all speech has been reported or filtered through the narrator, who is prone to parody or stylization. Leal gives speeches, and the author has a bit of fun reproducing his speech, a parody of political oratory. But Leal is the future; he represents prosperity, the new order, and he will guarantee the continuity of the family through his marriage with its highborn daughter.[16] But he represents the future: prosperity, political connections, and, in marrying Maria Eugenia he guarantees the continuity of the criollo family. Leal's origins are obscure; he is of mixed race, though what his racial mixture is remains a mystery. He serves as a counterpoint and a solution to the decadent Alonsos. The Peruvian critic Angelica Palma suggested we should feel sorry for Leal, and Palacios concurs that the reader should feel compassion for him since there is no room for him in Maria Eugenia's soul. "Poor Leal! How can we not pity the pompous senator, since, every night a sacrificed woman awaits him in his own house, stony with contempt, sharpening her aversion behind the door?" (459). This critic concludes that the best novel would be about Leal's life after the marriage.

Mercedes Galindo, whom Maria Eugenia nicknames Semiramis, favors all things French, and sees Paris as the symbolic center of her life. Mercedes is a big spender and she is unhappy with the current economic climate. The Abuela thinks she is a bad influence on Maria Eugenia, but the heroine is enchanted by her, and she is drawn to her and her material trappings and her Oriental boudoir.

Abuela Eugenia represents the spirit of the colony; she is the matriarch and the authority figure who will eventually bend Maria Eugenia to her will. She is the stereotypical impoverished but proud widower who has to maintain the family's reputation and integrity.

Tia Clara is the archetypal maiden who was jilted in her youth. Once a beautiful young woman, her physical appearance has deteriorated. Her life consists of domestic chores and performing religious activities. She is the stereotypical *beata*.

Tio Eduardo and his wife María Antonia are the greedy and mercenary relatives who rob the heroine of her inheritance. María Antonia takes an immediate dislike to her niece and relishes breaking the news that the object of her affection married another woman.

Perucho is the young suitor who becomes part of the landscape while Maria Eugenia is at the hacienda. He takes care of all her needs and he becomes her plaything. Besotted by his cousin's beauty, he compares her with the beautiful girl whose picture appears on the Ross Pills label. Palacios claims that the relationship between Perucho and Maria Eugenia forms the most erotic part of the novel as Maria Eugenia conflates and confuses Gabriel with Perucho (*Mitología* 311).

The Part Not Written

There is a two-year gap during which the heroine ceases to write. Another part of the novel not written by María Eugenia is the letter "written" by her lover, Gabriel Olmedo. In this letter, Olmedo beseeches María Eugenia to run away with him and not submit herself to lifetime prostitution, which is how he describes what her marriage to the ambitious upstart Cesar Leal amounts to. His letter offers her all she has dreamed of, all she admires and wants to emulate in her friend Mercedes Galindo's life but without the abuse Mercedes' philandering husband heaps on her. María Eugenia, to the disappointment of many of the novel's readers, does not run away with her lover. Doing that would make her a concubine and a social outcast. But her lover's letter is a projection of all her desires, and Gabriel's criticism of society and religion is probably the part of the novel that reveals the author's true feelings and articulates her philosophy. It anticipates the religious quest she will undertake later in her life while living in several sanitariums and studying religion, the lives of the mystics, and Buddhism.

In a postscript to the novel María Eugenia vows, "to tell my story to the end" (351) and these last few pages of her musings take on melodramatic twists and turns, as she announces her sacrifice and her resignation. "As in the ancient tragedy, I am Iphigenia" (351)[17].

In the letter María Eugenia writes to Gabriel, his name appears eighteen times in the letter's sixteen paragraphs. Putting her classical education to good use, she compares him to Solomon, Jesus and Messiah. The letter clearly shows that the heroine is well educated as she references works taken from the classical tradition, bucolic literature, Bible, Spanish Golden Age, mystic poetry, and the *Song of Songs*. Maria Eugenia becomes a nymph at San Nicolas, where she communes with nature in language that has mythic and pagan overtones. In her own letters the author described her pleasure in communing with nature.

Betrayal and Sacrifice

The first letter in the novel is the breathless and detailed missive the protagonist dispatches to her friend, which gets the novel off to its empathetic start, introduces the characters and sets the background. In her letter to her friend Cristina, a hopeful María Eugenia declares the two of them will be the heroes of their own stories. If anything, the criticism leveled at de la Parra through her young heroine only added to her conviction that the time had come for women's rights. Although María Eugenia's Abuela thinks she is rebellious, there are truly no rebellious gestures on the part of the heroine. She acts out in petty ways to annoy her Tia and her Abuela, but there is no final rebellion or rejection of the societal code. Although she is angry when she discovers that her Tio has taken over the hacienda meant to be her inheritance, she never questions the decision or confronts the man. Rather, she stews about her diminished prospects and writes in her diary to vent her anger and disappointment. There is never any hint that María Eugenia realizes that her rights have been violated or that she has been betrayed by her own family. Her writing becomes a search for self-knowledge, during which she eventually accepts her weakness and inability to rebel.

Iphigenia is a novel about betrayal. María Eugenia dreams of a carefree life upon her return to Caracas, counting on her inheritance and her property for her financial support. Her Tio, however, takes control of the hacienda she was to inherit. Her late father had mismanaged the property, and his brother had seized control. Her late father betrayed her by living a spendthrift life in Paris, a pattern María Eugenia blithely repeats. In response to her long letter to her friend, María Eugenia feels betrayed when she receives Christina's short reply informing her of her impending marriage and changing lifestyle. Tia Clara never marries because she is betrayed by her first love. María Eugenia's own true love Gabriel marries another woman out of expediency. Mercedes lives a double life alternating between Caracas and Paris, where different marital standards are observed, and she is abused by husband. All marriages in this novel prove to be unhappy ones. In the end, the heroine betrays herself.

Janet Jones Hampton reads the novel as a descent into self-betrayal. "The novel is structured as a document of self-destruction. Both the letter and the diary entries, written in dialogue form, reveal the discrepancy between the image María Eugenia holds of herself and the reality of her existence. This rift between perception and reality is underscored in María Eugenia's identification with the Greek Iphigenia. She differs completely from the mythological maiden who selflessly submits to be sacrificed to the gods at the hands of her father in an effort to save him and her nation. The self-centered protagonist, however, never displays genuine sacrifice or loyalty. María Eugenia evokes such literary references as Shakespeare's loyal, tragic lover Juliet; Penelope, the faithful wife of Odysseus, of Greek mythology; and Shulamite, the beloved of King Solomon, as the models of identity she seeks. While these figures expand her options of choice, they also constrain by obviating María Eugenia's responsibility to create an identity for herself." (79)

According to Francisco Rivera, *Iphigenia* is a novel about the auto-negation of a young woman who loses sight of her ethics and "annuls" herself. She becomes a non-entity and sacrifices herself so that she can fulfill society's expectations (113). In effect, throughout the course of the novel, María Eugenia slowly transforms herself into her Abuela, and follows through on the advice her Abuela has given her.

Iphigenia as Testimonio

One way to look at this novel is to examine it through the lens of testimonial literature, as one critic suggests "*Iphigenia*, a testimonial novel in four parts, explores the themes of gender and feminine identity" (Jones Hampton 79). Following María Eugenia as she makes her way through her conservative household, she invites the reader into her world by sharing her letter, her diary and her thoughts, the novel does indeed take on some of the characteristics of testimonial writing.[18] Testimonios tell the stories of marginalized women whose stories need to be told. While contemporary testimonios involve real women, Jesusa Palancares, Rigoberta Menchú and Domitila Barrios de Chungara, to name a few, *Iphigenia* presents us with a fictitious heroine. But the author wanted to present us María Eugenia's life for the same reason testimonial literature is written today: to examine a social problem and to have us become aware of that problem by examining the life of a witness who is unable to speak for herself. The author described her novel as "a true picture of the feminine soul in these times" (Hiriart 32). The novel offers a psychological analysis of a young girl, her internal observations, her continuous self-examination, and her place in her social economic class. *Iphigenia* is the story of María Eugenia and her voluntary sacrifice inspired by her fear of poverty. While other novelists of the time placed their plots in other centuries and other countries, de la Parra took the bold step of presenting a type of woman who lived in the Venezuela of her day. If poverty and the lack of education that force women into oppression in contemporary society give rise to testimonial literature, then de la Parra revealed how limited options for young women in her own day led to a different kind of servitude and gave women no voice to protest those practices.

Testimonial literature is the result of many hours of interviews, and the language of the informant is often colloquial, earthy and represents the language of the people. The protagonist is usually a woman who stands for many women, and as Domitila Viezzer asserts, "What happened to me could have happened to hundreds in my country," (*Testimony of Domitila, a Woman of the Bolivian Mines* 13). Despite the controversy raised by Rigoberta Menchú's book, readers are convinced that even if some of her assertions can be disputed, the book needs to be read because it is not the story of one person, but the story of the persecution of indigenous Guatemalans. In the examples of testimonial literature I have given, it is women who interview other women, so that the way the book is written, how the informant is interviewed, and the process of writing the book, the relationship between subject and author all contribute in shaping the outcome of the text.

Lydia Cabrera, the Cuban anthropologist and intimate friend of the author claimed, "It seems that all novels written by women have something of the autobiographical in them, but *Ifigenia* is not autobiography. *Mama Blanca's Memoirs*, that enchanting book with all the freshness of newly-cut flowers, is" (Hiriart 119). The characters de la Parra described in her works are based on her relatives, her contemporaries and her ancestors, whose values were determined by the society they lived in. De la Parra was a keen observer and a gifted storyteller. On her return to Caracas she often asked people to repeat what they had said so she could write authentic dialog. Her domestic settings brought the reader into the world of Caracas' family gatherings. The women she met in Caracas are reflected in her characters and they provided her with a rich source of psychological observations. Through the observations of María Eugenia, the reader is led through a world the author saw as unfair to women. "Teresa understood and knew how to analyze the female soul in all its manifestations. The author convinces us, we become her confidents, her accomplices and we approve of the theories María Eugenia unloads. Her thoughts are the thoughts of modern woman and in the climate of the day they must have seemed like heresy" (Díaz Seijas 73-74). While the ideal of a liberated woman, an independent woman, a well-educated woman does not appear in the novel, she appears in de la Parra's lectures. Velia Bosch suggests that had de la Parra lived longer, the historical novel she wanted to write about the life of Simón Bolívar told through the eyes of his lover Manuelita Saenz, the female protagonist would have been the anti-Iphigenia (*Obra* 8).

A Political Novel

Iphigenia can be considered a political novel for its depiction of frustration, dashed hopes, and the struggle of the criollo class to keep up appearances. The author offers up a sequence of events in which the heroine gains self-knowledge but nevertheless capitulates to societal demands and submits to a marriage of convenience to insure the economic health of her extended family. The first person narrative is particularly appropriate for the heroine's free association and epiphanies.

One characteristic of Latin American women's writing, and especially de la Parra's, is how it achieves a tone of intimacy. This narrative strategy is evident in the letters of Sor Juana Inés de la Cruz through the testimonial novels being written today, in which a woman interviews another woman, so that her exploitation can be made public. In Clorinda Matto de Turner's *Birds without a Nest* and Gertrudis Gómes de Avellaneda's *Sab,* the authors establish fictitious cases and characters based on the social reality of their day to expose exploitative situations such as slavery and priestly abuse. Through these novels, the authors offer solutions to societal problems. "America's women writers have themselves acted as agents of change in an ongoing process of cultural transformation often by unsettling old fictional patterns and creating new ones" (Reynolds 6).

While María Eugenia is not a real woman being exploited in the same way as Jesusa, Rigoberta and Domitila, given that de la Parra could not directly criticize Venezuelan bourgeois society and the sacrifices it extracted from its young women, she leveled her criticism through a novel in which a young girl serves as an example of societal pressure to marry for money. De la Parra's real criticism, however, is more patently evident in her lectures, but these ideas were never as widely spread as those in her popular novel.

Iphigenia is the imaginary biography of a young girl who struggled to be different and independent, who, in the words of Rosario Castellanos, was looking for "another way to be." Recent critics believe there is much work to be done in evaluating de la Parra's work and her message, and she belongs in the ranks of other women writers of the world whose messages still need to be heard. Her style and her imagination make her an important author Venezuela can contribute to world literature. Her subject matter, her style, her use of irony and above all, her preoccupation with the feminine world places de la Parra alongside Katherine Ann Porter, Virginia Woolf and Edith Wharton. These authors share an expressive force and a special outlook on life and the world, especially in the lives and worlds of women. They write about well-defined female characters. They are masters of irony. Without openly criticizing society, through their sharp observations and fine descriptions, they reveal prejudices and norms that keep women from living as autonomous beings.

By writing about one young woman named María Eugenia, de la Parra was writing about many Venezuelan young women who were being sacrificed to middle class patriarchal values. They were banking on their good names and their reputations. Teresa de la Parra thought the practice needed to be exposed, the public needed to be educated, and she accomplished this through the introspection and confession of a young girl typical of the time. As the author said, "María Eugenia is a synthesis, a copy of several women I had closely watched suffer in silence, and whom I wished to study, give voice to, as a protest against the current oppression "(Fuenmayor 165) . De la Parra gave voice to those who could not speak for themselves, which is the object of testimonial writing. Her objectivity and her travels gave her the necessary distance to see the problem. María Eugenia spoke to all the women of her class.

De la Parra responded to the problematic reality of her times by writing a confessional novel whose heroine has to accept lies, and lies to herself and prepares herself for a world of appearances. Are her readers still her collaborators or do they feel betrayed by her about-face? The readers who had become the good friends of the heroine felt cheated by its ending. They wanted a romantic and happy ending. They expected a sequel in which at the last moment María Eugenia does not marry César Leal. The author wanted to chronicle her times faithfully and she wanted to reveal the circumstances under which many Latin American women lived. She thought that middle class women suffered more than lower class women because they had less freedom to choose their marriage partners. She wanted to reproduce the feminine experience of her time through a woman who sacrifices herself to the status quo.

The first person narration alternates with other points of view and reflects the social and political realities of the Venezuela of its time: the discovery of oil and the Gómez dictatorship. The twenty seven years of the Gómez dictatorship suppressed women. Modernity in Venezuela begins with his death in 1935. De la Parra was critical of contemporary institutions and questioned the status quo in her letters and in her conversations. The protagonist's reading was not typical for young girl of her day, usually limited to romantic novels with little reference to popular culture. She is left with her good name and little else. She is well-born (Eugenia) and that is her only bargaining chip. Knowing that an intelligent woman is not an attractive commodity, she negates her education at the end and denies ever reading Dante. At first active, accomplished, rebellious and irreverent, she becomes passive and dependent. De la Parra was the first to reveal the deceit of romantic love. What matters to María Eugenia's family is not her passion, but economic consolidation. *Iphigenia* does not propose rebellion, but a submission, and the novel discredits the romantic notion of happiness through love.

Despite the many literary movements in Europe that Teresa de la Parra was aware of, there are no traces of these influences her work, although the writer incorporated the rebelliousness of the 1920's; women wear short dresses, cut their hair, and drink and smoke. While educational reforms in Argentina in 1918 and in Peru in 1919 allowed women to attend universities, the most important change in Venezuela was the discovery of petroleum in 1914. This discovery occurred during the dictatorship of Juan Vicente Gómez, and it was also the time when labor unions were formed and oil concessions were sold to foreign interests. Critics point to Jose Rafael Pocaterra and Teresa de la Parra as the first post-modernists in Venezuela, not because they broke with literary tradition or began a new literary movement, but because they were unique cases. They provided new models after which it was impossible to return to old examples and old styles of writing. After oil was discovered in Venezuela, Caracas was transformed and de la Parra felt that these changes were for the worse. When she returned to Caracas she felt the city had lost some of its old charm. When she described these negative changes in *Iphigenia*, she was taken to task by Venezuelan critics.

Iphigenia as a Bildungsroman

Iphigenia is a novel of development that follows a young girl's initiation into the adult world, a novel in which the growth or formation of a character from late adolescence to early adulthood is revealed by both the narrator and the characters around her that help mold her growth as the narrative moves from letter to a diary and personal confessions.

According to Edna Aizenberg, *Iphigenia* is a failed *bildungsroman*. In the male *bildungsroman*, the hero undergoes an apprenticeship and achieves self-actualization. Heroines, however, end up frustrated, sacrificed or dead. *Iphigenia* violates and transgresses the paradigm of the *bildungsroman*, in which "A regulated development within the life of the individual is observed, each of its stages has its own intrinsic value and is at the same time the basis for a higher stage. The dissonances and conflicts of life appear as the necessary growth points through which the individual must pass on the way to maturity and harmony, (Swales, quoted in Aizenberg 540). Aizenberg examines the central components of a *bildungsroman* as they apply to *Iphigenia*: youth and orphanhood, provincialism, the immediate society, intergenerational conflict, self-education through experience or prohibited readings, an amorous test, and the search for values and a vocation. María Eugenia is an orphan whose formative years are supervised by two venerable matrons and whose apprenticeship is learning to navigate the social and domestic rituals appropriate to the Venezuelan upper class, restricted by *Kinder, Kirche and Kuche*. According to Aizenberg, María Eugenia embarks on a secret process of auto-illumination. She first falls in love with Gabriel Olmedo, but later decides to marry César Leal, which leads her to question her own values. When she capitulates to what she calls the Sacred Monster: society, family, honor, religion, morals, duty, conventions and principles, her initiation is over. But María Eugenia keeps reminding us that she has become a good liar; lying is a skill she needs to conceal her fragmentation (Aizenberg 542). Should we believe her decision? When she begins to write, it is a liberating and cathartic exercise for the protagonist. Towards the end, those same sheets of paper on which she poured her thoughts and feelings now remind her of tombstones on which she is about to write her epitaph.

According to Aizenberg, *Iphigenia* is also qualifies as a failed *Kunstleroman* since the heroine finds no solace in literature and she will not be able to dedicate herself to her writing (546). She has no self-awareness of herself as a writer, even though the letter she writes is consciously literate, with characters, drama, suspense, and is structured like a novel. She never imagines that she could earn a living as a writer. Because the family is in mourning for her grandfather and father, she is prohibited from playing the piano. She knows that the Venezuelan Teresa Carreño is a famous piano player and a would-be role model, but the piano is off limits to her during the mourning period for her father. She lacks the models and she lacks the examples. There are no feminine voices available to her except for the black laundress Gregoria, who adheres to laxer societal rules, and the unhappily married Mercedes.

As the heroine of her own story, the narrator goes through various stages of development. The stages are associated with characters in fairy tales, mythological beings, and literary characters. She begins as a Cinderella, an orphaned girl who has been touched by the magic of Paris. She becomes the captive princess waiting to be freed. Like Penelope, she weaves and unweaves her thoughts while she reads, writes and waits. Much later, she compares herself to Juliet, waiting for her Romeo. Ready to embark on her marriage of convenience, she becomes a timid shepherdess before the man who will dominate her. Her last and most tragic role will be that of ancient Iphigenia.

The novel is a dissection of criollo bourgeois values and attitudes towards women; a young girl's search for love and independence. The heroine settles for a marriage of convenience based on her experience with poverty and dependence on others. The novel ends with the heroine committing herself to sacrifice, but the heroine ends the novel contemplating this end. The reader never knows if she indeed goes through with the marriage. The ending runs counter to the romantic ending the reader expects. Perhaps this was de la Parra's way to shock the reader to focus on the reality of the social situation she felt was impeding women's progress. María Eugenia works hard to find herself, and when she does, she faces the bitter reality of her situation, a life of resignation, and the negation of self: a life like her maiden aunt's. If this is a novel of achieving self-knowledge, what María Eugenia learns is that she must give in to societal pressure. She may have sought refuge in her writing, but she abandons even that outlet for self-expression outlet for two years.

Innovation and Reception

Venezuelan critics began to write about de la Parra, but usually confined her within the circle of other Venezuelan writers. According to Yolanda Pantin and Ana Teresa Torres, editors of *El Hilo de la Voz,* nothing during the time De la Parra wrote prompted Venezuelan women to write, except an internal need to write. De la Parra inaugurated a fundamental tradition in Venezuelan narrative. She discarded epic themes and the theme of grand social processes. The new theme she introduced in Venezuelan literature was a young girl who wrote by herself, and who wrote about herself. This, according to these editors, was a new and risky project (54).

Venezuelan literature was considered to be stagnant, played out and backwards, divided between the followers of romanticism and Latin American modernism. De la Parra burst into this tired literary scene and created a new style and introduced a new theme by having a well-to-do young lady, who writes out of boredom, reveal the foibles of her society with grace and irony. The author used this bright and hopeful young girl to speak in a language free of the criollismo and rustic Venezuelan regionalism and free of romantic language to focus on the larger themes of the novel, which touch on the themes of sexism, racism, consumerism and women's commodification as she witnessed it in her contemporary society. The playful and witty word-play in María Eugenia's letter to her friend are evident in the first lines of the novel, with its zeugma, "When we said goodbye on the station platform in Biarritz, I remember that I, full of sorrows, sighs, and packages, told you while I hugged you 'I'll write soon, soon, very soon!" (7).

De la Parra's heroine, María Eugenia, describes herself and her world. This was an unusual and groundbreaking move for a writer, especially in Venezuela in the 1920's. The 1920's and 1930's produced several outstanding Latin-America women poets: Delmira Augustini, Juana Ibarborou, Gabriela Mistral, and Alfonsina Storni, to name just a few of the most well-read ones, or the most frequently translated into English.[19] Only de la Parra and the Chilean María Luisa Bombal are cited by literary historians as outstanding women novelists during the same period. Both authors provided an outlet for women's voices. Their heroines speak in the first person about themselves, and for themselves. Maria Eugenia is aware that she is an author, and a good one at that. Her reading is wide-ranging and she writes about how she has matured into a literary critic. In the letter to her friend Cristina she boasts, "I no longer consider myself a secondary character at all. I am quite satisfied with myself, and I have declared myself on strike against shyness and humility; I have, moreover, the presumption to believe that I am worth a million times more than all the heroines in the novels we used to read in summer- novels which, by the way, must have been very poorly written" (10). Not only does María Eugenia strive to entertain her friend through the dramatic report of her Parisian adventures, to which she now compares her humdrum existence in Caracas, but she is aware of her own voice as a writer and she shares her insights as a literary critic. Through Maria Eugenia, de la Parra created a new voice and a new narrative structure through which women could express themselves.

In her self-defense de la Parra discussed the theme of *Iphigenia* and as it applied to the situation of the contemporary young woman. In the first of her *Three Colombian Lectures* she talked about her first novel. She then segued to women's place in contemporary Latin American society

"This worthy and urgent topic that required remediation (*Obra* 473). She saw the necessity to create a feminine writing tradition. "Many are the moralists, some with amiable equanimity, the majority, or with violent anathemas, the minority, who attacked the diary of María Eugenia Alonso, called it Voltarian, treacherous and very dangerous in the hands of the contemporary young miss. I don't believe that this diary will influence today's young women for the simple reason that it will only serve to make them reflect. Almost all of them, especially those born and raised very strictly, carry a María Eugenia Alonso in full rebellion within themselves, more or less hidden, according to their oppression, who every day say loud and clear what she told them in her writing. María Eugenia Alonso's diary is not revolutionary propaganda, like the foreign moralists claim, no, on the contrary, it is the exposition of a typical case of our contemporary illness, that of Hispanic American Bovarism, that of being sensitive to the quick change in temperature, and the lack of fresh air in our environment. Whether the moralists like it or not, you don't wipe out an epidemic by hiding the cases, like they do in some ports where at the cost of truth and public health they pretend to have a clean bill of health. Epidemics are cured with air, light, and modern hygiene that neutralizes the causes, which can also be modern, that produce the illness. The crisis women must overcome can't be cured by preaching submission, submission and submission, like during the times when a tame life could be enclosed behind the doors of a house. In today's life, a car driven by its owner, a radio near her bed, access to the press and travel leave no respect for closed doors. Like radio signals, which it so closely resembles, it penetrates through walls, and whether you like it or not, becomes part of family life. In order for women to be strong, healthy and free of hypocrisy, they must not be judged against this new way of life, on the contrary, she needs to be free, conscious of dangers and of responsibilities, useful to society even if she is not a mother, and financially independent through her work and her collaboration alongside man, who is neither her owner, her enemy, nor a candidate for her exploitation, but her colleague and her friend" (*Obra* 473-7).

Change was inevitable, not only in women's lives, but in women's representation in literature.

De la Parra experimented with new ways to present narrative, and *Iphigenia* was not a novel narrated in a conventional rectilinear style common at the time. There is a two- year gap in which María Eugenia ceases to write, followed by a period of time in which she discovers and re-reads her diary. De la Parra jokingly referred to "the part not written" as the best part of her novel. The narrator establishes complicity with the reader through the device of a letter written to her best friend. The reader is privy to the letter, her diary, and the letter from her lover urging her to elope. Through the construction of an intimate tone, the reader lives in the same space and time as the narrator.

De la Parra contributed to the creation of a female aesthetic and made a lasting contribution to a literary tradition. What Reynolds refers to as "folkloric modernism" constitutes a means to construct radical fiction informed by an anthropologist's sense that trivial or superficial features of everyday life (gossip, cookery, family anecdotes) contained deep structures of culture (Reynolds 7). These inside narratives tell us the culture's political history. Reynolds continues, "Women debate, directly of covertly, salient political questions, they engage in the public psychology of their day" (7). The writing reflects the microscopic observation of manners and the everyday rituals of the female world. There was a need for this kind of fiction to be incorporated into the larger patterns of literary history.

Some of the literary techniques de la Parra incorporated into her novel include the use of stream-of-consciousness, the epiphany, and the use of myth. The drama that plays out in the narrator's mind is the writer's focus, and thoughts and images travel through her mind in illogical succession. James Joyce and Virginia Woolf were the first writers to transfer this mental phenomenon and the use of interior dialog to English literature and exploit it as a literary technique. The "action" takes place and the plot develops through the mind of the characters, who tend to have emotional and intellectual adventures rather than physical ones. The epiphany is a spiritual revelation or a breakthrough, and María Eugenia's epiphany occurs when she realizes that she can't fight the system. Her conscious employment of mythology, her use of María Eugenia as the modern Iphigenia is a reminder of the role of sacrifice in contemporary times.

The reaction to *Iphigenia* depended on the nationality of the readers. Europeans found it charming and funny. They were taken by its exotic setting. Venezuelans thought the novel could harm young girls, that it was Voltairian and therefore revolutionary. The novel was realistic; Venezuelans critics were afraid that young women would read it and identify with the heroine. María Eugenia's caustic commentaries on respectable marriages of convenience and her descriptions of Caracas leveled her criticism on institutions and places rather than on her sometimes naïve yet very perceptive narrator. María Eugenia depicts the city she has come back to in a less than favorable light and she returns not to the wide, long, elegant streets of her infancy, but to a Caracas whose streets are hung with telephone lines, "And as if the lines were not enough, the intruding telephone posts opened their arms and, feigning crosses in a lengthy Calvary, stretched one after another, until they were lost in the remote confines of the horizon.. Oh! yes, Caracas, of the delightful climate, of gentle memories, the familiar city, the intimate and distant city, turned out to be this flat town...a kind of Andalusian city, like a melancholy Andalusia, without a shawl or castanets, without guitars or music, without flowerpots and flowers on the balconies...a drowsy Andalusia that had dropped off to sleep in the sultry heat of the tropics! " (38).

"As early as 1923, a prominent Venezuelan critic, Don Lisandro Alvarado, had pointed out that *Ifigenia* revived the age-old and bitter philosophical struggle between philogynists and misogynists. In 1926, Teresa could no longer stand the misogyny she divined behind those "brilliantly prepared arguments" and exploded in an article, published in Caracas, called "*Ifigenia:* The Criticism, Critics, and Would-Be Critics."

Stressing somewhat bitterly her humble approach to writing as an "amiable and conciliatory recourse, at times very sincere," which she permitted herself to "recommend to all authors," she lit into a group of critics she labeled "false intellectuals" (Lemaitre 98)." One time, for example, one of them said to me with a patronizing air, that my novel *Ifigenia* was full of "femininities." I believed sincerely that he meant great praise and started to express my thanks with my most pleasant smile. But in time I realized that "femininities" did not constitute a good quality, but rather a grave defect. Then, with the same smile I was prepared to give him thanks for the praise, I thanked him for the warning and promised in the future I would never commit "femininity." The truth is that I could never change myself, because I have not really managed to understand what they wanted to tell me."[20]

Unamuno's advice to de la Parra was to "throw away the mirror and disregard the negative criticism." This was advice she found hard to follow: "No, I did not invent the mirror, don Miguel. If, like Narcissus, I spend my days in its insipid attraction, it is out of sheer nonsense, out of an obstinate spirit of association; the inertia of the blank page." When Unamuno questioned de la Parra on her use of the words "resignation" and "sacrifice" in her novel, she responded," Most certainly! I think also that in all resignation, as in all sacrifice, there is a divine scorn, towards something or someone, a divine, inactive scorn that asks neither vengeance nor justice, and which sleeps tranquilly with the sweet dream of serenity."

(Lemaitre 108). These words go a long way towards explaining María Eugenia's last speech in which sacrifice and resignation echo as the heroine gives in to her fate.

By 1926 there was negative criticism out of South America," In the establishment circles of Venezuela and Colombia, everything, from the realistic, moody description of Caracas in the beginning of the book to the descriptions of misery underlying family life throughout it, was seen as an insult. As late as 1928, harsh religious judgments by a Colombian Jesuit came down on Parra's use of the words "obligation, honor, family, religion, morality, society and social need." Not only did he think that María Eugenia was immoral, but that her author was equally so. From his point of view, the novel clearly posed a danger to readers without strong moral principles." (Lemaitre 103). *Iphigenia* was a success in Europe, where it was considered exotic and picturesque but it irked Venezuelan readers who interpreted de la Parra's descriptions as a mockery. Furthermore, they were offended that it was written by a writer who was unfamiliar with the customs of her own country, since the writer had lived abroad for several years.

The criticism only served to create a clandestine following for *Iphigenia*. The initial attacks on de la Parra's morality hurt her, and she resented being identified with her heroine María Eugenia, who she considered to be a weak character. "For to her, the book was written by María Eugenia, not by herself; it lived a separate life of its own. The voice of the narrator is capricious and charming, and we learn not to trust it (Lemaitre 103)." De la Parra claimed she had not set out to create "serious literature" but wanted rather to describe intimate details about everyday life. Nor did she want to be remembered as the author of a harmful book or a book that brought dishonor to her family's name. But sometimes de la Parra could be unreasonable. "When, in December of 1926, Chilean critic Armando Labarca published an article in *El Universal* praising *Ifigenia* for its author's gift of observation of the ridiculous aspects of people and things, of gentle conventionalisms, de la Parra refuted that she had not made anything or anyone in her novel look ridiculous. The exasperated columnist mollified her by writing another column praising her for her charming and contradictory letters" (Lemaitre 104).

There was an attempt to stop *Ifigenia's* second printing by an anonymous person who wrote under the pseudonym of Carlos Villena. The writer mailed a letter to the Venezuelan embassy in Paris. The attack concerned Tio Pancho's remark about how Venezuelan women, in their spouses' absence during the war, took lovers of mixed race. Although the character Mercedes Galindo defended the virtue of her female ancestors and insisted on the purity of her descendant's blood, (after all, she is "white on all four sides"), the anonymous attacker saw the remark as sacrilegious. Villena's attack took on a racist dimension," The book, already close to completion, very likely took on a collaborator in its manufacture, probably Jewish, who conceived of the ending, pretending therewith that the spirit of sacrifice can exist beyond the Christian religion, and even beyond all religion" (109). The attacker turned out to be Dr. Ignacio Vetancourt-Aristeguita, a journalist and secretary of the Venezuelan delegation to Peru and Bolivia. He cited María Eugenia's preference for the company of the Negro laundress, Gregoria, to reinforce his racist comments.

Eduardo Guzman Esponda wrote a review of *Iphigenia*, "La novela de una caraqueña," published in *Sante Fe de Bogotá*, Bogotá, in 1927. De la Parra asked Guzman-Esponda to show more respect for the word "spinsterhood." As far as being afraid of spinsterhood, as you put it, that's not the reason- that's not why María Eugenia marries Leal. Admit that this word deserves more tact and reverence. Admit it deserves a nicer word that evokes the charming attitude of love. Since the beginning of time it's been this fear that secretly teaches maidens to smile, to silently make the arrangements for funerals and wakes, discreetly plan weddings, and with her blessing she gives the bride a deep peace that smoothes the past and colors the roses in the dark destinies that were accepted rather than chosen."

De la Parra has been called the most complex writer of Hispanic America literature (Díaz Sánchez 17). Her masterpiece is *Iphigenia* - an imaginary biography of a woman who wants to be someone else but doesn't know how to do it (14). Despite criticism that she painted Caracas in a bad light, Díaz Sánchez admires that the writer conveyed the true feel of Caracas with its interior gardens in the Spanish style, its church bells, and the narrow silent streets under the tropical sun.

The clash of cultures is evident in *Iphigenia*. Caracas is presented as a quasi-medieval place, a colonial world with squat houses whose inhabitants, especially women, lived their restricted lives behind grilled windows. Although the city had undergone some changes, the contrast between the realities of the Venezuelan capital and the life de la Parra lived in Spain and her experiences in Paris provided a shocking contrast. Ultimately, de la Parra left Caracas to return to Europe to seek a cure for her tuberculosis. Her impression of Caracas is indelible in *Iphigenia,* whose heroine stands in for an entire class of women who lived in the capital at the time. Critics concentrated on the externals, and took offense at her description of the city, saying she had shown Caracas in a poor light.

The hypocrisy, the backwardness, the machismo and the political situation in Venezuela shocked her, and the author was taken to task for exposing them.

The author was delighted when the three dozen copies of *Iphigenia* she brought to a book festival sold out immediately while other books lingered on the shelves. She planned for illustrated luxury editions of *Iphigenia* in German and Russian, and for a second edition of the novel in Spanish. The Parisian fashion houses de la Parra mentioned offered to furnish her with the ensembles María Eugenia wore in the novel.[21]

The real drama of María Eugenia, according to the writer and critic María Fernando Palacios, is poverty.[22] It is poverty that destroys the heroine's dream of an independent life. The myth of the *criollo* woman is further explored by this Venezuelan essayist and poet. Her extensive work, *Ifigenia: mitología de la doncella criolla*, Angria Ediciones, 2001, connects the Maiden archetype to criollo society and its expectations for women's roles. This book represents a new approach to criticism for a novel buried under its load, and it is an approach rarely used in Venezuelan criticism. Palacios examines the novel through the myth of the maiden, the bright and luminous aspect as well as the dark and dangerous side of this complex image. In this case, there is less of the classic aspect and more emphasis on the criollo. Veronica Joffe's review of the literary critic and professor's study of the novel as she reads and examines it, its author and its country, and in doing so Joffe claims that Palacios reads herself and we can read ourselves as readers, (and Venezuelans). The study itself becomes a novel, the charming and sad novel *Iphigenia*, of Teresa de la Parra, of Venezuela, of the author, and of ourselves as readers. As we continue reading, the study becomes more like Teresa's novel; it becomes a novel continued by María Fernanda, and it accomplishes everything a serious study should do: it speaks of life and of ourselves. It speaks to us and is about us. Palacios interprets the novel as a novel of destiny, a fight for the narrator's soul. In her letter to Guzman Esponda, Paris, June, 1926 she explains that the protagonist is moved by "those dark destinies that were accepted rather than chosen" (435). The heroine's ultimate sacrifice is her refusal to flee; instead, she accepts matrimony, and accepts her role as a tragic victim.

In Venezuela, the *criollos* are the descendants of the conquistadors. María Eugenia Alonso describes " almost all of those *criollos,* descendants of the conquistadors, who called themselves "Mantuans" in Colonial times, who founded and ruled the cities; who engraved their coats of arms on the doors of the old mansions; who, with their blood, forged the independence of half the American continent; who declined afterwards, oppressed by persecutions and party hatreds; and whose granddaughters or great-granddaughters, today forgotten or as poor as I am now, awaited with resignation the hour of marriage or the hour of death, making sweets for dances, or weaving floral wreaths for funerals" (*Obra* 60).

Palacios' work is divided into four chapters: "The Mythology of the House," "The Cage of Eloquence," "The Maiden" and "Sacrifice". Palacios studies the speech and the humor of the novel in the "Cage of Eloquence" and also examines its common speech, and the Caracas roots, which is the privileged vehicle of the humor of Teresa de la Parra: "I mean a language that is united to a life where the *castiza* note sounds, with its archaisms and its simple country talk, and the illustrated petulance and the finicky, prudish, hysterical tone of household exaggerations. And the less festive, more serious tone, when she confronts the theme of sacrifice, here found in the agonizing figure of Tio Pancho, who represents one of the main themes of the novel: decadence. The novel joins decadence to a this jovial character and his squandered life. On the other hand, there is the sacrifice of María Eugenia as a criollo Iphigenia, but there are also the streets of Caracas, with the poor porters of its port, with the poverty that is the heroine's inheritance that contrasts with the heroic vision and the terrible seriousness with which the book ends. The final discovery: Venezuelan's love of the heroic can't accept the realistic vision of a marriage of convenience, so it turns it into a tragic sacrifice, analogous to the sacrifice of a war hero. María Eugenia, claims Palacios, does away with the last of her fictions: the myth of the sacrificed maiden. In order to live with the weight of reality María Eugenia moves from the fantasy of captivity to an expanded state that imitates the lofty heroic and sacrificial figure of Iphigenia. But, says Palacios, not as a fantasy that becomes dangerously suicidal. The sacrificed woman remains like a hidden and resentful wound, and that is worse. Palacios views the ending of the novel as disturbing. It is not an exemplary ending, but rather a frightening image of woman and of the criollo household and woman's role in it.

Humor

The humor in the novel begins with the chapter titles, a parody of 17th century novels, much like the chapter titles of *Don Quixote,* and the sentimental and picaresque English novels. Chapter I of the Second Part, for example is titled, "Having now sent the interminable letter to her friend Cristina, María Eugenia Alonso resolves to write her diary. As will be seen, in this first chapter, the genteel Mercedes Galindo appears at last."

On board she meets a flirtatious Colombian poet who is attracted to her, and he comments on her languid pose, as she rests her chin on her hands on the ship's guardrail. He showers her with flowery poetry in an attempt to seduce her, and praises the whiteness of her hands. "Now they look like two lilies holding a rose," my friend recited again. "Tell me, María Eugenia, haven't your cheeks ever been jealous of your hands?" "No, I responded. Everyone here lives in perfect harmony" (20).

María Eugenia tries hard to be a naughty adolescent. She scandalizes her grandmother with her outright rejection of Catholic dogma. Defending herself against her Tia Clara and her Abuela, who consider her too outspoken and rebellious, she responds, "Do you want me to tell you what I think now, Abuela? Do you want me to admit it? Very well! I think that morality is a farce…Yes, I had three years of philosophy in school, and the teachers who graded my homework and compositions used to fill the margins of my papers with praise" (121). When her Abuela wonders, "How do so many things occur to her at the same time?" multilingual María Eugenia explains, "Yes, thank God, I do have a rich vocabulary! I do know how to express myself elegantly, and even in ordinary, domestic conversations, with good taste, in three languages…" (123). She likes to show off her own knowledge of languages. Her Abuela objects to her unladylike outbursts. "Eureka!!" I exclaimed, since this, although a little pretentious, was the only interjection Abuela had left me" (105).

María Eugenia's Paris fashions are too immodest for her conservative relatives and seem out of place in Caracas. To bolster her argument concerning modesty, she paraphrases a parable from the *New Testament*. "Tell me, do lilies wear clothes, Tia Clara? Do they dress? Do doves dress? Without dressing they preach purity and they are the symbol of chastity. If doves wore clothes, we'd be scandalized to see them fly, because they'd probably lift their dresses with the movement of their wings, and this from below would make a very indecent display (107).

Through her protagonist, de la Parra injected humor to call attention to social issues. Since humor was a rare feature in Venezuelan literature, and the author was sad that the humor and irony in *Iphigenia* went over some readers' heads. Others, however, found the novel funny. María Eugenia tries hard to be a naughty adolescent. She flirts with a Colombian poet, she is sure that the three years of philosophy she studied in school gives her the right to mock morals and customs, and is proud that she can express herself elegantly, and with good taste, in three languages. She quotes from the Bible to defend her immodest clothes, and is sorry she did not pay enough attention at a feminist lecture by British suffragette Pankhurst due to the hobnailed shoes and thick cotton stockings the speaker wore.

Appearances are important to her, and contemplating her future as a wife and mother she ponders, "I might have a daughter, who instead of looking like me, might look like her aunt's, an irreversible disaster, which would probably leave me forever inconsolable" (227).

Febres notes that when a writer is called a humorist, it tends to put her in a superficial, frivolous, and shallow category. But humor and irony can be used to call attention to social issues, and *Iphigenia* succeeded in doing this. María Eugenia is not a romantic heroine. She is a bored young lady, but she is not indifferent or bitter and is always engaged with the people around her. She is not just a rebellious young woman; she is more complex than that. De la Parra broke new ground by treating contemporary issues in a humorous way.

The author was proud that the Infanta Eulelia, the King of Spain's Tia, herself a writer, was amused by *Iphigenia.* The Infanta invited the author to take tea with her and told de la Parra how she laughed out loud at some passages in the novel, such as the one about the cutwork tablecloth Abuelita wanted María Eugenia to work on. The Infanta laughed so loud, in fact, that her maid came running to see what the matter was. In this passage, the Abuela is praising Tia María Antonia, who is described as morally superior. María Eugenia describes her Abuela talking as she works her needle, "Morally María Antonia is irreproachable. I know, because Abuela says so often, imperceptibly separating five threads of her needlework: Ir-re-proach-a-ble (29)."

Humor in the novel is injected through digressions, a slow pace, circumventions, and dialog with the reader, interruptions, exclamations, reoccurrences, and instances that may seem unnecessary to the reader and take our attention away from the plot. De la Parra infuses the heroine's letter and diary entries with historical, mythological and religious references, sometimes to give her thoughts deeper meaning and at other times to satirize, mock, or call attention to events. She is well-versed in the teachings of the Church Fathers, and she disagrees with St. Jerome, "who apparently wrote horrors about the chic woman of his day" (18). De la Parra is not so much a funny writer, as she is a witty one. When French editors wanted to shorten the length of *Iphigenia's* text she responded by saying, "What can I cut from María Eugenia? Her dress and her hair are short already...perhaps I should remove an arm or a leg?" (56) A keen observer of her social scene, she continues to be praised by literary critics for her graceful style, her wit, her ironic handling of situations, and her endearing, but never cruel or bitter, sense of humor.

A Message for Contemporary Women

Virginia Woolf argued that woman needs a room of her own and that women should not be the mirrors to men's lives. In the ancestral house in Caracas, with its barred windows shuttered to signify mourning, María Eugenia writes in her room. Although she has a room of her own, the room that belonged to her maiden Tia Clara, she lacks the financial independence Woolf argued for. What does María Eugenia do in this room of her own? She writes. First she writes a letter to her school friend Cristina to catch her up on her wonderful adventures in Paris and to complain about her boredom. María Eugenia sets out to summarize her thoughts and activities to Cristina as is done in "authentic novels." She continues, "Besides, I have lately discovered that I have a gift for observation and great ease in expressing myself" (10), drawing her friend into the joy of this self-discovery.

The heroine, who has reinvented herself from a sheltered Catholic schoolgirl to a chic young lady in cosmopolitan Paris, returns to live in a conservative household in a developing country. She learns that she is penniless, having spent the last of her fortune on couture clothes and gifts for her family. She soon realizes that she must make a good match and marry a man who will provide for her but keep her house-bound. She has a chance to flee with the man she loves (who has also opted for a marriage of convenience), but that would make her a social outcast. It is curious that the religious sense or moral issue of running away with a married man does not enter into the heroine's choice, nor in the heroine's choice of marrying a man she does not love, thus perpetuating a pattern of failed marriages of convenience, another of the themes of this novel.

According to Mariano Picón Salas, many Hispanic-American women, still imprisoned in the most trivial routines and conventions, were waiting for such a message. And *Ifigenia,* unique for its grace and adolescent malice… conquered the entire Hispanic world. It was read simultaneously in Mexico, Bogota, Montevideo, in Santiago de Chile. I knew an elderly Chilean philosophy professor who confessed to me, like on who has committed a delightful sin, that he devoted to the small and fantastic María Eugenia Alonso a moment he had stolen from Kant (186).

Orlando Araujo states that what "was most objected to in her time is what today's reader most appreciates: her irreverence toward accepted norms, the irony with which she portrays a city and its inhabitants at a social and spiritual crossroads between the coffee and the petroleum industries… In 1924, *Ifigenia* was a true challenge both to the "manners" of the time as well as to genre writing. That a young woman should speak with such freedom and should mock a society that admired and envied her, must have been intolerable to many people of her class and to the literary mediocrities who observed from afar... Yet there is no bitterness or venom in her work, no satire, no bad humor: she says things with a smile, or with peals of laughter... and thus she sweeps aside the conceited incompetent who, in her time, administered the word at festivals and conferences. The irreverent words were being written by the daughter of one of the best families in Caracas, envied for her refinement, education and intelligence" ("Sobre *Ifigenia*" in Bosch, *Teresa de la Parra* 155-156).

Despite the fact that the heroine succumbs to societal pressures, the novel was criticized in Venezuela and Colombia as being a bad influence on women readers. María Eugenia's diary is written in the intimate confessional tone and at times dramatic tone usually associated with female writers, but by using different points of view and by maintaining a narrative distance from her material, de la Parra was able to articulate the social realities that hampered women of her class and exposed mistreatment of women in Latin American society. The protagonist's inner journey represents a first-person exploration of limited options. The novel explored many themes that many Latin American women were facing: unhappy marriages, women's passivity and lack of self-expression, unfulfilled love, economic dependency, dread of spinsterhood, and the fear of appearing intelligent and well-read.

De la Parra created a way to interpret and report women's experiences, thus producing a key novel in the development of Venezuelan fiction. Through this novel she hoped to voice the frustrations of many women caught up a changing society. The narrative style progresses as the heroine matures. The narrator defines herself by focusing on different angles of herself at different turning points in her life. The end is profound and painful. The free-spirited young woman who was full of hope is gone. She disappears into the text, much as the actress walks away from the set in Ivan Feo's 1986 film based on the novel.[23] The open-endedness of the novel leaves the reader to judge its ending. The novel suggests more than it says. What, exactly, happened during the heroine's two-year silence? The reader has been accustomed to expecting irony and ambiguity and is called upon to play an active role imagining both the lapse in the narrator's writing and in constructing the novel's ending. Does she really marry Cesar Leal or is the ending another example of María Eugenia's dramatic outpouring and identification with a Greek heroine?

The novel's focus on woman's place in Venezuelan society forms a contrast to what women's roles should be, roles better fleshed out in the *Three Colombian Lectures* and in her letters. In her lectures, de la Parra explores the idea of the commodification of women in a hostile environment created by a society in which women have limited choices. Since de la Parra was not free to criticize openly, she offers plenty of examples to prove her point. The protagonist becomes a young version of her Abuela. Her transformation questions the values of marriage and the institution of the family. María Eugenia is on the verge of becoming her husband's property. She also changes outwardly. Her fashion sense, once so important to her, will have to adhere to her husband's tastes. Intellectually, she has to pretend she knows less than she really does. In *Iphigenia*, María Eugenia resists these traditional pastimes at first and mocks them, but then she eventually takes them up.

As Annis Pratt pointed out, "When a woman sets out to manipulate language, to create new myths out of old, to write an essay or paint a painting, she transgresses fundamental social taboos in that very act.. the outcries evoked by the mildest of women writers who dared to make even the slightest rebellions against gender norms: to use our drives for authenticity in order to shape feminine archetypes into fiction, to bring elements of our inner world into consciousness and give them shape in the social form of the novel, is an act of defiance with perilous consequences (*Archetypal Patterns* 11.)

According to Edith Dimo and Amarilis Hidalgo de Jesús Teresa de la Parra subverted the canonical masculine literary models that had been established in Venezuela. De la Parra created a starting point for women writers and a process through which female experience could be recorded, in addition to autobiographies, testimonios, diaries, letters, historiographic models, historical documents, and popular culture, among other genres (*Escritura y desafío: Narradoras*7). The process allowed for a production of a subtext through dissident discourse, and the insertion of the Latin American woman into the historical-social context. It legitimized the female as a subject.

Before Teresa de la Parra, the first texts written by women published in Venezuela relied on realist masculine models, but these were lacking in the discourses that foregrounded alienation and introspection as existential female conditions. According to the editors, Venezuelan narratives written by women are fundamentally based on Teresa de la Parra, since she began a literary tradition that reflects the subversive context of literature. *Iphigenia* is the motive text, the springboard that challenged the conventional order of seven decades, and integrated the participation of the woman-writer in the historical-social process of Latin America.

Notes

[1] All translations taken from *Obra: (Narrativa, ensayos, cartas)*, Ed, Velia Bosch are mine.

[2] Febres, Laura. *Perspectivas críticas sobre la obra de Teresa de la Parra*. Caracas: Editorial Arte, 1984.

[3] Ramón Díaz Sánchez. *Teresa de la Parra: Clave para una interpretación*. Caracas: Ediciones Garrido, 1954.

[4] "Mujeres del Avila" (intervista de actualidad) *El Nuevo Diario*, Caracas 23, Feb. 1923.

[5] An introduction and translations to the short stories "The Story of Miss Dust Mote, Sun Dancer", "The Genie of the Letter Scale", and the "Hermit in the Clock" appear in chapter 10.

[6] Louis Antoine Lemaître. *Between Flight and Longing: The Journey of Teresa de la Parra*. New York: Vantage Press, 1986.

[7] These views are more fully explained in the *Three Colombian Lectures: The Role of Women in the Formation of the American Soul*.

[8] *Iphigenia* is autobiographical insofar as it includes the lives of the stories of her female ancestors, according to Lemaitre. *Iphigenia* is the modern woman's refutation of everything old fashioned (Lemaître 15).

[9] All translations from *Iphigenia* are from *Iphigenia: The diary of a young lady who wrote because she was bored*. Trans. Bertie Acker. Austin: University of Texas Press, 1993.

[10] María Fernanda Palacios. "Pobreza y dependencia en Ifigenia." *El Universal*. Caracas. Verbigracia, No. 11, año IV. 6-12-2000. 1-2.

[11] The letter is over 80 pages long in the English translation.

[12] María Eugenia refers to Mercedes as Semiramis. She was the Assyrian queen who built the Hanging Gardens of Babylon, known for her beauty, wisdom and sexual excesses. Mercedes is the prototype of the affluent Venezuelan who visited Paris regularly, and her taste reflects the current taste for all things Oriental.

[13] In a letter to de la Parra, Miguel de Unamuno suggested she write more poetry. De la Parra responded, "Since my entire life I've written only, and only after great effort, two or three poems, I judge to be mediocre. Lyric poetry bares the soul and requires great purity and modesty or it risks becoming comical."

[14] "Aphrodite, as the goddess of sexuality is lacking not only in *Iphigenia*, but in Teresa de la Parra's world as well." (Palacios 247).

[15] For an excellent discussion of Gregoria, see "Intersections of Race and Romance in the Americas: Teresa de la Parra's Iphigenia and Ellen Glasgow's The Sheltered Life." *Mississippi Quarterly*, Summer/Fall 2005, Vol.58, Issue 3/4. 737-759.

[16] Eugenia means "well-born" in Greek.

[17] Palacios dismisses the heroine's role as a sacrificial victim, since a sacrificial victim should have an affinity with divinity (439).

[18] Jara, René, and Hermán, Vidal, Eds. *Testimonio y Literatura*, Minneapolis: Institute for the Study of Ideologies and Literature, 1986.

[19] "Important women intellectuals, including Teresa de la Parra (Venezuela, 1889-1936), Maria Luisa Bombal (Chile, 1910-1980), Elena Garro (Mexico, 1920-1998), Rosario Castellanos (Mexico, 1925-1974) and Clarice Lispector (Brazil, 1925-1977), have used access to education to create literary works and essays critical of the limitations place on women. Recuperation of works like theirs constitutes a major project within feminist criticism" (Gollnick 115).

[20] *Ifigenia, Los críticos, y los criticones*. *Obras Completas*. 468.

[21] De la Parra was known for her exquisite taste and love of elegant fashion. The Parisian fashion house Drecoll, whose leading designer was Maggy Rouff, offered to outfit the writer in María Eugenia's outfits as de la Parra had described them in the novel.

[22] "Ifigenia, la novela que somos," Verónica Jaffe's review of María Fernanda Palacios *Ifigenia: Mitolgia de la doncella criolla*, Ediciones Angria, Caracas 2001. 479.16.

[23] Iván Feo directed the film *Ifigenia* (Venezuela, 1986), based on Teresa de la Parra's novel. His solution to the ambiguous, open-ended and problematic ending of the novel is to have the actress who plays María Eugenia contemplate her wedding dress, disrobe and walk off the set.

CHAPTER THREE

LEARNING FROM MAMA BLANCA

"If women's writing is, or should be, supremely simple and transparent, *Mama Blanca's Memoirs* was hailed as exemplary" (Sommer, in *Mama Blanca*, xvi.).

In her second book, *Mama Blanca's Memoirs* (1929), Teresa de la Parra offered a rare and privileged insight into life on a sugarcane plantation, describing a seemingly idyllic and bucolic way of life that was rapidly disappearing during her own lifetime.[1] It is a nostalgic work that reflects her affection for Venezuela's past she lovingly wrote about in her lectures and letters. To read *Mama Blanca's Memoirs* is to enter into an exotic, lost world told through a series of vignettes about life as remembered by a five-year-old girl who lived on the hacienda Piedra Azul. She is now in her eighties, and she reminisces to a young woman who will edit the memoirs.

De la Parra composed a series of vignettes set in the past, rather than a novel set in the present. For some critics, *Iphigenia: the diary of a young lady who wrote because she was bored* (1924), was the immature work of a rebellious young girl and *Mama Blanca's Memoirs* was the more objective work of a mature writer (Rivera 10). Early critics called the second work a childhood reminiscence marked by simplicity, tenderness, religiosity and ingeniousness.

More recently, critics call for a reappraisal of the work as an understanding of the American world, especially when it is studied alongside Rómulo Gallegos' *Doña Barbara* (Bosch xxxi). Both *Doña Barbara* and *Mama Blanca's Memoirs* were published in 1929, but de la Parra's work lacks the foundational fictional quality and historic sweep of Gallego's Nobel Prize winning novel. There are no complex characters or symbolic names in de la Parra's utopia. Both works are located in the rural, agrarian world of the late twentieth century hacienda. *Doña Barbara's* setting is the world of progress, civilization and the city; its prose is hymn-like, solemn and descriptive. Mama Blanca's world is intelligently funny and colloquial. While the characters in *Doña Barbara* are archetypes, the memorable characters that inhabit Piedra Azul go through the everyday rituals of life on a plantation.[2]

In *Mama Blanca's Memoirs*, the mother had been married at 15 to a man twice her age and in rapid succession gave birth to six girls. The daughters in *Mama Blanca's Memoirs* are deliberately ineptly named, and the vignettes are written in a gentle tone. As a member of the Criollo cultural elite, the author had enjoyed a carefree and happy childhood on her family's hacienda, Tazón, from the time she was two until she was nine. In *Mama Blanca's Memoirs* the family sugar cane hacienda is renamed Piedra Azul, and the stories recreate a turn-of-the century rural way of life. Growing up as one of three daughters in a conservative and patriarchal Venezuelan family, de la Parra recalled the experiences of the landowning class and the people who served them. After being educated in Spain, she returned to a Venezuela that was moving away from agrarian life. Her second book preserved the memories of life in the 1850s, 70 years before the work's publication. She wanted to show the contrast of hacienda society and the changes taking place that would impact the lives of both agricultural workers and the land-owning gentry.

De la Parra's chose to focus on society rather than on nature in her works. While *Iphigenia* was about a young woman's rebelliousness in Caracas and her capitulation to societal expectations, in *Mama Blanca's Memoirs* the author chose to depict the insular but interesting society of a sugar plantation situated not too far from Caracas, describing the idiosyncratic characters that provided the memories. The five-year-old Blanca Nieves will write a memoir as an adult which she will share with an unknown editor, the narrator.

Diversity made life on the plantation entertaining. The owners of the plantation are criollos, descendants of the Spanish settlers and conquistadors of Venezuela. But all kinds of people lived and worked on the plantation. De la Parra believed the future success of America was its ability to become a melting pot, and the inhabitants of Piedra Azul represented such a variety and mixture of races.[3]

De la Parra wrote the book between 1926 and 1928 while she was living a cosmopolitan life, mingling with diplomats, intellectuals, artists, and journalists in Europe.[4] Old and new ways of writing were battling for recognition. In her letters she wrote that the literary and artistic trends of the time such as cubism, Dadaism, and modernism did not move her. In fact, they left her cold. She began to write *Mama Blanca's Memoirs* in Maracay, but her peripatetic life brought her to Paris, Geneva, several cities in Italy, Paris again, Havana, Caracas, Vevey and Corseaux. She returned to Europe and moved to Vevey, near Lake Laman, Switzerland. A life of shuttling back and forth seemed to have inspired her to re-create a lost world, and she turned her geographical distance into literary advantage. She continued to write *Mama Blanca's Memoirs* while she was still in "voluntary exile" in Vevey, Switzerland, which she likened to a religious cloister. It was a welcome retreat for her.

In 1927 she wrote to her friend Rafael Carias, to whom she entrusted her manuscripts, that she was wholly devoted to this book, "though not as difficult, will definitely be better than *Iphigenia*." On Christmas Eve of that year she wrote to Enrique Bernardo Nuñez that she had finished the book. "I have written it with great affection and find it entirely to my liking, which is why I am so fond of it." The last installment of the book appeared in July, 1928 in the *Revue de L'Amerique Latine* and the book was published the next year in Paris in both Spanish and French. At this point in her career, she was well-known in many countries.

De la Parra was troubled by the reaction to her first novel, *Iphigenia*. She was dismayed by its reception in Caracas, and wrote about her disappointment in her correspondence to her friends. She felt too many readers had missed its ironic intention. She defended herself by writing letters in newspapers to her detractors. Her second work would be a more conservative, less self-reflective work. The publication of *Mama Blanca's Memoirs* appeased some readers but irked others. In fact, the readers who liked *Iphigenia* disliked *Mama Blanca's Memoirs*. The nostalgic tone in *Mama Blanca's Memoirs* seemed inappropriate to some readers, given the political situation in Venezuela and the riots that accompanied National Student Week of 1928.[5] That year she wrote to Carlos García Prada,[6] an assistant professor of Spanish at the University of Washington, about the criticism, "I wrote my second book, *Mama Blanca's Memoirs*, which, unlike *Iphigenia*, was very well received by the traditionalists but disappointed the female readers of *Iphigenia*, who missed María Eugenia Alonso, the heroine sacrificed to custom (*Obra* 600)."

While *Iphigenia* depicted a reality that needed to be questioned and changed, *Mama Blanca's Memoirs* more "colonial" world was to be savored and longed for. De la Parra took the adverse criticism of *Ifigenia* to heart, as we can see in her letters. In that novel, she dared to write about a current contemporary problem and was taken to task for it. To compound the problem, her critics found it difficult to separate her personal life from her narrative. In writing *Mama Blanca's Memoirs*, de la Parra mined the past and produced charming vignettes and unforgettable characters critics could not take issue with. Still sensitive to the negative criticism leveled at *Iphigenia*, de la Parra vowed to write a nostalgic novel. While still working on finishing the novel, *Mama Blanca's Memoirs*, de la Parra wrote to a friend, assuring her that it would be "the most criollo of criollo literature" (*Epistolario Intimo* 70).

Annis Pratt studies women's writing and restoration by way of memoir, their use of a confessional tone and how history is transmitted through a feminine subjective perspective. While history is the axis, it is filtered through an individual. In women's writing, there is a tendency to reject inherited language and discourse. Pratt points out the importance of silence, spontaneity, and the oral aspect of women's writing. These novels reevaluate the past from the present, after insight and maturity. It is exactly this aspect of Mama Blanca's storytelling that lends it credibility and charm. It is the story of six daughters in a typical patriarchal family which in reality is ruled by a charming young mother. De la Parra's style in this work is by turns graceful, humorous and witty. Some of the chapters detail the experiences of women of the landowning class, offering one vision of feminine existence. This assemblage of short chapters with a common thread adheres to what Reynolds terms "Folkloric modernism," a means to construct radical fictional shapes which were informed by an anthropologist's sense that trivial or superficial features of everyday life (gossip, cookery, family anecdotes) contained deep structures of a culture (7).

De la Parra had also been accused of exposing her family in her first novel. One of the criticisms leveled against *Iphigenia* was that the author exploited her family and took advantage of her position in society. Readers assumed that the novel's feisty heroine's outpourings were de la Parra's own "confessions." The story was about six sisters who grow up on a sugar cane hacienda. De la Parra had two older brothers, Luís Felipe and Miguel, notably absent in this work. Her family's economic situation and social status was aptly reflected, however, since both Tazón and Piedra Azul were eventually sold and the family moved to Caracas.

García Prada was taken with both of de la Parra's works and wanted to translate *Ifigenia* into English to use as a model of good literature for his Spanish students. De la Parra wrote to García Prada in May 1931 from Paris. She thanked him for his warm reception of both her books, and was honored that he wanted to translate *Iphigenia* for North American readers. She felt, however, that *Mama Blanca's Memoirs* would be a better choice. It was shorter and easier to translate, and her later work would better suit García Prada's didactic purposes since they were "loose sketches" rather than a novel (*Obra* 598). In June 1931 she authorized García Prada to edit the book, in whatever form he saw fit for pedagogical purposes, adding, "I am pleased it will be a way to teach about our Criollo life. I believe international conflicts stem from misconceptions. Your teaching in North

America is useful and good. Every book that sheds the light of affection, no matter how humble, can contribute to this enterprise. Maybe you are right, my six little girls in *Mama Blanca's Memoirs* can convey some of this affection to your students of Spanish literature, bless them, and it would give me great satisfaction (*Obra* 601-602)." García Prada noted that *Mama Blanca's Memoirs* filled a void. Before this work, there were few novels written that described childhood experiences, especially with compassion, grace and empathy. "For those of us who lived in the small towns of tropical lands, these memories are our memories. By sharing hers, Teresa has also told of the memories of thousands of Hispanic Americans (15)." In his introduction to de la Parra's letters in *Obras Completas,* Mariano Picón Salas wrote that *Mama Blanca's Memoirs* should be required reading in all Venezuelan schools. She was, according to this renowned critic, the perfect Venezuelan delegate to world literature.

It was this same idea that inspired García Prada when he made *Mama Blanca's Memoirs* a required text for his students in the United States, realizing that it would show them a glimpse into hacienda life. The hacienda had become a symbolic space for Mama Blanca, providing her with memories that endured after her family's exile from it. For North American students, the book offered an introduction to a way of life they would not be familiar with. "No other book of the type of *Las Memorias* is now available for school use in this country. The editors believe its wealth of local color makes it admirable as a medium for bringing North American Students into contact with certain aspects of the rural life of South America, so different from that of the United States (*Obra* preface)." García Prada edited the book, wrote an introduction, and added notes and vocabulary exercises. *Las Memorias de Mamá Blanca* was adopted as an official text at the University of Washington and later at the University of Chicago.

De la Parra agreed to send him her photo, and commiserated that it was difficult to find the works of Latin American authors, and she hoped to assemble a library of contemporary works. She appreciated his suggestions on translating *Ifigenia* and she hoped that Macmillan would eventually publish it. De la Parra wrote to García Prada thanking him for writing three essays on Gabriela Mistral's work and sharing them with her. She informed him that Waldo Frank had not begun the translation of *Mama Blanca's Memoirs* yet because he had not found a publisher. She did not want to hurry with an English translation if a publisher could not be found.

In December 1932 de la Parra wrote from Leysin to the unknown writer of the prologue and the illustrator of *Mama Blanca's Memoirs*. "The illustrations brought tears to my eyes and I'm longing to return to the world of the hacienda where everything is full of life, smells, colors, movement, bathing in the river. I agree with what you say about *Iphigenia*: I strove for a musicality I now find false and displeasing. I would have been better off without the unnecessary lyricism, but it was a true reflection of my writing at the time and the excessive romanticism we fall prey to in the tropics (*Obra* 626)." One of the changes made to the text of *Mama Blanca's Memoirs* was the inclusion of half-page ink drawings.[7]

Macmillan published the text as part of its Hispanic Series in 1932, only three years after its original publication.[8] De la Parra found herself in good company. The first book in the Macmillan series was *Selections from the Prose and Poetry of Rubén Darío,* and the book after de la Parra's was *Don Quijote de la Mancha.* In the English preface to the 1932 edition, García Prada refers to de la Parra as "the brilliant Venezuelan authoress" and defends his choice by stating, "No other book of the type of *Las Memorias* is now available for school use in this country. The editors believe its wealth of local color makes it admirable as a medium for bringing North American students into contact with certain aspects of the rural life of South America, so different from that of the United States" (v). In the Spanish introduction to the work, García Prada places de la Parra in "the glorious group in which Gabriela Mistral and Alfonsina Storni shine…in which once resigned and silent women could now express their noble, original, and restless souls" (3).

The editor goes on to describe the author's background. This information is taken from a letter she had written to him after he asked her to supply him with biographical information in preparation for the volume. While de la Parra wrote that she attended a religious school in Spain, the editor erroneously states that, "Teresa ingresó un convento, y allí pasó algunos de sus años, en un ambiente sosegado, católico y severo," implying that the author actually entered the convent as a nun, and not the convent school as a student. In fact, de la Parra's strict upbringing was due to the fact that her Venezuelan family was aristocratic and conservative Criollos. After her father's death, her mother moved the family to Spain to be closer to her own mother and for the sake of the children's education.

García Prada rewrote the biography de la Parra had supplied him and continued to explain her physical, spiritual and moral charms, and her pure ideals. He described her as a lover of truth, simplicity and humility (6). An additional editor, Clotilde M. Wilson, Ph.D. Instructor in Romanic Languages in the University of Washington, was listed. When critics from Latin America, France and Spain had been charmed by the delicacy and exquisiteness of *Iphigenia*, the editors stated that they liked *Mama Blanca's Memoirs* better, and were glad that the writer had not rested on her laurels after writing her first book. They hoped that de la Parra would go on to write more books, but if not, the two books she had written offered two unforgettable realities and several unforgettable characters to her Spanish-speaking readers. The editors thanked the author for "allowing them to use the book and to introduce into it the changes necessary to make it appropriate for class work" (vi).

The vocabulary section explains words that appear in the text, much like any other book that focuses on words in the target language that may be strange or difficult for the student. The section that includes the words designated as "Amer," or Americanisms have to do with sugar cultivation, its processing, and products, such as *alfodoque,* a paste made with molasses, cheese and ginger; *bagazo*, sugar cane as it comes crushed from the mill; it is often dried and used for fuel; *cachaza*, scum or first froth or cane juice when boiled to make sugar; and *cozallo,* sugar cane leaf fresh or dried. Other words introduce tropical plants native to the region, such as *bejuco, cuzí*, and *parcha*. The *maraca* is described as a musical instrument that like the castañet is used to mark dance rhythms; it is a sort of small gourd, dried and filled with pebbles. Commenting on Noche Buena, the name of the cow, the editors explain that in the tropics December nights are starlit, this cow's name is quite poetic as those of her companions. Students who read this text would be introduced to life on a tropical sugar cane plantation and would also get a good idea of the importance of sugar manufacture in this part of the world, along with the economic system of the hacienda itself, the tasks its laborers performed, and the daily life of the plantation owners.

Mama Blanca's Memoirs has traditionally been lauded for its fresh use of language. "Her admirable stylistic mastery is based on simplicity, narrative efficiency, fidelity to speech and to feelings (Liscano 126)." De la Parra succeeded in preserving the daily speech of the members of the hacienda: the lyrical and cadenced speech of Carmen María; the archaic 16th century Spanish speech of Vicente Cochocho; the comical, ungrammatical, article-free Spanish Evelyn from Trinidad speaks; Daniel's songs that demonstrate the skill Venezuelan cowboys use in composing spontaneous verse.

A lover of language, de la Parra reveled in words. Indeed, in one chapter of the work, she claimed the dictionary to be the best book in the world, a book refreshing to the spirit for its amiable incoherence and its lack of logic. She was especially fond of the spoken word and recreated and expanded anecdotes, such as Cousin Juancho's appropriation of the wedding incident in *El Cid* to tell the story of Carmen María's and Juan Manuel's own minor catastrophe of the overturned carriage during their wedding. Her sources for the vignettes and their language were Teresa Soublette, her great-aunt, Mama Panchita, her great-grandmother, and Emilia Ibarra, her patron and the daughter of one of Bolivar's aide-de-camps. *Mama Blanca's Memoirs* was the reconstruction of lost worlds through women's oral narratives. As she had discussed in the *Three Colombian Lectures Lectures,* one of her aims was to preserve history through women's eyes.[9] Traditional Venezuelan language with its rich colloquialisms had been downplayed, under-appreciated, and stereotyped: it was looked upon as the language of women, children, and country folk. De la Parra wanted to exploit its richness and bring it to the fore.

She was a staunch defender of colloquial Venezuelan speech. In her letters she deplored Thomas Mann's language in *The Magic Mountain.* The subject matter of this book should have intrigued her, since at the time she was taking a rest cure in Leysin, trying to recover from tuberculosis, like Hans Castorp in Mann's novel. In another letter, she sparred with Unamuno on her choice of word for "bored" in *Iphigenia*'s title and told him she would not capitulate to the rules set by the Reál Academia de la Lengua in Madrid. She set out to recuperate the lost Criollo heritage through its language and its stories. She was partial to this class and described it, "Like Ñusta Isabel, they had known glory and had learned how to lose it with grace and dignity (xi)."

The immediacy of the first person narrator in *Iphigenia* is transferred to an unnamed, more mature narrator in *Mama Blanca's Memoirs*, who becomes the conduit for the manuscript entrusted to her by a kind old woman. Although Molloy calls the premise of a manuscript a tired device, she concedes that it is perhaps a conspiratorial female pact, a text that asks for our collaboration (iv). Underlying the charming vignettes is a sense of loss, melancholy and nostalgia. Basing the vignettes on the past did not keep de la Parra from gently criticizing current institutions like marriage and government.

De la Parra was an idiosyncratic woman who was not bound to the conservative mores of Venezuela and of her family. Nonetheless, she was loyal to the socially conservative principles of her class and often described her family in Caracas as "living a colonial life." De la Parra was conservative by virtue of her family's background, her upbringing, her Catholic education in Spain, and her way of life. When she returned to Venezuela at eighteen, she listened attentively to stories and anecdotes from her grandmothers and old servant women. These made their way into both her books and her *Three Colombian Lectures Lectures*, reflecting on the love of Venezuela's colonial past.   Venezuelan critics in particular are fond of de la Parra's second book for various reasons. *Mama Blanca's*

Memoirs is a depiction of the "lives of our grandmothers....devoted to security, submitted to pain, quick to gladness, attached to the quotidian. Teresa de la Parra is one of the most feminine authors. No one exceeds her in this gift. The language in *Mama Blanca* is clean and clear as water. What took the form of confession and impetus in *Iphigenia* is now art and maturity. There is serenity in this in this book that transcends and remains" (Uslar Pietri 7). This critic described the work as a gallery of portraits. He points out that the prose is light, ironic, never dogmatic or militant. Uslar Pietri thought that the work was meant as a tribute to Emilia Ibarra, whose patronage provided de la Parra with financial and moral support.

The premise of the work is a flashback. A twelve-year-old girl enters Mama Blanca's house uninvited, and befriends the seventy-year-old woman. Years later, Mama Blanca will entrust the young woman with her manuscript. According to the old woman, it was ironic that Piedra Azul, the hacienda where she spent her early childhood, suffered from a surfeit of daughters. Mama Blanca herself had always wanted a daughter and now she has one in the form of the little girl who visits her and listens to her stories. This unnamed character edits and publishes the five hundred bound sheets of paper that Mama Blanca wrote for her children but not to them, sure that her children would not take her writing seriously.

In the flashback, Mama Blanca tells how she wrote the memoirs. The unknown editor dedicates her book to "someone like Mama Blanca." The old woman wrote the reminiscences during a "time before bells and locks existed." Mama Blanca "possesses the priceless gift of narrative evocation," and when the editor met her, the old woman was living a life of genteel poverty and gentle resignation, after squandering her fortune and playing the lottery. The manuscript, written at odd moments, was not meant to be shown to anyone else. Publishing the memoirs, in effect, is an act of betrayal on the editor's part. Nevertheless, she does publish the work, for she "senses" Mama Blanca urging her on.

The first vignette, "Blanca Nieves and Company," establishes the characters and the setting. In it we learn that Bianca Nieves is the young Mama Blanca (the third daughter of six) who, in her old age, has finally grown into her name, Snow White. The first-person narrator sets the scene of the six little girls, all misnamed, who live a hermetic but idyllic life on a coffee and sugar plantation along with their young imaginative mother, their godlike father, their mulatto nursemaid from Trinidad, and a host of servants and plantation workers. Mama Blanca recalls that she and her sisters were not at the center of the universe; rather they were at the center of the cosmos. On the surface, the only trouble in this paradise is that the girls have disobeyed their father by being born girls.

The second vignette, "Visitors," describes how the sisters are bathed and dressed as the family prepares to receive guests to Piedra Azul. It is essentially the story of the mother, Carmen María, born in 1831, a true romantic soul who is married at fifteen to a man twice her age. Every fifteen months a pregnant Carmen María gets into her carriage and heads for Caracas, where she will give birth to yet another girl, and deprive her husband of a much wished-for male heir. Critics disagree over the importance of Carmen María's position in the hierarchy of Piedra Azul. Although some critics claim that her role is to hold together the plantation's social life, José Balza calls Carmen María "a pleasant shadow" (*Mama Blanca's Memoirs* 160). According to Garrels, the mother is "stylized, romantic almost to the point of sentimentality... the beautiful mother of Blanca Nieves...conducts the social life of the hacienda (160)." Although the father projects an authoritative figurehead administering the plantation astride his horse, it is really the mother who keeps the social life of the plantation running smoothly.

The characters de la Parra describes in her works are based on her relatives, her contemporaries and her ancestors, whose values were determined by the society they lived in. De la Parra was a good listener, a keen observer and a gifted storyteller. In her *Three Colombian Lectures*, de la Parra writes about Francisca de Tovar, who was affectionately called "Mama Panchita," who lived between 1787 and 1870. It was her story, handed down orally to de la Parra's grandmother that made colonial history come alive for the author. Mama Panchita married a Basque when she was fifteen. Her husband was a rich merchant employed by the Compañía Guipuzcoana, which exported cocoa from Caracas. Mama Panchita was beautiful, rich and frivolous, "A good eighteenth century daughter." She slept her siesta surrounded by slaves who kept the mosquitoes at bay. Like Mama Panchita, Carmen María spends hours lying in her hammock, reading French romance novels, while being groomed by her black servants.

The third section, "María Frizzletop" is about the young Blanca Nieves, the only daughter who has straight hair, and her mother's attempts to curl it. The natural curls and ringlets of the other daughters is a point of pride for the family. Having to set Blanca Nieves' hair in papers creates a time when mother and daughter can tell old stories and give them new endings. The Mother's language before the mirror is rich and flowing as she tells her daughter myths, the fables of Samaniego, de la Fontaine, and the fairy tales of the Brothers Grimm. Among the favorite stories are *Paul and Virginie* and *Beauty and the Beast*. Blanca Nieves enjoys retelling and embellishing these traditional stories. Violeta, the tomboy sister, teases

Blanca Nieves and insults her first by mocking her straight hair, and then by refusing to listen to her made-up stories.

By having the little girls who live in Piedra Azul ask their mother to change the endings to the stories she tells them, de la Parra shows how young girls are initiated into the literature the narrator later uses for telling her own stories. The use of religious vocabulary in this novel, unlike in *Iphigenia,* is ironic and it is used to objectify situations. For example, religious language and religious history are used as a simile: for Blanca Nieves, getting her hair curled is compared to an *auto da fe.* Her personal situation is made universal. Other similes borrow vocabulary from the kitchen. The outcome of Blanca Nieves' curls is compared to an artichoke. At the same time she satirizes the characters through the use of history and myth. The little girls are compared to princesses of Castilla and Aragon. Carmen María's language is resonant and lyrical. When the family moves to Caracas, Blanca Nieves recalls her mother's speech as she "totted up the market accounts, delicately prolonging the final syllable of the various purchases: 'plantains-s-s…meat…potatoes-s-s…coffee…spaghetti-i-i.' (106).

Evelyn, the mulata nanny from Trinidad hired at the suggestion of the Anglophile Uncle Juancho to teach the little girls English, winds up speaking a strange version of Spanish to them instead. Instead of teaching them English, she speaks to the girls with "a Spanish devoid of articles" (53). Evelyn's speech adds a touch of humor throughout the story as she disciplines the girls, "Careful with pretty dresses from Caracas. Not sit on ground (112)."

"Here Comes Cousin Juancho" takes place when Blanca Nieves is five years old. This chapter is devoted to her chronically unemployed but charming relative who "works in the field of discussion" (50). Like the author, Cousin Juancho is a lover of language. The loquacious ne'er do well is a master of mishaps. He is a calamity-prone creator of chaos who provides hours of amusement for the family. Juancho is a walking encyclopedia who suffers many misadventures, but thanks to him, the narrator comes to appreciate *Don Quixote* in her later life, and when she visits Spain, the landscape becomes alive thanks to her uncle's love of literature. As she recalls Juancho, the sixty-seven-year-old Mama Blanca points out that she has grown into her name, which made no sense when she was a child. As a girl, she was dark-skinned and dark-haired, but now her hair is white. The last story Juancho tells is the reconstructed tale of 15-year-old Carmen María's and 31-year-old Juan Manuel's wedding in 1846. As a grownup, Mama Blanca realizes Juancho recreated and

embellished the marriage of El Cid's daughter. The amiable character in
Iphigenia, Tío Pancho, bears a striking resemblance to Cousin Juancho.

Among the memorable characters in the work, Vicente Cochocho
stands out.[10] He is an especially beloved character among Venezuelan
readers. In Cochocho de la Parra created a unique character: a barely
clothed, part black, part Indian factotum the size of a seven-year-old who
is named after a louse. "Believe me when I say that the most
unrepresentable persons are generally the most interesting (62)." Evelyn's
race hatred is discussed in relation to Vincente, who is at peace with
himself. The narrator believes Evelyn's one-quarter blackness is at war
with her three-quarters whiteness. This section ends with Vicente being
lovingly compared to a plant that yields fruits and flowers.

Vicente has many talents and skills, but his most cherished talent is
later revealed in Part II: he speaks seventeenth-century or Golden Age
Spanish. He is a repository of the language of the chronicles, which are
evident in his words, in his forms of address, and in his tone. Mama
Blanca appreciates this gift, since she is a champion of the oral tradition.
"The written word, I repeat, is a corpse (68)." Vicente pronounces his
courtly language to the beats of the maracas he is famous for playing at the
local fiestas. He is a fount of wisdom, a healer and a naturalist. He lives on
in the narrator's memory. "Our association with Vicente gave us a better
training in philosophy and the natural sciences than any textbook could
have done (67)."

The multitalented Vicente is also the local coffin maker and
practitioner of herbal medicine. As far as mores are concerned, de la Parra
compares Piedra Azul to a brilliant European court complete with its
sexual intrigues. The universe of Piedra Azul has its own norms, rules,
codes of conduct and prohibitions, and the lovable Vicente managed to
break all of them, to the mother and father's chagrin and delight of the
girls. While free love was accepted at Piedra Azul, Carmen María is
scandalized to learn that Vicente lives in his humble, rented hut with both
Aquilina and Eleuteria. She insists that Vicente marry one of them, though
all three seem to live in perfect harmony. Evelyn thinks Vicente's behavior
is depraved. De la Parra, who never wrote fondly about the institution of
marriage, here clarifies her opinion. "As it inevitable and unfortunately
happens everywhere, at Piedra Azul, too, most of the men, once the knot
has been tied, gave themselves over to infidelity with remarkable
dedication and plurality (75)." This is de la Parra at her best; a sharply
perceptive social critic who mocks contemporary mores with gentle
humor.

Vicente was also a brilliant military strategist who formed a militia when the revolution broke out, and protected the plantation from the opposing forces. According to Elizabeth Garrels, the action of the work takes place in 1855 (137). This poignant, lovingly written section about Vicente ends with his going off to war. Juan Manuel's mocking him by addressing him as Captain Vicente Aguilar in a deprecatory tone only serves to ennoble him and make him more endearing to the little girls. Juan Manuel's unkind farewell elevates Vicente in the girl's eyes and lowers their esteem for their father. "We, being small, sympathized when father was cruel (81)." Vicente never returns from the battle, and Mama Blanca beatifies him by rewording the Sermon on the Mount: "Heir of glory, you rule today among the blessed, and yours, all yours, is the Kingdom of Heaven" (82). Each vignette in *Mama Blanca's Memoirs* can be read independently, but the placement of Cochocho's death is put off until the end.

"No More Mill" is a section filled with nostalgia and a deep sense of loss. This chapter describes the girls' daily treks to the plantation's sugar mill, a much anticipated treat. Once more, the power of the spoken word plays a role here, but in a negative way, and allows de la Parra to slip in one of her gentle barbs against politicians. Violeta's words, "like those of certain congressmen and senators, disrupted the calm course of life. Peaceful multitudes then had to suffer the consequences (87)." Although she was a defender of women's rights, she urged them not to contaminate themselves through political careers. One day, Violeta lets loose a nasty word. As a result, the girls are punished by not being allowed to go to the mill. "To our rustic souls the mill was club, theater, city (84)." When the mill was turned off, the little girls could splash and play in the stream. Banishment from the mill was special in the narrator's memory and it taught her a valuable lesson. She speaks ironically of Evelyn, whose "good influence filled our childhood with joys and saved it from the bleak, cruel boredom that afflicts the soul of those children who have everything.... (88)." The little girls did not play with store-bought items; rather, they assembled found objects. The seventy-five-year-old Mama Blanca reminisces that, "surfeit never dulled the edge of desire (89)." Experiences such as banishment from the mill and the lack of material goods made her still grateful for simple gifts like rides in the country and small presents.

"Rain Cloud and Little Rain Cloud" are about a cow and her ill-fated calf. After the mill, the second favorite place for the young sisters was the milking shed. Papa had ordered the girls to drink a glass of fresh milk first thing every morning at six o'clock. This section describes the "Republic of Cows" with its ruler Daniel, the cowherd from the plains.

Daniel is a *llanero*, a cowboy from the plains of Aragua, where writing songs and making music goes hand-in-hand with cattle ranching. Daniel is crafty and rapacious, but with a touch of gallantry. Mama Blanca describes the cowshed as a Marxist utopia. Personifying the cows, she reminisces, "Nobody complained and nobody was resentful; there was no class warfare. To each according to her needs, from each according to her ability. All was peace, all was light (91)." One cow is named Estrella, like one of the sisters. It seems natural to name the cows after the girls since both are "daughters of the hacienda." Once again, the father is outwitted by one of his workers, and his authority is undermined because, "Don Juan Manuel, the supposed center and owner of Piedra Azul, is like a distant God whom no one truly obeys" (Fombona xxiii). Daniel sings to the cows, who are spellbound by the lyric pleasures of poetry and music. When Daniel is fired because Papa suspects he is swindling him, he is quickly rehired because the new dairy man refuses to sing to the cows, and the spoiled cows refuse to cooperate and give up their milk. When a calf dies, Daniel consoles the mother by placing the salted hide of the dead calf over another calf, which she quickly adopts. In true *llanero* fashion, he composes verses on the spot, a plaintive song filled with philosophy and consolation, which serves to confuse the little girls who miss the central metaphor: "All milk is turned to cheese/ And all sorrow is allayed (100)."

"Aurora" is the last vignette named for the sister who regretfully turns out not to be misnamed, for Aurora dies in the dawn of her youth. The family is in the midst of loss and change. Mama Blanca describes her sister's death as a fall from grace, and the girls are subjected to a series of unfortunate events. The godlike father, we learn, is not the sole proprietor of the plantation. His two brothers are the co-owners, and rather than divide Piedra Azul, they sell it. The family must move to Caracas. Aurora's death, the sale of the plantation, and the family's move to Caracas changes their lives forever and for the worse. "Aurora's death was the bitterest of all the misfortunes that followed our moving to Caracas but it was not the only one. The path that led from the country to the city was uphill and rough (103)."

Losing the plantation is compared to losing a decisive battle, losing an empire, and being cast out of paradise. Upon moving to Caracas, the girls immediately notice "the absence of water and the preponderance of cement, boards and bricks (103)." The family can only afford one maid now. Used to an abundance of fresh food supplied to them daily, food must now be purchased, and there is less money for it. The ex-princesses have to compete for attention with their cousins, and they stand out with their rustic ways. The family moves to a world of bricks, cement and melancholy, a decidedly negative view of modern city life. The children had been kept away from Caracas, which was previously treated like a site of contagion. Juan Manuel had insisted his daughters play outdoors and drink fresh milk, but now he has forced them to move to a place where the environment is constrained and restrictive. They lack a vocabulary for the unknown objects they encounter in the city. To them, sidewalks are "trails," lampposts are "iron trees," and a couple strolling arm-in-arm are "a team of people." They mistake the cathedral for a sugar mill and enter it running and shouting. They are forced to wear impractical and uncomfortable hats weighted down with useless trimmings rather than the practical and lightweight hats they wore to keep the sun out.

Evelyn returns to Trinidad, the new nursemaid can't manage the unruly girls, and she gives notice after the first day. The girls are sent to be educated and civilized at a private school, which Mama Blanca recalls as "an asylum of melancholy and learning." Two genteel ladies administer the school from their house. Two years pass after "our golden age of paradise lost." Mama Blanca recalls this time, an "abandoned trove of happiness" when she was seven or eight years old. The girls beg their mother for a visit to the plantation, which only makes things worse, as she had warned them it would. Everything on the plantation had changed. The house has been remodeled, the gardens and orchards are no longer where the girls remembered them, and the mill had been modernized. The spring had been walled up. Vicente never returned from his last battle. The girls are sorry they came back to witness the changes.

Blanca Nieves recalls the trauma of leaving a perfect world, and her introduction to money. She has never seen a coin, but she needs money to buy sweets from the corner vendor. Carmen María needs cash to buy food that used to "appear.' But all these memories of a paradise lost are fondly recalled by a smiling Mama Blanca who is never bitter about her loss. At a time when Venezuelan literature lacked humor, de la Parra's wit and grace injected a much-needed light note. In her essay "El humor en Mamá Blanca" Laura Febres points out the prevalence of the word "smile" in this work, a word that appears in the introduction, and unifies the narrator and little girl who will edit the manuscript. The very door of Mama Blanca's house seems to be in the shape of an inviting smile. Laughing water falls upon the foliage in the patio, and Mama Blanca tells her stories with a hint of a smile. Febres makes note of the repetition and variation of the words "smiling and laughter" in the introduction.

Another source of humor lies in the names given to the little girls, names that are the opposite of their natures. The mother refuses to accept reality. There is a concordance of the names of the cows, but a discord to the girls' names. The cows and the girls are related; the girls live on the hacienda and consider the cows to be their nurses and the calves to be their brothers. Animals and children live in harmony with nature. Sometimes objects take on a new life on the hacienda. The Anglophile Cousin Juancho brings an English garden umbrella to Piedra Azul so the family can take tea outdoors. This is a foolish notion, since the last thing the family wants to do is sip hot tea in the tropical sun in the afternoon. The umbrella eventually gets put to good use as a surrey for the ox cart.

Digging under the surface of the entertaining narrative, Juan Liscano's "Testimony" describes *Mama Blanca's Memoirs* as a delicious chronicle of "nineteenth century Venezuela with its agrarian economy, caudillo uprisings, large coffee, cocoa, and sugarcane haciendas, aristocratic, Francophile minorities, malnourished, illiterate peasants, and exhausted treasury and nonexistent industry (119)." Beneath the nostalgic and poignant vignettes filled with charming characters that plays tribute to mellifluous Venezuelan speech, there are signs of subversion and disobedience. The girls see Evelyn as a strict taskmaster who denies them the pleasure of going to the mill, asking countless questions of the workers, and bathing in the millstream when the mill is shut down. Far from ruining their fun, Evelyn gave meaning to their childhood. The little girls did not experience boredom like spoiled children do. They are not victims of satiety or disenchantment. Evelyn's prohibitions only serve to make simple pleasures more desirable

Teresa de la Parra decries lost traditions, while at the same time she realizes that the kind of life the family was able to enjoy is no longer possible. The aristocracy can't afford to keep the haciendas running under the old ways. When the little girls return to the hacienda, which has been sold to a rich owner, the modern changes that must be made to keep the hacienda profitable are looked down on and described as negative improvements. While modernization allows for efficiency and productivity, it infringes on rustic life and changes the ways people on the hacienda relate to each other.

Venezuela's enormous haciendas produced coffee, cacao and sugar. The low price of coffee in the international market occurred during the era of Cipriano Castro (1899-1908). His response was to modernize the country and move it from feudalism to capitalism. The dictatorship of Juan Vicente Gómez (1908-1922) and the return of political exiles from abroad corresponds to the period when Rómulo Gallegos and Teresa de la Parra were writing. Under Gómez, landowners lost their buying power, lost their interest in cultivation, and land was sold to foreigners whose main industry was the promotion of oil extraction and the creation of oil related jobs. The haciendas fell into ruin or were abandoned. Jobless peasants moved to the city, which led to the creation of slums in Caracas and an unfortunate pattern of unbridled growth without planning or development, which de la Parra vividly describes during María Eugenia's visit to La Pastora (*Iphigenia* 69). Under Gómez, the exploitation of petroleum led to unprecedented economic prosperity for some and an overriding spirit of materialism, also reflected in *Iphigenia*. Gómez's successors, Eleazar Lopez Contreras (1936-1941) and Isaias Medina Argarita (1941-1948) continued the trend of courting foreign capital and paying off foreign debt with petroleum, creating the conditions that are explored in the later novels known as the *novela petrolera*.

As she had already pointed out in *Iphigenia*, life in a *casona* in Caracas forced women to live indoors and created a restricted environment in which they could only view the world behind the bars of their windows. While rules of conduct for women, especially highborn criollo women, enforced this code, de la Parra was ambivalent. She recognized that the criollo existence of the past had its romantic moments, but she realized that the twentieth century made new demands on women and called for changes in their education and their expectations. It is this ambivalent attitude that gives *Mama Blanca's Memoirs* its bittersweet tone. Lemaître's biography of the author, *Between Flight and Longing,* is aptly titled. In both her fiction and nonfiction de la Parra struggled to balance her longing for the past with the necessary changes the present demanded.

Teresa de la Parra is part of an "other" Venezuelan literature still in the process of discovering itself (Bohórquez 8). She succeeded in modifying the literary tradition of her time which relied on the stylistics of *costumbrismo, criollismo,* and *realismo. Mama Blanca's Memoirs* used the language of de la Parra's childhood. "It was a tender language of absolute beauty, rediscovery and a vindication of life and humble people. I would discover in Teresa de la Parra that literature was more than possessing a style, more than being a rhetorical exercise (Bohórquez 48)." This Venezuelan critic explains de la Parra's legacy to the Venezuelan novel as creating a space for the voices of women, children and country folk. She gave them a body and desires. Piedra Azul represents the reign of the feminine. It has ties to the colony through its orality, its old-fashioned virtues, and its theme of childhood innocence. It is opposed to the city and its technology. Bohórquez points to how de la Parra redefined conventional gender identifiers and stereotypes. The feminine in Vicente is displayed in his magical curative powers, his spirituality, and his relationship to clay and the moon, whereas the masculine is associated with Evelyn and Violeta. In the novel *Iphigenia*, Abuela who is apparently maternal on the surface, really has the power and the authority of the male. De la Parra presented a new vision, a more complex one, concerning the sexes. While the author claimed that she did not have a feminist agenda, she wrote using a critical and plural discourse that explored other forms of expressing and imagining the feminine condition. Thanks to her, Venezuelan literature reinvented itself, and was given a feminine aesthetic. Her writing explored the quotidian and the relationship between tragedy and comedy. Her work expressed a rejection of conventional forms and stereotypes. She was constantly searching for ways to renew and create new ways to write, from the intimate and the personal, to the collective and the oral, but she has yet to be assimilated into a literary tradition, Bohórquez laments.

British critic Guy Reynolds points to the creation of a female aesthetic and women's contribution to a literary tradition as they act as agents of change in an ongoing process of cultural transformation often by unsettling old fictional patterns through writing "inside narratives" that inform the culture's political history (7). The microscopic observation of manners and the everyday rituals of the female world should be incorporated into the larger patterns of literary history, he claims. Observations such as these form an important aspect of the vignettes that shape this novel.

De la Parra recaptured the dignity and beauty of the lost colonial past through fable, fairy tale, biography and through a combination of techniques, forms, and modes of expression, and introduced a new structure in the place of old established discursive forms. She goes beyond the exotic vision of *criollismo,* a new narrative form which had been incorporated by the vanguard, and she did this because her travels gave her the necessary emotional distance. She was a modern, well-read woman who observed a world in transformation. De la Parra applied historical, mythological and religious references to daily occurrences to give them universal meaning. The friendship between Mama Blanca and the narrator forms an alliance that leads to the publication of a manuscript that preserves a moment in time. She combined the "rich and concrete Spanish she learned during her stay in Madrid, with the lively criollo Spanish of Venezuela, tempered with a touch of the French spirit refined and educated Latin Americans softened the harshness of the Castilian soul (Picón-Salas, 775).

A modern literary structure is imposed on the manuscript. The result is a work written in the seductive and poetic tone of a memoir in which Mama Blanca lovingly calls up the inhabitants of Piedra Azul. Even the lowliest of them is ennobled. Vicente is as ugly as a flea, but his talents are not to be underestimated. He is a philosopher, natural healer, funeral director and military leader. People who might have been considered ugly and barbaric are seen in a new light. De la Parra's literary influences were Proust, Colette, Valery, and Rolland. Her narrative style sought for an alternative to the contemporary avant-garde aesthetic.

Customs on the hacienda are not described in the exotic way that had become the norm. Progress and modernization, though inevitable, are tragic and melancholic. As a character, Mama Blanca is dignified and noble. The beauty of the past contrasts with the vulgar present and its values of economic success and luxury, which fails to take the spiritual into account. Mama Blanca is wise, intelligent, musically gifted, and spiritual. Through her, the past is privileged. She remains a romantic character whose stories are poetic versions of childhood memories of a paradise lost. Piedra Azul is a secret universe she wants to share, but she knows she has to find the right audience for her story.

Mama Blanca's Memoirs is an oral book, even though it is based on a manuscript. It is certainly more orally inspired than *Iphigenia*. The narrator retraces a colonial past and tries to retrieve it. It could be considered an oral history, a rewriting of countryside speech, due to the musical language and lyrical cadence of its prose. Writing in an oral fashion means a return to the language of mothers and grandmothers, a return to fairy tales, fables, and legends. There are intertextual references to *Beauty and the Beast, Paul et Virginie*, the *Romancero Español, El Cid*. The connected episodes are structured around narratives that evoke popular and oral culture. The language is composed of daily speech, proverbs, refrains, and folklore. There are descriptions of handicrafts, the manual arts, herbal medicine and sugar refining. The little girls thrive on the hacienda and their imaginations are put to good use.

There are lyrical descriptions of places the little girls of fond of: the mill, the millstream and the milking shed. The hacienda is an enclosed, pastoral paradise, sufficient unto itself, a place of uncorrupted nature. The dialog is fresh, spontaneous, and funny, conveying the tone, rhythm, and humor of oral speech. De la Parra loved the Spanish language and rejoiced in its musical elements. She recuperated oral tradition through the integration of older, colonial Spanish, as though she meant to promote it as an ideal language. *Mama Blanca's Memoirs* suggested new ways of seeing and understanding the colonial past. In this search, de la Parra bypassed an old literary order and created a new aesthetic for Venezuelan writing. It could have its own form and speak its own language, with a new structure, and memorable characters retrieved from history. The memory of the hacienda and its inhabitants takes shape as a symbolic space in memory, and her use of memoir influenced contemporary Venezuelan woman novelists such as Antonia Palacios, Antonieta de Madrid, Ana Teresa Torres and Milagros Mata Gil[11]. Beyond the scope of women's writing, Bohórquez posits that de la Parra initiated a new way of writing which was further developed by novelists such as Miguel Angel Asturias, Alejo Carpentier, Lézama Lima and Juan Rulfo.

Modernization allowed efficiency and productivity as it altered rustic life and changed the ways people on the hacienda related to each other. In the city, life in the colonial *casona* in the capital forced women to live indoors and created a restrictive life in which women could only view the world from behind the bars of their windows. While rules of conduct for women enforced this code, de la Parra recognized this, and in her lectures pointed out that it was not the way for women to live in the twentieth century. This is the ambivalent attitude that gives *Mama Blanca's Memoirs* its edge. The dilemma the work poses is how to balance longing for the past with the reality of the present.

Notes

[1] All English quotes are from *Teresa de la Parra, Critical Edition, Mama Blanca's Memoirs, The Classic Novel of a Venezuelan Girlhood*. Trans. Harriet de Onís. All translations from *Teresa de la Parra, Obra,(Narrativa, ensayos, cartas)* and other Spanish texts are mine.

[2] For an analysis of *Doña Barbara* and Gallegos's choice of names for the characters in the novel, see Ching, "Civilized Folk Marry the Barbarians." Santos means saint or saintly, Luzardo comes from "light" and refers to the Enlightenment, Doña Bárbara evokes barbarism, Señor Danger represents U.S. intervention, Altamira means high view (looking forward) while Barbara's land is called El Miedo (fear), (203-204). Elizabeth Garrels called the work an "anachronistic colonial fantasy". Garrels has determined that the action in the work unfolds in 1855 but that it "exists in blissful ignorance of history and material reality" (138). In his discussion of Guiraldes, Gallegos and Rivera, Raymond Leslie Williams points out that these three novels are novels of adventure – the protagonists travel from a city to a rural area. "*In Las memorias de Mamá Blanca*, the protagonist eventually travels from the hacienda to the city, although the novel deals primarily with her experience as a child on the hacienda" (54).

[3] In her letters de la Parra disagreed with Gobineau's theory on the superiority of the Aryan races.

[4] De la Parra was included in the group of the "señoritas," that is to say rich Latin American women who wrote because their economic backgrounds allowed them to, as opposed to women who wrote for a living. Sommer describes Teresa de la Parra at the time she wrote her *Three Colombian Lectures* was as a "disturbingly

beautiful woman who moved easily through colonial manors in silk pajamas and cigarettes, and took advantage of modernity to publicly reminisce about tradition."
[5]During Juan Vicente Gómez's regime, Caracas was swarming with popular and student demonstrations. Gómez's police shot at demonstrators with machine guns, closed the universities, and sentenced the young people to hard labor on the roads or to prison or exile. Teresa wrote to Gómez to express her sympathy. (Bosch 133).
[6] Carlos García Prada edited Teresa de la Parra's *Obras Completas* in 1965. While the edition offers a very thorough compilation of her work, it is not complete.
[7] Drawings: "La hacienda de Piedra Azul" (26), shows a typical tropical Venezuelan plantation with tile roofed buildings and a mill in the background. "La cabaña de un peón era para mí la de Pablo" (47), is a picture of a thatch-roofed peasant's hut that Blanca Nieves identifies as Paul's hut, taking her inspiration from Paul et Verginie. "Vicente era quien se subía a los arboles" (81), depicts Vicente high up in the limbs of a tree. In "Cuando Cochocho volvía del Mercado" (88), has Vicente returning from the market in a donkey cart while a black servant balances a large basket on her head walks in front of him. "Nos bañábamos a pleno sol junto al chorreón" (105) shows two little girls splashing in a pool formed by the millstream's waterfall. "Daniel era llanero" (114), depicts the dairyman as a cattleman, along with another cattleman on the plains. "El nuevo vaquero se fué" (122) shows the newly-hired dairyman departing from the hacienda with all his belongings in a sack he carries on his back. The last ink drawing is of the "Templo de Santa Teresa, Caracas," a typical colonial Catholic church (135). This drawing serves as a contrast to the rural hacienda, now that the family has moved to the capital.
[8] *Las Memorias de Mamá Blanca*, por Teresa de la Parra, edited with introduction, notes, exercises and vocabulary, by Carlos García Prada and Clotilde M. Wilson, Macmillan Hispanic Series, New York: Macmillan, 1932.
[9] The editors of *El hilo de la voz* single out Teresa de la Parra and the poet Enriqueta Arvelo Larriva (1886-1961) for the quality of their work and for their awareness of being authors. They do not write to cultivate *belles lettres*, nor for didactic ends; they write because they want to (53). Both authors decided to construct their own systems of writing, aware that a hostile world surrounded them. (53). According to Raymond Leslie Williams, "women writers such as Teresa de la Parra...published novels meritorious of more recognition than they received at the time. The presence of de la Parra and other women writers offered an initial feminine response to what was predominantly a masculinist aesthetic (38)
[10] Garrels writes that Vicente Cochoco is "one of the most studied and compared figures in Teresa de la Parra's work" (158). Describing Vicente Cochocho's historical dimension, Garrels says he protects the hacienda and the boundaries of the fable. Mariano Picón Salas describes him as "a humanized dwarf straight from one of Velasquéz's paintings (*Obras*, 776). García Prada in his introduction to *Obras Completas de Teresa de la Parra* claims" Above all (the characters) is the zambo Vicente Cochocho, one of the most simpatico characters in all Hispanic American novels of yesteryear and today (15). A zambo is a mixture of Indian and black.

CHAPTER FOUR

CRIOLLO CONSUMERISM

María Eugenia Alonso, like the Greek Iphigenia, is sacrificed to appease patriarchal values. The heroine submits through obedience and subservience, and is sacrificed for her family's sake in a marriage of convenience. To the chagrin of her readers, who witnessed the witty and headstrong young girl's maturation through a long and newsy letter to her best friend Cristina, and through a meticulously kept diary, María Eugenia capitulates when her family "sells" her in marriage to the highest bidder. The eighteen-year-old Venezuelan had returned to Caracas from Paris following her father's death, only to learn that she is broke. Her greedy and unscrupulous Uncle Eduardo had appropriated her inheritance, the San Nicolás hacienda. She realizes that she owns nothing but her family name and her spotless reputation. She recognizes that she is a commodity, "…my person acquired a notable likeness to those luxury items that are exhibited at night in store windows to tempt shoppers…," as she sits in front of the window and yells out that she is for sale, " I am for sale!…Who will buy me? Who will buy me? I am for sale!… Who will buy me?" *(Iphigenia* 218). The answer is César Leal, who drives a Packard in the 1924 edition and a Cadillac in the second edition.

Gabriel, the man she loves, has traded his family's good name and political connections to marry an unattractive, graceless, but rich young woman, María Monasterios. Her family has made lots of money in the petroleum industry, and the declining aristocracy in Caracas needs to tap that wealth.

De la Parra was among the first to introduce commercial references in her text, writing during a transitional period in Venezuela's history as the country moved from an agrarian economy to an oil-producing one. While in Paris, María Eugenia, fresh out of convent school, learned to be a good consumer. Her need to buy Gurlain makeup delays the mailing of the long epistle to her best friend *(Iphigenia* 17). While she was in Paris, María Eugenia walked its boulevards freely, window-shopping and outfitting herself in the latest fashion. This kind of activity would be unthinkable when she returned to Caracas.

During the 1920s advertisements and products aimed at women encouraged them to change their bodies and their appearance through clothing, cosmetics and hairstyles. María Eugenia bought into this program only too well, spending the last of her money on Louis XV style shoes. Popular in the 1920's Louis XV heels were named for the King of France 1715-74, and were a style of high-heeled shoe with curved heels. She has her dressed made from Lanvin, a Parisian designer who created clothes for film stars such as Mary Pickford and Marlene Dietrich. He also designed clothes for European royalty, including the queens of Italy and Romania. She buys and wears hats intended for widows, but nevertheless buys them so that people will address her as "Madame Alonso" (*Iphigenia* 15). Autonomy and freedom in Paris can be purchased with the 50,000 francs she has access to, shopping in the city's boutiques. According to Elizabeth Garrels, in 2005 dollars, the 50,000 francs María Eugenia spent during her three-month stay in Paris amounts to between $32, 280 and $36,010   (*Ifigenia*)[1] In Bertie Acker's translation, based on the 1924 edition, María Eugenia has 20,000 francs at her disposal (14). In the second, Bendelac edition, de la Parra more than doubled María Eugenia's disposable income (Garrels 8).[2]

When María Eugenia returns to live with her conservative grandmother, the matriarch is appalled that her granddaughter had spent the remainder of her money and she gives her a lesson in money management and wealth accumulation: "So you spent the eight thousand bolivares!. But two thousand pesos drawing nine percent would have brought you about fifteen pesos a month, my daughter; maybe they could have been invested at ten percent, even twelve and then it would have been seventy or eighty bolivares a month (*Iphigenia* 48). María Eugenia reckons otherwise. "Oh!! Grandmother's extreme devotion to those two thousand pesos, the last shred of my patrimony, was grating horribly on my nerves, now that the many thousands that San Nicolás represented had just disappeared before my eyes." (*Iphigenia* 48). María Eugenia reveals in her diary that in 20th century Caracas, money makes all the difference between freedom and choosing one's mate, or a life of obedience and submission to a man her family has chosen for her. *Iphigenia* is a novel that begins in frivolity and ends in disillusionment. It is the *bildungsroman* of a young girl who falls from wealth to poverty, from hope to despair. The intelligent, well-read young woman who can express herself in several languages, the adolescent who transformed herself into a chic young lady through clothes, makeup and a fashionable hairstyle, now must pretend that she was copying recipes all along to please her future husband.

Her grandmother gives María Eugenia her antique emerald earrings as a wedding present. They represent the grandmother's last remaining articles of value. María Eugenia sells them so she can buy a silk trousseau like the kind she saw and coveted in Paris. She realizes too late that the earrings had sentimental value that can't be replaced. Her attachment to these dainty silk garments ultimately foils her attempt to elope with Gabriel. Trying to find a suitcase in the dark on the night she plans to elope, she knocks over an object that will awaken her Aunt Clara and force her to put an end to her plan to flee. She will be forced to marry César Leal, a man with money and government connections instead. She confesses that she was seduced by the sound of his Packard (*Iphigenia* 219). As a senator, Leal needs a wife who is beyond reproach. He will live in the public eye while María Eugenia remains behind the scenes. When she appears in public, she will be expected to dress modestly and shun makeup. Even before their marriage, Leal has laid down the rules concerning how she will dress and what she can read.

Her visits to Mercedes Galindo, whom she nicknames "Semiramis" gave de la Parra the opportunity to write about the Latin American obsession with all things from the Orient. Mercedes represents fun, travel, fashion, all things exotic, freedom and wealth, but she herself is a commodity trapped in an unhappy marriage. Her nickname suggests why Maria Eugenia's family is displeased with their friendship. Semiramis was the Babylonian queen known for her sexual excesses. Though Mercedes does not appear to be outwardly unfaithful, there is a hint that when she and her husband are abroad, usually in Paris, she enjoys freedoms not allowed in Venezuela. This arrangement is a trade-off for her husband's abuse. Mercedes' attachment to her luxurious lifestyle is at the expense of a married life with a man she loves. María Eugenia is intrigued by the suggested decadence of Mercedes' lifestyle and is seduced by its visible Oriental trappings and Mercedes' indolence. Mercedes has sold out; she is locked in a loveless marriage but is resplendent in her harem-inspired boudoir. We later discover that Mercedes has a reputation for flirting and that she has lovers when she is in Paris, far away from family censure. When Mercedes invites María Eugenia to accompany her to Paris and escape her boring life, her conservative family will not allow it.

Aside from the numerous product placements and product endorsements, de la Parra pokes fun at the modernist obsession with the Oriental style that was being promoted through Latin American literature. The aesthetics of *fin-de-siecle* modernism was reinforced by the many visits to Paris prosperous Venezuelan families of means were able to take. María Eugenia's visits to Mercedes allow de la Parra to comment on fashion and makeup in the conversations that take place between the two women. There are references to the serial romance novels published in women's magazines which were avidly read at the time, which fueled romantic dreams in young women, and provided escapism for married women.

De la Parra used canonical genres for expressing women's ideas about nation, gender, ethnicity and class in this novel. The naming of expensive products in the letter to Cristina and in the diary prefigures the current commercial women's genre referred to as "Chick-Lit". María Eugenia's letter to Cristina gives the heroine an opportunity to express her opinions on fashion and makeup and the products she uses. This letter as well as other parts of the novel are sprinkled with references to coveted products. She mentions Guerlain liquid rouge twice (17, 224). Guerlain was a famous perfumery established in Paris in 1828. In 2007, Guerlain produced the most expensive lipstick in the world, which cost $62.00 (Garrels, 12). In her more carefree days María Eugenia used dark red Guerlain lipstick (20, 65), but she later changes to the softer tones of Saint Ange lipstick (213,241, 248). "Rouge écletant de Gurlain" was an explosive, vivid shade of red lipstick. "Rouge vif" was a softer tone. She also uses Faber #2 eye pencil, (231). Before she left for Caracas, she had clothes sewn for her in Biarritz, and bought dresses by Lanvin, (50), and she wears shoes with Louis XV heels (49,81). Once, she had the opportunity to listen to a lecture by Pankhurst, an early feminist, but the speaker's thick stockings repulsed her to the point that the fashion-conscious María Eugenia could not pay attention to the speaker and her message. María Eugenia prefers to wear number 100 gauge stockings (81). The deniers refers to a unit of weight for silk. The lower the denier, the sheerer the stocking. The higher the denier, the thicker and more durable the stocking. She opts for charmeuse fabric that costs 30 bolivares a yard, (76) and wants to follow the hairstyles and clothing as seen in *Vogue* (133). *Vogue* was first published in New York in 1916.

Her grandmother takes Ross Pills, or Dr. Ross Pills: *Píldoras de Vida del doctor Ross*, were laxatives sold throughout Latin America (172) and Scott's Emulsion (215).

In the early pages of the novel María Eugenia writes to her friend that she dislikes the smell of the ointment Elliman's Embrocation (8). She grows used to the smell two years later, when she has to rub it on her grandmother. Aunt Clara takes Rubinat Water, "a very bitter purgative... so repugnant that the very sight of it gave María Eugenia chills, nausea and vertigo (254) In one of his many humorous asides, Uncle Pancho suggests María Eugenia have a drink of Rubinat Water before she reads Leal's bombastic, multi-page article in the newspaper, a wry comment on the article's content. *Nirvana* perfume by Bichara is mentioned three times (228,229,231). Nirvana de Bichara was a perfume introduced in 1913. Bichara Malhame was a Lebanese who established a successful perfume company. His clients included Sarah Bernhardt, Gabriel Fauré and Gabriele d'Annunzio. The scent Leal wears is Origan by Coty, his signature scent, which is mentioned twice on the same page, (45). One of Leal's many gifts to Maria Eugenia during his courtship is Boissier bonbons and fondants, mentioned three times on page (238) and again on page (241), which is "the best kind of candy in the world," and the same kind of candy Mercedes Galindo had previously offered her friend from a Bohemian chocolate box. Bossier was a famous French candy firm, established in 1827.

Mercedes smokes Egyptian cigarettes (132), and the conversation at her party is enlivened by cocktails and Medoc wine (140). Her house is filled with silver objects and porcelains from Saxony and Sevres (109, 145). Whenever possible, Mercedes interjects French words and phrases where, as Maria Eugenia herself points out, when a perfectly Spanish word would do. Mercedes also resorts to French when she doesn't want the servants to know what she is talking about.

When the heroine is reunited with Gabriel, the man she has fallen in love with, she supposes he has become a rich doctor who has dozens and dozens of Japanese silk shirts (274). The always fashion-conscious heroine takes notice of what Gabriel is wearing even as her Uncle Pancho is on his death bed. "Then I started to mentally enumerate all the shirts Gabriel had worn in the two days he's been taking care of Uncle Pancho. I remembered I'd seen the raw silk, one; and the white silk with thin blue stripes, two; and the other one like it but with lavender stripes, three; and the green checked, four; and finally the white one today, five" (274). She will not marry Gabriel, but in preparing for her marriage to Leal, her own lingerie is of Milanese silk (252), her trousseau has been ordered from Paris and is made of Parisian silk (258), and her wedding gown will be made of Chantilly lace (242, 258).

The products named in the novel were consumed in bourgouise Venezuelan households. Integrating them into the work helps to draw the reader immediately into María Eugenia's world through sights and smells:"…you can't imagine how bored I've been this past month, locked up in this house of Grandmother's, which smells of jasmine, damp earth, wax candles, and Elliman's Embrocation" (8). María Eugnenia's fondness for wearing Chinese kimonos and visiting Mercedes as she lounges in her Oriental boudoir reflects the modernist movement's affinity with all things eastern and foreshadows de la Parra's interest in Eastern religion, which she turned to and studied when she became ill. Her interest in Eastern religion and philosophy also found its way into her short stories and is frequently alluded to in her letters.

María Eugenia makes lists of the clothes she owns. She had purchased a dozen black mourning dresses in Biarritz, which she donated to the chambermaid. Her stay in Paris had taught her what was chic, and these mourning dresses were not. On board the ship taking her from France to Venezuela she boasts, "I who had not been seasick for a second, did nothing but parade my repertory of wraps, dresses, and gauzy shawls that I learned to tie very gracefully... I wore a black and white one in the morning, a lilac one at noon, a gray one at night...(17) Such was the association of Maria Eugenia, the narrator of the novel, with the author of the novel that the Parisian fashion house Drecoll offered to outfit the writer in Maria Eugenia's clothes as de la Parra had described them in the novel. (*Epistolatio íntimo 71*).

De la Parra exposed the commodification of women in Venezuela, and the novel's family discourse centers on transactions, property, estates, and rents. María Eugenia feels free because she equates wealth with freedom: "It was Mr. Ramírez with the twenty thousand francs, and the permission to go out alone, who suddenly revealed to me that delicious sensation of liberty" (140). Her father's profligate spending and financial mismanagement, however, left him and his daughter penniless. Remembering their happy, carefree days together in Paris, she reflects, "Poor Papa... Those brief days, when your prodigal spirit and jovial spirit seemed to be reborn for a moment in my soul, were the only inheritance that you were to bequeath me " (16). Her grandmother reminds her that once upon a time, the Alonsos were rich, "so very rich that they were perhaps the foremost capitalists in Venezuela" (54). María Eugenia thinks back to those days when it was a pleasure to have money and to be a man. As a penniless, landless woman, María Eugenia is a "zero" who must remain in the custody of her family until someone buys her. Her body is her capital: "A woman is never poor when she is beautiful," her Uncle Pancho reminds her. The young heroine is obsessed with modern ways and smart appearances and reinvents and reveals herself through the products she buys, and defines herself through them. As a young adolescent who lacks role models, she constructs a chic identity based on Parisian fashions. Eventually, she has to tone down her appearance so that she will be appealing to a man who can provide her with a secure life. The reader learns that her future husband will dictate how she will dress, how low her necklines will be, and when she will make public appearances. De la Parra exposed a dilemma many Venezuelan upper class young women faced.

By the time María Eugenia rediscovers her diary after two years of not writing in it, she has turned into a young version of her grandmother. She now takes pride in doing the needlework she so detested and mocked, takes meticulous charge of the linens, counting and sorting and storing every piece. With the glamorous Mercedes back in Europe, she has no one to visit and gossip with in the afternoons. She had been banished to the estate which should rightfully be hers so that she can't correspond with her beloved Gabriel. While at the hacienda, she learns that Gabriel has married a rich girl. Back in Caracas, she gradually abandons her dream of living a carefree, chic and adventurous life and takes on the values of her grandmother's generation. De la Parra wanted to combat centuries of hypocrisy through this novel, by showing Venezuela's so-called modern society rooted in its colonial surroundings and values. On her return to Caracas, de la Parra was shocked by its social hypocrisy, its backwardness, its inherent machismo, and the political situation in Venezuela.

European habits, culture, mores modernity are contrasted to the current situation in Venezuela, which María Eugenia found wanting. Since de la Parra had studied in Spain and lived in Paris, she was in a good position to point out the differences between Europe and Venezuela and her stay abroad had given her a new lens from which to observe her native land. De la Parra adored Venezuela and so identified with the country that she erronously claimed she had been born there, when in reality she had been born in Paris while her father was serving in France as consul. She moved beyond the exotic vision of nationalism through criollismo, the new narrative form which had been introduced by the vanguard. She chose to describe her times, and could do this because her travels gave her the necessary emotional distance.

De la Parra was a modern, well-read woman who wanted to describe a world in transformation. According to some critics, she was the precursor of a narrative style which would be further developed by novelists such as Miguel Angel Asturias, Alejo Carpentier, Lézama Lima and Juan Rulfo. She described the changes Venezuela was undergoing as it became a petroleum-producing country. Some of these changes are revealed through María Eugenia's letter to Cristina, and later in her diary. Both forms serve to establish a pact with the reader. María Eugenia writes from her locked room, sharing her observations with us. We witness the young heroine struggling to find her own way but ending up like her grandmother. The heroine is inevitably led to accept her family's decision that Leal is a good catch, despite his being an outsider, and not a member of their set. It was the grandmother who had held the family together. While wealthy Venezuelans toured Europe and returned, María Eugenia's grandfather,

Martin Alonso, described by his wife as one of Venezuela's first capitalists, who made his fortune importing spices, tapestries, paintings, rugs and china, went to Europe and "lost his judgment" never to return.

The novel is about the lives of the impoverished but proud founding families, the criollos or mantuanos and the new class of Venezuelans who make their money through the newly developed oil industry and who invest their money to make capital. The story of the decaying Caracas aristocracy, the founding class, whose "granddaughters and great-granddaughters, today poor and obscure... without ever being ashamed of their poverty, wait with resignation the hour of marriage or the hour of death, making candy for parties or knitting wreaths of flowers for burials " (60). This was Aunt Clara's fate. María Eugenia remembers that as a young girl she sat in the living room with Aunt Clara and a gentleman who made her paper dolls and brought her candy. But Aunt Clara did not marry this man, and in her letter to Cristina María Eugenia writes, "I felt a stirring of the spirit of that inheritance that Aunt Clara was leaving me....Oh! Cristina... Aunt Clara's legacy!...It was a countless throng of long, black nights, invariable, that went by slowly holding hands beneath the snowy lace of the white curtain!...(42). Two years later, run down with nursing Uncle Pancho, about to marry César Leal, she looks at herself in the mirror: I looked pale, lifeless, hollow-eyed, almost ugly, and above all, I saw a striking resemblance to Aunt Clara's faded features. I also recalled the expression I heard so many times about Aunt Clara, "She was a flower that lasted only a day. She was precious at fifteen; at twenty-five she wasn't even a shadow of what she had been (344). Afraid to lose her looks, "my only guarantee and my only reason for being, the only thing left for me would be the same existence that Aunt Clara led, forever humiliated and dependent on Uncle Eduardo and his family"(346). About to marry César Leal, María Eugenia is torn between her convictions and her need to avoid Aunt Clara's fate. Feeling disgusted with herself, she writes, "My behavior, my cowardly behavior, criminal to myself, was at the same time horribly disloyal to the man who in one week was going to give me a luxuriously appointed home, filled with everything I needed, and his name and his support, and a position in society, and a secure future sheltered from want and humiliating dependency" (348).

The novel is an indictment of an economic system that allows women to be in men's economic thrall. All the women in the family are at the mercy of the men who frittered away their fortunes. Uncle Pancho explains the process: Aunt Clara has nothing because she gave her money to her brother, a happy, wild, generous soul and a lady's man. Grandmother has next to nothing because her son Eduardo lost her money on a mining venture. Mercedes is in an unhappy marriage, "her husband was a libertine and a gambler, who after having thrown away almost all her fortune, now treated her very badly" (98). María Eugenia recognizes the irony of her own situation: "the frightful fact: my absolute poverty, without any remission or hope other than the support of the same ones who perhaps had robbed me!" (59). Uncle Pancho confides that Eduardo has stolen from her and points to the simple economic truth that troubles Venezuela, "For women without a dowry or a fortune of their own, as almost all woman are in our society, it is always men who are obliged to totally support them" ...and he concludes that "a woman's worth is whatever value a man takes it into his head to place on her" (75). The solution is to find a man who will place a high value on Maria Eugenia. Since the family has lost money on several speculative ventures and perhaps the future of San Nicolás hacienda is none too stable, María Eugenia is the last thing of value for the Alonso family. She is her grandmother's prized object, as Uncle Pancho reminds her: "You are her pride now, rather like what a new hat brought from Europe must have been in her youth" (79).

Neither Mercedes nor María Eugenia can imagine having to work for a living. But then again, both lack positive role models to emulate. The novel offers a discussion of the two branches of the criollo group, one spending, indulgent, luxury loving and unproductive, the other good managers who keep the ranch going and the family solvent, but not without a good injection of capital, by way of seizing María Eugenia's property and forcing her to marry a rich, politically connected man.

When Maria Eugenía thought she was rich, when she was a carefree young woman roaming the boulevards of Paris, fashion was a means toward freedom. She fashioned a new self, using and adorning her body. In 1986, Iván Feo, a Venezuelan screenwriter and director, adapted the novel for a TV film. His screenplay faithfully follows the plot of the novel, for there is no "action," in the novel. Feo, however, skirts the issue of an unhappy ending in a curious way. After keeping vigil in her room the evening before her wedding night, the actress who plays María Eugenia removes all her clothes and walks off the film set. Having stripped herself of all the clothing and makeup involved in her self-fashioning, the heroine is left with nothing but her body.

In *Chick Lit: The New Woman's Fiction*[3] the editors of the volume point to "... Edith Wharton and Jane Austen as acknowledged precedents "of the genre and how "much of the chick-lit genre revisits the "class without money" conflict that pervades the novel of manners tradition (41). The genre is focused on the courtship of young, single women. "Chick

Lit" also owes a debt to Frances Burney and Jane Austen, who offered "vicarious moral improvement as well as entertainment for their readers (Wells 53). "Every heroine who tells her own story to the reader is, in a sense, writing her own novel, yet in no case does she acknowledge this (Wells, 56). Often seen as shallow entertainment "Chick Lit" nevertheless crystallizes some of the most important cultural issues facing women by calling attention to the dailiness of women's lives. It can also be a vehicle for describing political and feminist issues. The genre is playful, nuanced, self-consciously ironic and at times more complex than it seems. One of the characteristics of "Chick-Lit" is the naming of fashionable items, not through description but through brand names. The act of making lists of the clothes and other products the heroine wears and uses becomes a way to reinforce her sense of identity. The heroine becomes linked and "branded" to what she wears. ("Fashionably Indebted", Jessica Lyn Van Slooten. 224)

María Eugenia's trendy Parisian clothes, her makeup and hairstyle, her outlook as an educated woman and her aspirations to be a free woman clash with what was stylish and acceptable for a young woman of her class in Caracas. Her family wants to mold her into a suitable young woman who will appeal to a man who will marry and support her. Life in Paris had afforded María Eugenia with an array of luxury products that exhilarated and transformed her. In buying the products that were essential to her new persona, she spent all the money she had left. She used the money to create a fantasy-persona and she defined herself through her purchases. She dreams of a lifestyle she will take to Caracas, thinking that can afford to appear wealthy and stylish. Shari Benstock in her "Afterword" notes Chick-lit's use of the diary form, journals, letters and e-mail that links it to the epistolary tradition and to the novel that emerged out of private modes of writing commonly associated with women. She also traces contemporary Chick-lit to the novel of psychological development that emerged in the early twentieth century. Women such as Virginia Woolf and Dorothy Richardson moved away from the social considerations of the novel of manners to explore the internal, mental and emotional life of a central female protagonist. They used stream of consciousness, interior monologue, and ironic distance, all of which were used by de la Parra in her first novel.

During the time Teresa de la Parra corresponded with Vicente Lecuna, the foremost Bolivarian scholar of his time, she contracted tuberculosis, and corresponded with him from a sanitorium in Leysin, Switzerland. Her health would not allow her to finish the novel she hoped to write about Bolívar. She wrote to Lecuna that she was "Living a life of absolute bed rest, solitude, silence in the pure air of this prison of snow. I have renounced all my desires and it is like living in a Buddhist paradise" (*Obra* 558). Traveling from one sanitarium to another, seeking a cure for tuberculosis, the author's own life turned from one of conspicuous consumption to a life of contemplation and a disregard for materialism. One day after de la Parra returned to Paris, her friend Clemencia Miró asked her if she needed anything from Luasanne. De la Parra responded, "I do not need anything from Lausanne nor from any other place. I am the woman who never needs anything. I found this out a while ago the hard way, and it's very sad" (*Obra* 603). Her resignation is an about-face for a public figure known for her good looks and good taste.

Notes

[1] Garrels, Elizabeth. *Ifigenia: Diario de una señorita que escribió porque se fastidiaba.* Doral: Stockcero, 2008.
[2] In *Obra*, María Eugenia writes that she has cincuenta mil francos (50,000 francs). In Bertie Acker's translation, she has twenty thousand francs (14).
[3] Ferris, Suzanne and Mallory Young. *Chick Lit: The New Woman's Fiction.* New Cork, Routledge. 2006.

CHAPTER FIVE

A DISCUSSION OF RACE IN THE WORKS OF TERESA DE LA PARRA

Although de la Parra did not deliberately set out to portray the racial changes in her homeland, her two novels, lectures, diaries and correspondence nevertheless reflect the social, political, economic and racial realities of Venezuela in the 1920s. She challenged dominant discourse concerning race by writing about relations in her fiction and her letters. Having spent her childhood on a hacienda in Venezuela, she came into contact with the workers there. She was educated in Spain, and traveled throughout Europe after returning to Venezuela for a few years. *Iphigenia* provides an insight into issues of race and class relations in a criollo Caracas household, while M*ama Blanca's Memoirs* explores issues of race and race relations on a sugar plantation near Caracas.

Criollo families were proud to trace their white ancestry to the first settlers to Venezuela from Spain. They referred to themselves as *Mantuanos* because during the formative colonial era they wore capes, or *mantas*. *Iphigenia* allows the reader to listen in on family discussions concerning race in a bourgeois Caracas household, while the sugarcane plantation which is the setting of *Mama Blanca's Memoirs* offers an opportunity to witness race relations and racial attitudes among the plantation owners and their workers. Both the urban and rural settings in these novels examine interactions and relationships between the races and provide a range of racial/racist discourse that reflect attitudes towards racial mixing as Venezuela was transitioning from an agrarian society to an economy based on petroleum. As Doris Sommer has summed up, Latin America's novels, or "foundational fictions," were created with an eye toward nation-building. Latin American writers created the nation in the act of writing, shaping its values and projecting an ideal history through fiction. De la Parra, on the other hand, challenged the very society she was a part of and held a mirror up to it.

While racial issues are not the primary focus of the novels, nevertheless we gain insights into racial attitudes interspersed throughout the character's dialogs and in their behavior towards each other. The characters in de la Parra's novels reveal that while social hierarchy in Venezuela continued to be based on skin color, other factors were beginning to determine status and social standing. The criollos, the landed aristocracy who were losing their land and their status, were proud of their white lineage and fiercely clung to it. References in de la Parra's two novels attest to variations in skin color and its influence on the social hierarchy that had been in effect since the founding of Venezuela. Whiteness is privileged. The criollos seem comfortable with the "pure black" servants and descendants of slaves. What lies in the middle, however, causes discomfort for the Venezuelan elite. During de la Parra's lifetime, economic affiliation to the oil industry and political affiliation to the government were becoming important status symbols that were displacing and challenging established hierarchies based on lineage and landholding.

The cocoa, coffee and sugar haciendas in Venezuela owned by criollos depended on black slave labor. The importation of African slaves had an enormous impact on the racial makeup of the country. Slavery in Venezuela was outlawed in 1854. In the third of her *Three Columbian Lectures* de la Parra delivered to a standing-room audience in Columbia in 1930, she outlined her next project, a historical novel about Simón Bolívar focused on the women who influenced his life. She cited the relationship between Bolívar and his black wet-nurse, Matea, as the first of many women who had an impact on the Liberator's life. "From his black wet-nurse Matea, to Manuelita Sáenz, his last love, Bolivar can take no action without the image of a woman who inspires him, consoles him during his periods of great melancholy, and who lends him their eyes so that he can look within to discover his genius (*Obra* 514)." De la Parra was convinced that Bolívar had soaked up the poetry of rural life on the hacienda in Matea's arms. Relying on the oral stories and memories handed down from her female relatives, de la Parra believed that slaves who worked on these plantations were treated as an extension of the family. In the author's nostalgic evocation of plantation life on the Bolívar hacienda, Matea took the young Simón to the slave's quarters where he heard folk-tales, ghost stories, and legends, de la Parra asserts. When a triumphant Bolívar returned home to Caracas after the founding of the Gran Colombia in 1827, his attachment to his black nursemaid was stronger than ever. He noticed Matea's white kerchief and ran through the cheering crowd and singled her out to embrace her.

In de la Parra's second lecture, devoted to the role of women during the colonial era, she distinguished between the insular lives of wealthy criollo women who lead reclusive, private lives and the more public existence women of mixed race were allowed to lead. Relying on nineteenth century traveler's accounts written by Ulloa and Jorge Juan, de la Parra summarized these descriptions for her audience. According to these chronicles, the mulattas, quadroons and quinteroons nursed sick soldiers in the ports. Once their patients were cured, they often married them. If their patients died, the women of mixed races were the ones who performed the funeral rites (*Obra* 497). Mulattos were also called *pardos* in the 18th century, and *pardo* came to describe all people of mixed race during Independence. *Trigueño* was later used to describe dark-skinned Venezuelans.

Iphigenia's narrator, María Eugenia, reminds the reader that she is blonde[1] several times. Her family also reminds her that her hair and skin color add to her value as a marriageable woman. Her grandmother urges her to marry a rich man, and various relatives explain that her family name and skin color are both marketable commodities. Racial attitudes and prejudices crop up very early in the novel. Upon her arrival to La Guaira, the port of Caracas, María Eugenia's Uncle Eduardo greets her and warns her that this place will make a bad impression on her: "It's horrible, extremely narrow streets, poorly paved, blistering sun, and lowering his voice mysteriously he added, 'many blacks! Oh, it's horrible (*Iphigenia* 21)." María Eugenia, who is unused to the racial mixtures she will encounter responds, "It doesn't matter, Uncle, it doesn't matter. Since we'll be only passing through, it's not important *(*21).*" But in passing through, she does notice the port's stevedores, half-naked mestizos and mulattos bent beneath the weight of their loads, and she shares her impressions and her unease in the letter to her friend Cristina, reflecting "They were not really blacks as Uncle Eduardo had just said; no none of them had the unity of characteristics or the uniformity of appearance I had seen in pure blacks. Rather, each one individually and all as a group constituted a variegated mixture of races… (*Iphigenia* 27)." Throughout the novel, the disdain for racial mixing is represented as though it were a bad experiment. As Ileana Rodríquez observes of the Criollo's reaction to the Venezuelan mixed-race majority, "The mulatta nation is an absurdity, a nightmare, the grotesque"[2]

Arriving at her grandmother's house, the heroine is greeted by "a group of black, wooly heads belonging to the four retainers who constitute Abuela's domestic service (*Iphigenia* 39)." This group, on the other hand, is described as being more "pure black." One of them, the laundress Gregoria, who is later described as "poetically black" and "brilliantly black," becomes María Eugenia's confidant. She is the family historian and María Eugenia considers this black woman to be one of the most intelligent and wisest people she has known in her life. The relationship with this down-to-earth black woman, who disdains convention unlike the heroine's succumbing to it, will deepen throughout the novel. It is Gregoria who smuggles what her Abuela would consider questionable books for María Eugenia to read and who delivers her mail. Gregoria is the link to the outside world for the young woman who is forced to live a restricted life and seldom leaves the house unescorted. She learns the facts about her family from this wise servant who knows all the intimate details that her prim Abuela and Tia won't reveal to her.

De la Parra was sensitive to the roles loyal female black servants played in criollo society, as we have seen in her treatment of Bolívar's nurse. In *Iphigenia* Gregoria and the heroine form a feminine bond and Gregoria, unlike the unhappily married Mercedes, the jilted Tia Clara, the spiteful María Antonia, and the hyper traditionalist Abuela offers the only positive female role model for a young girl who needed one.

After María Eugenia comes through the port of Caracas and becomes aware of the racial mixture of the dockworkers and the harsh life people of color endured on the waterfront, she asks her more liberal Uncle Pancho to escort her to the slums of Caracas. Her outings are restricted to wherever he takes her, since she is not allowed to go out unchaperoned. The two visit La Pastora, the highest and most backward neighborhood in Caracas, a slum where brown-skinned inhabitants live in poverty. The naïve protagonist claims she wants to experience the community's painful but colorful destitution, at first treating the excursion as a lark. When she arrives, she sees ugliness and poverty all around and notices little black and mulatto children, some with deformed bodies. After having lived in Paris and strolling through its wide boulevards, she is shocked to see that "on the sidewalks, beside closed doors, blocking the way, were little naked children of the neighborhood, little blacks or little mulattos who barely knew how to walk... (*Iphigenia* 69)." By now accustomed to the loyal, subservient and uniformed black servants who wait in her Abuela's household, she describes the children's mothers who live in La Pastora as "mulattas, petulant, wearing ribbons of violently brilliant colors (*Iphigenia* 70)."

The visit to the slums, which seems to have been planned as an educational outing, includes a racist rant on the part of her uncle. Trying to engage Uncle Pancho in a philosophical conversation in order to try to make sense of what she sees, her uncle makes his patently racist feelings known. He claims these people's aspirations "are imprisoned in a body that tyrannizes them and binds them with chains as it proclaims aloud the mortifying inferiority of its origin. Yes, the mulatto is the patient melting pot where painfully the heterogeneous elements of so many renegade races are fused (*Iphigenia* 70)." María Eugenia's naivety is evident when she later blithely reports what she has seen in a letter to her friend "And after philosophizing in this way, we remained silent a long time, watching on both sides of the carriage that mystery of humble life that showed itself to the street through open doors, shutters and windows, until finally, we had seen enough of the suburb, and we went out into the countryside (*Iphigenia* 70)." The baffled heroine's telling silence speaks volumes. The lesson she has learned from her uncle is that blacks and mulattos are backward, ignorant and poor.

If the national narratives of Latin America projected ideal histories through the novel, de la Parra defied this tradition. For a number of reasons, one of them being that the author depicted a backward and unfashionable Caracas, her first novel was attacked by Venezuelan critics. The novel's heroine was attacked as though she were a real person. Critics missed the irony and ambiguity de la Parra is now famous for. They did not read between the lines, and could not separate the author from the protagonist, assuming they were one and the same. De la Parra countered that María Eugenia was a representation of general thought within her social set at that time. Although de la Parra relied on her family history, she depended on her fertile imagination and her sharp observations of daily domestic life to write this novel. According to Lydia Cabrera, de la Parra's companion, it was *Mama Blanca's Memoirs* that contained autobiographical elements and family memories. Nevertheless, the views on race relations expressed in *Iphigenia* represent a consensus of the racial attitudes de la Parra heard and experienced when she returned to Venezuela, especially those of the landed aristocracy who were clinging to their pure white identities and were fearful of an unstable and mixed racial order.

Alone and bored, María Eugenia strikes up a friendship with Mercedes Galindo,an unhappily married woman whom her grandmother disapproves of. The heroine first glimpses the genteel and elegant Mercedes and notices "her white and well-cared for hands (*Iphigenia* 96)." As elegant and beautiful as Mercedes is, María Eugenia hastens to add, "But I am much prettier than she. It's beyond question: I am taller, blonder (*Iphigenia* 106)." When Mercedes introduces her to an eligible bachelor, Gabriel Olmedo, her first reaction to this aspiring suitor is one of disappointment, because "in the first place, his eyes and hair are black as coal...he's not bad looking if you happen to like brunets, but since I don't like jet-black hair except on a cat's back, his hair, the color of a crow's wing, made a poor impression on me last night (*Iphigenia* 109)." She eventually falls hopelessly in love with this man, but Gabriel is ambitious and marries the daughter of a politically connected oil speculator and becomes very rich himself. His wife-to-be María Monasterios is described as "dark, chubby and short (*Iphigenia* 131)." In other words, just the opposite of our heroine. María Eugenia is forced to give in to her family's demands to marry, and agrees to a loveless match to a newly rich man who can offer her a comfortable life. Her first impression of César Leal, her husband-to be, is that he is too fat, too dark complexioned and too old.

The perception of a character's whiteness changes throughout this novel. When she sees the now-married Gabriel once more at her uncle's sickbed, María Eugenia has second thoughts; he has suddenly lightened in her eyes. In contrast to Leal, "how white Gabriel is! I didn't know that either… no, I had never noticed. Judging by his face I thought he was brunet, but no, he is white, white, very white (*Iphigenia* 273)." When Gabriel folds the sleeves of his shirt back, she notices that, "his arms are white, like my arms, and Abuela's arms, for she's very blonde, too. The back of Gabriel's neck is extremely white, like his arms (*Iphigenia* 373)." The heroine reminisces over her lost love for Gabriel, whom she first dismissed as too dark and now perceives as "very light skinned and very well groomed… he seems very whiter yet… (*Iphigenia* 273)." Gabriel reminds his former beloved of the love sonnet she had written to him. He is also reminded of her desirable white skin and blonde hair, and drawing her closer, declares, "Well, that little blonde beautiful head, and those pretty white hands know how to write ardent love sonnets (*Iphigenia* 281)[1]."

The criollo characters establish a black/white hierarchy. All references to dark skin and dark hair are negative ones. While her grandmother and her aunt urge María Eugenia to marry Leal, her free-spirited uncle opposes the match. "I know both of César Leal's sisters. They are tall, skinny, dark-complexioned girls with pimply faces (*Iphigenia* 225)." Reluctantly coming to grips with the rapid changes in social standing, their Abuela admits that it's harder and harder to find an eligible bachelor without vices who belongs to their social group, and concedes that although Leal's family are a long way from first-class, she laments that things have changed and exceptions must be made.

During the dinner conversation at Mercedes' house, Uncle Pancho suggests that Venezuela is going through a period of sociological gestation, a period of racial fusion, whose principal manifestation must always be anarchy. His theory is that, "Caudillo spirit" is the result of the uneasy fusing of the races.[3] This "caudillo spirit" reflects the reality that political conflicts did not end with the Independence movement led by Bolívar.

Mercedes, who is fond of speaking French, joins in the argument "I consider myself pure white. I'm sure of it. Ah! Ma généalogie, mon cher, c'est quelque chose de très chic (*Iphigenia* 142)." Uncle Pancho suggests that during the War of Independence "Bolívar, in his proclamations, for reasons of state, managed to exalt and to make brown-skinned people fashionable. I say no more. You know how women are about fashion (*Iphigenia* 143)." Mercedes, fearful of offending the servants who will overhear these racist remarks, asks Pancho to speak in French. The fun-loving and dissolute Pancho counters that "free trade" was established during the wars of independence and that after the war old maids and the nuns who had been expelled from their convents suddenly had mysterious adopted children. Not only does the uncle dispute Mercedes' pure white lineage, but he suggests that while husbands were away from home fighting the Wars of Independence, miscegenation took place, and that white married women and former nuns had sexual relations with men of color, resulting in mixed-race children.

When her very traditional grandmother and her strict maiden aunt disapprove of Mercedes, María Eugenia defends her friend, boasting that she is "white on all four sides," repeating Mercedes' claim to her pure white lineage. Growing ever fonder of Gregoria, María Eugenia chats with her and suggests, "In your youth, Gregoria, you must have been really wild (*Iphigenia* 288)." To which Gregoria responds, "Yes, I may be really black, and really ugly, and everything else, but I always had someone interested in me. Black women who are married put on airs, and they're ashamed of their color and they have to put up with insults and beatings from their husbands (*Iphigenia* 288)." Gregoria is proud of being an independent woman, a loyal servant, and a good Christian. "I've always been glad I was born black and poor because black and poor I could love whomever I pleased (*Iphigenia* 289)." As Rodriquez points out, "The image of old servants as companions, the presence of these ancient guardians as historical continuity, is one of the architraves in the construction of both gender and nation – of gender because physically and spiritually they support the white feminine protagonists (80)."

There is also reference to "la aya mulata" or mixed-race nursemaid in the prize-winning short story *"Mama X "*which de la Parra later inserted into *Iphigenia*. The reference to this woman is just one example of the diverse racial makeup of the Venezuelan population. Chapter 6 of *Iphigenia*, into which the "Mama X" story was inserted, describes a little black girl, María del Carmen, the cook's daughter, whose head is crisscrossed by an intricate hieroglyphic of tiny braids that are linked together. The criollo narrator of the "Mama X" story is unhappy at her private school and contrasts her unhappiness to María del Carmen's blissful existence. She would happily trade places with the little girl, since the white narrator hates her school and her family circumstances. "Really, after all, it wasn't worthwhile to have been born white, with blonde curls, rosy lips, and a rich father, to have sailed for more than two weeks to reach this disastrous conclusion...(*Iphigenia* 186)." While Gregoria's character points to the advantages of being a black older woman, the white narrator of the short story imagines the advantages of being a black little girl.

There are two characters, both mulattos, in de la Parra's novels who are accused of race hatred. The heroine dislikes her Tia Antonia, who is held up as the model of female rectitude, but she describes her in a deprecating manner, using mulatta as an insult. "She's a nobody, she's a mulatta, an illegitimate child, full of evil and racial hatred (*Iphigenia* 118)."

Although *Mama Blanca's Memoirs* is set in an earlier time, de la Parra integrated her childhood memories of growing up on a hacienda near Caracas, very much like the setting of the fictional hacienda Piedra Azul in the novel. While the descriptions of race relations in *Iphigenia* reflect a composite of racial attitudes de la Parra experienced on her return to Venezuela, the narrative in *Mama Blanca's Memoirs* reflects the racial attitudes she was exposed to growing up as a little girl amidst the household help and the workers on the plantation. She remembered what life was like on one of these plantations, from the owners to the workers of the sugar mill, to the hired hand who tended to the dairy cattle and the house servants. In *Mama Blanca's Memoirs* Evelyn, the mulatta nanny brought in from Trinidad to teach the little girls English, is accused of being racist. The very strict Evelyn tries to keep the girls away from the lovable Vicente Cochocho, the jack-of-all trades is a zambo, a mixture of American Indian and African. Looking back on the harsh treatment Evelyn meted out to Vicente, the elderly narrator Mama Blanca admits, "At bottom, as I understand it now-the war to the death that Evelyn carried on daily against our beloved Cochocho had its origins in a complex, personal race hatred. For that reason it was relentless and without quarter. Evelyn's three-quarters of white blood cursed her quarter of Negro blood. As she was unable to bedevil the Negro in herself, she took it out on Vicente. She never passed up the chance to discredit him in the eyes of his admirers-that is to say, in our eyes- but without success. On the contrary (*Mama Blanca's Memoirs* 64)." As a child, the narrator could not understand the nanny's hateful behavior. As a grownup, the narrator interprets the nanny's cruel treatment of the mixed-race Vicente Cochocho as a function of Evelyn's hatred for her own blackness.

De la Parra references Gobineau in her letters. He wrote about the advantages of a pure Aryan race, and she disagreed with his theories. Joseph Arthur Gobineau (1816-1882) was a French diplomat and man of letters and the proponent of the theory of Nordic supremacy and anti-Semitism. His "Essays on the Inequality of Human Races" (1853-1855), separated mankind into White, Black and Yellow races, and he believed that race mixing would lead to chaos.

She held hope for the people of the Americas, who would eventually form a mixed race. She wrote to her friend Dr. Luís Zea Uribe in 1933 that she opposed Gobineau's theories and urged him to suggest further readings on issues of race to her. In this letter she recalled the nobility of the poor and humble blacks who grew up in the countryside in Venezuela. They were full of love and charity, they were generous and they filled her childhood with fond memories. She reminded her friend Zea that she brought one of them to life through the fictional character Vicente Cochoco, whom she invented for *Mama Blanca's Memoirs*. She pondered, "What would Gobineau, who believes that civilization depends on the symmetry and orderliness of the Aryan race have to say about this ungovernable yet lovable creature with his lyrical zest for life? (*Obra* 584)." As Sommer points out, "Miscegenation was the road to racial perdition in Europe, but it was the way of redemption in Latin America, a way of annihilating difference and constructing a deeply horizontal, fraternal dream of national identity (39)."

After living in Venezuela for a few years, de la Parra settled in Paris, where she participated in its intellectual life, took classes at the Sorbonne, and was exposed to other ways of thinking. While she used her novels to interpret literary representations of race in her contemporaries, the author also looked inward, leading her to reflect on her own racial and ethnic prejudices. One result was that she removed the word "Jew" used as an anti-Semitic slur from the 1928 Bendelac edition of *Ifigenia*. The second edition left out the word "Jew" in expressions like "Jew usurer", to describe Uncle Eduardo, and other instances of the word "Jew" used as a racial epithet (Garrels *Ifigenia* 9).

De la Parra formed a close friendship with the Cuban painter, anthropologist and ethnographer Lydia Cabrera. When she contracted tuberculosis, Cabrera recounted the Afro-Cuban stories she had heard during her childhood to entertain her. She urged her friend to collect and publish the folk stories of Cuban blacks, folkloric tales that were in danger of disappearing and worthy to be preserved and published. Inspired by her friend, Cabrera collected and wrote the *Contes Negres de Cuba* (1936), and dedicated the work to her.

Unable to voice her own opinions openly during the Gómez dictatorship and its censure in Venezuela, de la Parra was able to portray attitudes towards racial mixing through the observations and attitudes of the characters in her novels. Using her own experience and observations, she proved that race and color were subjective and slippery labels that depended on the speaker's viewpoint, and illustrated how contemporary society reacted to racial mixing in the face of a new and dynamic economy in Venezuela.

Although de la Parra relied on some of her family history, she relied on her fertile imagination and her sharp observations of daily domestic life to write this novel. Nevertheless, the views on race relations expressed in *Iphigenia* represent a consensus of the racial attitudes de la Parra heard and experienced when she returned to Venezuela, especially those of the landed aristocracy who were clinging to their pure white identities and were fearful of an unstable and mixed racial order.

The perception of a character's whiteness changes. When she sees the now-married Gabriel once more at her uncle's sickbed, María Eugenia has second thoughts; he has suddenly lightened in her eyes. In contrast to Leal, "how white Gabriel is! I didn't know that either... no, I had never noticed. Judging by his face I thought he was brunet, but no, he is white, white, very white" (*Iphigenia* 273). When Gabriel folds the sleeves of his shirt back, she notices that "his arms are white, like my arms, and Abuela's arms, for she's very blonde, too. The back of Gabriel's neck is extremely white, like his arms "(*Iphigenia* 373). The heroine reminisces over her lost love for Gabriel, whom she first dismissed as too dark and now perceives as "very light skinned and very well groomed... he seems very whiter yet...," (*Iphigenia* 273). Gabriel reminds his former beloved of the love sonnets she had written to him. He is also reminded of her desirable white skin and blonde hair, and drawing her closer, declares, "Well, that little blonde beautiful head, and those pretty white hands know how to write ardent love sonnets" (*Iphigenia* 281).

The criollo characters establish a black/white hierarchy. All references to dark skin and dark hair are negative ones. While her Abuela and Tia urge María Eugenia to marry Leal, her free-spirited uncle opposes the match. "I know both of Cesar Leal's sisters. They are tall, skinny, dark-complexioned girls with pimply faces" (*Iphigenia* 225). Coming to grips with the rapid changes in social standing, their Abuela admits that it's harder and harder to find an eligible bachelor without vices who belongs to their social group, and concedes that although Leal's family are a long way from first-class, things have changed and, exceptions must be made.

During the dinner conversation at Mercedes's house, Uncle Pancho suggests that Venezuela is going through a period of sociological gestation, a period of racial fusion, whose principal manifestation must always be anarchy. His theory is that that "Caudillo spirit" is the result of the uneasy fusing of the races.[7] Mercedes, who is fond of speaking French, joins in the argument "I consider myself pure white. I'm sure of it. *Ah! Ma généalogie, mon cher, c'est quelque chose de très chic*" (*Iphigenia* 142). Uncle Pancho counters that during the War of Independence "Bolívar, in his proclamations, for reasons of state, managed to exalt and to make brown-skinned people fashionable. I say no more. You know how women are about fashion" (*Iphigenia* 143). Mercedes, fearful of offending the servants with these racist remarks, asks Pancho to speak in French. The fun-loving and dissolute Pancho counters that "free trade " was established during the wars of independence and that after the war old maids and the nuns who had been expelled from their convents suddenly had mysterious adopted children. Not only does the uncle dispute Mercedes' pure white lineage, but he suggests that while husbands were away from home fighting the Wars of Independence, miscegenation took place, and that white married women and former nuns had sexual relations with men of color, resulting in mixed-race children. When her very traditional Abuela and her strict maiden Tia disapprove of Mercedes, María Eugenia defends her friend, boasting that she is "white on all four sides," repeating Mercedes' claim to her pure white lineage. Growing ever fonder of Gregoria, María Eugenia chats with her and suggests, "In your youth, Gregoria, you must have been really wild" (*Iphigenia* 288). To which Gregoria responds, after some Wagnerian laughter, "Yes, I may be really black, and really ugly, and everything else, but I always had someone interested in me. Black women who are married put on airs, and they're ashamed of their color and they have to put up with insults and beatings from their husbands "(*Iphigenia* 288). Gregoria is proud of being an independent woman, a loyal servant, and a good Christian."I've always been glad I was born black and poor because black and poor I could love whomever I pleased" (*Iphigenia* 289). "The image of old servants as companions, the presence of these ancient guardians as historical continuity, is one of the architraves in the construction of both gender and nation – of gender because physically and spiritually they support the white feminine protagonists " (Rodriguez 80).

The first edition of *Iphigenia* was published in Paris in 1924 by the Casa Editorial Franco-Iberoamericana. Four years later, a revised edition was published in Paris by I.H. Bendelac. This edition omitted some segments and added others. Most of these changes are word changes and do not change the novel in any fundamental way, as Elizabeth Garrels points out in the "Advertencia" to the Stockcero edition (ix). All the changes were annotated by Jorge Gaete Avaria, "Registro de variants, supresiones y adiciones en "Ifigenia" in María Fernanda Palacios' edition of *Obra Escogida I* (Caracas: Monte Avila, 1992, 485-504. Garrels chooses the 1928 edition because de la Parra had by that time processed the criticism, both good and bad, her novel had received. Garrels questions to what extent the changes were a reaction to the criticism (x). Some of the changes involved omitting racial and ethnic slurs. The first edition used "Jew" as an anti-Semite slur, which does not appear in the second edition. Garrels suggests that after living in Europe for five years, de la Parra became sensitized to the use of this word and eliminated it. Garrels, however, finds this a curious decision, since the rest of the old discourse concerning race continues as in the first edition (x).

The novel also offers a study in class and color and there are discussions about marrying the 'right' people. Mercedes Galindo is very white, "white on all four sides." Social pacts and alliances and the bettering of the country depend on achieving the right mix and there is an unwritten code of *mestizaje*: a poor white criollo like Maria Eugenia can't marry a poor ambitious *mestizo* like Gabriel Olmedo, but she can marry a rich *mestizo* who is allied with the government. All leads to the establishment of a new social order and new alliances between the races mixed with a dash of tropicalismo, "a cocktail where all our psychological conditions are mixed with a little bit of bitterness, leafy and luxuriant; it is the potent sap of the new land; it is the sun; it is the tropics" according to Gabriel (142).

Blacks are servants, confidantes and the repository of truth. Gregoria brings María Eugenia books. She is her accomplice. Gregoria is a prototype for the black servant who allies herself with her young white charge. One of four servants of the household, she is the most liberated character in the novel, and probably the most respected role model for María Eugenia. She is "the laundress and historian... who would tell me stories, who took care of her physical and spiritual well-being. She has a poetic soul, which scorns human prejudices with the elegant harshness of a cynical philosopher, has for all creatures the brotherly charity of St. Francis of Assisi. This free partnership has made her soul generous, indulgent, and immoral (*Obra* 39-41). She disdains conventions. Gregoria becomes her confidante and procurer of books from the circulating library, smuggling the off-limits contraband to Maria Eugenia in her shawl.

Gregoria also mails the interminable, that is to say, over 80 page-long letter to Cristina. "Gregoria knows my dreamy tendencies and instead of frustrating them, as Tia Clara does, no, Gregoria feeds them (102). Gregoria represents "simple, uncomplicated wisdom (103). She is smart and knows how to carry on a conversation, she is gifted with a lively imagination and the gift of mimicry. After talking to Gregoria, the grandmother's and aunt's trivial conversations pale by comparison, so to speak.

Notes

[1] Amidst all the talk of blonde hair and white skin as privileged traits, it is ironic that when Iván Feo feo adapted *Ifigenia* for a film version in 1986, he cast a brunet for the leading role.

[2] *House/Garden/Nation: Space, Gender and Ethnicity in Postcolonial Latin American Literatures by Women*. Durham: Duke University Press, 1994. 80.

[3] "Caudillos, usually from the llanos, continued to raise personal armies and to destabilize the government... Venezuela's history showed a pattern of implacable dictatorships alternating with impractical and short-term regimes (Sommer 279).

CHAPTER SIX

THE THREE COLOMBIAN LECTURES:
MOTHERS, SISTERS AND LOVERS

As a noted novelist and gifted public speaker, de la Parra was invited to deliver three lectures in Bogotá and Barranquilla, Colombia, in 1930.[1] She also delivered the lectures later in Cuba. The lectures were not published until 1961 in Caracas by the Venezuelan critic Arturo Uslar Pietri.[2] The *Tres Conferencias: Influencia de las mujeres en la formacíon del alma americana* or *Three Lectures: Women's Influence in the Formation of the American Soul,* described the important roles women played during the Conquest, Colony, and Independence eras in Latin America. According to Antoine Lemaitre, de la Parra's biographer, "Teresa's Colombian lectures stand abandoned and cut off, like a prologue without a text and burdened with representing the last valuable expression of Teresa as an artist: her last creative work" (*Between Flight and Longing* 141). According to Elsa Krieger Gamberini, the lectures were treated as trivial essays with no substance, essays that were reductive and repetitive in nature (177). Gamberini goes on to point out that early critics of the essays were mostly male until the 1970's, when new critics began to value the feminine for its difference and to read the author's work with literary criteria giving way to a more open reading that addresses the feminine text as subject (192). Maria Antonia Palacios, de la Parra's Venezuelan biographer considers these lectures to be her best writing.

In these lectures de la Parra declared herself a "moderate feminist" as she highlighted the important roles the founding mothers played in Latin American history and in the formation of its ethos and culture. She wanted to uncover the hardships that had been imposed on women starting with the conquest of Mexico. As Spain conquered more of the Latin American continent, women played important roles, but the stories of half the human race had been ignored by Latin American historians. Historians and chronicles tended to write about battles and victories. In recuperating the voices of the "founding mothers," de la Parra began her lectures describing the invitation to visit Colombia and her initial reluctance to accept it. She had just returned to Paris after a visit to Italy and was looking forward to getting on with her writing.

A key to understanding de la Parra's writing and her interest in promoting women's lives and concerns resides in her own idiosyncratic life. Unlike most women of her class and generation, she was economically independent, free to travel and devote her time to writing. After having written two successful novels and other fiction, de la Parra began to devote herself to studying Latin American history in order to recuperate women's roles in its development. De la Parra identified with her Venezuelan heritage and recalled stories she heard from her female relatives.[3] As she described herself to García Prada in a letter: I spent most of my early childhood on a sugar plantation in Caracas. Many of the memories from my early childhood are contained in *Mama Blanca's Memoirs*. My father died when I was eight years old and my mother moved our family to a province in Spain to live near our maternal grandmother to be educated. Both my grandmother and mother belonged, in their outlook and in their customs, to the established colonial society of Caracas. Therefore, in my late childhood and adolescence I had a strict Catholic upbringing. Corpus Christi processions, Holy Week, Marian feast days, and other holy feast days of the Catholic Church, along with walks in the country, were my only celebrations and social outlets. I returned to Venezuela when I was eighteen years old. I spent a lot of time in the countryside reading as much as possible. It was in Caracas that I first came into contact with the world and society. I observed the continual conflict of the new mentality of young women who traveled and read, but who lived bound to old assumptions and to the customs of an earlier age. They were ruled by the old values but did not believe in them and longed, in their hearts, for an independent life and ideas, until they married, gave them up, and reverted to the old ideas, thanks to motherhood. This eternal female conflict with its end in renunciation gave me the idea for *Iphigenia*. Because the novel was critical of men and opposed established ideas, it was not well received in my country. Conservative Catholics in Venezuela and Colombia deemed the novel to be dangerous to young girls, since they enjoyed seeing themselves portrayed by the heroine with her aspirations and her limitations and sided with her. The novel was attacked and defended by both sides, which contributed to its readership. In 1923 I moved to Paris, and I have lived here since. In 1928 I wrote my second book, *Mama Blanca's Memoirs*, which, unlike *Iphigenia*, was very well received by the traditionalists but disappointed the female readers of *Iphigenia*, who missed María Eugenia Alonso, the heroine sacrificed to custom. I am currently studying colonial Latin American history, which I would like to write about some day (*Obra* 599-510). Her first opportunity to put her study to use came when she delivered her lectures, which aside from relying on accepted written history at the time, were infused with passion, biblical references to parables, and oral histories. As an independent woman living in Paris, she had attended lectures and attended readings, and she took elocution lessons (Palacios 65).

Previously, de la Parra had written articles for literary journals and a newspaper in Caracas. In 1927 she traveled to Cuba to represent Venezuela at the Interamerican Conference of Journalists, where she gave a talk on "The Hidden Influence of Women during Independence and on the life of Bolívar." This led to her next project, a novel about Bolívar told from the point of view of his confidante, Miguelita Sáenz. She continued her study of colonial history, which she kept up with until her dying days. While composing the lectures, she outlined what she hoped would be her third novel. She had done the historical research, but wanted the novel to be different from the official version of Bolívar's biography, since it would include the perspectives of the women in his life and their influence on his career. Various biographies had been written about Bolívar, but de la Parra wanted her readers to experience history from a woman's point of view. She planned to visit the places where Bolívar had traveled, soak up the atmosphere, and convey it in her novel. Although she corresponded with the foremost Bolivar historian, Vicente Lecuna, her later letters to him reveal that the interest in the project either waned, or she felt overwhelmed by the material and put it aside. Her illness may have contributed to the fact that she never wrote the novel. She identified with Bolívar, who died of tuberculosis in his 40's, the same disease that would take her life in 1936 when she was forty-seven.

We can deduce how she would have mined the historic material through her correspondence and from her references to the book in her lectures. In the *Third Lecture* in Bogotá, in which she reviews the role of women in Venezuela's fight for independence, and in her letters written during the time of her illness (1932-1936), she describes Bolívar and his relationship with Manuela Sáenz. She explained to Lecuna that she wanted to write a novel about Bolívar showing how the women in his life, starting with his black nurse Matea and ending with his last love Manuelita, affected him.[4] At every point in Bolívar's life, from his military success to his bouts of depression, a strong woman had given him a new perspective so that he could re-focus his efforts and look within himself with a fresh pair of eyes (514).

In another letter to Garcia Prada, written in December, 1932, de la Parra wrote about her reaction to delivering the lectures and how disappointed she was that her audience wanted to know more about her personal life than the topic she actually delivered and wanted to raise their awareness about. Some critics, and by extension her audience, had confused the character María Eugenia in the novel *Iphigenia* with the writer and hoped to hear more about the controversial author's personal life. "When I traveled to Colombia in 1930, the public wanted to hear more confessions and were disappointed when instead I chose to speak about historical characters, Fanny de Villars, Doña Marina, Doña Manuelita, and Inca Garcilaso's mother" (630). The reading public adored confession and *Iphigenia* was popular in some circles because readers thought it was about her.

She disabused her audience by stating, "I do not recognize myself in my novels. The first was written by a contemporary young girl whose address we don't know; the second was dictated by a dead grandmother who was hospitable and loving as are many women who live under their tile roofs, so that they are the absent authors of these stories or novels, in my way of thinking. Situated as they are at the extreme stages of life, they came to me for a while, one told me about her life anxieties, the other recalled her melancholy life, and having taken me into their confidence, they discreetly departed when it was time to edit the books" (473).

Others critics accused her of writing novels that were disguised autobiographies that exposed her family. Her childhood years were spent on a sugar plantation very similar to the setting of *Piedra Azul* in *Mama Blanca's Memoirs,* but as she herself wrote, she had little in common with the heroines of her novels. She never married and lived an independent life that allowed her to travel, giving her a new perspective from which to study life in Caracas at the turn of the century. She was well read and loved to visit museums and monuments in Spain, Italy, and France. Boredom was not an incentive to write, and thanks to an inheritance left to her by her patron Emilia Ibarra de Barrios Parejo, she did not have to work for a living.

In her lectures in Bogotá she talked about the social conventions and the restrictions that stood in the way of women's progress. She is considered as the first writer in Venezuela to write about the inner life of women living in a patriarchal world and exposing their limited choices. De la Parra bridged the gap between Venezuelan and European traditions, and she wrote during the dictatorship of Juan Vicente Gómez (1908-1935), as Venezuela experienced changes during the emergence and development of its oil industry in the 1910s and 1920s.

In the *Three Colombian Lectures,* however, she focused on the historical role women played during the Spanish conquest, through Latin

America's colonial era and into the time of the wars of independence. She stressed the common heritage of all Latin American countries: they shared the same language and religion. She talked about prescribed and acceptable roles for women as mothers, nuns, or spinsters. After publishing *Iphigenia,* her patriotism had been questioned. The lectures provides her with an opportunity to acknowledge her patriotism and rekindle her ties to Latin America, as she called to mind celebrated forgotten or marginalized heroines and women she considered to be female martyrs, such Ñusta Isabel, Inca Garcilaso de la Vega's mother and the role her own foremothers played during revolutionary times. Highlighting female achievements throughout Latin American history, she pointed to the need for more positive feminine role models, for she believed women decided the direction of human societies. Her feminist message was not strident, but rather tame and "moderate" to use her own term. In her letters, de la Parra wrote about being invited to speak in Colombia and her different reactions to this invitation. On the one hand, she saw the invitation to speak as an attractive, yet dangerous offer. She was full of doubt. She wondered how to address a public who perhaps liked her from afar because they liked her novels, but would not like her after they had seen her close up. She had not spoken publicly since May 1921, when Prince Ferdinand of Bavaria and Bourbon visited Venezuela. She had been the subject of "ad feminam" criticism" the condescending attitude of some male critics who were interested in de la Parra's "feminine charms" rather than in her "female" fiction, like her translator Miomandre (Ibieta 425).

She received the invitation to speak in Colombia while she was living in Paris. The thought of crossing the ocean, traveling up the Magdalena River, traveling through the Andean jungle, and visiting cities known and unknown filled her with anxiety. But the tropics beckoned, and she accepted the invitation. She wrote the *Tres conferencias* on her return from a trip to Italy in 1929-1930, over a period of three or four months. Ismael Arciniegas and Luis Eduardo Nieto had overheard her say on the ship that was stopping in Barranquilla that she longed to return to Colombia. "This led her to write the best pages in her life "(Palacios 106). Palacios praises the *Tres conferencias* for their remarkable for narrative skill, and how, as a speaker, de la Parra vividly evoked eighteenth century city life in Latin America. The lectures are complex, suspenseful, and have the subtlety of a great novel, and she enchanted her audience like Scheherazade had done with her tales. Her sense of history was not strictly historical, it was submerged in sentiment. She preferred to talk about daily occurrences, privileging everyday, colloquial language and praised women for their gift

of continuity and hailed them as the true founders of families. She
described the contribution of women's roles, and envisioned them of
having many things in common no matter where they lived in Latin
America. She relied on stories and fables to tell her version of history and
idealized women who had been martyred, defeated or marginalized.

Newspapers promoted the excitement surrounding her talks. Bogotá's
El Tiempo's headlines read: "Bogotá gave Teresa de la Parra a reception.
There were people on top of railway cars. It took twenty minutes to get
through the crowds... In the photo she is surrounded by elegant women,
distinguished by her physical and intellectual stature. Below it reads:
"Teresa de la Parra in the Hotel Augusta, moments after her triumphal
arrival" (Bosch 133) Luís Eduardo Nieto Caballero reported that at every
train station her train had to stop for parades in her honor. Spectators
handed her bouquets or asked for her autograph (Ramón Diaz Sanchez
140). Three thousand people greeted her. She read the three lectures six
times at the Teatro Colón. A true believer in the spoken word and the
power of oral tradition, the opportunity to address an audience of this size
made her feel proud.

The First Lecture

She broke the ice with her audience in a self-deprecating manner: "I know
that in Colombia you like my books. I know you like them with that sweet,
disinterested and domestic way one loves dogs, flowers, caged birds, in
short, the way one loves familiar and useless things" (*Obra* 472). She
played into her audience's hands describing her love for Colombia. This
humble beginning would take a radical turn as de la Parra led her audience
through a brief history, a kind of crash course, of women who played key
roles in shaping Latin American history. The first lecture began with a
meek, shy, soft- spoken and humble tone, allaying the audience's fears that
she might be a rabid feminist. She confessed that was afraid that she would
not live up to her audience's expectations. Realizing that they wanted to
hear about her personal life, she told them that she hoped to return in thirty
years or so to tell the tale of her youth. Sadly, however, she died in Madrid
in 1936, just as Spain's Civil War broke out.

She prefaced her first lecture by glossing over her two novels, insisting
she did not see herself in either of them, and had nothing in common with
the characters. The rebellious young woman María Eugenia had been
attacked by the critics, and she used this criticism to launch into her first
message: today's women can no longer lead a sheltered life. They need to
have a useful life and they need to work, and she clarified what she meant

by work: she did not want women to be employed in badly paid and menial jobs, but rather wanted them to have careers that required training and preparation. Neither did she want women to have political careers. She jokingly compared politics to coal mining. In both jobs, she claimed, you are bound to get your hands dirty. Rather than see her as reactionary or conservative or indifferent to politics, however, Palacios suggests that because de la Parra witnessed the goings-on in diplomatic circles, she was aware of their hatreds, exaggerations, and the falsehoods (105). She declared herself to be a "moderate feminist." It is not surprising that de la Parra distrusted politics, living as she did in the time of Gómez's long and repressive dictatorship. "If her feminism seems tame when compared to today's standards, it should be noted that it was deemed as rather advanced and polemical for its time. Her strengths lie in her delightful, ironic style and her authentic portrayal of a woman's search for a viable identity. For these reasons, aesthetic as well as thematic, her work remains provocative, relevant, and appealing to the modern reader (Ibieta 423).

She continued to soften any anti-feminist feelings in her audience. Before visiting Colombia, de la Parra had travelled to Havana and happily reported that, when in 1928 she was as a guest of a Cuban family (the Cabrera family) for a few days, she observed women's life in Cuba and shared her reactions to it: "A great number of Cuban women work and study without having lost their femininity or their respect for principles and traditions" (*Obra* 475). The lives Cuban women led made for good role models. Having jobs did not keep them from getting married. She extolled the benefits of a modern education for women insofar as it not only helped them live independently, but because it helped them help to others.

De la Parra contrasted the lives of two contemporary poets: her friend Gabriela Mistral, the Chilean writer who would be awarded the Nobel Prize in Literature in 1945, and the Chilean Delmira Augustini, who made a hasty marriage and was shot to death in a jealous rage by her former husband. Augustini suffered the same fate as the protagonist of *Iphigenia*, who was forced to marry according to social convention. The consequences of Delmira Augustini's choice, however, led to a truly tragic outcome.

She reviewed how she struggled with the title of her lectures. In an argument concerning labels that continues unresolved to this day, she considered whether she should call her lectures "The Soul of Latin American, IberoAmerican, Hispanoamerican, Indoamerican or the unwieldy- sounding Indohispanicamerican Women," and finally decided on "American Women." The first lecture was to be a survey of notable women who lived during the time of the Spanish conquest of the Americas. These were the women who "preached in silence, the women of the conquest, obscure Sabines, silent anonymous laborers of concord, the true founders of cities and households, their work effective across the generations in their silent enterprise of fusion and love"(*Obra* 477).

The Catholic Queen Isabela of Spain brought the Renaissance to the American jungle. De la Parra considered her to be the mother and godmother of criollo America, a woman who combined feminine graces with masculine virtues. The criollos were the descendants of the conquistadors, the white landed gentry. In Venezuela, they called themselves "Mantuans," because they wore *mantos,* or cloaks in public. In colonial times this class founded and ruled cities, engraved their coats of arms on the doors of their old mansions, and forged the independence of half the American continent. But the criollos later suffered a decline, oppressed by persecutions and party hatreds, and forgot the roles their grandmothers or great-grandmothers had played to liberate the Americas. The Spanish queen had a chronicler, José María de Heredia, but there were countless American princesses whose lives went unrecorded, Indians who were baptized and given Spanish names, heiresses to lands they shared with their white husbands. Bartolomé de las Casas, the Spanish religious and chronicler, knew of over sixty Indian women who were married to European men. According to de la Parra, the mixing of the two races was possible thanks to the "miracle of feminine love." She cited the example of Gonzalo Guerrero, the Spanish captive who married an Indian woman and refused to be repatriated when Cortés tried to rescue him as an example of a European man who married an Indian woman. These Indian women were" tropical Nausicaas." After the brutality of the conquest, they showed European men how to find the gold within themselves.

Indian woman who lived through the conquest were "crucified" during the encounter and the mixing of races. Colonial women lived lives as mystics and dreamers. Women who lived during the independence movement inspired and facilitated Latin America's break from Spain. Women who lived in Mexico City, Bogotá, Lima, Quito, Caracas, Buenos Aires and Havana shared a common legacy; it was as though they lived in the same city and could be sisters.

Sor Juana Inés de la Cruz, the anonymous colonial poet Amarilis, the unjustly treated Ñusta Doña Isabela, (el Inca Garcilaso de la Vega's mother), and the nuns who lived in convents represented a cross-section of society. Queen Isabela encouraged Spain's age of discovery. The much-maligned Malinche continues to be a source of inspiration for poets, playwrights, historians and novelists, as Cortés lover, the mother of a *mestizo* child by him, and as someone accused (unjustifiably so) of helping to bring about the fall of the Aztec empire. Sor Juana Inés de la Cruz continues to inspire study and controversy in her role as a brilliant baroque poet and an unappreciated and stifled genius, although there is no evidence that she was a painter, as de la Parra claims in the lecture. Amarilis was one of perhaps many literate women who lived in a patriarchal society and who wrote behind the scenes. She and perhaps many others like her were never given credit for their work. Doña Isabela was a Peruvian noblewoman who gave birth to the first Latin American poet and historian, el Inca Garcilaso de la Vega, but she was cast aside by her Spanish husband when he married a Spanish wife.

De la Parra believed that Doña Marina was the power behind Cortés good fortune in the conquest of the Aztec empire. Several of the chronicles she read in preparing her talk acknowledged that Marina was the interpreter and mediator for Cortés, helping to uncover plots against him and his men in Cholula. But little had been written about Marina herself; one can only guess at what remains untold. Even Bernal Díaz del Castillo, who treated Marina kindly in his version of the history of the conquest, left much of her story unwritten. Chronicling military feats, victories, battles, and scenes of death and destruction drowned out the authentic voices of women. Their efforts were not as heroic, or worthy of epics. Their contributions were anonymous, reflected only in their children, their legacy in the mixing of the Indian and European races.

After establishing that Cortés was a Don Juan and a picaresque character, she launches into an impassioned version of Marina's history. She was sold as a slave by her mother and stepfather to other Indians, dispossessing her of her title and inheritance. But this only served to make her more adaptable. She was intelligent and spoke the language of the Mayas and the Aztecs, whom Cortés would try to conquer. Soon she learned to speak Spanish, "as though she had been born in Seville" (481).

Doña Marina's example was not unique, since other Indian women were sold as slaves, offered in sacrifice, or forced to marry men they did not choose. They were naturally attracted to the new religion in which men worshipped the Virgin Mary, whom they interpreted as a feminine idol who held a child in her arms. "Allying herself with Cortés in the cause of the white men against her own people, doña Marina, obeying the revolutionary imperative, with the wings of love, initiated the future reconciliation of the races and initiated in America furthermore, albeit in a rudimentary form, the first feminist campaign" (482). Bernal Díaz described doña Marina as being "meddlesome and outspoken." What he probably meant to say, posits de la Parra, was that this Indian woman was useful, alert, witty, discreet and flirtatious. She served to advance the narrative of Bernal Díaz's chronicle, and she imagines Doña Marina to be a charming and generous creature, an idealistic woman who welcomed change. Moctezuma's scribes depicted her as a powerful presence at Cortés' side, working as an emissary and translator. Yet after the birth of their son, Martín Cortés, and after conquering Mexico, Cortés married the mother of his child to another soldier, Juan de Jaramillo. When Doña Marina was reunited with the parents who sold her into slavery, she forgave them. De la Parra converts Doña Marina into "a new Joseph sold by her brothers, a symbol of mercy" (483). This is the first example of de la Parra's use of biblical examples to construct vivid analogies to make history come alive to her audience.

Bernal Díaz's chronicle was written in response to Cortés' own chronicler Gómera, another one of many chronicles in which women had been excluded. Bernal Díaz's chronicle was full of lively details, and doña Marina's role casts her as "the flower of a narrative that is not only historic, but something grander and more beautiful: a prose romance" (484). True history, de la Parra concluded, was really about recording everyday details like the kind that enliven Bernal Díaz's chronicle, such as references to the soldier's nicknames and the colors of the horses. Other chroniclers had missed out by not reporting the work of women, an onerous exclusion, since "Excluding them, they severed one of the threads of life" (484).

Doña Marina was only one example of Indian princesses who joined with Spanish conquistadors whose unions were dissolved. Such was the case of Ñusta Isabel, a niece and grandchild of the last kings of Peru, whose husband abandoned her and their six-year old son, the future author of the *Florida of the Incas* and *The Royal Commentaries of Peru*. El Inca Garcilaso de la Vega was born in Cuzco in 1539 to Sebastián Garcilaso de la Vega, who was related to the famous Golden Age poet from Toledo, Garcilaso de la Vega, and Isabel Chimpu Ocllo, a noblewoman and the niece of Huaina Capac and Atahualpa. When the Spanish conquistadors in Peru were ordered to marry, Garcilaso's father chose the Spaniard Doña Luisa Martel instead, marrying Isabel to one of his soldiers. De la Parra took up the story of Ñusta Isabel as told by her son in his *Comentarios Reales*.

It would be up to this *mestizo* poet to describe his childhood memories and the martyrdom of his mother, who was persecuted by Garcilaso's enemies. Mother and son were reduced to being prisoners in their own house, eating whatever their servants could supply. All the while, Isabel conducted herself as a wife and Inca princess, keeping the household accounts on *quipos,* the Inca recordkeeping system of knotted ropes. Her son learned the history of her people, their legends and myths. In his memoir, the young Garcilaso recalled how he had no words of rancor for the father he loved and no bitter words for his step-mother. But his grief overwhelms him when he remembers his mother, to whom he dedicated his book, "To my mother and lady, made more illustrious by baptismal water than by the royal blood of so many Incas" (*Obra* 489). The young Garcilaso traveled to Spain to reclaim his mother's land, but Isabel died during the process. Her son immersed himself in Spanish Renaissance life and wrote *The General History of Peru.* His *Royal Commentaries,* according to de la Parra, (who agrees with the historian Prescott), were his best work because they were based on the stories and legends told to him by obscure and forgotten Indian grandmothers.

The conquest period brought about a new race that mingled "feminine goals with masculine virtues." If men came to the New World to find gold and riches, it was the Indian women who led them to find their ideals and their true selves. Indian women also smoothed the path for the acceptance of Christianity.

De la Parra calls upon her relationship with her contemporary, a nun named Madre Teresa, from the Convent of Concepciones in Caracas. This relationship serves as a springboard for describing convent life during colonial days. A decree in 1872 expelled the Jesuits from Venezuela, which resulted in the closure of three convents in Caracas. Hundreds of women were literally thrown into the streets, and de la Parra tells how the inhabitants of Caracas came to the nuns' rescue. She also mentions her Criollo female ancestors who contributed to the cause of the Venezuelan revolution. While the male heroes of the revolution were acknowledged and revered, de la Parra wanted to emphasize the impact of the women who worked behind the scenes to make Venezuela a free nation. She deplored the decree of 1872, the cruel evictions of the nuns, and described how families converged on the plaza to take them into their homes.

Her family members were conservative criollos, and this influenced her beliefs and her way of life. The section on Madre Teresa and the description of convent life is both passionate and nostalgic. Her relationship with Madre Teresa and her childhood memories could have been the basis for a book, and perhaps Madre Teresa served as one of the models for Mama Blanca. This nun, claimed de la Parra, had the ability to transport the listener back one century,

Convents in Latin America often housed the unmarriageable daughters of the elite. But life in the convent could be a place to live a sheltered and comfortable life. Some convents had a ratio of five or six servants for every nun. De la Parra chose Sor Juana as the prototype of the nun who chose convent life in order to pursue intellectual pursuits. Another worthy woman who spent her life in the convent was Madre Castillo, an extraordinary nun from Tunja, Colombia. She entered the convent barely able to read and write. At the behest of her confessor, she eventually wrote an astonishing *vita,* a divine visionary revelation in the baroque style popular in XVI century Spain. Convent life in the tropics was often led outdoors, and there were frequent visitors and exchanges of food. This led to "rhetoric of messages, food, and gift-giving" (498). Convents played an important social role in colonial times. The nuns offered prayers and recited rosaries on behalf of supplicants. On feast days and holidays they provided musical entertainment and contributed to the festivities and ceremonies whenever an archbishop, viceroy, captain-general or marquises visited. Sor Juana wrote many poems for Laura, the Marquesa, who was posted in Mexico City, especially sonnets lamenting her death.

De la Parra ends the first lecture by admonishing her audience to reject neither the Spanish nor Indian legacy that is a part of the America soul and an important aspect of their heritage. "Like Garcilaso, the mestizo, let us keep it in the Castilian language without denying anyone, blessing the harmony of the union and with faith for the future and in forgiveness for the blood spilled and tears wept" (*Obra* 489).

The Second Lecture

During the three-hundred year span between the Spanish conquest of the New World, the formation of the Spanish colonies, and the time leading up to the wars of independence from Spain, women had no chroniclers. Reiterating her message from the first lecture, de la Parra reminded her audience that this period was a time of fusion, of the co-mingling of races. Women's history during this period was silenced, since women's lives had been restricted to the home or the convent. On the surface, the colonial era may seem to be indolent, tolerant, and voluptuous, partly due to the tropical climate, but behind this façade lay faith and sacrifice. This colonial time also forms part of her inner geography and provides a key to who she was, as she explained to her audience. De la Parra confessed, "I feel very much at home in the present period, and have great admiration for it, but who among us has not lived in Colonial times thanks to a friend, a relative, or a servant who is blissfully inept to live in this present century?" (*Obra* 490).

There were few records, letters or books about women in the archives during the colonial period. Any trace of women's lives lived on through oral tradition. It was a society enveloped in silence. These times reflected a conversational, familiar tone, much like an old grandmother's stories, or stories told by a black household slave who often confused his personal memories with those of his master's. Although she claimed she felt at home in the present, de la Parra wrote nostalgically about the Colonial period, describing her own anachronistic childhood as a "colonial upbringing." Indeed, she attributed the stories told to her by her Criollo female relatives as the impetus that led to her writing career.

Following the 1872 decree, the Federal Government in Venezuela closed the three convents in Caracas. These were live repositories of three centuries of colonial life, housing sixty-four nuns, some of whom were forced out by soldiers armed with bayonets. Since each nun had a black servant, an additional sixty-four women were now homeless. The nuns were taken in by their own families or other families, and continued to live their cloistered lives, praying, sewing, and cooking. De la Parra describes them as "lovers of silence who lived an interior life, and although it may seem like a contradiction, they were the precursors of the modern feminist ideal" (493). They lived their monastic lifestyle, and reconstructed their rituals while they lived with families.

Visiting one of the nuns she befriended, Mother Teresa, was like stepping back in time. One reason women entered the convent was to live the life of the mind, among books. The woman who wanted to dedicate her life to study was considered to be a strange species and was consequently marginalized. De la Parra quotes the Spanish proverb, "A woman who knows Latin will come to a bad end." In the convent, on the other hand, women could live in silence among books. She offers Sor Juana Inés de la Cruz as an example of the mystic intellectual, one of many who lived their lives in the convent. Unlike the great Baroque poet, there were other women whose lives and work remain unknown to us. But Sor Juana, who de la Parra described as beautiful, witty, passionate, full of life, and talented, was a genius. She was a poet, musician, painter, humanist, and scientist. "Had she been born in France at that time, she would have been one of the most brilliant literary geniuses and one of the most seductive women in the court of Louis XIV. But she was born in the colonies, however, and cognizant of her talents, she silently offered them up to God in the convent" (495). The young Juana Asbaje was summoned by the Viceroy to appear before the most learned men in the colonies who put her knowledge to a test, which she passed with flying colors. Her fame reached the court in Madrid. At that point, she retired to the convent and became one of the greatest colonial poets.

The Claretian nun Madre Castillo, like her Spanish predecessor, Teresa de Avila, was ordered to write her *vita*. Only their confessor or bishop could publish what nuns wrote. Madre Castillo entered the convent in Tunja, Colombia, high in the Andes, to pray and contemplate. As a novice, she could barely read. Her fellow sisters judged her to be strange, aloof, and visionary. Her confessor ordered her to write, and write she did, in the Spanish sixteenth century manner tinged with the baroque stylings of Góngora. De la Parra concluded that life in the colonial convents wasn't as repressive and closed off as we may think. After all, *gongorismo* made its way easily to this Andean nun's cell.

Because they were in the tropics, life in the colonial convents was lived outdoors, and there were many exchanges with secular life outside. The writings of eighteenth century visitors such as Ulloa and Jorge Juan described how in Mexico City and Havana each nun had six or seven servants living with them. A Franciscan brother sent from Spain to look into this excess was scandalized by the veritable "army of servants," the five hundred lay women who lived with the nuns in one convent. When the nuns were ordered to dismiss half their servants, they refused to comply.

Convents played other important roles in colonial life. Nuns composed music and songs and performed when important personages such as the viceroy, the virreine, or the bishop visited. Sor Juana was famous for her role in these festivities, and in Sor Juana de la Parra saw the seeds for the love of all things imported from across the sea, manifested in the preference in Latin America for all things French during her lifetime.

The daily lives of some criollo women were described by male travelers to Cartagena and Caracas. They reported that women of this class never ventured into the street, attending mass at 3:00 a.m. The traveler Jorge Juan tells of the daily life of Criollo ladies in Cartagena, distinguished women who lived in "ivory towers." Though they did not have a public life, they were hospitable to a fault, excellent and generous hostesses to their guests.

The mulatas, quadroons, and quinteroons led more public lives and nursed sick Spanish soldiers in the port. Once their patients were cured, they often married them. If their patients died, they performed the funeral rites. There was another set of marginalized women. These were the maiden aunts whose were not wives or nuns. Some of these women had been jilted by their lovers. De la Parra called them "marginalized mystic dreamers," who were in some instances more maternal that one's mother, and who could be counted on in times of illness or death.

The life of the anonymous colonial poet who called herself Amarilis remains shrouded in mystery. She wrote an epistolary poem which, according to de la Parra, should be more widely read in Spanish-speaking countries. "But perhaps her greatest charm is that she had the good taste to stay in the shadows, thereby offering a good example to the vain half-talents who display their works" (501). Amarilis may have been born in Peru; she may have traveled to Colombia. De la Parra wondered, how did she live? Did she marry? Can her descendants be with us today? She continued to tell the story of Amarilis: we only know that she wrote in 1621, she read the classics and she fell in love across the miles with Lope de Vega, whose fame was at its height. She wrote a poem in which she poured out her romantic longings to him, addressing him as Belardo. Lope responded with two letters that he never mailed to her. They were later found in one of his books. The great Spanish literary critic Menédez Pelayo judged Amarilis to be one of the freshest and most charming colonial voices, but de la Parra insisted that when Amarilis' epistolary poem is compared to Lope de Vega's works, Amarilis' work is superior. De la Parra recited the poem to her audience, stopping here and there to explicate a line or expand on a theme. She concluded that there were many other "Amarilis," that is to say, women who wrote, who lived their lives behind the grilles of their windows, who wrote their own poetic letter dedicated to a "Belardo" but who eventually gave their letter to someone who did not deserve it nor inspire it. And how many, because they could not write prose, never wrote at all? "It is to these women that I owe, no doubt, the almost mystical love for the old criollo tradition that is fast disappearing" (504).

The example of a woman who wrote during the colonial period provides the opening for de la Parra to talk about the ancestor whose tales about colonial life allowed her to see the colony with her own eyes. Francisca de Tovar, who was affectionately called "Mama Panchita", lived between 1787 and 1870, and it was her history, handed down orally to de la Parra's grandmother that made the cycle of prosperity, persecutions, tragedies and declines of the criollos come alive for the author. I suspect this ancestor may have been another inspiration for *Mama Blanca's* protagonist. Mama Panchita played childhood games with her neighbor, Simón Bolívar. She married a Basque when she was fifteen, a rich merchant employed by the Compañía Guipuzcoana, which exported cocoa from Caracas and imported revolutionary ideas from France. Mama Panchita was beautiful, rich and frivolous, "a good eighteenth century daughter." She read nothing but her missal. She slept her siesta surrounded by slaves who kept the mosquitoes at bay. When her husband did not join the revolution, their property was confiscated. She donned her last pair of silk stockings, her latest cashmere shawl, and, surrounded by her children and her slaves, set off for a life in exile in San Juan, Puerto Rico. She returned to Caracas years later, a poor widow who continuously complained that the revolution had ruined her, and blamed her former playmate, whom she refused to call "The Liberator", or "Bolívar," but rather "that kid Simón." Whenever Bolívar was praised in the press or in person, she discreetly murmured, "I never saw anything special about him. He didn't even cut a fine figure" (50).

De la Parra regretted that as a child she did not pay enough attention to the stories her female relatives told her, and that so many of her forbearer's anecdotes went unrecorded. Another inspirational relative was her maiden aunt, Teresa Soublette, who like Amarilis, could have been the lover of some Lope de Vega or other. The wheelchair-bound Teresa led recitations of the rosary, crocheted, and read unceasingly. Young historians consulted her to get their facts straight. She taught her young black servant how to read and write French. These were the days of the Gran Colombia, and Soublette corresponded with her relatives in Bogotá. This lecture concludes with an anecdote and a Biblical analogy that demonstrated Soublette's graciousness and spirit of forgiveness. She had invited some Colombian students to dinner and went to great lengths to prepare a delicious meal for them. She waited three hours for them to arrive, finally sitting down to eat, sure that the wayward students had met with some accident, and thinking about their poor mothers who must be worried to death. The example of the students' disrespectful behaviour prompts de la Parra to end the second lecture with a reminder that it is fitting from time to time to dine at "the noble criollo table of full of atmosphere, tradition and landscape. Modest but bountiful, it awaits us in a shadowy corner like the table set by the father in the parable of the Prodigal Son" (508).

The Third Lecture

The Third Lecture contains the seeds of a book de la Parra planned to write about Bolívar. After preparing to give the three lectures, what Palacios calls a "dangerous fantasy" to write a novelized biography of Bolivar materialized (109). In a letter to Lecuna she likens it to a disease like TB which will attack her (110).

The oratory in the last lecture is leaner; there is more dramatic tension, and more attention to historic detail. She was fascinated by the women who influenced Bolivar's life and who in turn influenced the revolution.

She presented Manuelita Sáenz as an untraditional woman whose vision was fired by the admiration of and protection for her lover. Simón Bolívar captured her imagination, and in 1930 de la Parra began corresponding with Vicente Lecuna, the foremost Bolivar historian. She planned to write a biography of Simón Bolívar, but she wanted to tell it from the point of view of his lover Manuela Sáenz. Although she accumulated a wealth of material and considered Sáenz to be a key force in the life of the Liberator of Latin America, the biography was never written.[5]

By the late 18th century European ideological movements and the American Revolution and the French Revolutions gave rise to the independence movement in Latin America. There was widespread discontent with the Spanish economic and political regime. In 1810 Venezuela declared its independence from Spain, and in 1811 it adopted a republican constitution. Full independence was achieved under Bolívar's leadership. Venezuela lost nearly one third of its population during the wars of independence. The remainder of the 19th century and early part of the twentieth in Venezuela was characterized by unrest and strife. Further deterioration led to the repressive administration of Juan Vicente Gomez (1908-1935), during de la Parra's life.

Her narrative powers are at their most vivid as she invites her audience to conjure up a visual scene to evoke the era of independence, asking them to visualize that time along with her as she describes scenes as though they were watching a movie rather than listening to a lecture. She calls up the architecture of the colonial houses, and the mild climate as two slaves dressed in white carry a woman in a sedan chair through the streets of Caracas, clad in a black mantle and mantilla. She is a *mantuana*, a noble criollo woman so named because aristocratic women could venture into the street only if they wore a *manto,* or mantle. It is seven o'clock in the evening and the lady has dined, the rosary has been recited, and slaves are putting her children to bed with their songs and stories. She is about to attend a *tertulia,* (a gathering to discuss politics and philosophy), perhaps at the house of the Marques or the count, her third or fourth cousin. No matter; he is the richest man in the city. The slaves set the chair down. A capuchin monk emerges from the convent on his way to confess a house-bound sinner. As night falls, the night watchman shouts "Light the lanterns!" A black slave emerges with an oil-lamp. Now a young *mantuano* emerges, dressed in a silk vest, lace shirt, velvet breeches, and silver-bucked shoes, wearing a white wig. He too, is on his way to the Marques' reunion. His cloak conceals three books that would incur the wrath of the Inquisition. One of them is the *Declaration of the Rights of Man*, recently translated in Bogotá. This scene is being repeated in many cities whose

lands are ripe for independence, be they viceroyalties, captaincies or
provinces. Most of the noble young men have studied in universities in
Mexico City, Lima or Bogotá. Some have gone off to study in Europe.
Women are welcome to attend these gatherings where fresh ideas are
discussed, and where the seeds of revolution are being sown.

The expulsion of the Jesuits and the absence of their influence
contributed to the revolutionary spirit and paved the way to independence.
Their expulsion was "a sentimental catastrophe in that it ruptured colonial
life that had been centered in the church and in the convent. Their
departure left a huge void which could not be filled by the other orders.
The exiled Jesuits were in the majority Criollo sons, brothers or relatives
who now faced a life of poverty. In sum, "It was the Dark Age for the
Company of Jesus" (511). The triumvirate of God, Country and King, a
creed fostered by the Jesuits, had been dissolved. Having lost "the
directors of their consciences" and "sovereigns of their souls" women
lapsed into a comfortable syncretic Catholicism. The relaxation of
religious beliefs led to a creolization of religion, and Indian and African
beliefs and observances began to mix with Catholic ones. De la Parra cites
the example of a friend who observed the traditional meatless Friday, but
only when her cook could purchase the freshest fish. She believed in God
and the saints, but not in priests. After the expulsion of the Jesuits, the
XVIII century Criollos were unwilling to accept secular priests or other
religious orders other than their beloved Jesuits.

In crept the works of Montesquieu, Voltaire, Rousseau and the French
encyclopedists. Secretly disseminating books by these authors became a
sport; reading them was a delight. De la Parra describes how women took
part in hiding, reading, and circulating prohibited works. It became stylish
to learn French. Corneille's tragedies were popular. Once again de la Parra
insisted that there were many unknown and uncelebrated heroines, besides
the well-known Pola Salavarrieta, who also deserved to be remembered
for their roles in revolutionary times. Policarpa Salavarrieta (1795-1817),
also known as La Pola, was a seamstress who worked on behalf of
Columbian independence as a spy for the revolutionary forces. Shot to
death by a Spanish firing squad, she became a martyr and national heroine.
During the past three centuries women had worked anonymously in the
shadows, but the fight for independence changed that. As an example, she
cites "La Emigración," an event that took place in Venezuela in 1814, in
which 40,000 people, most of them women and children, marched out of
Caracas, led by Bolívar, rather than remain in a city governed by the old
regime. The men were still at war, and only the archbishop and the

cloistered nuns stayed behind in the city. In another biblical simile, de la Parra compares Bolívar to "a new Moses" leading his people to freedom.

At this juncture, de la Parra proposed that behind Bolívar were women who played an important role in his life. "From his black wet-nurse Matea, to Manuelita Sáenz, his last love, Bolívar can take no action without the image of a woman who inspires him, consoles him during his periods of great melancholy, and who lends him their eyes so that he can look within to discover his genius" (514). Bolívar soaked up the poetry of rural life on the hacienda in Matea's arms. Slaves who worked on these plantations were sometimes treated like extensions of the family. Matea took young Simón to the slaves' quarters where he heard folktales, ghost stories, and the legend of the tyrannical conqueror Lope de Aguirre. Later in his life, Bolívar would come to depend on Teresa del Toro, Fanny de Villars, Josefina Machado, Manuelita Sáenz, and other women who either provided the respite or the stimulus he needed at the time.

Bolívar fell in love with María Teresa del Toro in Spain, married her when he was nineteen, and returned to live on his plantation in San Mateo. Eight months later Teresa died of yellow fever, and the inconsolable Bolívar returned to Spain. In time, he inherited his uncle's vast fortune and traveled to Paris, where he fell in love with his cousin Fanny de Villars, who became his lover, friend, and counselor.[6] Villars was married to a French count and she presided over a salon frequented by Chateaubriand, Beauharnais, Madame Recamier, Madame de Stael, and Alexander von Humboldt, among other notables and intellectuals. It was here that Bolívar absorbed his romantic notions. Villars transformed the sorrowful young widower into an elegant youth who gambled fabulous sums and gave lavish gifts. He became a dandy and wore a hat which became known as the "Chapeau Bolívar," whose design was probably Fanny's invention. These distractions did not assuage his grief, however. He wrote to Fanny that although he could now fulfill his every whim, life without Teresa was a desert.

Fanny was determined to become "his new Teresa." She introduced him to Baron von Humboldt, who had just completed his five-year travels through tropical lands that in turn led to a scientific revolution in the natural sciences. Humboldt described his love of Latin America, which he described as a terrestrial paradise, his friendship with intellectual Criollos, and his belief that these lands needed to be emancipated to Bolívar. The young Bolívar listened in astonishment and began to envision America's potential with fresh eyes through von Humboldt's descriptions. Shortly after Napoleon's coronation, Bolívar visited Humboldt, who once again stressed the need for Latin America's independence, and bemoaned the lack of leadership needed to accomplish the task. The twenty-year old Bolívar decided that he would be that leader. He took his reluctant and tearful leave of Fanny, reunited with Humboldt in Paris, traveled to Italy to make a sacred vow to liberate the Americas from Spanish rule, and set off for Venezuela.

She confesses that "In order to talk about women's influence in the heroic life of Bolívar one would have to write at least one book" (523). During the rest of her talk de la Parra recreated Bolívar's story, his new-found mission to liberate the Americas, the love, pity and spirit that propelled him toward this objective, and how he was supported by the women in his life during this enterprise. Women who lived in the American capitals heaped praise on him. Like a god, he was drunk with pride. Popular with the ladies, he was known to change battle plans in order to keep an amorous tryst. In 1827 he triumphantly returned to Caracas to cheering crowds. His attachment to his black nursemaid was stronger than ever; he noticed Matea's white kerchief and ran through the crowd, singled her out and embraced her.

The lecture devolves into a rather rambling overview of Bolívar's biography, which allows de la Parra to usher in the fascinating story of Manuelita, the last and most "picturesque" of Bolivar's loves, whom Bolívar himself called "the Liberator's Liberator" and who saved his life on two occasions.

Manuelita was very different from the quiet Teresa del Toro, and "represents the violent protest against woman's traditional servitude whose only future is the sometimes-closed door to matrimony" (524). She was a woman of action, a product of post-war thinking following the Independence movement. De la Parra tells how Manuelita was born in Ecuador, Argentina or Peru, to a distinguished and wealthy family and while still a child she was married "to an Englishman whom she did not love and who bored her to tears" (524). De la Parra had gotten her information about Manuelita from the Peruvian writer Ricardo Palma, but some of these so-called facts later proved to be false, like the story about Manuelita's understanding and generous English husband, the Englishman Thorne (Lemaître 180).

From her balcony she glimpsed Bolívar entering victoriously into Quito. She fell in love with him. Divorcing her husband was impossible. She confessed to her husband that she had fallen in love with Bolívar. "The Englishman accepted her decision with resigned sadness" (524). Her contemporaries, however, did not support her. A daughter of war, she was a freethinker and an atheist. Accompanied by her two black female servants Natán and Jonatás, she dressed like a man, rode on horseback and fought valiantly. One contemporary's account recalls her dexterity with both sword and pistol. She acted as Bolívar's bodyguard, and when Peru and Columbia became hostile to Bolívar, she was exiled from both countries.

This was a sad time for Bolívar. The Gran Columbia had been dissolved, and his last years were bitter ones. Manuelita lived on Bolívar's plantation in Bogotá as though she was his wife. Women did not approve of her, but this mattered little to her. De la Parra recounted how Manuelita and her two maids violently disrupted a display of allegorical fireworks in the form of caricatures of Bolívar labeled "Despotism" and "Tyranny."

Following his death, Manuelita was considered Bolívar's widow, and the Colombian government tried to oust her from Bogotá. She was determined to stay and got into bed with two pistols. Her maid-accomplices were arrested, and she was eventually carried out of the house, still lying on her bed. She spent the last of her days in Paita, Colombia, supporting herself by making medicinal elixirs which her maid sold in the street. Shortly afterward, her husband, Mr. Thorne, died in Ecuador and bequeathed her his fortune. Manuelita, however, felt that accepting her legal husband's fortune meant being unfaithful to Bolívar's memory, and she renounced her inheritance, choosing to support herself. Simón Rodríquez, Bolivar's tutor, visited her, as did Giuseppe Garibaldi and Ricardo Palma. Customers came to her door asking, "Is this where the Libertadora lives?" And Manuelita, from her wheelchair would respond," Come in. What can the Libertadora do for you?" (527) Proud to the end, she kept her title of La Libertadora, a strong woman who crafted her own code of conduct and lived by it to the very end. De la Parra agreed that many would find Manuelita paradoxical, her behavior scandalous, and her moral code contrary to public opinion. She concluded her third lecture with yet another biblical analogy. She defended the heroine by challenging her audience: "Let him who, living in poverty, and is capable of renouncing an inheritance to make a cult of memory, cast the first stone at doña Manuelita" (528).

By the end of the third lecture, de la Parra's oratorical powers reach their height. A series of three lectures that began in a timid, self-effacing way, in which the speaker felt the need to defend herself by distancing herself from the feminist movement, ends in climactic fiery rhetoric as she dares her audience to cast a biblical first stone at an unconventional woman who flaunted society's rules so that she could be by the side of the romantic revolutionary she loved. Her defense of this armed, cross-dressing woman who fought by the side of her lover, who saved his life on at least two occasions, and who would rather be loyal to his memory than accept her husband's money in her infirm old age merits our sympathy, our understanding, and our esteem, she insisted. If her audience was not persuaded, at the least de la Parra brought doña Manuelita's uncompromising life to their attention, and offered her as the last example in a list of heroic women who helped to shape the Americas.

De la Parra's lectures provided an overview of women who had been overlooked or forgotten by history. She used her fame and her attractiveness to propose her theories and spread the word about the vital roles women played in American history. Her first attempt to show the need for reform in women's lives was implied in *Iphigenia* but had met with mixed results. Women readers had identified with María Eugenia's plight in the novel, but conservatives were outraged. Sensitive to the attacks, she played it safe in her second novel, *Mama Blanca's Memoirs*, which was based on Venezuela's past rather than its present. As a public intellectual lecturing outside her country, de la Parra felt she was on firmer ground spreading her ideas abroad. While her letters shed light on how she wrote her fiction and give us her points of view, her insights, and her thoughts on her craft, her lectures gave her the opportunity to articulate explicitly what she implied in her novel. By focusing on women's activities and contributions in the formation of Latin American history, she reminded her audience that despite the constrictions of gender roles in the patriarchal societies in which they lived, women of the Americas could and did find ways to overcome these obstacles and set examples for alternative female identities and roles. Her own life was a case in point.

Notes

[1] All translations are mine and are taken from *Tres conferencias: influencia de las mujeres en la formación del alma americana*, in Velia Bosch, *Teresa de la Parra, Obra: (narrativa, ensayos, cartas)*. Caracas: Biblioteca Ayacucho, 1991. pp. 471-528.

[2] Arturo Uslar Pietri, ed. *Tres conferencias inéditas*. Caracas: Ediciones Edime 1961.

[3] According to Lemaître, de la Parra had a quiet sense of self-worth. Her companion, Lydia Cabrera said that de la Parra considered her aristocracy a spiritual value (xi).

[4] *Our Lives are the Rivers*, by Jaime Manrique, (Rayo, Harper Collins: NY 2006), is a historical novel that interweaves the story of Bolívar and Manuela Sáenz. The alternating chapters in the novel are told through Manuela's voice and the voices of her two black slaves, whom she affectionately refers to as her "two girls," Natán and Jonotás. *For Glory and Bolívar: The Remarkable Life of Manuela Sáenz*, Pamela S. Murray, Austin: U Texas Press, 2008 provides a comprehensive

biography of Sáenz. On July 5, 2010, Venezuela honored Sáenz with a full state burial when her "symbolic remains (soil from the mass grave where she was buried) were laid to rest alongside Bolivar's in the National Pantheon.

[5] The sad story of Bolívar's poignant journey between Bogotá and Santa Marta would later be chronicled by Gabriel Garcia Márquez in *The General in His Labyrinth*, trans. Edith Grossman, New York: Knopf, (1990).

[6] Fanny de Villars was only the first of many amorous liaisons. Ramón Urdaneta's *Los amores de Simón Bolívar y sus hijos secretos* (2003), chronicles the "Liberator's many love lives." According to Urdaneta, there were at least eighteen women who had intimate relations with Bolívar, and Urdaneta dedicates a chapter to each woman. There is an additional chapter dedicated to other (supposedly undocumented) lovers, and another chapter titled "The Children of Simon Bolívar." If Urdaneta's data is correct, Bolívar sired over a dozen offspring in as many unions.

CHAPTER SEVEN

THE FIRST LECTURE:
THE CONQUEST

I feel as though I'm dreaming, finally finding myself in Bogota in front of my old, dear friends, without feeling the fear I felt from afar; on the contrary, I am confident and happy like it's the happiest of moments of my life.

This visit to Colombia had beckoned to my heart for a long time. I answered those calls, but from afar, with gestures and smiles, because like shy and timid lovers, I was afraid to get too close. This fall the call took on a voice so urgent and promising I set aside all fears and placed myself under the influence of the star that protects the enterprising, and prepared for my visit not wanting to arrive, as you can see, empty-handed.

The beckoning call I mentioned arrived in the form of a letter. It was early November. I had just returned to Paris after my first long trip to Italy. I was planning to spend a quiet winter in my corner in Neuilly—perhaps a winter of reading and work, one never knows in Paris—when one morning I awoke to a messenger bearing a letter from Colombia. It was from a group of friends who live in Bogota. They extended the following invitation: To travel to Colombia to present a series of lectures about myself, the story of my literary career and my books.[1] It's not easy for me to express how perplexed I was about this thought-provoking and risky invitation. I've never spoken in public before and for several days I floundered in a sea of doubt and temptation. I kept turning the idea over in my mind and pondered the dilemma, "How was I going to deliver a lecture? What role would I play before my public, if they loved me from a distance was it because they hadn't seen me up close? And what about the literary career, so sporadic and fragile?" But on the other hand, the idea of crossing the ocean during long, peaceful days, slowly cruising down the Magdalena with the jungle on either side of its banks, and the Andes, to arrive at many familiar and dreamed-of cities filled my soul with exquisite excitement. The tropics called to me through my window as the golden leaves swept through the foggy Paris October.

From a distance I recognized the Colombia of the first romantic visions of my childhood: the Cauca Valley, the big plantation house, the shimmering bathing pond with roses, Mayo the dog, Feliciana, the black servant, and in the distance, at the top of the path, the window framed with flowers where María, dressed in white, is bidding Efraín farewell.[2]

Faced with the bright dream of the journey and how to achieve it, its consequences slipped away... One of the more serious aspects was deciding on a subject for the lectures. Accepting the invitation was almost an obligation. When a book finds such good friends in the reader's soul, like in all matters of intimacy, it flows from the ears to the lips with the secret thirst of trust. I know, I've seen it and now I can say, like a bragging child who's done nothing to deserve love, I know how much you like my books in Colombia. I know you love them with the kind of disinterested, domestic affection you love dogs, flowers, caged birds and, generally speaking, all things familiar and useless.

So I understand it was entirely natural, that today, on the day of my arrival to this paternal home, a trusting smile would form on my lips. Unfortunately, the lack of distance and the excess of witnesses haven't let me put together a lovely true story for the heart's needs. Within the next thirty, thirty five or forty years I'll return to these Colombian cities.[3] Then, as in Ronsard's sonnet, trembling with old age between the distaff and spindle in the candlelight, I'll tell you the marvelous story of my childhood. The incident in *Iphigenia* concerning the exquisite Colombian poet, as I see it, requires a name, which will then be revealed. [4] Taking advantage of that story and other extraordinary ones without the threat of anyone disapproving of me, my audience's eyes will reflect not the image of who I am, but the divine image of who I wanted to be.

This promise takes care of the first topic. Concerning the second topic, that of a literary vocation, I can only tell you that however much I sought it and studied it, as usual, I couldn't find it. This literary vocation would be lost to me and leave me helpless, so at times some detractor—there are always tactless rumor-mongers who tell us nice things—when one detractor spread the rumor that I didn't write my books, I was happily the first to believe him. Having lost my vocation, I was freed from a huge responsibility, having also lost the books. Are they in effect works that came about without the vocation that backs them up and protects us from ourselves? Up to a point, it is true that the books aren't mine. Besides the name on the cover that lingers like a distraction, I don't recognize myself in my books. The first one was written by a contemporary girl whose whereabouts are unknown, the second by a deceased grandmother who in her lifetime was charming and hospitable like so many others sheltered beneath the tiled roofs in these good American cities. These stories or novels are the result of these two missing authors. Situated at the extreme opposites of life, they visited me for a while, one shared her anxieties, the other the sadness of having lived, and, after telling their stories, they discreetly left to edit their books.

As for the third topic, books, or to be more precise, the theme of *Iphigenia*, the subject of criticism of the modern girl, it seemed interesting to treat it transcendentally because it lent itself to discussion about the urgent need for change. That I won't deny.

There are many moralists with loving equanimity at best, or with violent anathema at worst, who attacked María Eugenia Alonso's diary, labeling it Voltairean, perfidious and dangerous in the hands of contemporary young ladies.

I don't think that diary would damage today's young girls for the simple reason that it simply reflects them. Almost all of them, especially those who are born and raised strictly, carry within them a María Eugenia Alonso in full rebellion, more-or-less hidden, depending on how oppressed they are, who speaks out loudly and daily what the young lady put in writing.

Maria Eugenia's diary is not about revolutionary propaganda, as some reactionary moralists see it; on the contrary, it's the exposition of a typical case of contemporary illness—that of Hispanic American bovarism, that of sharp inconformity to the sudden change in temperature and the lack of air in the environment.[5] Whether the moralists like it or not, the epidemic can't be hidden, as when in seaports, at the expense of truth and public well-being a clean bill of health is sought at all costs. Epidemics are cured with air, with light, and with modern hygiene that counteracts the cause of the illness.

The crisis today's women face can't be cured by preaching submission, submission and submission, as was once done when a domesticated life could be contained behind the doors of a house. In today's life, with the owner driving her own car, with the telephone next to her bed, the press, travels, closed doors are not respected. Like the radio, which makes for a good metaphor, it penetrates the walls and whether you want it to or not, it mixes with the life of the household. For a woman to be strong, healthy and free from hypocrisy she can't be subdued in modern life; to the contrary, she needs to be free for herself, conscious of the dangers and responsibilities, useful to society even if she isn't a mother, and financially independent through her work and collaborating alongside man—neither her master, enemy, nor a candidate for exploitation, but her companion and her friend. Work doesn't exclude mysticism or exemption from sacred duties; to the contrary, it's a discipline that purifies and strengthens the spirit. But mysticism, submission and passivity imposed through force, through customary inertia, results in silent reaction, awakens the chain reaction of hate which was good in other times and sours the souls in the face of peace, taking out their reprisals and revenge when they can, and ending up under white headstones. The real enemies of female virtue are not the dangers of healthy activity, books, the university, laboratories, offices, or hospitals; it's frivolity, the empty, flitting, mundane world of the housebound girl or the unhappily married woman. Educated in an old fashioned way and already infected by cynicism, they should distract themselves through work and study that would be a thousand times more noble and healthy. When I say work, I don't mean humiliating and badly paid jobs where poor helpless girls are cruelly exploited. I'm talking about jobs that require training, in careers, work or specializations appropriate to women with fair pay, according to their abilities and the tasks performed. I would not want, as a consequence of my tone and argument, to be considered a defender of women's suffrage. I am neither a defender nor a detractor of women's suffrage for the simple reason I don't know enough about it. Knowing that it cries out so that women can have the same duties and political responsibilities as men frightens and stuns me, so, I've never understood to what end this voice proposes. And it's because in general I believe contrary to the suffragists, that women should be very grateful to men who've taken on the oppression of political office. It seems to me that, along with coal mining, it is one of the hardest and dirtiest jobs there is. Why wish to claim it?

My feminism is moderate. To try to prove, ladies and gentlemen, this delicate point, that of new rights that modern women should have, not through destructive and sudden revolution, but through noble and conquering evolution and education, and taking advantage of the forces of the past to talk about this subject, I began to prepare in three lectures a kind of historical overview of feminine oppression in our countries, or the happy and hidden influence of women during the conquest, the colony and Independence. Since I believe there really exists a common spirit in all our Catholic and Spanish countries, and since I believe that promoting it through their union is an embracing patriotism, I included all our countries in this historical overview and I called it "The Influence of Women in the Formation of the American Soul."

But having finished my historical overview, due to unforeseen circumstances, I had to travel to New York and Havana before taking my trip to Colombia. I hoped to gather in those two cities new and interesting insights about modern women, the object of my final lectures and in effect,

I got them, but at the same time my writing vocation abandoned me. You can't work in New York on account of the excessive movement and noise, even less in Havana, due to the *dolce far niente*.[6] What were left to me were my oppressed women. Frankly speaking I'll tell you that deep down in my soul I prefer them. They possess the grace of the past and the infinite poetry of voluntary and sincere sacrifice.

As a brief summary of my impression as a traveler I will say only that Havana is one of those places where one can observe the happy evolution of Latin American women towards a useful and appropriate end without losing the characteristics of femininity and with good results. Cuba has a strong traditional and folkloric criollo character and miraculously defends it against spiritual invasions. Cuba's watered-down Americanism has not yet reached the soul of any of its social classes. People from Havana are genuinely Creole, despite the presence of the English language, tourism, dollars and constant travel. A great many Cuban women work and study without losing their femininity or respect for established principles and traditions. I lived in the home of a family friend whose garden bordered the university's garden. I saw about the same number of girls as boys pass through the university's doors. I became acquainted with a respectable middle class family. There were five sisters ranging in age from twenty to thirty. Three had graduated and worked successfully in clinics and hospitals. Two of them were students. The five of them were well-behaved, attractive, feminine, and the three doctors helped out their elderly parents and the two sisters who were students with their tasks. Their work did not deter them from marriage: two of them had boyfriends they received in their home in the evenings according to criollo custom. The difference between this education and traditional education that persists to this day in Havana in the ruling classes is, in my way of thinking, notably different. The "well brought up" young lady from Havana, the wealthy heiress, who plays bridge and tennis, who is dressed by Patou,[7] who owns a car she herself drives, sometimes fresh out of the convent where she was raised under strict conditions is generally speaking elegant, easy to get along with and charming, but her culture, her character and above all her morality is lacking in preparation for the modern world and is also inferior to those of the young lady who is disciplined by her work.

Gabriela Mistral,[8] who perhaps will visit you in July or August revealed this wish in a letter in which she calls Colombia "the healthiest place in the tropics." Gabriela undoubtedly will talk about this burning issue much more skillfully and a thousand times better than I can, since she is militant in all her ideas. It was precisely in drawing a parallel between her life and Delmira Augustini's,[9] the two best American poets of our century, that I can show the redemption and dignity of independently wealthy women and work. Just briefly, let me offer you this example.

Delmira Augustini, young, pretty, agreeable, born into a strict bourgeois family, represents the case of María Eugenia Alonso brought to a tragic end. In obeying the custom that every woman should marry, she married while still young in a so-called good match. The drama of misunderstanding began within a few days of the marriage. On one side is a vulgar and despotic master, on the other, the silent disdain of one who feels herself to be superior but sees herself as a slave. Mutual hatred, mixed with passion, divorce, and finally one day, during the divorce trial, the husband shoots her and then kills himself, the only way he knows to subdue her and satisfy his thirst for domination.

Gabriela Mistral, poor, born into honorable and modest circumstances without wordly conventionalism worked since she was a young girl. With each passing day, she brings her ideals and adapts and humanizes them to the world's needs, suffering and fighting in her work as an apostle, Socialist, Catholic and the defender of liberty and the race's noble spirit. She will speak to you with her trustworthy voice of the now necessary and just feminism. I myself, in the meantime, if you will permit me, and it's time for it, will look to my selfless women or "The Influence of Women in the Formation of the American Soul." I confess that editing this title cost me much reflection, numerous conversations with myself and generally speaking, all the cruel anxieties that usually torment us in the dilemma of gaining clarity of expression and therefore losing out to elegance. I did not know if it would be correct, and above all, if it would sound right in Colombia to say "American Soul" instead of "Latin American Soul" Iberoamerican, hispanoamerican, indoamerican, or indohispanicamerican. None of these combinations seemed good to me either in form or substance. They are not light, they lack wings, they lack grace. They sound, I don't know why, like foreign criollo snobbery that has been naturalized abroad , the origin of some good things, but also of many bad things and sins against good taste. On the other hand, having so many different baptismal names seemed sad to me. Taking the different expressions into account, I saw that each one contained, when contrasted with the others, a formula of disintegration. I thought randomly about the power of words to determine facts, I thought about the sweet intimacy of things with their names, I thought (finally) that our beautiful nameless homeland, so extensive, so diverse and so miraculously similar without the mystery of why it's so alike, without enfolding arms or the paternal table of having only one name, now being relegated to the status of an abandoned girl without a last name and in danger of losing her inheritance.

I resolved to leave out the compound name and just say "American Soul" with a loving smile, assured that everyone would understand me.

I believe that while politicians, the military, journalists and historians spend their lives putting antagonistic labels on things, the young, the common people and above all women, who are many and very disorganized, are in charge of shuffling labels and establishing a cordial confusion. I refer especially to an annoying antagonism, the work of the press and not of the living language that has come to contest Indoamericanism or Hispanoamericanism. I don't want to address here the evils that enclose these two opposing formulas like two torches of discord within the same household: on one side is the inhuman and insensitive disdain of the white man who still thinks of himself as lord and master; on the other hand is the romantic Indianism, the blind hatred the mestizo feels towards the intrusive race, the hatred that daily incites a popularized and unfair version of the Spanish conquest through blood and fire; as if only destruction were the case, as if the conquest of America was an isolated incident in the history of the world and not the eternal and hateful law of all wars and all invasions! This issue has been much discussed which brings up the excellent and overly praised Father Las Casas.[10]

I think Father Las Casas was an apostle and a saint. He knew how to bravely condemn the cruel spirit that animates war and the iniquitous abuse of the strong against the weak. But like many pacifist and socialist leaders looking beyond their love of pity and justice he loved even more his own eloquence, which belonged to the school of Savonarola.[11] A brilliant polemicist, he unfortunately lived during a time where there were no political gatherings and no press. His energetic campaigns were enriched with statistics of mortality passed on as historic documents that served, in the hands of foreigners—that is to say, in the hands of Protestants and the northern races, twice the enemies of the Spanish Empire—to systematically discredit us. And often we ourselves use them to fuel racial hatreds.

The contemporaries of Las Casas preached mercy and peace in silence. These were the women of the conquest. Obscure Sabines,[12] anonymous workers of concord, the true founders of cities through their founding of households, their work proved more effective across the generations through their silent enterprise of synthesis and love.

As we all know, one woman, Isabela the Catholic Queen [1451-1504] gave birth to the epic of the Conquest. Reading Columbus's mind she steered the splendid tumult of the Renaissance from Spain to the jungles of America. From afar, through time and distance, she is the European godmother of our America. Her symbolic figure, softened afterwards by the indolence of colonial life, already contains all the characteristics of the classic Creole nation of our grandmothers of yesteryear. In their memory I want to evoke an example of the queen as described by Jose Maria Heredia[13] in the prologue of his translation of the *Conquest of New Spain*. I do it out of faith and devotion to the race like one invokes a patron saint in the prayers one knows by heart and recites daily.

Heredia says that Queen Isabela died on November 26, 1504, in her castle in Medina del Campo. A brave and chaste woman, she united feminine graces with manly virtues. Her spirit was superior to that of her age. She was intensely fond of knowledge and books. The intrepid and wise queen conquered Granada and understood Columbus. She dictated her will on her deathbed with the serenity of an ancient philosopher. That famous will, overflowing with love, intelligence, and magnanimity, was the seal to her noble life. Isabela was good. In the throes of agony she still thought about the people of Castile and her children in the Indies with maternal concern. All of Spain wept for this matchless woman. She had been the best and the greatest of all the sovereigns. Nature herself was moved by her death. The earth trembled. The sky covered her simple funeral with mournful pageantry. She wanted to be put to rest in the land she had conquered. Under the storm, lightning, thunder and rain, a funeral hearse took her to Granada. Isabela's reign was the dawn of that glorious Spain that sank into the sea with the Invincible Armada.

Compared with Isabela the Catholic, on this side of the ocean we see the founding women pass by, discreetly veiled by the tales of the Chronicles of the Indies. Their humble lives, full of suffering and love, are not told. One barely notices them. Almost all of them are Indians who have been baptized and given Spanish names. Many are princesses. The most famous ones are Doña Marina;[14] Doña Catalina; Doña Luisa; Doña Isabela the Guaiquerí,[15] the mother of Fajardo, the conqueror of Caracas; the other Doña Isabela, Inca Garcilaso's;[16] sad mother and the other poor slaves or heiresses to chiefdoms they shared with their white husbands and with them governed their lands, teaching them how to use cotton trousers and make henequen sandals and straw hats.

The white ruler, completely adapted to the Indian environment, is not, ladies and gentlemen, a romantic legend; it's a typical case of conversion through the miracle of feminine love. Even Father Las Casas himself, in praising the beauty of certain Indians, counts up to sixty of them married to Castilians in the city of Vera Paz alone, and the story of the Spaniard named Gonzalo Guerrero is extremely eloquent and moving. After having been shipwrecked on Vicuesa's expedition, Guerrero lived among the Indians for eight years.[17] His companion, Aguilar, who had managed to escape one day, returned to the tribe with the money necessary to pay Guerrero's ransom and warned him that he would lose his soul by living with the idolatrous Indians. Guerrero sent him away saying (and these are the words of the chronicler}: "Brother, I am married, I have three children and I am a chief here when there is a war. Go with God. My face is tattooed and my ears are pierced. You see how lovely my three children are. For the love of your life give me those green beads you brought for them."

So that in the town of caneyes and bohios, in front of coconut trees and the ocean, mixing cacao and vanilla or cooking casabe,[18] the Indian women, tropical Nausicaas,[19] prepare—along with the meal for the recently arrived—the coming of the colonial epoch, our Creole Middle Age. That Middle Age will have, almost unconsciously, the cult of Nature for its religion. She, Nature herself, will catechize the new barbarians while these catechize the Indians. Their Gothic cathedrals will be the boughs that in founding the haciendas will line up and rise in transparent vaults, harmonious and tall. Within them will come the fertile blessings of cacao, coffee, bananas, cotton, tobacco, and sugar cane. Since there are blessings for all, all will be brothers in the holy abundance. All of them will pray daily with the old don Juan de Castellanos[20] their Colombian creed of the grateful conqueror (the same lines I repeated as I entered Colombia through the Valley of Cauca and through the fields of Quindio):

> Land of gold, land of plenty
> Land to build a lasting home
> Land with abundant food
> Land of great towns, level land
> Land of bright and serene blessings
> Land that has brought an end to our grief.

As often happens on travels and during all undertakings that tug at the heart, this, when you least expect it, makes us change our course. The Spanish and Portuguese conquistadors who left the Peninsula were military men or merchants like the Venetians, their rivals, and wound up, without knowing it, being the founding poets of a tropical Arcadia.[21] They came looking for gold and found ideals. After the brutal clash with the generous land they began to discover the gold within themselves. How many obscure adventurers, upon crossing the ocean, through a miracle of their surroundings were converted to Patriarchs and splendid Lords! Ah, not in vain did they sail through tropical seas under fragrant skies full of stars that multiplied and grew nearer to the ship. The traveler looked to the promises of fortune and love that America, across the ocean, promised. As members of the expedition the conquistadores, such rough warriors, quickly learned how to become gentle and docile lovers.

The women who take part in the formation of our American society, stamping on it its soft and deep seal, are numberless, they are everything. I think they can be divided into three big groups: The women of the conquest; the women painfully crucified by the conquest through the clash of the mixing of the races. Those of the colony: the mystics and the dreamers. Those of the independence, who inspired and made things happen. In Mexico, in Bogota, in Lima, in Quito, in Caracas, in Buenos Aires, in Havana, they share a similar process. It seems as though they are living in the same city, they are neighbors from the same neighborhood, they are sisters. If Colombia, Venezuela, Argentina, Chile, and Ecuador are the homes of the martyred heroines and lovers, and of the great women of the Independence movement, it is to Mexico and Peru where I've come searching for two humble indigenous flowers as the prototypes of the original painful primitives, along with Malinche, the Mexican Doña Marina who was revered and happy until the end of her days, the melancholy Ñusta[22] Isabela, the niece of the Peruvian monarch Tupac Yupanqui and the mother of the first American writer, the tender Garcilaso de la Vega. The life of the latter will be spent sweetly between love and tears. For the fruit of her tame abnegation she will reap only thanklessness and dislike. It doesn't matter; she will take refuge in silence and resignation. Her pain at being abandoned will bear fruit through her son who, through his longing and in his exile, will produce, many years later, one of the most beautiful books of classic Spanish literature: *The Royal Commentaries.*

The political genius of Hernan Cortes[23] is always spoken of with admiration—his extraordinary gift to negotiate with and come to agreements with the Indians. I believe, ladies and gentlemen, that Cortes's mysterious shrewdness was exclusively called Doña Marina. In the various chronicles of the Conquest of New Spain, that it to say, the two or three that I'm familiar with, to Doña Marina plays an important role as mediator and interpreter, giving accurate advice or discovering plots, like the one in Cholula, where Cortes's death and that of his whole expedition was plotted. Through the little that is said we can guess a lot from what is not said. It is absolutely certain that Doña Marina's influence on the Conquest of Mexico was more important, her mediation and her advice more subtle and frequent, than the historians tell us, even in Bernal Diaz del Castillo,[24] who treats her with such affection. They are untold because they drown in the din of military action. They are little tales not suitable to the official pageantry of history, whose field of action prefers scenes of destruction and death. Harmony, almost always woman's work, is anonymous; it lacks tragic elements, it does not make a good source for epics, and happiness, which is not so exciting, is not expressed in books, but rather through children, in the fraternal fusion of the races and in the humble goodness of the custom that smoothes over life's roughness until it makes it smiling and grateful.

Hernan Cortes was a Don Juan. Before undertaking the conquest of Mexico he had made numerous and famous love conquests. Born in Medellin, Extremadura, he was sent by his father to study at Salamanca. Instead of yielding to the study of rhetoric, Greek, philosophy and Latin, which in those days were taught by the humanists Nebrija, Peter Martyr and Lucio Marineo, Cortes, as an adolescent and student preferred composing verses and ballads, which he went about singing under the balconies and windows of Salamanca, repeating Latin themes. One night, the garden wall he was climbing to enter a balcony broke, and an injured Cortes had to stay in bed for several days with the usual scandal in the city and the desperation of his father, the modest squire Don Martin Cortes. Convinced that his son would always prefer the forest flowers of love in the randomness of picaresque life to the roses of wisdom, after giving him his blessing and a purse containing more reales than Castilian gold pieces, don Martin had his son embark on an expedition that was departing from Sanlucar of Barrameda bound for the West Indies.

Hernan Cortes was nineteen years old. First in Santo Domingo, later in Cuba, the growing colonies, Cortes's life is woven through with amorous adventures. Holder of lands and encomiendas[25] Velasquez awarded him for his services, pleasant, good-looking, expressive and attractive in his speech, "very frank," as the chronicler says, Cortes soon accumulated— along with the love of young women, widows and married women—more than one death blow that he hid under the shadow of his black beard. Established in Cuba in the city of Baracoa, "due to the heat of his heart and the heat of the climate" as the Chronicler says, Cortes was locked up in a church and was imprisoned many months for having given his word in matrimony but not keeping it, to Catalina Juarez, a poor humble woman from Granada who lacked a good reputation. Having obtained his freedom after many adventures, married to his poor woman from Granada, he was happily assured that he would be more content with her than if she were the daughter of a duchess.

Cortes was generous, gallant, and in love when he met Doña Marina. When the Conquest of Mexico was underway, some chiefs from the town of Tabasco took her as a gift to Cortes, "along with four lizards, some blankets, five ducks, two gold sandals and a few other items of little

value" says Bernal Díaz del Castillo. Completing his list of gifts, he adds:
"After they converted her, they gave the name Doña Marina to that Indian
woman they gave us as a gift. She was truly a great chieftess and the
daughter of great chiefs and a lady over vassals. She was attractive in her
person, which was pleasant, meddlesome and brazen. Doña Marina was an
excellent woman, a good translator, [26] and made for a good start to our
conquest, which is why Cortes always brought her with him."

Sold as a slave by her mother and her stepfather who gave her away
one night to another Indian tribe in order to usurp her title and her
inheritance, Doña Marina had passed through several hands and several
cities. Thus during her wandering life she learned, along with the gift of
adapting, the customs, aspirations, rivalries and languages of several towns
that Cortes would conquer. To her natural intelligence, she added the
broadness of vision from having travelled and the refined tact of having
suffered. She spoke Mayan and the Aztec language and very quickly
learned how to express herself in Spanish with as much fluency and clarity
as if she had been born in Seville.

It's not hard to imagine the dazzling impression that Cortes made on
Dona Marina's imagination. A powerful white god, son of the sun and the
moon (according to common belief among the Indians), an ambassador
from the unknown, captain of gods, he held thunder and lightning in his
weapons, he ran rapidly mounted on animals that seemed to have wings,
his stature and his beard proclaimed him to be invincible, and according to
ancient prophesies, he had come to destroy the empire and build upon its
ruins a new era. If, for the Indians Cortes was the Aztec anti-Christ, his
weapons, horses and soldiers were the monsters of an apocalypse of
desolation and death; for Indians like Doña Marina he was undoubtedly
the Messiah.

Doña Marina owed little or nothing to her own kind. Her mother had
sold her to strip her of her title. Through her tears during her bitter travels
from town to town she learned the condition of the humble women of her
race. Relegated to the lowliest of tasks, mistreated, sold by men from one
to another as sacrificial victims when they were children as slaves, for
marriage as adults, these women would without a doubt improve their lot
under those new lords who worshipped a female idol who held a baby in
her arms. On allying herself so fervently to Cortes and the whites' cause
against her own kind, Doña Marina, obeying revolutionary imperatives, on
the wings of her love began the future reconciliation of the two races, and
the first feminist campaign in America, albeit in rudimentary form.

She was "meddlesome and brazen" says Bernal Díaz del Castillo upon
introducing her. How much flavor these two adjectives contain in their

antiquated simplicity and how much we can read into them! "Meddlesome and brazen"—that is to say, helpful, alert, sharp in her words, discreet with a little coquettishness and inborn generosity. Aside from helping to advance Bernal Díaz's very vivid chronicle, we see her actions and get to know her until we've established an intimate friendship with her. Being the good woman that she is, she's an enthusiastic friend of novelty like all restless and creative spirits. She is credible for her idealism. Everything dazzles her. She is a sympathetic type. She's the classic full-blooded woman who is welcomed everywhere because she knows how to fit in and to patch up disagreements with the gladness of her spirit. The scribes or painters who were sent by Moctezuma to give him a detailed account of what the invaders were like, in a sky crossed by sparks which represent the shots of crossbows, winged spirits which represent horses or other mysterious forces, the scribes hastened to draw on this detailed letter Dona Marina's portrait like one of the major mysterious forces. There is no diplomacy she does not pass on or peace proposals where she doesn't preside alongside Cortes. She sweetens the bitterness as she translates their parliamentary discussions. This faith in her intervention, like a secret Providence, guides us through the countless crises that Bernal Diaz narrates. There is a critical point, after the taking of Mexico during which Cortes seems to have forgotten all the tact and political spirit he had observed until then. He goes too far with unnecessary harshness. He has the arrogance of the conqueror. He offends the sensitivity of all the people upon profaning the sacred person of Moctezuma. One can only guess at the disaster waiting to happen; discontent mounts; one can foresee "la noche triste" with its terrible sacrifices on the Spaniard's side to the god Huichilobos.[27] I feel like pausing in this lecture and calling upon the spirit of mercy and harmony: Where are you, Doña Marina?

Cortes's passions were violent and brief. His love for Doña Marina quickly turned to mild appreciation. Sometime after the conquest he married her to the Spanish hidalgo Don Juan de Jaramillo. "Doña Marina, who had a good reputation and already ruled absolutely over all the Indians of New Spain," says the chronicler, "accepted this marriage with resignation." What was left to her from that long war, in which she had been its mediator and counselor, was the memory of a great love, the restoration of her power before the Indians and her son Don Martin Cortes, a Spanish hidalgo and a Knight of Santiago.

Let's listen to how, with a biblical flavor, Bernal Díaz describes the scene in which Doña Marina and her mother, the Indian who had sold her when she was a child, accidentally come face-to-face.

"Cortes was at the Villa of Guazagualco," Bernal Díaz says. "He sent for all the chiefs of that province to discuss Holy Doctrine and its practices. Then Doña Marina's mother came and her maternal brother Lazaro, for thus he was called after having converted to Christianity, and with them came other chiefs. When the old woman saw Doña Marina she realized immediately that she was her daughter since she resembled her. The mother and the brother were afraid she would have them killed, and were crying. When Doña Marina saw them weeping she consoled them and told them not to be afraid, that when they sold her to the Xicalango they did not know what they were doing and that she would forgive them and she gave them many articles of clothing and gold jewelry, and told her mother that God had granted her a great mercy by keeping her from worshipping idols and now being married to a Knight such as her husband; that having a child by her lord Cortes, even if they made her chieftess of however many provinces there were in New Spain, she would not do it, that she would rather serve her husband Cortes than anything in the world and I certify that I saw this and swear by it, amen."

I don't know what you make of this passage. As for me, I find it charming. You see her like a character like in an old-time movie: there are quick movements and a comic ingeniousness at the dramatic moment. You see Doña Marina, a new Joseph sold by his brothers, a symbol of mercy, greeting her family who bring up her tragic past. As soon as she sees them she forgives them. With a generous display she fetches garments and jewels. They are objects that have come from marvelous, far-away countries. She tells them about her fantastic adventures. She introduces her new family. They all belong to the conquering foreigners. Since she is happy, she pardons their past wickedness and does so with a display of generosity.

During the course of his lively, evocative narrative, Bernal Díaz excuses himself at each step for his lack of style, for his careless writing. He assures us that he feels obligated to "draw from his memory those deeds that are not old tales, nor histories of the Romans, but things that happened yesterday as they say, because the learned and well-known writers, Gómara[28] among them, altered the truth when they wrote the chronicles concerning the Conquest of New Spain, that famous war in which he fought over one hundred battles. It pains him to see the memories of his youth being ill-treated and he tells them as best he can to restore them. Since he isn't a man of letters but rather a rough soldier, once his true history is written, he finds it so unpolished that he will die before he dares to have it published. It's so full of trivial details! In effect those are the ones that remain alive, whimsical and charming in memory, and in their humility is all the poetry of memory: the colors of the horses of the expedition, their nicknames, their habits or their qualities, the unexpected birth of a colt born aboard the ship, the foal of a chestnut mare, the amount of cassava and bacon brought by a soldier, a native of Havana named Juan Cerdeno, famous for his wealth. Juan Solis, he says, we called "Behind the Door" for his affinity for eavesdropping. Tarifa was "He of the White Hands" because he was useless in war and in performing tasks. Pedro Iricio was "Pasitilla" because he was the opposite of what we thought. Such numerous and evocative details flow in the flood of facts. Doña Marina's actions move along that bright turmoil. She will be the flower of a narrative that is not strictly history but something even loftier and more beautiful: a prose romance.

More than one person must think that in talking this way I'm falling down on the job, and so as not to talk nonsense, it would be better to stick to my job as a novelist. Well, no. I am sure that I don't talk nonsense and that it is almost a duty to proclaim the moral superiority of this narrative genre. Next to them, historical truth, the other, official one is a banquet for men alone. Sitting around a table, they formally say intelligent things and discourse eloquently on things the heart cannot attend to because they come from mandatory meetings. They are rumors of false feasts. Having excluded women they have severed one of the connecting threads of life. On the other hand, in the Roman histories and the gospels, living and moving histories par excellence, women are better represented like in Bernal Díaz, and not only women, but even the friendly and brotherly animals. Two thousand years have passed since the breaths of the mule and the ox in Bethlehem continue to warm our hearts. The drama of the passion was written by the Evangelists who were rough chroniclers in the manner of Bernal Diaz. No great writer of this epoch, not even the exquisite Plutarch, could have depicted it with such lasting force. In the story of the passion a rooster makes his entrance in a very important scene and women pass in the crowd following the adventures just like Doña Marina. No one stands in their way; on the contrary, they all go forward. It is they who are the heroines of the day. It's a street adventure to which all are drawn. Described and represented without interruption for twenty centuries the people represent it and continue to describe it even during Holy Week, keeping the same loving tradition of love and reality that small details lend it. Let us listen, for example, to the *saeta*[29] of *The Seven Falls* gathered by the Andalusian folk. Although this may seem like a digression, I can't help but recall it in honor of these stories whose importance I must insist on. Just like in life, tragedy does not disregard the anonymous or the unexpected.

Jesus is climbing a steep slope with the cross on his shoulders. As the scene is decorated with everyday objects the hill is not in Jerusalem; no, it's any street or alley in Seville. It's called the Street of Bitterness. Dressed as a Nazarene, bloody and disheveled, here comes Jesus, walking along, slowly making his way through the crowd.

> On the Street of Bitterness
> Christ climbs barefooted
> In his purple tunic
> His brow crowned with thorns
> And the cross on his shoulders.
> The sun blinds him
> Shining off the horse's armor
> On the helmets and spikes.
> Christ sees Judas
> Who sold him
> After kissing him
> Lovingly on the cheeks
> And recalling this first betrayal
> He falls for the first time.

The blood that flows down his forehead and into his eyes keeps him from seeing clearly. The objects that impede his steps and the painful memories that quickly run through his mind cause him to trip and he falls again and again until he's fallen six times. When he thinks of Peter's betrayal, his tears mix with blood. At a certain point they obscure his vision so that he takes the most serious fall of all. It's the fall in honor of St. Peter. When finally he turns a corner and suddenly meets the Virgin Mary, the impression is so intense you can't describe it in words. A great silence ensues. The only witnesses worthy of appreciating it are not men, but the elegance of the breeze and the flight of the birds as they fly across the sky.

> Distraught and sobbing
> The Virgin Mary
> Weeps so, her eyes
> Are fountains of living water
> The mother of God: My son!
> Jesus says: My mother!
> And nothing else was said
> Because they could not speak.
> Seeing them, in the sky
> A swallow stopped,
> The doves were silent,

The breeze ceased,
And that is when Christ fell
For the seventh time.

I think it's impossible to write a better historical scene. I say "better" because the moral end of history is that of loving definite people or things, this fusing the present with the warmth of the past; the more lovable or worthy of our love these things appear, the better history will be. I don't say this because of the common urge everywhere to belittle respected and official things; but while I believe that the historian's truth is relative, the truth of tradition or history of non-historians is absolute, because they come closer to reality and approach it with more grace. Besides, tradition goes away. One must doubly love it because of its ideal usefulness and because it is dying. The press has devoured it. Memory does not force itself to retain what is written and if it is retained, it imitates the written form. No one could tell a story like Bernal Díaz or like the anonymous authors of the *saetas* who write not as one writes, but rather as one speaks. This was proved to me a little while ago in my own country which is where anyone can best discover genres that are undergoing changes.

Once in Caracas, a group of friends hired some famous black singers to play some typical songs. They were *llaneros*.[30] Pleasant and brimming with regional pride, they offered to sing the most typical music and lyrics from their repertoire. In effect, they sang for us *galerones, joropos* and *corridos*—scenes of the war of independence in the llanos. Well, there wasn't one word they took from the press. They said "vigorous paladin" and "the father of the country," "the glorious centaurs" and "the eponymous hero." It was like a session of the Academy of History to the accompaniment of guitar and maracas. Since the common folk know how to lend grace to everything they do, especially when they aren't conscious of it, that was one entertaining academic session.

Having observed, ladies and gentlemen, that distinguished orators never preach by example, these remarks concerning history having been made, I want to do nothing less than that; let's go back to history, for a while, have no fear:

The Indian princesses, in accordance with their laws and customs, often formed relationships with the conquering Spanish men. These unions, especially Morganatic[31] ones that the Spaniards didn't always sanction with the Catholic sacrament, could always be severed depending on their whim or on the day it did not suit them. Submission and one-sided faithfulness, the eternal law of the strongest, foreseen albeit in a rough form, is a certain kind of chronic illness that still lingers in all parts of our own charming society. Although often the conquistadors confirmed their unions according to the Church, thus founding illustrious mestiza families in Spain and in the colonies, as we have seen in the story of Doña Marina, at other times they sought their definitive homes with European women who were younger or offered more advantages.

This was the case of the Conquistador Garcilaso de la Vega and the sweet Ñusta Isabela, the niece and grandchild of the last Peruvian kings, who ended her days abandoned.

Garcilaso de la Vega, like almost all the great captains of the Conquest, was from Extremadura. A descendent of the most illustrious Spanish families he counted among his ancestors the poet Jorge Manrique, who wrote the couplets; to Garcilaso, the poet of the eclogues; and the other Garcilaso, who performed great deeds in Granada. While two of his older brothers were fighting in campaigns in Italy and Flanders at the side of Charles V, he, seeking more action, embarked for America. At first as part of Alvarado's fabulous expedition, and eventually with Pizarro in the Conquest of Peru, he led the astounding life of the great conquistadors. Once the war against the Indians, who used to be the owners of great lands, half kings and half gods, was over, Garcilaso achieved in his lifetime, in this new land of treasure and marvels, the dreams of the most ambitious *condottieri* of the Renaissance.[32] As a splendid lord installed in his palace in Cuzco, the ancient capital of the Inca Empire, he welcomed daily at his open table fifty dinner guests he clothed and lodged, and gave horses to whichever friend or acquaintance passed through Cuzco, and he was lord of vast *encomiendas* and he was generous and kind to his Indian vassals.

The terrible civil wars between Pizarro and the Viceroy of Lima had not yet broken out, and during the time of peace, the streets and plazas of Cuzco seemed to reflect on the melancholy remains of Inca society all the splendor of Florentine life. While the noble Indians, the venerable elders, were poor and sad wrapped in their vicuna and rabbit fur blankets, the Spaniards celebrated with processions, floats, tourneys, and horse races so costly and luxurious that in one of them someone wore a Moorish turban with gemstones worth three hundred thousand ducats. Due to the anxiety of the time, the need for luxury united with the need for danger. The slightest insult led to a challenge and frequent deaths and ambushes for reasons of vengeance or honor.

In this atmosphere of anticipation, Ñusta Lady Isabela lived as owner and lady in Garcilaso's palace in luxury. All the Spanish *encomenderos* who made up the aristocracy in Peru treated her with great respect and courtesy. She honored her guests, kept up a correspondence with the archbishop and was highly esteemed by Garcilaso. She kept a table that was open to all in the generous palace, an early version of our colonial households, and she occupied the place of mistress of a Creole household, affable and hospitable.

When the war between Pizarro and the Viceroy Nuñez de Vela broke out, Garcilaso had to leave Cuzco and fight on the side of the Viceroy. In the huge house, empty and abandoned, Doña Isabela was left alone with her six-year-old son, the future author of the *Florida (of the Incas)* and *The Commentaries*. Seventy years later, old, poor, a recluse in his house in Cordoba, Spain, Garcilaso, the mestizo poet, described his childhood memories, so tender and full of life, and his mother's martyrdom during those years of blood and fire. Persecuted by Garcilaso's enemies, who wanted to behead both mother and child, the house was sacked and the furniture burned, dead with fear, the two of them hiding in a secret room of the big house, the cheiftess and her son lived on corn and whatever their Indian or Spanish servants secretly brought them. More than once, during the night, through two holes in the window, the child Garcilaso saw his father's enemy, the terrible and handsome old Carvajal, pass by in the street. Riding on his brown mule, shining in the shadow of his snowy-white beard, wearing a purple robe and a taffeta hat with white feathers, seeing to the preparations of war and meeting out pardons or death, the old man trotted through the silent, narrow streets.

The time of terror having passed, Doña Isabela and her son continued to live in the house in Garcilaso's absence, in her role as wife and Inca princess. When at Christmas or on St. John's Day the encomenderos arrived to pay their tribute, her son helped her with the accounting with the *quipos,* which was the Inca way of keeping accounts with knotted strings. The afternoons were spent with long family visits, during which relatives arrived, the old *pallas* or Inca princess who were still alive after the war between Atahualpa and the Spanish. Brought together during these gatherings, sitting near his mother, the boy heard about the splendid past, the celestial prophecies that predicted the downfall of the empire, as Garcilaso himself tells us in his words: "Remembering the good things they lost, they always ended in tears and weeping as they said, 'We went being from rulers to being vassals.'" When he was alone with his mother, she would tell him, her voice trembling with emotion, the sweet legend of Manco Capac and his wife, the Children of the Sun, who brought civilization to the world and founded Cuzco. In the gentle nights, full of fireflies, his mother took him by the hand and showed him the shape of the celestial alpaca whose members formed the Milky Way up above; she showed him in the shapes in the moon the traces of the kiss of the goddess who was in love, and how rain fell from the maiden's pitcher when her brother broke it with his thunder.

One day, when the Civil War was over, Garcilaso de la Vega returned to Cuzco. He was the same rich and privileged captain. His son, the mestizo child, went to greet him carried on the shoulders of servants, as was the custom for Indian princes during solemn occasions. But oh! His father returned married or about to be married to a noble Spanish woman. After the horrors of the war, along with his absence came humiliation and abandonment. It's the old story, the result of long separations that come between faithfulness and changes of the heart.

When he tells about his childhood memories of that great betrayal during his childhood, Garcilaso, the old writer, has not one bitter word regarding his father whom he intensely admired. Not one hurtful word about his stepmother who passes by in silence. His grief spills over when it comes to the memory of the poor abandoned Indian. His *Comentarios* are dedicated "To my mother and lady" – he says—"made more illustrious through the waters of baptism than through the royal blood of so many Peruvian Incas." What a lovely, filial dedication of hope and forgiveness.

When, a few years after his second marriage, the old Garcilaso died in Cuzco, his mestizo son, still an adolescent, went to the Spanish court to claim the rights to the lands and encomiendas that belonged to his mother from the king. The procedure took a long time, Doña Isabela died in Peru, and Garcilaso, all alone, in the flower of his youth, esteemed and respected in Spain,proved his valor in the wars against the Moors. He travelled, lived in Italy and on his return to Spain became an ordained priest and devoted the rest of his days to the life of the spirit. He withdrew to his farmhouse in Cordoba, surrounded by some servants and owning a little land, his kingdom from that point on became the inner life. After completing his humanistic studies, badly learned during his adolescence, his poetic soul opened up to all the trends of the fifteenth and sixteenth centuries. Along with the Greek and Latin classics he studied the Scholastics, he read the most famous writers and poets of the Renaissance and he translated the three *Dialogs of Love* by Leon Ebreo in a delicious way. In the autumn of his life, his soul as a solitary artist turned toward his American homeland. She would become, from afar, in his maturity, the true promised land of his spirit. While with his own hands Garcilaso sowed the seeds of the cacao bush in his garden in Cordoba and tried to acclimate the flowers he picked during his childhood in Cuzco, he began to write in his charming and graceful style, *The General History of Peru, The Civil War Between the Spaniards*, and the *Florida of the Inca*. The historian-poet of America is a folkloric narrator. But where his joyful prose soars to its creative heights is in the *Royal Commentaries*. The memories of his childhood, recollections of the memories of memories others told him, in these come together and unite in love, just as in his own life, the main trends that will shape the future of the American nations. *"The Royal Commentaries,"* says Prescott,[33] the Angloamerican writer, "are the product of the Indian spirit." In effect, if you listen carefully, beneath the clear prose you can hear the sound of tears, a complaint coming from beyond the tomb. It is still the echo of the maternal voice when she pointed out the stars at night and told him the simple legends of Inca tradition. Because they were told to him orally, due to the lack of a written word, they would have been lost forever when the last traces and accents of the maternal words were in the ears of the mestizo child. But that child, from his exile and in his old age, led on by his nostalgia, would have to return to his childhood, gather the ancient voice with filial love, and encircle it religiously in his crystalline prose and make of it a symbol. That trembling of tears, like a distant sound of the quena or indigenous flute is the cultivated lament that in the deepest part of the race allows us to see our obscure and unrecognized Indian grandmothers. A note of sadness in a minor key, it is the most genuine and delicate of all that resonates in the turmoil of our American soul. Like Garcilaso, the Spanish mestizo, let us keep it in the Castilian language without denying anyone, blessing the harmony of the union and with faith for the future and in forgiveness for the blood spilled and the tears wept.

Notes

[1] De la Parra's two novels were *Ifigenia: Diario de una señorita que escribió porque se fastidiaba* (1924) and *Las Memorias de Mamá Blanca* (1929).

[2] *María* is a romantic, sad and classic novel written by the Colombian Jorge Isaacs (1867) whose main plot is the pain and love that unite the two lovers, María and Efraín.

[3] She never returned to keep this promise. She died at the age of 47 of tuberculosis.

[4] On board the ship that is taking her from Paris to Caracas, María Eugenia, the narrator of *Iphigenia*, flirts with a Colombian poet. When he tries to kiss her, she knocks his glasses off.

[5] *Madame Bovary* (1856) is Gustave Flaubert's first published novel and is considered his masterpiece. The story focuses on a doctor's wife, Emma Bovary, who has an adulterous affair and lives beyond her means in order to escape the banalities and emptiness of provincial life. It is also a criticism of 19th century bourgeoisie society.

[6] "Dolce far niente" is Italian for "It's nice to do nothing".

[7] Jean Patou (1880-1936) was a French fashion designer. He was known for introducing sportswear for women and inventing knitted swimwear and the tennis skirt.

[8] Gabriela Mistral (1889-1957) was a Chilean writer who won the Nobel Prize for literature in 1945.

[9] Delmira Augustini (1886-1914) was a famous Uruguayan poet.

[10] Bartolomé de las Casas (1484-1566) was a 16th-century Spanish historian, social reformer and Dominican friar. He became the first resident bishop of Chiapas and the first officially appointed "Protector of the Indians" His most famous work was *A Brief Account of the Destruction of the Indies*, (1552).

[11] Girolamo Savonarola (1452-1498) was a charismatic preacher from Florence.

[12] The Sabines were an Italic tribe that lived in the central Appennines of ancient Italy. The legend says that the Romans abducted Sabine women to populate the newly built Rome.

[13] José María de Heredia (1842-1905) was a Cuban-born poet who translated and annotated Bernal Díaz del Castillo's *Historia Verdadera de la Conquista de la Nueva España* (*The True History of the Conquest of New Spain*) into French, in four volumes, *Veridique Histoire de la Conquête de la Nouvelle Espagne* (1877-1887).

[14] Malinalli Tenepatl, better known as Malinche (1502-1529) was given as a slave to the Tabasco Maya caciques after a war between the them and the Aztecs. She was then given to Hernán Cortes along with nineteen other women. She served Cortes as an interpreter and counseled the Spanish on their military and social costums. She also had a son with Cortes. For a better history of Malinche, refer to Sandra Messenger Cypess, *La Malinche in Mexican Literature: From History to Myth*. U Texas P. 1991 and Camilla Townsend, *Malintzin's Choices: An Indian Woman in the Conquest of Mexico*. Albuquerque, U of New Mexico Press, 2006.

[15] The Guaiquerí was an Indian tribe. They were the first inhabitants of the Island of Margarita.

[16] Inca Garcilaso de La Vega (1539-1616) was a Peruvian historian and writer and was best known for his work *The Royal Commentaries of the Inca* (1609).

[17] See my article, "From Cult to Comics: The Representation of Gonzalo Guerrero as a Cultural Hero in Mexican Popular Culture," *A Twice-Told Tale: Reinventing the Encounter in Iberian/Iberian American Literature and Film*, U of Delaware Press, 2001 pp. 137- 148.

[18] Caneyes were sheds made of palm tree leaves. These sheds had no walls and were supported by columns of wood. Bohíos were typical Latin American cabins made of wood and tree branches. These bohíos were round and had only one door and no windows. Casabe was a kind of bread made of yucca.

[19] In Homer's *Odyssey,* Book VI, Odysseus is shipwrecked naked on the coast of Phaeacia. Nausicaa, the daughter of King Alcinous and Queen Arete, gives him clothes.

[20] Juan de Castellanos (1522-1607) was a Spanish poet, priest and chronicler.

[21] Virgil (Publius Virgilius Maro (70 B.C.-19 B.C) was a classical Roman poet who wrote about Arcadia, an imaginary land of leisure and song whose inhabitants lead simple lives close to nature in his Eclogues.

[22] Ñusta is an Incan title of nobility.

[23] Hernán Cortes (1485-1547) was a Spanish conquistador who led an expedition that caused the fall of the Aztec Empire.

[24] Bernal Díaz del Castillo (1492-1581) was a Spanish conquistador and chronicler of the Indies. His greatest work was *The True History of the Conquest of New Spain* written in the 1560's and published in 1632.

[25] Land, along with Indians granted to a colonist.

[26] Cortes referred to her as "mi lengua"—my tongue.

[27] A misspelled reference to Huitzilopochtli, the most important Mexican god, who was associated with the sun and war. Bernal Díaz's tells the story of "la noche triste" when Cortes was defeated by Aztec warriors June 30, 1520.

[28] López de Gómara (1512-1572) was a Spanish historian and writer. His greatest work was *The History of the Indies and Conquest of Mexico* (1552).

[29] Sacred song in Flamenco style.

[30] Llaneros are people who live in the savannas and inter-tropical zone in the Orinoco River basin.

[31] A Morganatic marriage is a marriage between a nobleman and a woman of lesser lineage or vice-versa.

[32] Condottieri were the mercenary soldier leaders of the professional, military free companies contracted by the Italian city-states and the Papacy. In Renaissance Italian, condottiero meant "contractor".

[33] William Hickling Prescott (1796-1859) was an American historian and Hispanist. Prescott specialized in the history of late Renaissance Spain and the early Spanish Empire. Some of his most important works were *The History of the Conquest of Mexico* (1843) and *The History of the Conquest of Peru* (1847).

CHAPTER EIGHT

THE SECOND LECTURE:
THE COLONY

Our Colonial Hispanic American era, that is, the three centuries between the Conquest and the Wars of Independence, was a time of synthesis and love during which the reign of sentimental feminism of the old-fashioned kind ended when the Wars of Independence began. As we turn our attention to that time, for we know little about it, we should note the grace that unites all the nations of Spanish America. It's as though this period left no traces of itself in archives, letters, or famous books because the sweetness of its life accustomed its inhabitants to silence, and its soft and repetitive rhythm came down to us charmingly through its oral tradition. When discussing the Colony, one needs to adopt a familiar and conversational narrative tone, like the tone a talkative and plainspoken grandmother who has lived a long life and has read little talks in, or the tone of an old black servant, who, having always been a member of the same household or having lived on the same plantation, confuses his own memories with the memories others shared with him. Thus to speak of the Colony is to narrate, often to speak of itself, about itself, that is, about its own impressions that we have randomly collected here and there.

Ingenuous and happy, childlike, and like countries that lack a history, the Colony is thoroughly wrapped up within the Church, the home and the convent. I believe it can be summed up as a feminine voice behind a shutter. It has nothing to do with politics, the press, wars, industry or commerce; it is an unchronicled women's domain left behind by men and their rule. It can be compared to a communal life, and a somewhat mysterious one like the lives cloistered people live and is without a doubt one of the most thought-provoking we know of in the history of the whole world and in the evolution of a society that matures in silence. Somber and chivalrous, like the Middle Ages, fine and delicate like the French eighteenth century, it has something more of the transcendental than the beautiful smile of a French Marques who read Rousseau. The Colony was not skeptical. Indolent, tolerant and voluptuous, due to the demands of the climate, behind its indolence lies faith, the slowly simmering sacrifice of life, the tragic love full of Spanish-style jealousy and a need to dream and be fed by far-off ideas, uncertain of what it is waiting for as it gently sways in a hammock.

My fondness for the Colony would never bring me to say, as others do, that I would like to have been born during that time. No. I feel very much at home in my own time, and I think highly of it. I believe that in this moment of our brief existence we have a good and lofty vantage point from which to spend some time liberally and distractedly looking toward other horizons. Despite what its detractors have to say, it is a brave time, restless, intelligent, generous and tolerant in the sense that it embraces with the same enthusiasm one intolerance after another.

Like our cherished and likeable friends who are punctual but a bit egotistical, it brings together so many good traits we can't help but love them. It knows how to eliminate our small tragedies and it has freed us of our many great terrors, which keeps our heart scrubbed, comfortable, and half-empty like the restroom of *The Palace*. I am grateful daily for the material and moral comforts it bestows on us, and I am grateful, too, because in the midst of its dizzying pace it still preserves peaceful places like the Quinta Bolivar, which, though it seems far removed from the present, speaks to me so well of good Bogota taste; it is in these places that we can willingly and gratefully listen to the sounds of the past. I say grateful because as much as we live in the present, the more we can savor the past. Who of us has not lived during the Colony thanks to a friend or relative or old servant who is miraculously and wondrously ill-suited at living in the present? As far as I'm concerned, I have to say that most of my childhood was colonial, and the need to react to it during an age in which we are all revolutionaries—as much as in our spirit of justice as in our vanity—was what inspired me to write.

I don't know whether this was a good or bad influence, this colonial vestige that was part of my upbringing , retrospectively filled with charm in my memory and just as in Caracas as in Bogota as in the rest of America, it constitutes for me the present form of the homeland. Independence, like all revolution and abrupt change, only changed on the outside. The colonial spirit continued to reign throughout the entire nineteenth and up to our time. An enemy of revolutionary ideas, which formed the basis of the revolutionary movement, it contradicted its own goals.

In Venezuela—since I am especially talking about my own family memories, but am convinced, fraternally speaking, that you share some of these memories—that colonial spirit was unjustly and disdainfully labeled the Gothic party.[1] It was charged with safeguarding tradition. It was made up, for the most part, of the same liberators who had been ruined by the war. Silenced by narrow-mindedness and short-sightedness, impoverished, removed from power, pulled from the roots of that painful independence brought about by the best of its blood and its fortunes, the Gothic party knew how to purify itself through adversity; despoiled, denuded, removed from all its material power, it continued to direct itself morally in its own house. Its influence was healthy and its stubbornness was tempered by its tenderness and generosity. Everyone's home belonged to everyone. They knew how to be poor with nobility and good humor. They attacked their triumphant political enemies with home-grown satire, a weapon the ingenious use so they can amuse themselves without having to pay admission to the play. This never led to shame since the simplicity of life without excess abundantly provided all that was necessary. There was enough to maintain the decorum of the open table set with enough Creole dishes on the starched white linen tablecloths that had been laundered in cedar and vetiver. From the heavens the sun daily warmed the bathwater in the yard, and the flasks of liquor mixed with herbs from the fields replaced the the flasks that held cologne water. Since bad taste almost always proceeds from the abuse of abundance, that poor Caracas aristocracy, that of all the nineteenth century, molded itself to the discipline of sobriety, paying no attention to the poverty in its bosom , generating a certain kind of good taste. One of the finest manifestations of that good taste was the spontaneity and the generosity of its hospitality. When in 1872 the Federal Government ordered the three old nun's convents to be shuttered with the added prohibition that the communities could not re-form themselves elsewhere, almost all the good families in Caracas hurried to offer a room that could serve as a cell for one of its newest members of the family.

In Venezuela today there are no political parties to divide the country into two camps like in the past century: one can speak about them as one speaks of the dead, dispassionately and without giving offense. In Venezuela, those who represented the Federal Party in the nineteenth century or claimed they did, for surely what has been called an affinity for progress, lacked, however, a poetic spirit.

They believed that achieving progress involved destruction. They relentlessly destroyed as much in moral as in material ways to impose a progress on the sentimental ruins that was a caricature; since it had not sprung spontaneously from its surroundings; it lacked an inner voice. One of these acts of vandalism was this decree of 1872 that ordered the secularization of the nuns, and thanks to it the three old colonial convents were destroyed. It is hard to describe the pain and the outcry this measure caused in Caracas. The convents were the repositories of three centuries of colonial life. Located downtown and surrounding the Plaza Mayor, later the Plaza Bolívar, along with the Cathedral they lent a rustic architectural tone that harmonized so well with the climate, the sky, and the landscape. The decree gave rise to a muted indignation hardly anyone dared to protest publicly because one paid dearly for protesting. One of the Mothers Superior, who was surely related to the President and was an educated nun, wrote a magnificent letter of protest demanding her rights be protected and defended, and requested they be moved to a community outside the city. The President replied that he could not grant her wish, that the communities had to be forcibly dissolved, which according to his thinking was how one should serve God in the spirit of the century. Once again, the Mother Superior responded that she did not have enough authority to lift the rule of the cloistered status of her nuns; on the contrary, she ordered them to defy the State and while waiting for whoever came to force them to comply. As it turned out, when the authorities arrived, the Mother Superior had the nuns lined up, praying and chanting "The Magnificat," and they left their convent for good, escorted at bayonet point. Their host families awaited them In the Plaza. The three convents housed sixty-four nuns. All of them, even the provincials, even the oldest of them who could not recall having any friends or family in the city, were immediately and warmly received in people's homes. Surely, along with the nuns the families received living proof of the great despotism of the opposing party and satisfied at the same time the tenderness of their hearts and the demands of political passion, since those Goths possessed the blessings of the pure of heart. In the inner patios of the house, in the shade of a royal palm or an orange tree, each nun reconstructed her cell with its enclosed walls, an altar, an image, a prayer bench and a humble cot. The altar was adorned with two candles and with either artificial or fresh flowers from the garden. Since family life was not so different from life in the convent, while life with its gatherings, visits from fiancées and windows open to the street went on in the outer patio, in the innner patio the nun continued to live her cloistered life wearing her Carmelite habit, her soundless sandals and the rosary beads that clicked as she walked. There, in the shade, she sewed, prayed, cooked meals for the household and prepared the chocolate and cookies the convent was famous for.

I got to know one of these formerly cloistered nuns. Her memory led me to read many obscure things. I've learned that it is not the tame idealism of women, who, as homemakers confined to their homes shaped the character of our society, but rather that of a prevailing number in the Colony, who due to biases and prejudices, without necessarily being religious, were drawn to mysticism and entered the convent. They were lovers of silence, of the eternal inner life, and though it may seem contradictory, they were the forerunners of modern feminist ideals.

The nun who formed some of my first childhood memories, who was a symbol of colonial feminine idealism, was named Mother Teresa. She was one of the last survivors of that cruel dispersion. She lived in an old house owned by the widow who took her in and who was as old as her house. My sisters and I used to visit them often because we lived nearby and doubtless because being five and seven years old we were already moved by the spirit of wild tourism that enriches our contemporary time. To push open the entry door and suddenly enter into Mother Teresa's patio was like flying from one country to another; better than that, it was like traveling from one century to another. You did not have to have a sense of history to understand it. We even ignored the existence of history. We appreciated the value of that house like a good archeologist appreciates inscriptions on rocks. We appreciated it in a welcome way without the intervention of intelligence, so often dry, but rather with emotion, always pleasant. The smell that greeted us was the damp odor common to leaky houses visited by many cats. Our eyes were greeted by the tangled vegetation in the patio. Clumps of grass grew on the damp tiles as far as the eaves, gutters were weary of draining water, and in the salon, the saints were dressed in their stiff damask finery. Everything in that house bore the clean charm of old age. Mother Teresa, a sort of majestic imp in her dark habit, her oval face snuggly enveloped in her white snood, was the natural inhabitant of that humble museum. The landlady was dull, the nun was austere, and between them there existed a happy and hearty note that recalled St. Teresa's[2] and all the colonial convents of America. And this traditional note was kept up at all times by the servant.

When nuns entered the convent they brought their dowries and their servants with them. This happened throughout the Continent during colonial times. In Caracas, in earlier times, when slavery still existed, the slave was a black woman. On the day of her profession ceremony after the nun took her three vows, she presented a letter of manumission to her black servant. The voluntary slavery of the free woman served to set her slave free. Such was the rule of the Discalced Carmelites in Caracas, "the garden of perfection and the hacienda of virtue" as it was poetically described in the sixteenth century by the writer Oviedo y Baños.[3] When they were expelled, sixty-four nuns and their sixty-four servants were turned out into the street. It was difficult for the servants to find shelter, since, accustomed to convent life, they found it hard to adapt to ordinary household service in homes they felt lacked the status of monastic life.

Mother Teresa left her hacienda along with her servant, who, faithful even in adversity when we knew her, was still helping to prepare sweets, respond to the recitation of novenas, and recite the rosary when no one else in the neighborhood came to pray. She was a jovial mulatta whose laughter rang out at the slightest comic detail she heard in a novena or in one of the *Lives of the Saints* of the Christian calendar. Since she treated the saints with excessive familiarity, she offered continuous and enriching acts of faith, because she removed them from their hieratical status and brought them to life.

When she declared, for example, that St. Anthony was a cheat because he accepted an offering but did not grant a favor, or when she seriously believed that the best way to worship St. Pascal[4] was to pray while dancing—since he was a native of Baylon—with a broom in her sturdy hands, she indiscreetly and abruptly opened the gates of heaven. The saints appeared behind her gaily enjoying themselves and innocently dancing some sort of black dance. I must tell you that this way of honoring St. Pascal while dancing was not limited to that maid, but was a common devotion among the black population of Venezuela. In Caracas it's not uncommon to hear a knock on the door and encounter a black woman or a mulatta between the two doors in the entryway, who, after a polite greeting declares, "I'm here to ask for a donation because I am collecting money to sponsor a dance I offered up to St. Pascal when my child was very ill." The donation is given and the dance is held and the celebration takes place without much devotion but with lots of liquor.

Both the nun and her maid alike aged without growing old. The nun was serious. She never talked about the convent. She possessed the magnificent dignity of those who have suffered persecution without complaint because they know complaining won't help. Between the two of them, one was amusing and the other was intellectual, like St. Teresa or Sor Juana[5]. I believe that in her silence Mother Teresa had the soul of a poet and she entered the convent to live among the lilies of the Lord but also to live among books. In those days, and even in the midst of ours, a woman who devoted herself to studies was a marginalized phenomenon. This prejudice was very rooted in men's souls and it persists to this day. In order to be pardoned for living among books one must appease men by writing about love. "The woman who knows Latin comes to a bad end," goes the refrain, and some still believe it today. Once her fame was established, the disdain for the studious woman either led to excessive admiration or relegated her to a kind of curiosity rather than to her admiration.. Both misunderstanding and pride were bad for a delicate soul. In the convent, on the other hand, one could live impunity among books and in silence. Going back two centuries we find this case in the story of the life and vocation of Sor Juana, the prototype of the intellectual mystic typical of colonial convents.

Sor Juana was without a doubt one of the most perfect examples of feminine genius that has ever lived. When one reads her biography or her works, it is astonishing to see the richness of so many gifts come together in one person. Beautiful, very intelligent, passionate and full of life, she possessed many talents. Aside from her poetic genius she was a musician, painter, a great humanist, knowledgeable in both the natural and the physical sciences. Had she been born in France during the same time, she would have been one of the most seductive women in the court of Louis X IV. Having been born in the Colony, burdened by her amazing gifts, she silently offered them up to God in the convent. Although she was a local woman with a modest background, her fame as a charming young woman spread to the Viceroy of Mexico's palace.

At the time she was called Juana de Asbaje, she was worldly and not quite twenty years old. One day the Viceroy invited her to his palace and by separate invitation also called in the most renowned theologians, doctors and learned men: in all, there were forty of them. Their task was to outwit the young girl with learned questions about all kinds of knowledge, to see how she would answer and to determine if her knowledge had been taught to her, was inborn, acquired or false. I like to think that Sor Juana was so clever, she must have answered some questions in an ironic manner when her memory failed her and when she could not reply with certainty upon seeing that great shower of erudition fall upon her. Since she was also very pretty she knew how to soften that intimidating knowledge with smiles. The fact is that she escaped from that trap into which more than one of her examiners fell into. For superior souls, victory brings with it at times a sadness more subtle than the pain of defeat. Defeat provokes a reaction and makes hope shine anew. Juana de Asbaje, the wise child, grew weary of her great intellectual triumph, which was spoken of throughout the land and whose echoes reached the court at Madrid, and from that day forward she preferred to live a sheltered life to one of worldly success. She retired to the convent, calling herself Sor Juana, giving herself up entirely to study until she became one of the greatest poets the Colony produced.

In the peace of her cell the growth of her intelligence united harmoniously with the growth of her virtues, those two enclosed and neighboring gardens. She grew in wisdom while she grew in sanctity. Her love of God became a life- long courtship, that exempted her from disappointment throughout her life, without the fear that old age would fade it. The love verses in which she passionately expressed the laments of divine passion, well polished, were impressed on her mind, so that God, the silent audience, could read them. Books could only be published by order of the confessor or the bishop. In Castille, St. Teresa wrote out of obedience, and out of obedience wrote Madre Castillo, the extraordinary Colombian Claretian nun.

This nun's case demonstrates the cultural inclination that existed in colonial convents. Madre Castillo was born and died in a provincial city, the delightful town of Tunja. The only trip she took during her life was in her adolescence, when she travelled from her home to the Claretian convent. I believe that Tunja, nestled in the colonial Andes, must be especially propitious for dreaming and for contemplation. The conquistador and chronicler, the intellectual and poet Juan de Castellanos,[6] who was a worthy precursor of Colombian culture, spent his last days in that town. There, after taking orders as a priest, he wrote the 150,000 verses of his memoirs which he called *The Elegies of the Worthy Men of the Indies*. This charming extravagance, a chronicle that sets to rhymed verse even the most prosaic of everyday details, must have been inspired by the poetic atmosphere of the city. Many highly regarded and enlightened critics, Menendez Pelayo[7] among others, complained that Castellanos described things that were anti-poetic in verse. On the contrary, I believe he did well to heed the atmosphere's advice and lent his poetic talents to poor, prosaic things.

A century later, in the same city, Madre Castillo also felt the need to retire to pray and think. When she began her novitiate she barely knew how to read. Enclosed within her cell, or sitting aside in a corner of the cloister, she was always alone with a book in her hands, keeping silent for many years. The other nuns, judged her an eccentric, labeled her proud and visionary. This misunderstanding was a thorn in her side. One day her confessor ordered her to write and she broke the silence. Everyone marveled at her erudition. The bishops thought it was a case of divine revelation and ordered her to write her *vita*. This she did in the smooth style of the sixteenth century. But like all true artists she perceived the spirit of the age and reflected Góngora[8] in her verses.

Rejoicing in the Eucharist she writes passionately with love:

The soul burns in a fire
Hydropic in its burning

And later:

To sustain me you sent
Your love's seal in a host

How could *gongorismo* travel so easily on sailing ships and on the backs of mules to find its way to an Andean nun's cell?

Aside from culture, there was much gayety in the airy colonial convents. The hypocrisy of certain lay brothers and sisters and that of some contemporary religious orders is not colonial, but is rather influenced by Jansenism[9] Already St. Teresa of Castille had on many an occasion lent an energetic tone to faith. Once, a plague of unnamed insects descended on her community. The insects were so insistent that having given up hope of exterminating them, St. Teresa took an extreme measure. She ordered all the clothing in the convent to be burned, a strong measure given that, the convent was poor and all the nuns' habits had to be replaced. The day of the inauguration of the new habits was celebrated with a jolly procession in thanksgiving during which the nuns recited the following verses they composed:

You grant us new garments
Oh, Heavenly King
Deliver this habit
From evil creatures.

Good humor not only travelled to the colonial convents, but it also developed rapidly here on its own. Autonomy grew along with a good sense of humor. The tropics are an enemy of reserve and the etiquette of strictness, which are good traits in northern climates. Warm climates love social gatherings in the open air and are opposed to all kinds of isolation. Some travelers who came to America in the eighteenth century and wrote their impressions of their journeys, like Ulloa and Jorge Juan,[10] were shocked by the relaxed rules in the religious communities. These lapses, as Ulloa writes, consequences of the climate, were innocent enough. One of them was the innumerable visits in the visiting room. There were worldly gatherings in which theological themes were discussed, but less weighty matters were considered. Another relaxation of the rules was the number of slaves or secular servants attached to the communities. There were convents in Mexico City and Havana in which each nun had five or six servants in her service. Good mystics and good criollos, they thought without a doubt that it was unedifying to squander their material efforts on their own behalf, but they should rather save their efforts when the occasion presented itself and put them to better use in the service of God. Meanwhile, the six servants did all the work.

The excess of servants in Mexico provoked a famous case between a convent and a provincial from the Order of St. Francis, named Brother Mateo de Herrera, who arrived from Spain to visit the communities. The provincial was scandalized by the number of servants he counted in one convent: there were five hundred of them, a veritable army, and he decided to reduce their number to a minimum. The nuns indignantly opposed him, the provincial insisted, all the nun's relatives came to their support, a heated discussion ensued and the case came before the Royal Audience. There was a hearing. The Viceroy was named as the arbiter and he decreed that the number of servants be reduced by half. But since the nuns refused to fire even one servant, they brilliantly won the case.

Gifts accompanied by loving messages travelled from the houses of the wealthy families to the convent and from the convent to the houses of wealthy families and back. There were trays of almond cookies, dried fruit, meringues and fine chocolate. Filling the tray and sending messages was one of the delightful tasks of the aforementioned servants. Sor Juana, who also passionately loved the Marquesa de Paredes, one of the vicereines, almost daily sent her gifts of sweets or hand-made items along with a verse. Once she sent her an embroidered slipper and a chocolate cake and she glossed that gift with a ballad that read:

Throwing down the gauntlet, my lady
Is the signal of a challenge,
Throwing down a slipper
Is the signal of defeat.

I don't know if Sor Juana's verses were delivered in a sealed envelope or if they were recited out loud and postmarked by the messenger. I can imagine the quatrain above being recited at an open door, the chocolate and the slipper resting on a tray firmly held in the hands of the messenger. These messages between friends were a very important form of expression during colonial times, and there were no phones and no correct forms for letters except as messages of love. A well-conceived, well-formed and well-delivered recited message went a long way and it was an art style full of subtleties and shadings which a slave who was an accomplished messenger could deliver. Depending on the circumstances, it could be a greeting, a congratulatory message or condolences, sensational news, observations on the weather, or complaints or declarations of love or endearments. All of it was adorned in a unique Spanish rhetoric, partially declaimed and partially in black dialect, in which from time to time, even in Caracas, one could hear the "s" pronounced.

I got to hear one of these messages during my childhood. They continued to arrive until 1910. They were sent by elderly women who held nothing but a sacred repugnance for the telephone and were delivered by a black servant woman who wore the traditional white kerchiefs slaves wore. Convents played a very important role in the daily and social life of the Colony. The turnstile, according to one contemporary writer, turned more than once on its axis, not only to bring out and take in gifts but also used to ask for donations or to distribute alms. "To Mother Superior" a voice outside would plead, "that she should have the goodness to offer a rosary for one in great need. Here are the alms offered for the holy souls." And the turnstile revolved.

On certain holy days, depending on the schedule, comedies, dramas and regional performances were on the program. Nuns played music and sang sacred songs. They assisted the archbishop and the Viceroy or the Captain General, depending on the city. In Mexico, in Sor Juana's day, the Viceroy and the Vicereine, the Marquesa de Mancera, never failed to attend these. Sor Juana did it all with passion, for she loved this vicereine dearly, the one who came before the other one, the one she wrote the poem about the slipper for. The first one was named Laura and she died during her reign. Sor Juana, who praised her while she was alive, mourned her death in countless sonnets and poems written in hendecasyllables.

One of these sonnets begins:

> They die with you, Laura, for you died.
> The effects that desire you in vain
> You deny my eyes your sight.
> The beautiful light you once bestowed
> My sad lyre you set singing dies.
> Lamenting echoes acclaim you.
> Even these ill-formed flourishes are
> Black tears that flow from my sad pen.

I see in the homage Sor Juana paid the vicereines the same tendency we still have in America to passionately admire everything that that reaches us from across the sea. When you analyze it, it's a form of naïve idealism. Since nature in the tropics predisposes one to dream of grand things, Europe is imagined as larger than life, is given an enormous shape with fantastic proportions, the same as we would forge the sky. People across the sea are imbued with the same prestige. They are like a kind of cherubim with wax wings. The melt when brought closer to the heat of reality, but faith does not die. It's reborn under another influence, another manner or another personality since nature is ever ready to forge or shape new skies.

In our own time we give preference to Paris. During colonial times it was to the courts of Austria and the Bourbons. The birth of a prince or the king's birthday was, along with Holy Week, one of the most important and solemn ceremonies of the year. Bells pealed, there were fireworks, the noble mantuano ladies [11] came out into the streets and everyone had a great time. The deposition and incarceration of Ferdinand VII[12] by Napoleon wounded the colonies in its fondest, most mystic heart. The colony had humiliated itself before its sacred king. They were disappointed when they realized that his reign was a house of cards, and gave up on him up on him in their dreams. They had forgiven him for many things, but they could not forgive his reign in a house of cards.

Women, being the most sensitive and thirsty for the ideal, were more prone to deify anything. Both Jorge Juan and Count Segur,[13] who came to Caracas and to Cartagena de Indias in the eighteenth century wrote about the warm, enthusiastic greetings with which the Creoles welcomed the Europeans. Segur, who travelled to Caracas complaining about the uncomfortable trip and the narrow-mindedness of the colonial authorities, changed his tune when he arrived in the city. He saw beautiful women approach the windows to greet the French officers and it seemed to him that Caracas was an enchanted valley where one could enjoy the sweet life. Everyone, he said, hurried to offer him their home, and ladies opened the shutters with a smiling invitation. He was so charmed by the genuine hospitality he never forgot the days he spent in Caracas. Neither did he forget the Aristiguieta sisters, Bolívar's cousins, with whom he danced frequently, and whom he called, since there were nine beautiful sisters, "The Nine Muses."

For his part, Jorge Juan recalled that here in Cartagena de Indias, distinguished criollo ladies never went into the street. They only ventured out night. They attended Sunday mass at 3:00 a.m. Their noble rank as mantuanas did not allow them to leave the house without a cloak, and since the heat of the sun made it uncomfortable to wear a cloak, they stayed at home during the day. Lying in their hammocks wearing bright clothes and high-heeled slippers, they gazed at the palms, the sea, and the sky through their windows and dreamt of far-off things.

When a foreigner approached their ivory towers they welcomed him with excessive kindness. They offered him fruit, flowers or homemade sweets. They were great smokers and one of the most courteous gestures was to offer a well-lit cigar to the person they wanted to honor. It was considered polite to light a cigar and offer it to the guest.

The mulattas, quadroons, and quinteroons, whose distinction in rank was very important, could, without lowering their rank, circulate in the streets, wearing a simple taffeta bodice, a blouse and a white kerchief. They considered it great fun to go to the port and watch the galleons arrive. In their goodness, the *chapetonadas*, for so they were called, would take the *chapeton* or recently arrived European, who were often ill with fevers that attacked them in the tropics when they disembarked, into their own homes. When the *chapeton* was cured, he often married one of his nurses. If he died, the charitable mulattas cried over him and mourned him loudly and vigorously, held the wake, gave him a proper burial and ordered nine masses said for his soul.

During colonial times, there were many of these mantuanas who were dreamers confined to their homes and saw nothing on the horizon save but what they could glimpse from their window. Undecided, vague mystics without vocations for the convent or matrimony, either ambitious or disappointed by their first love, they lived on the margins.

Living in abnegation and having planted the seeds of affection in the family, they grew old as unmarried women. More maternal than their own mothers had been, for the most part, the old maiden aunts created our typical Creole sentimentalism with a fierceness that comes to the rescue in times of loneliness, illness and death.

There is an anonymous colonial poet who may have been Colombian and who wrote only under the pseudonym Amarilis.[14] We don't know much about this mysterious person except what we learn about her in a lovely poem so frequently typical of the Creole dreamer. The remarkable Amarilis, who flits like a shadow over colonial literature without leaving behind even one letter, is worthy of having an entire book written about her. And her epistolary poem should be better known in the Spanish speaking world. But her main attraction is that she stayed in the shadows, as vain and mediocre talents did not, thus teaching us a lesson about good taste.

It is believed Amarilis was born in a province of Peru at the beginning of the 17th century since she was writing in 1621. According to one source, she left Peru when she was very young and traveled to Santa Fe de Bogota where she lived for the rest of her life. But, how did she live? Did she ever marry? Are her descendents living here? Or did she always dream of impossible loves? She was very young, and very well-read, a passionate reader of the classics and of her contemporaries; she fell in love with Lope de Vega,[15] whose fame was at its height, from afar. She got to know him through his writings and in her admiration of him and thinking herself to be his kindred spirit, she developed a true romantic passion for him.

To make him aware of her love, she secretly composed a letter in verse in which she simply told him of her love, her life, her surroundings and of those who loved her. She also told him that she had chosen him as a lover but due to her blessed, happy state she could not hope for a real love or happy endings. She signed herself Amarilis and addressed Lope de Vega as Belardo.

A charmed and moved Lope de Vega responded, but since he did not know where to send the letter, he saved the letter in one of his books. Menendez Pelayo judged the verses of the first writer—that is, Amarilis—to be the most refreshing and charming in colonial literature when he compared the two letters, but this time—forgive me, Lope—her poetry was judged superior.

Amarilis begins her long letter with her autobiography, telling Lope de Vega the history of her grandparents, who were the conquerors and founders of her city. She writes fluently and is well-versed in history and mythology. She recounts how she and her sister were orphaned and writes him that she is rich, beautiful and happy.

> We two sisters were born of noble parents
> Who died suddenly when we were young
> Clothed in children's garments.
> The heavens and our aunt
> Softened the loneliness of our fate.

And at this point she hits the typical note of the criollo family:

> The sky shares its beauty
> And other good things,
> The many plantations
> Support us
> And we live happily together
> Sharing one soul to govern us
> There is no "mine" and "thine,"
> But a loving peace, sweet and tender.
> My Belisa is praised
> For that is her name, and Amarilis mine.
> We share a mutual fondness.
> I was drawn to the sweet muses,
> My young sister was more spirited
> And is renowned for her charms
> And the graces she is famous for,
> And she deserves
> The joyful praise.
> I followed another path:

Happily living in celibacy
In my virginal state,
My love consecrated to God
Hoping that in his goodness and greatness,
He will offer me his hand,
Safeguarding my spotless purity.

She continues a long time describing her hopes and her platonic love and praises him and admits that she is in love with him from afar without ever having seen or touched him, in a lofty and extraordinary way:

To sustain a hopeless love
Is so rare that I should like to know,
If it is present in any heart,
To live in such a blessed state,
To love so richly
Or if it is impossible.

Here her lyric soul appears. She is eager for the abnegation and the responsibilities I spoke of earlier, which represents the ideal femininity so disparaged and so misunderstood in its pure form:

I heard, Belardo, your conceits,
Your sweetness and your miraculous style,
And admiring your marvelous wit
I could not restrain nor harm myself
By revealing myself to you.
I heard your voice, Belardo, what more can I say?
No, Belardo, you should be called a miracle,
For that is the name heaven gave you,
And love, which never gave me peace,
Revealed itself to me bit by bit.

Amarilis declares herself to be ignorant about love and says she only speaks to the heavens. She asks Lope for the gift of a poem: a poem about the life of the saint she is devoted to:

My sister and I worship a saint
No one has written about.
From from your hands
Your sweet muse will breathe it to life.
And write it in a lofty style
So it will be renowed everywhere.
Oh, what a fellow you are my Belardo
Your temples crowned with laurel!

And taking leave of him she reminds him:

> Finally, Belardo, I offer you
> A pure soul conquered by your fame.

Upon rereading the letter she is unhappy because she has not done the best she could; she is distressed but she seals it and sends it along with the best intentions:

> Tired verses, what passion turns you
> Into subjects of native simplicity
> To land in Belardo's hands?
> At least, even if you are as bitter as unripe fruit,
> You will be tasted, although without desire,
> And your taste be rough and dull
> The graceful wit which will honor you at his table
> Will forgive your attempts;
> Sail forth, Godspeed the sail,
> Guide a soul who wingless flies.

How many Amarilises have lived since then in our cities watching life go by between the bars of their windows and between the pages of their books? How many, silent and imprisoned for many years, never sent their letter to a Belardo, eventually writing it in prose and addressing it to someone who did not inspire her or was worthy of it? How many others, unable to write, never wrote at all?

Among the vestiges and relics of my semi-colonial childhood I relish the influence of two such dreamers. It is to them that I owe, without a doubt, that almost spiritual fondness I feel today for the old Creole tradition that is rapidly disappearing. Their examples provide an intimate view of both sides of the independence movement. The first one was a hardened Royalist and the second one was a highly praised patriot. I heard about the Royalist, and the stories about her came so alive for me that thanks to them, I experienced colonial times with my own eyes. Doña Francisca de Tovar[16] lived up towards the end of the eighteenth century. As she grew older, thanks to her children, grandchildren and great grandchildren, she was called by the typical Creole name Mama Panchita.

As I said, I learned about her through her daughter, my maternal grandmother, who despite being a literate woman knew how to tell a lively tale like illiterate people are prone to do. The adventurous Mama Panchita lived from 1787 to 1870, more-or less-spanning a cycle of prosperity, persecution, tragedies and downfalls. It was her story as told to me by my grandmother that entertained me during my childhood. I can state without exaggeration that hand-in-hand, the two of us walking in the shadow of Mama Panchita, I relived the days of Caracas when Humboldt[17] visited, the period before the Revolution, the earthquake of 1812. A heroine in war, Mama Panchita was even more heroic in peacetime, precisely because of the unpopularity of her heroism. Surrounded in her own home by patriots and illustrious leaders, in her defeat she continued to be a Royalist and never gave it up until the day she died. She was Count Tovar's niece and a contemporary of Bolívar, with whom she played la cebollita[18] and Blind man's Bluff in the Plaza San Jacinto in her childhood. Mama Panchita was married at the turn of the century when she was fifteen to a Spanish Basque named Don Francisco Ezpelozín, a high-ranking employee of the Guipuzcoana Company.[19] The vessels of the Guipuzcoana Company brought the best cacao from Caracas to Spain. But through contact with France they also brought the germs of the Revolution to the Colony. It is thanks to the Guipuzcoana Company that the magnificent culture and the adventurous heroism that produced Miranda[20] and other liberators sprang forth. At the beginning of the nineteenth century, Mama Panchita, who was a rich and beautiful mantuana and surely frivolous like the good eighteenth century daughter that she was, was at the height of her splendor. The Basque don Francisco owned many plantations and sailing vessels outright. I suspect Mama Panchita did not read any books except for her missal during high mass on Sundays, and this, rather superficially. Dressed in bright flounces, she took her siesta surrounded by slaves. While one of them groomed her hair, another massaged her arms, a third kept the mosquitoes at bay and a fourth helped her put on her stockings, which were a great luxury in her day and were always of pure silk.

One day, to her bad luck and to the luck of her stockings, the damned revolution began. Good-bye forever to peaceful siestas! Don Francisco, her husband, wise like a rich man, believed that "the best" is the enemy of "the good" and decided to remain strictly neutral. But the bloody war started and the revolutionaries began to destroy, and attacked the neutral parties. You were either for the revolution or you were against it and the suspects were made to say "orange" or "Francisco" to hear how they pronounced the word.[21] Persecuted by the patriots, Don Francisco's goods were confiscated since he couldn't even pronounce his own name the right way, and he had to hide to save himself. In vain Mama Panchita pleaded with her fraternal cousins, the Tovars and Mendozas of Independence fame, that they be allowed to keep a small plantation and be left to live quietly in peace since they were peaceful people. The cousins all tersely and dryly responded that they had to manage as best they could since the

Republic needed money, and besides, who told her to marry a Spaniard? After many risks and facing danger Don Francisco managed to escape, and Mama Panchita, surrounded by her children and the last of her remaining slaves, her last cashmere shawl and her last pair of silk stockings, sailed to San Juan, Puerto Rico. And so came the long years of exile. When she returned to Caracas, already widowed and poorer than a church mouse, she had to live in a hut in a garden that once belonged to the Tovars, who themselves were also ruined. She spent her well-documented old age courteously protesting against the new regime. Truth be told, the Republic was not doing so well. Mama Panchita seized on the slightest opportunity to attribute whatever was going wrong to the revolution and to her former friend and neighbor she assured us she knew better than anyone else and whom she never called "the Liberator" or even Bolívar, but that kid Simón who lived on the Plaza San Jacinto. Whenever he was praised, be it in the press or aloud, she prudently lowered her voice and murmured so that only whoever wanted to hear it could, "I never found him to be special. He didn't even cut a fine figure."

She kept track of the cruel deeds and repeated them to whoever came to dinner, an indifferent audience who did not want to hear about them, heard her out with indifference and answered her ironically. She assured them that Bolivar dipped his pen in the warm blood of a Spaniard when he signed the Treaty of Trujillo. Her nephews and nieces, grandchildren and great-grandchildren, responded that if he ran out of ink it was because until then the Royalists had eaten and drunk everything.

I sadly confess that for the most part, I did not memorize Mama Panchita's bloody, unedited anecdotes that I heard in my childhood, and they are lost forever. The same way I lost others, the memories of my old illustrious aunt. I listened to them like old things, like rain as background noise. It was this second relative, this worthy aunt, the real dreamer, the one I knew personally, an old maiden aunt who could, like Amarilis, had been the silent and chaste and untouched lover of some Lope de Vega or other. I never learned her story, if there was one, but the love stories of unmarried women who did not die young and gloriously like Maria Bashkirtseva[22] are not interesting to anyone. The family does not remember them. Over the chaste heart that withers with its secret, the days fly by like snowflakes and the secret lies hidden beneath the snowdrifts of time. This old dreamer's name was Teresa Soublette. She was my great grandmother's sister and Teresa Aristigueta's niece, one of the nine muses Segur wrote of in his *Memoirs*, and er of Carlos Soublette's youngest daughter, who was one of the generals who liberated Colombia in Boyacá. Soublette's character is, family ties aside, one of the best examples of the leaders of our Independence. But as Paez[23] said about himself, Soublette lived too long. He got caught up in the pettiness of the times lost his reputation.

As head of the Conservative party, as I previously mentioned, he wanted to rule in a Utopia. So convinced were the liberators of the sanctity of their cause that, once the Revolution was over, they believed they had cleansed the whole world. Their candor cost them dearly. Soublette, as President of the Republic, was surrounded by the failure of his idealism, having forever fallen from power, although his hands were clean, he wound up in his last years being cruelly persecuted. This same persecution continued to plague his reputation after his death.

Here's an example: When the opposition in Venezuela published at its own expense the memoirs of the great O'Leary,[24] who as we all know was one of the main leaders in the history of the Independence, they edited out all references to Soublette. And these mutilated editions went to press and continue to circulate since then. This man, who was so prominent, such an important a part of the book of history since he was Bolivar's cousin and his comrade in arms and O'Leary's own brother-in-law! When he died, his remains were not brought to the Pantheon,[25] where even the most minor military officers are buried—not the ones of the independence, but rather what was later called "The Federation." So great were the hatreds between the parties and so bitter the dissent that it led Bolivar to claim, "I plowed the sea."

When I met Aunt Soublette she was handicapped and used a wheelchair. She had sparkling eyes and was intelligent and had her wits about her and complained about the many injustices committed against her father's memory. To enumerate them, she relied on delightful anecdotes that neither she nor her listeners appreciated back then. That illustrated litany was her favorite subject matter. I think she could have complained about some other personal and deeper sentimental injustices that she would not talk about in the same way.

Sitting in her wheelchair, she led the recitation of the rosary, crocheted bedspreads, debated about politics and read unceasingly. From time to time historians consulted her about a fact or came to hear an anecdote about her father. She would recount it in detail and with devotion. Although her intellectual resources were modest, she used her intelligence to not only to teach her servant, a young black woman she had brought from a plantation, to read and write, but she taught her all the French she knew. These lessons took place behind closed doors. Not wanting to be mocked bythree generations of nieces and nephews, she hid her Ollendorf[26] and her accomplice's notebooks in which she wrote her

themes, conjugations and first drafts and to whom she passed on the sacred
thirst for knowledge. Everyone knew her secret but everyone chose to
ignore it. The poor meager French she knew was undoubtedly one of the
keys with which throughout her long life she entered the country of her
dreams. Before she died, so it would not be lost, she humbly shared it with
her black servant.

Another key that opened the door to her dreams was the monthly
correspondence that put her in contact with Colombia, the country sacred
to her idealism. When Venezuela and Colombia were part of the same
country, which we continue to be, despite these disputed and imaginary
boundaries, and this superficial thing we call government and politics, a
branch of the O'Leary Soublette family moved to Bogota. Doña Carolina
O'Leary who was from Bogota, as you all know, and Aunt Teresa
Soublette, from Caracas, although the two of them never met, kept up a
lively correspondence. This correspondence lasted from their childhood
until one of them died, a period of about eighty years. I don't know the
Caracas Carolina O'Leary built up in her yellowed letters. Aunt Teresa
Soublette's Bogota was the imaginary ideal city of arbitrary perfection
whose falseness was obvious to see. How often did her sentimental soul
meet up with the shock of reality when she was faced with the frivolous
and disrespectful and unrefined surroundings of Caracas. She assured us
that in Colombia correctness always reigned, that everyone respected the
memory of General Soublette, that families prayed the rosary without
complaint and interruption; she knew this very well through Doña
Carolina O'Leary's letters. While she gazed at the portrait of her
correspondent surrounded by her children and grandchildren and deduced
all this, she threw it in our faces as she sighed, "In Bogota, my children,
listen up, old people still matter." One day, fate dealt her a cruel blow that
did not damage her deeply- rooted faith. Doña Carolina O'Leary sent
students to visit her in Caracas. Aunt Teresa wanted to entertain them as
was the proper thing to do and she invited them to lunch along with her
nephews who were in the third grade. The day before she had herself
brought into the kitchen, and seated in her wheelchair, and like General
Soublette in Boyacá, she directed all the action necessary to prepare a very
eclectic menu. They prepared *hallacas*, which is what tamales are called in
Caracas, chicken soup, meringue pies and bien me sabe of coco.[27] All in
all they prepared the best and the most exquisite dishes of that golden age,
since like the good daughter of a worthy, she earned money in those days
preparing desserts for parties. When lunchtime arrived, she was all dressed
up in black, wearing her jet necklace, her hair well-brushed, straight and
parted down the middle, she was seated in her wheelchair, ready to be

surrounded by her guests, presiding at the table, she waited for her two guests to arrive, she waited for them in the vestibule, as is the custom in Caracas. Twelve o'clock came and went, twelve thirty, one o'clock, two o'clock, three o'clock and the students were nowhere in sight.. They were probably having cocktails somewhere with friends their own age, and completely forgot the invitation. They "played rabbit", as they say in Paris, when someone fails to show up for an appointment.

At three o'clock, not giving up her dignity in defeat, Aunt Soublette finally gave the signal to serve lunch without the guests. Adolescence is a cruel age. When we arrived at the table victorious and dying of hunger we took advantage of our victory and our spoils like true vandals. "You see, Aunt Teresa, "we said, as we unwrapped our hallacas, "See what your beloved Colombians did? They didn't even respond! They're worse than us! Why do you keep saying that they are so refined, so attentive to their elders and that we should learn from them? Good teachers indeed! It's the same all over."

But she, heroic to the end, hid her disappointment, not wanting to give in. "Something must have happened to those boys, "she declared, "They've had an accident, as sure as I'm alive, and I'm worried for their their poor mothers' sake."

Of course nothing had happened to them. They forgot; it was one of those truly involuntary lapses which, if Freud dug deep into their subconscious, would attribute it to the violent fear of having to spend time with a poor old romantic woman. She also resorted to a Freudian explanation in order to keep her idealism alive. She came up with an explanation and continued to practice her comforting religion: disappointments and the moral isolation of old age were the result of the surroundings. In other places, in Colombia, above all, the dead, elders and all the spiritual values they represented were paid their due respect. Her contagious idealism won the day. As far as I'm concerned, she taught me about Colombia through force of repetition and made me fall in love with it with the same romantic drive and with the same passion for her fondness of the Bogota of her dreams. Aunt Teresa was right. As for her unappreciated lunch, I think I have repeated the moral of it to myself many times: when we want to produce a work of art or something of value, let's not go down the flashy, strange path that may prove to be confrontational, but let us sit down from time to time at the noble criollo table, the nearby traditional table of the countryside. Modest and substantial, it always waits for us in its shady corner like the father's table in the Parable of the Prodigal Son.[28]

Notes

[1] The Gothic Party (Godos) was the Venezuelan conservative party, founded on September 4th 1845. Its supporters followed a liberal economic policy and they did not believe in revolutionary changes.

[2] Saint Teresa of Avila (1515-1582), a Spanish mystic, theologian, Carmelite nun and Catholic saint who wrote her autobiography and *The Interior Castle* and *The Way of Perfection*.

[3] Oviedo y Baños (1671-1738) was a Venezuelan writer. He wrote *The History of the Conquest and Population of the Venezuelan Province* (1723).

[4] St. Pascal (1540-1592) was born in Torrehermosa, Spain. He was known for seeing the apparition of Jesus Christ in the Eucharist. Among the miracles attributed to him was the multiplication of bread for the poor, and the healing of sick people. "Baylon" sounds like "bailar" to dance, in Spanish.

[5] Sor Juana Inés de la Cruz (1648-1695) Mexican self-taught scholar, Baroque poet and nun referred to as the first feminist writer in the New World.

[6] Juan de Castellanos was a Spanish poet, soldier and eventually priest, who settled in Tunja and composed the longest poem in the Spanish language.

[7] Marcelino Menéndez Pelayo (1856-1912) was a Spanish literary critic. He undertook three extensive works that would occupy most of his time until his death; one of them was the works of Lope de Vega (1890-1902).

[8] Luis de Góngora (1561-1627) was a Spanish Baroque lyric poet. His style is characterized by what was called culteranismo, also known as Gongorism. Culteranismo existed in stark contrast with conceptismo, another movement of the Baroque period which is characterized by a witty style, game with words, simple vocabulary, and conveying multiple meanings in as few words as possible.

[9] A Roman Catholic reform movement of the 17th and 18th centuries based on the theological views of Cornelis Jansen, who maintained that there can be no good act without divine will or the grace of God.

[10] Antonio Ulloa (1716.1795) was a Spanish writer and scientist. Jorge Juan (1713-1773) was a Spanish sailor and scientist.

[11] Mantuanos were the members of the criollo plantation aristocracy in the eighteenth century and these members of society wore capes or *mantas* whenever they went out.

[12] Ferdinand VII (1784-1833) was twice King of Spain: in 1808 and from 1813-1833. In 1808 the War of Independence broke out in Latin America. Spain was bankrupt, and the government was unstable because the king changed ministers every few months. He was taken prisoner by Napoleon, but restored in 1814. After his fourth marriage, to Maria Christina Bourbon of the Two Sicilies in 1829, he was persuaded by his wife to set aside the law of succession of Philip V, which gave preference to males of the family over females. His marriage had brought two daughters. The change in the order of succession established by his dynasty in Spain angered a large part of the nation and led to a civil war, the Carlist Wars. Under his reign Spain saw the loss of her possessions in the New World.

[13] Louis Philippe, Comte de Ségur (1753-1830), was a French diplomat and historian who fought in the American War of Indepedence.

[14] Amarilis was an anonymous Peruvian poet of the 16th century. This poet is thought to be a woman because of her only poem, *Epistola a Belardo* (1621), was sent to her great admirer Felix Lope de Vega. Amaryllis was also a botanic name taken from a shepherdess in Virgil's pastoral *Eclogues* and a given name for girls.

[15] Felix Lope de Vega (1562-1635) was one of the most important poets and dramatists of the Spanish Golden Age.

[16] Aristeigueta, Urdaneta, Soublette, Mendoza and Tovar were colonial last names of the Creole aristocracy. Teresa de la Parra had descendants from these families. Doña Francisca Tovar was de la Parra's great grandmother and Bolívar's neighbor and friend.

[17] Alexander von Humboldt (1769-1859) was a German naturalist and explorer who travelled extensively through Latin America and described it from a modern, scientific point of view and published his travels in four volumes over twenty-one years, *Le voyage aux régions equinoxes du Nouveau Continent (*1799-1804).

[18] In the game "la cebollita" children form a line and grab each other's waist. The first person in the line holds a pole and the rest pull each other until the child holding the pole falls down.

[19] A commercial company founded on September 25th, 1728, whose purpose was to monopolize Caracas province's commerce with Spain. The company operated from 1730 until 1785 and had much influence in the development of the economy and politics of the colony.

[20] Francisco de Miranda (1750-1816) was a Venezuelan general who was considered the precursor of the American emancipation from the Spanish Empire.

[21] Orange, "naranja "in Spanish, is pronounced in Latin American Spanish with the fricative glottal phoneme /h/ while in Spain it is pronounced with the fricative palate-alveolar phoneme /ʒ/ as in garage. In Latin American Spanish Francisco is pronounced with the fricative alveolar /s/ while in Spain it is pronounced with the fricative palate-alveolar /ʃ/ as in shoe.

[22] María Konstantinovina Bashkirtseva (1858-1884) was a Russian painter. She was also a famous writer known for her *Intimate Diary*.

[23] José Antonio Paéz Herrera (1790-1873) was a soldier and politician who became the president of Venezuela on three occasions (1830-1835), (1839-1843), and (1861-1863). He was one of the most distinguished precursors of Venezuelan emancipation.

[24] Daniel Florencio O'Leary (1801-1854) was an Irish militant and politician. In 1817 he sailed to America to join the fight for independence. In 1831, after Bolívar's death, General O'Leary traveled to Jamaica where he wrote his memoirs, which were then published by his son Simón Bolívar O'Leary, as *Memories of General O'Leary*.

[25] The Pantéon Nacional de Caracas is a building in the northern edge of the old town. It was originally built as a church, but is now used as a famous burial place. The entire central nave is dedicated to Simón Bolívar, with the altar's place taken by the hero's bronze sarcophagus, while lesser luminaries are relegated to the

aisles. The national pantheon's vault is covered with 1930s paintings depicting scenes from Bolívar's life, and the huge crystal chandelier glittering overhead was installed in 1883 on the centennial of his birth. Teresa de la Parra died in Madrid in 1936 and was buried in the Almudena Cemetery there. In 1947, her remains were brought to the Parra Sanojo chapel in Caracas, and later moved to the Pantheon in 1989, the centennial of her birth.

[26] Heinrich Gottfried Ollendorf (1803-1865), was a German grammarian and language educator who helped develop the first fully modern oral system of teaching how t o read, write and speak a living language based on the intuitive method and oral practice.

[27] *Bien me sabe* is a typical Venezuelan sweet made of coconut, eggs and other ingredients.

[28] The Prodigal Son, also known as the *Lost Son*, is one of the best known parables of Jesus. The parable begins with a young man, the younger of two sons, who asks his father to give him his share of the estate. The parable continues by describing how the younger son travels to a distant country and wastes all his money in wild living. When a famine strikes, he becomes desperately poor and is forced to take work as a swineherd. When he reaches the point of envying the pigs he is looking after, he finally comes to his senses and returns home.

CHAPTER NINE

THE THIRD LECTURE: INDEPENDENCE

Before we look at women's half-hidden but decisive influence during the Revolution or the War of Independence, I invite you to imagine the time. Let's look at it as though it's a movie. The outside view will reflect more vividly what is taking place in the soul. Let's imagine any street in any of our colonial cities—they are so alike! It's the end of the 18th century. It's dusk. On both sides of the street the eaves adorn the roofs with their red tiles. From time to time water from the roof tiles drips down to the gutter. The gutters and the eaves hang so low that from the window you can reach them with your hand. The wide windows have thick bars like a jail. After every three or four windows there is a nail-studded door. This is all the facades have to offer. The street is cobblestoned.. Grass grows between the thick rocks. It also grows on the tiles of the roofs. Sometimes it leaps up and attaches itself to a gutter. Lifting your eyes to the heavens, the sky is clear. The temperature is delightful and beyond the roof tiles you can see a steeple and the mountains appear in the distance.

Slaves dressed in white carrying a sedan chair are walking down the street. They approach. They pass by. A mantuana -- you can hardly see her face—is sitting in the chair, dressed in a black cloak and mantilla. She is a high-ranking lady who can only venture out into the street wrapped up in a cloak, from which we get the word "mantuana." It's late. The clock is about to strike seven. The mantuana has dined and recited the rosary; her male slaves have removed the tablecloths and cleared the table and the female slaves have put the household children to bed with songs and stories. Rocking with the gait of the bearers, the mantuana turns the corner. She is on the way to a gathering at the home of the Marques or Count, who is her first or fourth cousin. He's the richest man in the city. The street is empty for a while.

Now at the same corner the bearers just turned, a Capuchin monk appears. He is on his way to confess a shut-in. His sandals rustle and the rosary beads click with each step he takes. Once again the street is silent for a while. Now the only night watchman in the city pauses on the corner and cries with a plaintive sing-song voice, "Turn on the lights." You can hear his voice from corner to corner, "the lights, the lights," until it finally fades into an echo on the outskirts of town. Soon, the first window opens and a bare-armed black woman with a round neckline that shines along the border of her white camisole lifts her arm to hang a lighted oil lamp on one of the rungs of the bars of the window. Nightfall approaches. And the line of lamps illuminates the street that can't be left dark on moonless nights. Since the property belongs to everyone, they all help to keep it lit.

A mantuano approaches. He is young. He treads lightly. His shoes also click and his velvet pants make a sound with each step. He is also attending the Marques's "chocolate." He wears a white wig, a silk vest, a lace cravat, hose, and low-heeled shoes with a silver buckle. He carries books in his arms. He hides them from the civil authorities and the representatives of the Inquisition. One of these books, the most dangerous and sought-after of all, is a pamphlet called *The Declaration of the Rights of Man*. They are going to read it out loud at the Marques' salon.

The mantuano got it from Granada Nariño's[1] hand, who, hiding in his house in Bogota, translated it, and had it published and circulated from Mexico to Tierra del Fuego. For this, Nariño was arrested and sent to jail, and his goods were confiscated. Tonight's reading might cause the mantuano the same fate. What to do? What can be done? With this treasure, this dangerous object in his pocket, he happily walks on. Along with the treasure, he carries an illustrious name that history may or may not remember. Maybe not. Perhaps like the mantuana, the friar and the slaves he is condemned to an obscure death. His anonymous blood will flow in the torrent fed by failed conspiracies, like Gual y España's,[2] which will flow until it is finally staunched twenty-five years later at Ayacucho.[3]

The mantuano has turned the corner. Night has fallen. A peacock's cry can be heard among the trees. Two blocks further down, the Marques's gathering behind closed doors lasts until midnight. With minor variations, this scene repeats itself in cities that are ripe for independence, be they in viceroyalties, captaincies or simply provinces. During the second half of the century, the criollo noble aristocracy came into its own and found its spirit. Almost all the young men studied in universities in Mexico City or Lima or Bogota, which is where the most famous ones were. Some went to Europe.

If the rich, educated and proud criollos attacked the king's authority from afar, they were provoked by the *chapetones* or Spanish rulers who are often brutal and don't adapt to the circumstances. The rulers only think of enriching themselves at the expense of the criollos, who were able rulers of the land they owned. Sometimes, out of spite, the *chapetones* allied themselves with the dark-skinned population. Partial to them, they extend privileges to them instead of to the white criollos, who are their natural enemies. Feeling humiliated, their pride hurt, the criollos are bitter. The mantuanas stand out in this group of malcontents. They are the standard-bearers of this deep-seated hatred that is about to raise its voice in protest. Just as they showed during Independence, beneath their languid exterior they have fiery souls ready for uprising, sacrifice and heroic action. The secret clubs or gathering places where only men conspire do not yet exist. In the meantime, women attend these gatherings, and they are exposed to new ideas, and to the seeds of revolution growing behind closed doors in the salons and patios of the illustrious households. There, during these gatherings they inspire the men with their personal observations and their passionate words. One of them reports the latest display of insolent superiority that took the Captain General by surprise during High Mass on Sunday. Another remarks on the rudeness of some *chapeton* or other who failed to give way to her so she left the cathedral on foot and made her way across the plaza on her way home escorted by her slave, her chair and prayer carpet.

A lot has been said about the favorable effect of the expulsion of the Jesuits from America on the revolution. Women were the active agents of this influence. An example comes to mind. The count of Aranda, Charles III's minister, with his extraordinary reforms—outstanding for the spirit of the times—thought to apply them to Spanish colonial rule, unaware of the sentimental catastrophe it would cause first of all, and later the political catastrophe that he would unleash in America with the departure of the Jesuits. As in all exiles, it was accompanied by the confiscation of goods, and the expulsion of the Jesuits resulted in shattering, heart-rending scenes that were not easily forgotten, especially during that time of heightened sentimentalism when life revolved around the church and the convent. For the most part, those exiled were criollos, brothers and sons, and as they watched them embark, their relatives saw them leave forever as they headed toward a kind of death that awaited them.

It was a dark time for the Society of Jesus. They were rejected everywhere and the Pope would soon suppress the order. They were able directors of conscience, as they had always been, and at the same time they spread culture and provided all kinds of moral and material services. The Jesuits in the colonies had power and influence and ruled over the domain of the soul, especially the souls of women. In them they instilled the inseparable concepts of Father, Homeland and King. These three concepts formed part of the same creed. The concepts of Homeland and

King were synonymous with submission to Spain. When the king's minister expelled the Jesuits and persecuted them, the trinity was dissolved and the anarchy of the schism spread in women's consciousness. On the other hand, weighed down by their suffering, the exiled Jesuits, aware that they were criollos, began from afar to be the best active agents of the independence movement.

Here in America, women continued to mourn for their absent children, their brothers and the directors of their consciences. The other religious orders were ill-equipped to exercise spiritual direction since they were more subtle, and to a certain degree were responsible for the expulsion. They were never able to fill the Society of Jesus's void. Deprived of their spiritual directors, feminine piety—without losing its outward form—lost the rigor and austerity of Spanish Catholic discipline. Once released from its source, religion underwent the same transformation as the races. It became creolized. It, too, rocked in the hammock, fanned itself lazily, and thought about pleasant things that didn't mortify the flesh too much. The heat of hellfire diminished until it became a sort of uncomfortable tropical heat, bearable given a little rest, patience and conversation. Mortal sin became a vague abstraction and the dreaded God of the Inquisition became more like a strict plantation overseer, a father and godfather to his slaves, someone who gave gifts and was generous to the point of sponsoring and hosting the plantation's parties.

This comfortable, half pagan Catholicism isn't my invention. Perhaps it is unknown here in Colombia, except for the highest classes of society. It still exists in the majority of Latin American countries, and not just among people who mixed it with Indian and African fetishism. It would make for an interesting study. In Caracas, for example, I knew a dear friend whose house was full of images of saints. They usually had candles or oil lamps burning before them. She was pious and this is how she observed the Church's commandments: she went to mass on Mondays because on Sundays the church was too crowded; the crowds got in her way, they smelled bad, and they distracted her from her devotions with their comings and goings. She scrupulously observed Lent—not on Fridays when the throng of cooks left early to choose the best fish, but rather some other day of the week when without too much trouble you could buy a good, first-class fish. Her profession of faith was as follows (I have to warn you about its anticlerical animosity): "I believe in God and the saints but not in priests." If we were to examine the roots of "I don't believe in priests," we would find without a doubt the same protests as those of the Creole women of the eighteenth century who through their spirit of faith and opposing spirit never accepted secular clergy or other religious orders, who in their grieving conscience could not replace their beloved and mourned Jesuits.

During Holy Week, the holy images, the rosary and Mass took place, occupying the same space but without the rules of Council, theology or Latin. On their own, Creole women resolved difficult matters of casuistry and soon came up with their personal creed. It made itself very much at home and helped protect and disseminate Montesquieu, Voltaire, Rousseau and the other French encyclopedists's works. In a manner of speaking, it was a way to provoke the insolent *chapetones* who prohibited these works and the questioning they led to; that was enough. Secretly passing the books among themselves was a sport. Reading them was a delight, not so much because of their content, but rather due to the fact that they were prohibited by an authority that had no influence on their conscience. When all was said and done, it was inevitable that the contagion spread by the French Revolution and aided by Spain itself would expand as America responded to changes and reforms that were needed for its criollo dignity.

As for women's complicity in hiding, keeping secret, reading and circulating prohibited books, there is an important letter. It was written from Paris by the Chilean revolutionary or patriot Antonio Rojas. This was in the year 1787, that is, twenty years after the Jesuits were expelled. A young, beautiful Chilean woman whose name we don't know wrote to Rojas asking him for information and permission to open some boxes of books he left with her before he departed from Santiago de Chile. Rojas wrote from Paris: "What information and permission do you want? Aren't you the owner of the boxes?" And then he lists the titles of the books and the names of their authors with biting irony as if to arouse his friend's curiosity. "There are some folio volumes that are an example of the wretched *Encyclopedic Dictionary* which they say is worse than typhoid. Item: the works of an old man who lives in Geneva whom some call an apostle and other label the Antichrist; item: the works of a nobody who hits us over the head with his Julia,[4] item: the charming natural history by Buffon...." And the list goes on.

The attraction of the books depended on the language they were written in, and it became fashionable for the young to learn French. The ones who knew it declaimed Corneille's tragedies. The references to Tancrède fired their imaginations. "Injustice at last gives way to Independence," and the passionate Creoles will soon play the lofty roles Racine's heroines played, not in the theater, but in real life, facing death.

I don't mean to eulogize the heroines of the Independence like Pola Salavarietta,[5] who knew how to fight like a man and was shot to death and bravely died with dignity like those in the executions of May 2[6] and like the outstanding women of the French Revolution.

History has gathered the names that are familiar to everyone and will become more famous as the idea of nations and the fatherland grows stronger. It is the anonymous women, the admirable women who were working behind the scenes, I want to praise affectionately, as their memories deserve. During the three centuries they worked in the shadows, busy as bees; nameless, they left their gifts of wax and honey. With their sacrifice they wove the patriarchal spirit of the Creole family, and lending their voices to the language, they carved it with the cadences and sweetness of all their dreams. When Independence arrived, a gust of collective heroism awakens them. Propelled by it they flow through history like a river. It forms a mass, a volume of anonymous moving waves. One of the loftiest and most symbolic of these historic moments is referred to as "The Emigration in Venezula."[7]

It was in 1814. The Treaty of Trujillo[8] had been signed. That simply means that to be a patriot or a Creole was a crime one was willing to die for before the Spaniards, and to be Spanish or a Royalist was a crime that had the same consequences before the Creoles. The latter tried their prisoners by having the accused pronounce the word "naranja." If they pronounced the word with a "j" they would be shot immediately. The Spanish advanced on Caracas from all sides. They had just returned from beheading the inhabitants of Valencia and promised they would do the same to the inhabitants of Caracas unless they immediately surrendered. Caracas was still recovering from the wreckage of the earthquake of 1812. Bolívar lacked the resources to defend himself and he left the city to recruit an army. The entire population, not wanting to fall victim to the old regime, decided to march behind Bolívar. There were forty thousand people, mostly women and children, since the men were away fighting the war. Only the cloistered nuns and the Bishop remained in the devastated and deserted city. Crossing most of Venezuela, dead with hunger, weary, thirsty, the emigrants walked across the deserted plains under the heat of the tropical sun. On horseback, at the head of that walking and moribund multitude, Bolívar, like a new Moses, led them haphazardly, with no more hope than the faith he and his followers shared. After innumerable attacks and many adventures they finally arrived and Bolívar got an army together, and of the forty thousand women and children who left Caracas only a small number of them remained. The rest died of hunger, or of heatstroke along the way. Bands of buzzards hovered over the footsteps where the caravans had traveled.

Taking into account the other leaders of the Independence movement, besides Bolívar, whose life was the most important from his birth to his death, we can very easily appreciate the very important role women played in the Liberator's life and their definitive contribution to his character. A great lover, as he himself declared, only the women he loved passionately influenced his tastes, his personality and his decisions. Simón Rodríguez,[9] who was his teacher during his adolescence, also influenced him as he was paradoxical, idealistic and visionary and stood out from his contemporaries. From his black nursemaid, Matea, to Manuelita Sánz,[10] his last lover, Bolívar could not act without the influence of a woman who motivated and consoled him during his periods of melancholy and could lend him another pair of eyes so he could discover his true nature.

Orphaned in his childhood, left in the care of the slave Matea, Bolívar hears and sees for the first time the heartfelt poetry of rural life, noble and beloved in his homeland. At his plantation in the valley of Aragua, the typical Creole plantation, the almost- biblical plantation, the slaves are an extension of the family and their last names are Bolívar or Palacios, the same as their owner, who is the god and father of them all.

At dusk, having finished her work in the fields, Matea carries the young Simón to the slaves' quarters or patio. There, as night falls, under the sky and the ghostly lights of the wil o' the wisps, he listens to scary ghost stories an old black man recites. The subject of these stories is almost always the terrible crimes of the tyrant Aguirre,[11] the rebel conqueror and bandit, whose wandering soul still haunts through a light that blinks on and off but is much bigger than the firefly's. It's a traveling light. Sometimes he appears in the fields; other times he climbs to the top of huge tree you can see from the hacienda's hall over there in the distance that's called Guerre's Rain tree, "Saman[12] de Guerre." Thirty years later under the shade of that same legendary saman of his childhood—though the tree is old and gnarled, it is still alive today and still holds the soul of the conqueror who died in a sinful state—beneath this same saman Bolívar and his soldiers camped one historic night.

The much-honored Matea would live to be one hundred, and Bolívar, the future liberator, who was a difficult child, loved her tenderly. He would go on to become the disciple of his relative the lawyer Saenz, to Father Andujar, to the young and famous Andres Bello,[13] who did not leave the least trace in his spirit, and did not influence him in the least. Finally Bolívar falls under the tutelage of Simón Rodríguez, his mentor and good friend, whose eccentric, uncommon idealism would ignite Bolívar's soul and lend wings to his temperament.

The friendship of Rodríguez or the love of a woman—be it Teresa del Toro, Josefina Machado or Manuelita—was where Bolívar always found either the respite or the stimulus he needed for his exceptional undertakings.

Before we can call upon this group of inspiring women, we must paint a picture of Rodríguez. He always comes first. This Simón Rodríguez is the prototype of a man who comes close to being a genius without achieving it, is passionate about the people he is close to, and a joy to those who know him near or far. Wild-haired philosophers like Saint Simón—generous, paradoxical and original—lend spice to life. They redeem humanity from its avarice and egoism, which are the vices of cowards. His restlessness discovers new aspects in the most common of things and his presence is always accompanied by comical and unexpected circumstances. It was natural, then, for Bolívar, whose personality was well-balanced, to have dealings with his namesake professor Rodríguez who was, as we shall see, the madman *par excellence.*

Rodríguez was born in Caracas during the second half of the nineteenth century and his real name was not Rodríguez but Carreño,[14] from the same family as Teresa Carreño, the renowned pianist and author of *Urbanidad*. Rodríguez dedicated himself to philosophy when he was fourteen. Orphaned, he fought tooth and nail with his older brother, and having nothing in common with him, he changed his last name. He ceased being Simón Carreño and became Simón Rodríguez. He got a job on a boat sailing to Spain, disembarked in Cadiz, and without any resources save for his thirst for knowledge and his own two feet, during the next five years he walked through Europe. He lived in Paris on the eve of the French Revolution and breathed in its atmosphere, discovered Rousseau and decided from that day on to convert all humanity by preaching the love of nature.

After five years of travelling through Europe on foot he returned to Caracas, got married and within the next year-and-a-half he had two daughters to whom he gave the plant names Maize and Tulip, in accordance with Fabre d'Eglantine's calendar.[15] He then declared, "I don't want to be like trees that send their roots in one place but I want to be like the air, water and sunlight that unceasingly run free." And he returned to his wanderings, abandoning his wife and his two plants, who from that point on meant nothing to him. His last pubic meditation was published, a pamphlet titled, "Reflexions on the Flaws Vitiating the Reading and Writing School for Children in Caracas and the Means for Achieving its Reform and a New Establishment." As a result, and due to responses to this pamphlet, he acquired a reputation as a pedagogue and he looked for a disciple to practice Rousseau's theories as stated in *Emile*.[16] He would soon find his disciple in the young Simón Bolívar, to whose education he was entrusted.

Rodríguez was happy that the child met the indispensable requirements his Emile needed: he was rich, he was an orphan, he was noble and he was sane. In Rodríguez's opinion, he himself met the requirements of a teacher, which were that he was prudent, young, with a noble soul and an independent mind. Concerning this last requirement, he naturally did not include his wife and his two poor plants. To the end that his disciple remained in "his natural state"—since, as he said, "wisdom is connected to athletic prowess"—he retired with him to the country, taught him physical exercises, and as for the rest, he devoted himself to the difficult task of not teaching him anything at all. He would learn nothing. Thanks to Simón Rodríguez's methods, when Bolívar sailed to Europe, he wrote illegible letters written in a deplorable style full of misspellings while he was on board. But also thanks to Rodríguez he was already the untiring walker, the horseman and the swimmer no one could compete against.

Busy with Gual y España's suit, and persecuted by the Spanish authorities, Rodríguez abruptly interrupted his projects *a la* John Jacob Rousseau and brought the education of his Emile to an end; he was exiled and resumed his erratic life in Europe. Botanist, philosopher, physical scientist, pedagogue and businessman, as needed, he traveled widely through Germany, Russia, and Turkey, learned many languages and was deeply moved when he came across the story of Robinson Crusoe and decided to honor him. He would no longer be named Simón Rodríguez but rather Simón Robinson. He met up once again with Bolívar in Rome in 1805, where he would learn of Bolívar's epiphany and one afternoon, one of those marvelous Rome afternoons just before sunset, walking and talking on the Sacro Monte (on the Aventine Hill), the two are so caught up praising each other that Bolívar is transfixed, and the next moment, in a romantic delirium, turns the city of Rome and the setting sun into his witnesses and takes his famous vow to liberate Spanish America. A few months after Bolívar's departure Rodríguez remained in Europe and master and disciple would not see each other for another twenty years.

In 1824, attracted to the fame of one who was already known far and wide as the Liberator, Rodríguez returns to America to found, in the nations freed by his disciple, a great communist state in which only equality and happiness reign. To begin with, he has a project: to found an educational establishment. Bolívar lends him the necessary funds. Simón Rodríguez or Simón Robinson travels to Upper Peru and opens his establishment, promotes it, and enrolls many students and inaugurates it by walking through it entirely naked for the purpose of preaching and promoting the return of natural man. The students' families are outraged, they remove the students and threaten to sue him for immorality, and following the uproar, the school goes bust. With what he has left, he opens a sail shop in Chile and ends his days as a poor old man in the Peruvian town of Paita,on the shore. There, coincidentally, his neighbor will turn out to be Miguelita Sáenz, that madwoman and Bolívar's other great friend we will talk about later, the old paralyzed woman everyone in town continued to call "The Liberator." What would these two eccentric old people talk about in their declining years? When in 1864 Simón Robinson died, twenty years after his disciple Bolívar, the elderly Miguelita Sáenz took up a collection among the town's gentry to give her poor philosopher friend a decent burial.

Bolívar travelled to Spain for the first time when he was sixteen. It was there that he found his first and truest love. The unexpected departure of professor Rodríguez interrupted his studies. In order to complete them, or rather to begin them formally, his tutor sent him to Madrid to the home of Bartolomé Palacios, who was in Spain at the time and was the brother of Doña Concepción, Bolívar's mother. Once he arrived at his uncle's house in Madrid, Bolívar headed for the Royal Palace. The circumstances: Don Bartolomé Palacios was the close friend of Mallo, the Grenadine, who as an attractive and proud young man was in turn a close friend of none other than the Queen, María Luisa. Godoy, the all-powerful minister at the time, did not approve of this friendship, which was subject to gossip.

Meanwhile, despite Godoy, a group of Creoles introduced by Mallo frequented Charles IV's court. Bolívar was among them and he often played ball with the princes, and though he was a shy adolescent, he had good powers of observation. He observed the royal family's situation, which was not edifying, to be sure. From his home in Caracas, like others, he had worshipped them as though they were some kind of Divine Emanation.

If you examine this closely, from the details you can arrive at this conclusion: that Bolívar's first stay in Europe was a sad one, depressing and frustrating as far as he was concerned. As a meticulous and haughty Creole, his self-esteem often suffered. Despite the legend, which would like us to see him victoriously striking blows at the Prince of Asturias, the future Ferdinand VII, there is a side of him that is more human, and more interesting. Among the people in Madrid his own age Bolívar passed as someone from the Indies, a provincial who didn't attract attention, but that was not true. Adolescence is a cruel time. Unaccustomed to the environment and the surroundings, he was at an unthankful stage. He was on the small side, slender, his voice full of criollo sweetness and sing-song.

Perhaps his leadership qualities were treated ironically or were ridiculed. They made fun of him because he was different: his attitude, his accent, and his mannerisms. It is common at that age and common to those people who, because of their inflexibility or misunderstanding, cannot dig below the surface. Who hasn't felt at some point in their lives, when they moved to a new place and felt ill-suited to it and had to make adjustments, the object of a chilly reception due to reasons they don't understand? Bolívar did not shine in Madrid. On the contrary, compared to what he would later become in Paris, the worldly elegant man who lived on the Rue Vivienne, the poor adolescent who lived in Madrid was not happy with himself. This negative feeling and his disappointment with Queen María Luisa must have influenced his calling and determined the direction his life took in 1802.

Don Bartalomé Palacios left Madrid, and Bolívar moved out of his house. He shut himself up in the house of a compatriot, the old Marquis of Ustariz, a cultured man who awakened his soul to learning and provided him access to many books. Ensconced and isolated in Ustariz's household, Bolívar was the prototype of the typical cultured 18th century Creole. Bolívar studied so hard he got sick. In the isolation of his books, a romantic passion was growing in his inner life. Soon after arriving in Spain, while passing through Bilbao, he met a beautiful young lady form Caracas named María Teresa, the daughter of Don Bernardo Rodríguez del Toro, and the niece of the Marques of the same name, a magnate and leader of the Independence from Caracas. Bolívar was in love with the sweet Teresa who was still in Bilbao while he was in Madrid, and for many months he did nothing but study and think about her. A trivial incident would soon change his life and accelerate the pace of his romantic love to the point of violent passion.

One afternoon, riding his horse near the Toledo Bridge, two policemen detained him for no apparent reason. Bolívar, who was living with his tutor at the time, was far from wealthy, but nevertheless he wore shiny buttons on his lace cuffs. One of Godoy's decrees prohibiting wearing these had just gone into effect. The policeman detained him for the infraction. The real reason was that Godoy suspected he was carrying love letters from Mallo to the Queen. An indignant Bolívar refused to obey. The authorities were rude to him, Bolívar got off his horse, took out his sword and a fight ensued, and he could have suffered serious consequences unless he left Madrid immediately, which is what everyone told him to do.

It's interesting to note that with Bolívar's case, this marks the third time an inhabitant of the Indies was brought to the attention of the authorities of the Spanish Court for wearing an item of luxury. When Fernando Pizarro, the conqueror of Peru, arrived from America to defend his brother's case, he wore a multi-colored headdress. The austere Philip II, who usually dressed all in black, first reprimanded him for wearing the headdress and then refused him his claim. He was declared a rebel and wound up spending twenty years in jail. A similar incident happened to Jimenez de Quesada the poet-conqueror of New Granada. He came to court in America wearing the gold fringes he felt he deserved to wear, and which attested to his glory and fame and were legitimate. Quesada was escorted out with shouts of "the madman, the madman" and to the detriment of his reputation and he was not granted his petition.

Furious and humiliated, Bolívar headed for Bilbao and don Bernardo del Toro's house, and immediately declared that he wanted to marry his daughter, leave as soon as possible, and never return to Spain. Don Bernardo tried to calm him down, offered to fix things for him and asked him to wait awhile before getting married. Bolívar, meanwhile, was seeing María Teresa, which put an end to his studies and to his black moods in Madrid. All the fieriness of his lofty spirit was directed toward his fiancée. It is a grand passion. The rest of the world disappears from view, and he can't live, can't breathe, and wants nothing else but Teresa. Doesn't she make up for the hostile climate and his longing for his quiet house in Caracas and the lovely fields of the Valley of Aragua? There, among his planted fields, his cattle and his slaves, isn't he more-or-less a god? To marry Teresa as soon as possible and flee with her to his San Mateo plantation as soon as he can, this is the only thing his soul desires. The long months of waiting don Bernardo imposed were a torture tempered only by the hope of the marriage and the journey back.

Bolívar was nineteen when he married. At the height of his happiness, he sailed for La Guaira and his dream came true and he lived in San Mateo by the side of his beloved Teresa. But like the old song says, "Dreams of love last but a day; the sorrows of love last a lifetime." Bolívar would sing these verses and would cry for a long time. Eight months after their wedding, Maria Teresa died of a virulent fever (yellow fever) and her funeral cortege made its way through the halls of Bolívar's house.

It exploded in Bolívar's soul. Teresa's death made him despair and unlike before, when he wanted to fill his world with passion, now he longed to fill it with pain. In this frenzied state, not knowing what to do, he returns to Spain. He brings with him some mementos Maria Teresa's family gave him and returns to a place to mourn where they will commiserate with him and share in his desperation. But little by little it dawns on him that the family doesn't provide the solace his pain seeks, and he finds don Bernardo's home suffocating. In his quest for excitement, he thinks back on his tutor Simón Rodríguez. He remembers how many times they walked through the fields of his plantation and planned to tour the most famous cities in Europe together. Only Rodríguez the visionary would be able to understand him. He sought him out. He arrived in Paris and inquired as to Rodríguez's whereabouts. Where is Rodríguez? Where is Rodríguez? But no one knows. One day, at last, a friend he's just met named Carlos Montujar tells him that Simón Rodríguez doesn't exist. But in his place he may find Simón Robinson, who is in Vienna working as a chemist in a learned German's laboratory.

Bolívar immediately takes off in search of his beloved friend. Rodríguez, transformed into Robinson, is surrounded by formulas, salts, acids and test tubes. But alas, poor Bolívar, with his poem of infinite love he wishes to move the world with, would be subjected to another disappointment. Robinson hears him out but hardly commiserates. What? The death of one person? It's a natural occurrence. Nothing is left to the desperate one except his own death. And that is what he did. Robinson rescued him from his own death in a colorful and surprising manner. Let's hear how Bolívar tells how he sank to the depths and was resurrected. He does this in a letter addressed to his cousin Fanny de Villars.[17] In the pathetic tone of this charming letter, a document that describes Bolívar's romantic education, both he and Robinson come alive—not as historical characters, but in the way they will be written about later.

"I was expecting a lot," Bolívar writes in 1804 as he describes his meeting with Robinson in Vienna, "I was counting on the companionship of my friend, my childhood companion, the confidant of all my joys and sorrows, the mentor whose advice and consolation meant the world to me." Alas, in this case his friendship proved fruitless. Now MR loved only science. "I found him busily working in a learned German's laboratory. I hardly saw him one hour a day. When I met him he hastily said, 'My friend, have fun, get together with friends your own age, go to the theater, you need distractions. It's the only way you'll be cured.' I understood then that something was lacking in this man, the wisest, and most virtuous and doubtless the most extraordinary man one could ever hope to meet. Because of my suffering I contracted consumption and the doctors told me I would die. And that's what I wanted to do...."

After describing the ups and downs of his heartbreak and romance, he continues to tell his cousin how he came back to life. "One night," he said, "weak as I was, I could still carry on a conversation, and Rodríguez sat down next to my bedside. He spoke to me with the affection he always showed me during the most critical times of my life. He spoke sweetly and explained it was madness to give up and wish to die in the middle of my journey. He taught me that there are other things in life than a woman's love and I could be happy dedicating myself to science or giving in to my ambition. He talked me into it like he had always done. The next evening, I imagined what I could do—be it science or liberating nations. I called him and said, yes, without a doubt, I will recover and launch myself into my career, but I needed to be rich. I can't achieve anything without the necessary funds, and far from being rich, I am poor and sick and worn out. Oh, Rodríguez, I prefer to die! And I held out my hand, shook his hand hard and begged him to let me die in peace.

"Suddenly, I saw a change in Rodríguez's aspect. He raised his eyes and hands to the heavens and with an inspired voice asked, 'My friend if you were rich, would you agree to live? Say something, answer me.' I remained resolute. I had no idea what he meant: I answered yes. 'Ah,' he exclaimed 'then we are saved. What is money for? Well, then, Simón Bolívar, you are rich, you inherited four million.'"[18] He found out that while he was sick an uncle had left him an inheritance. Busy with his test tubes, Simón Robinson forgot to deliver such trivial news. Bolívar leapt from his bed upon hearing it. He was healthy and well. The injection of four million cured him. But it only cured his body. His spirit, like the old song says, was still sorrowful.

Simón Robinson wasn't mistaken when he said Bolívar's four million were going to be useful. It brought him to his cousin Fanny de Villars, his great inspiration, the one who showed him the way, revealed his character to him and sometimes supplied him with small details that gave him confidence that spread like a great fire within Bolívar. Fanny's love was not the kind of passion that absorbs and cancels. No. It was temperate and cheerful, a Paris love. Fanny was more than a lover, friend, counselor and inspiration. Thanks to her connections and her way with people she lent Bolívar a hand and put him on a kind of pedestal, that of Colombian Paris at the time. From there he contemplated the times, like one contemplates a panorama, takes control of his strength, lays out his future and takes flight. When Bolívar speaks of his love for Teresa del Toro he assures us that had she lived, he never would have stepped outside the bounds of that idyllic adolescence. The Daphnis and Chloe[19] of the Valley of Aragua, they would have ended up like Philemon and Baucus of the San Mateo plantation. Dedicated to his marriage, Bolívar affirms that by the end of his life he would have aspired perhaps to be the mayor of the neighboring town. Some might reject this assertion. I like to believe it because it seems plausible and it is sweet to think that while living a monotonous life, when we least suspect it, we meet a pleasant soul we fall in love with and makes us forget ourselves and leads us to walk with the herd.

Fanny de Villars was an Aristigueta on her mother's side and therefore was Bolívar's cousin. She was married to a Frenchman, the Count of Villars. In Paris she had, like years later that enchanting Cuban Creole did, a salon. Beauharnais,[20] Madame Recamier,[21] of Tama, of Madame de Stael,[22] of Humboldt[23] and Talleyrand,[24] all of them attended Fanny's salon, Fanny the beautiful Parisian Creole. All invited her, and all praised her. Capping the convulsions of the French Revolution, under the stepped up rhythm of Napoleon, Romanticism was being born. It was a gust that swept from here, from America, brought over by Chateaubriand[25] and to which the extraordinary voyage of Baron von Humboldt to the equatorial regions gave new impulse and wings. The moment could not have been more propitious for Bolívar, the Romantic prototype par excellence. Besides having the fire and grandiloquence typical of Romanticism, his background, his fineness and premature sadness, he was the incarnation of the hero who recently arrived from the American jungle. Seeing him arrive from Germany so young, sad, and rich, Fanny sized him up with a glance and decided to open doors for him. After having been Rousseau's Emile thanks to Simón Rodríquez, thanks to Fanny, he was about to become Chateaubriand's René. All was contributing to the transformation. Installed in an elegant apartment on Rue Vivienne, Teresa del Torro's widower became, thanks to Fanny's advice, one of the most refined and interesting young men in Paris, the kind who strolled through the Palais Royal, heard Talma, repeated Brunet's play on words, had their portraits painted by David, fell in platonic love with Madame Recamier or Paulina Borghese.[26]

Prodigal, elegant, praised by all, Bolívar led the life of a prince. He gambled away fabulous sums, lent money to his friends, gave lavish gifts and challenged Eugene Beauharnais for Fanny's love. He dressed fashionably and introduced his hat, his famous "Chapeau Bolívar,"[27] whose raised brim Fanny without a doubt came up with. People who live in Paris and have the gifts of talent, culture, originality or luck complain about French chauvinism because they either lack these gifts or haven't met their Fanny de Villars, the inspiration, the advisor on small details. Paris can be serious but always lighthearted, and there is no better advice than that which is given by a lovely woman endowed with a lovely voice and a smile.

Worldly success intoxicated Bolívar but it did not cure him. Once he achieved success, nothing else mattered to him. He lost interest. He continued to be sad. Luxury, praise, and pleasure produced a deep weariness in him. He visited Paris often to distance himself, he returned to Paris, and, nothing! Deep in his soul the restlessness of the unsatisfied had taken root. This is what he wrote when he wrote to Fanny, who inspired him, whom in his love letters he calls Teresa in homage and fidelity to his adored deceased wife. "The present doesn't exist for me," he writes one day after arriving in London. "The present is empty. The minute I want something, I satisfy it. Ah, Teresa, this will be the desert of my life. Paris can't put an end to the vague uncertainty that torments me." Success, admiration and honors are not enough. He needed to find another goal, and Fanny, the new Teresa, steers him on the path to Damascus[28] by introducing him and putting in a good word for him to Baron von Humboldt. Thanks to her insistence, he and Bolívar become friends. In the course of their friendship, Humboldt will reveal Bolívar's American homeland to him, just as Fanny had revealed his character and his triumphant gifts. During a voyage that lasted five years, the famous German who traveled through equatorial lands started a true revolution in the natural sciences and the world's geography, and enthusiastically described the indescribable riches and the marvels of those unexplored lands. He talks about the future that awaits them, and the absolute necessity of emancipating those lands.

He emotionally and affectionately described criollo society, so innocent and loving. As an outsider he can better appreciate the charms of simplicity and its generous and effortless grace. He took note of the intellectual movement he witnessed among the Creoles. There are centers of advanced cultures like Bogota and Mexico City. He's met poets like Bello and intellectuals like Mutis[29] and Caldas.[30] He fell so in love with the easy and contented life in these countries, true earthly paradises, that someday, if circumstances allow, he wants to spend the rest of his life there.

An astonished Bolívar listens. A miraculous light shines within him. Faith and enthusiasm grow in his soul as he converses with this learned man. How different from the depressing impression of his homeland and his view of himself in Madrid as a poor adolescent from the Indies! Despite his disapproval of it, Bolívar attended Napoleon's coronation, and shortly after that ceremony, which took place at Notre Dame, Bolívar visited Humboldt. Humboldt once again brought up the subject of the emancipation of Spanish America and said, "I see the challenge but I don't see the man capable of bringing it about." With the memory of Napoleon's apotheosis fresh in his mind, Bolívar, the alarming and ambitious twenty-year-old kept his peace but said to himself, "I can be that man."

And that was the end of the Paris days. Sighing and weeping, between tears and sighs he said good-bye to Fanny, the only person who knew about his undertaking. He travelled to Italy, visited Humboldt, who was in Naples once again, and accompanied by Simón Rodríguez he walked to Rome. He made his vow on Sacro Monte, once again bade Fanny farewell in a long, painful letter, and, at her urging, sailed to La Guaira, which is to say, to one of the most beautiful fates any man in history could have.

One would have to write an entire book to discuss the influence women will have on Bolívar's heroic life.[31] Tender and passionate, it's not just his great loves that guide him; it's also his affection, his piety and the spirit of protection toward his women friends. The applause of women in all the American capitals who cheered for and adored him like a god made him drunk with happiness and pride. Following his victories, he is a just like an adolescent, enthusiastically looking forward to a ball or some other function that will be given in his honor, the women who will attend to him; he will change the battle plan so he can keep a date, after leading his men from morning to night. He'll dance until morning and the mere presence of a beautiful woman makes him happy even if he doesn't know her.

Within his family circle with a smile, he listens to his sister María Antonia's warning, for she shares the same impulses and his gift of leadership, and one triumphant day entering Caracas in 1827, after having been gone a long time, a delirious crowd greets him, and in the distance he catches a glimpse of his old nurse Matea Bolívar wearing her white slave's kerchief. He stops everything and runs through the entourage to embrace his old black servant. On two occasions Doña Manuelita Sáenz, whom Bolívar himself called the Liberator, saved his life, and she was the most colorful of all the loves of his life. How different is the extraordinary Manuelita from Teresa del Toro, the typical romantic criollo who goes through life leaving no trace except for the sorrow her death caused. Since we can't mention all of them, after discussing the first two, I will briefly discuss—have no fear—Bolívar's last love. Doña Manuelita is interesting not only because she is a colorful character, but because she represents, in the context of women's objections to their traditional role as servants or as married women, a door not always open to them. A woman of action, she could not put up with either the deceit or the pretense of false love. A daughter of the revolution, she only heard the language of truth and the right to her own defense. She was the *après guerre* woman of the Independence. She preached her crusade through example without wasting time and without leaving behind a school of thought.

All we know is that she was born in Ecuador, Argentina, or Upper Peru, to a distinguished and rich family. Doña Manuelita, who was very beautiful and young, and when she was practically a child was married an Englishman she never loved and who bored her to tears. One day, from her balcony, she spotted Bolívar victoriously entering Quito and there and then she fell in love with him, decided to divorce her Englishman and marry Bolívar. But there was no divorce in those days. There was no lawyer, trial or wedding ceremony. But neither was there betrayal or games. Doña Manuelita told everyone about her decision, her husband first of all. The Englishman accepted her decision with resigned sadness. As you can expect, everyone was shocked. All her contemporaries shunned her. They did it out of their naturally conservative social spirit and the fidelity to their values. They were right. But that didn't intimidate Manuelita. Born and raised in the middle of the war, she believed, not illogically, that if you could reject the fifth commandment, "thou shalt not kill," with impunity, in her case you could overlook the indissolubility of marriage. And she attacked it alone, lance and pistols in hand, like she always did when there was a plot against Bolívar or herself. Some say Manuelita acted like she did because she was an atheist and a freethinker. On the contrary, I believe when she rode on horseback dressed as a man and accompanied by her two brave black equestrians, and threw herself into battle, in the depth of her conscience and remembering her Englishman, at the same time she challenged death she challenged hell, the height of heroism. One of her contemporaries provided this snapshot: "When I knew her, "he said, "she was about twenty-four years old. She had black, daring, sparkling eyes, her complexion was as white as milk, and she was of normal height and had a nice figure. She was very lively and gracious to her friends and charitable to the poor. She was brave and handled her sword and pistol well, rode on her roan horse, dressed like a man in red trousers and a black velvet jacket, her curly hair loose under a little hat with a feather that accentuated her enchanting figure."

It appears that as her prowess increased, Doña Manuelita's clothing took on a military appearance. She added colors and sewed on new braids and chevrons. I say this because Palma[32] paints us another portrait afterwards by another witness in which she appears dressed in a red jacket with yellow buttons and gold Brandenburg. Be that as it may, what is certain is that dressed in her uniform, her lance in hand and her two black equestrians, Nathan and Jonathan at her side, Doña Manuelita waged battle with the Peruvian and Colombian governments when these were hostile to Bolívar. Whenever he left the country, and on the least occasion, she would go forth feeling obligated to defend him *a la* Don Quixote with lance in hand. These sorties were never successful—on the contrary—but she never lost faith and pressed on. To avoid being spied on, both the Peruvian and Colombian governments exiled her.

Deep down, Doña Manuelita was always right. It was a sad time for Bolívar, a time when he was unappreciated; it was his Calvary, the final bitter days of his life. His project to unite the Gran Colombia was hindered on all sides by petty interests and it was dissolved and he was accused of being a tyrant and an autocrat. The minute he left one country to travel to another one, that country turned against him. This is what infuriated Doña Manuelita.

Bustamante's's[33] plot against Bolívar, who had just left Colombia, took place in Lima in 1827. Doña Manuelita found out about it in time; she ran to the barracks and assembled a battalion, but she failed in her attempt and the new government that sprang forth from the coup exiled her from Peru. She lived by Bolívar's side at the Quinta Bolívar in Bogota for several years, surrounded by all the famous men of the day, who treated her as though she were Bolívar's wife. The women shunned her, but that didn't bother Doña Manuelita. In her opinion, generally speaking, what women talked about wasn't so interesting. On the famous night of September 25, a group of conspirators, as you know, attacked Bolívar in his home in order to assassinate him. Doña Manuelita's admirable intuition figured out what was happening and she had him escape from a window. She chased after the conspirators armed with a pistol, opened the door to them and threw them off Bolívar's scent. From that night on, she was known, and she referred to herself as "La Libertadora."

When Bolívar was away or when Santander,[34] who was then vice president of Colombia, was behaving in a way she deemed disrespectful or inappropriate to the absent Bolívar, she decided to throw a big party to which she invited some notables. The party began with the execution of Santander's effigy. Following the execution they danced until dawn. That disrespectful ceremony leveled at the vice president created an uproar. The brunt of it fell on Bolívar who, for reasons of state, was forced to write a fiery letter in which he called the party an unfortunate and lowly act, and he tried, in a loving and appropriate way, to excuse the lovely madwoman. But in the same post he wrote a letter to Doña Manuelita in which he more or less told her she was the most charming and gracious woman he had ever met in his life.

Another time, when Bolívar was very ill during the feast of Corpus Christi, fireworks in fantastic shapes were set up in Bogota's main square. They held big surprises. Everyone anticipated them enthusiastically. Toward dusk, people came to warn Doña Manuelita that the forms represented "Mr. Despotism" and "Madame Tyranny," which were in reality caricatures of her and Bolívar. What's this about despotism and tyranny? Well, then, they're going to have to wait for the party. Overtaken by a fit of destructive revenge she called for her horse, donned her trousers, the jacket with chevrons, seized her lance and her pistols and, accompanied by Nathan and Jonathan, headed down the street in hot pursuit. They arrived at the square and the three of them destroyed the fireworks. In the darkness of night, all was in bits and pieces and not one of the allegorical figures was set off. General Caicedo,[35] who was president of Colombia at the time, turned a blind eye and didn't prosecute Doña Manuelita. The next day, a demagogue newspaper ranted against Caicedo's weakness.

"A shameless woman," the newspaper wrote, "who dresses in clothing inappropriate to her gender and forces her two servants to do likewise, an insult to decorum and a mockery of the law showed up yesterday in the public square, attacked the guards who were in charge of setting up the fireworks, fired her pistol and spoke against the government, the people, and freedom. This woman's very presence forms the criminal cause of Bolívar's conduct." And here they lit into President Caicedo, who knew what had happened, and instead of arresting the aggressor, he gallantly escorted her to her home to calm her down and explain.

Bolívar died poor and exiled, as we all know, and Doña Manuelita's grief never calmed her vengeful and vindictive fury. On the contrary, the first few days of her widowhood were tempestuous. More than ever she felt obliged to defend the deceased one. Since Bolívar's shadow had protected her until then, the government of Colombia resolved to distance itself at all costs from the Libertadora and the Libertador and told her nicely that she was exiled. Doña Manuelita ignored this and declared she would not leave her house in Bogota, where she was surrounded by the loving memories of the past, until the day she died. The government was determined. So was Doña Manuelita. They told her they would resort to force and they set a deadline. The deadline came and she said she was ill and got into bed with her two pistols, while Nathan and Jonathan, armed to the teeth, guarded the doors. When the authorities arrived, the two of them resisted, and not wanting to shed blood, they returned to deliberate with the minister and the President. After lots of back-and-forth and compromises, the two black women were taken by surprise and arrested and the exiled Manuelita was taken away, bed and all. Carried out feet first like a corpse, she left her house, never to return.

She was attached to the symbolic images and honored them. Once she was far from her home, she asked for her horse and headed to Cartagena, to Paita, where she lived out her days. She spent her long widowhood there and lived only to recall the past fervently. Poor and handicapped, she had to earn a living by making medicinal syrups which one of her black servants would sell through the town. Shortly after her exile, her husband, Mr. Thorne, died in Ecuador, and in his Saxon generosity forgave her, because he understood her. His forgiveness extended as far as naming her the sole heir to his fortune. Doña Manuelita believed that accepting the inheritance went against her dignity and the fidelity Bolívar's memory deserved. She therefore refused Mr. Thorne's fortune and continued to make syrups.

As we know, in Paita she met with Simón Rodríguez. Garibaldi[36] visited her in Paita. Ricardo Palma met with her in Paita and he described her as already grown old and sitting in her wheelchair beside the patio of her modest reed house. Palma recalls how at times, someone would come to see her or come by to buy syrup and would inquire from the doorway, "Is the Libertadora here?" "Come in; what do you want from the Libertadora?" she answered from her wheelchair. In her old age, proudly bearing the title of Libertadora, Doña Manuelita appears as an example of a strong woman who rebelliously fashioned her own code of honor and was true to it until she died. Some will find this affirmation so contrary to current opinion and others will find it scandalous. But let he, who living in poverty, is willing to renounce an inheritance in order to honor a memory, cast the first stone at Dona Mañuelita.[37]

Notes

[1] Antonio Amador Jose Nariño (1765-1823) was a journalist, politician and soldier from New Granada. Along with Pedro Fermín de Vargas, Francisco de Miranda, Madariaga y Francisco Antonio de Santacruz y Espejo, he was one of the precursors of the emancipation of the Spanish colonies.
[2] Gual y España's revolutionary movement to liberate Venezuela from Spanish colonialism began in La Guaira in 1797 and ended on May 8th, 1799.
[3] Antonio José de Sucre defeated the Spanish army at the Battle of Ayacucho in Peru on December 9th, 1828. It was the decisive battle that liberated Peru.
[4] *Julie, ou la nouvelle Héloise*, 1761, by Jean Jacques Rousseau, was an epistolatory novel based on the story of forbidden love between Heloise of Argenteuil, who became an abbess, and Abelard, a medieval French scholar, scholastic and philosopher. The novel was placed on the Index.
[5] Policarpa Salavarrieta (1795-1817), also known as La Pola, was a seamstress who worked on behalf of Colombian independence as a spy for the revolutionary forces. Shot to death by a Spanish firing squad, she became a martyr and national heroine.

[6] A reference to the random executions of the Spanish citizenry, May 2, 1808, following an insurrection during which they opposed Napoleonic occupation. Goya's famous painting, "The Third of May" (1814) depicts the cruel events.

[7] "La Emigracion a Oriente" took place on July 7, 1814 when the people of Caracas took the road to Chacao in order to escape the Royalist forces commanded by Boves. They walked for twenty days, with the majority dying along the way.

[8] The Treaty of Trujillo was signed on November 26th 1820, ending the war between Spain and Colombia and was signed by Pablo Morillo and Simón Bolívar.

[9] Simón Rodríguez (1769-1854) known during his exile from Spanish America as Samuel Robinson, was a South American philosopher and educator, notably Simón Bolívar's tutor and mentor. In 1794, he presented his *Reflection on the flaws Vitiating the Reading and Writing School for Children in Caracas and Means of Achieving its Reform and a New Establishment* to the council. It was an original approach to modern school reform.

[10] Manuela Sáenz Aispuru (1797-1856) was the illegitimate child of a Spanish father and Creole mother born in Quito. She was married to James Thorne, an English merchant twice her age. She was an Ecuadorian patriot and Simón Bolívars' confident and lover. She was known as the heroine of the South American Independence, and lived for twenty six years after Bolívar's death. On July 5, 2010 her "symbolic remains" were laid to rest next to Bolívar's in the National Pantheon in Caracas. See *For Glory and Bolívar: The Remarkable Life of Manuela Sáenz*, Pamela S. Murray, Austin: U of Texas Press, 2008.

[11] Lope de Aguirre (1510-1561) was a Basque Spanish conquistador nicknamed "The Madman." He was considered a paradigm of cruelty and treachery in colonial Spanish America.

[12] The samán (*samanea saman*) also known as the raintree, is a tree native to the subtropics. In Maracay, the capital of Aragua state, Simón Bolívar's army met during the war of independence under a tree known as the Samán de Güere, now a national symbol of Venezuela.

[13] Andrés Bello (1781-1865) was born in Caracas, Venezuela. He was one of the most important humanists in Latin America, dedicating his life to literature, education, philology, philosophy, and law. He was Simón Bolívar's professor.

[14] The Venezuelan Manuel Antonio Carreño wrote a book about good manners in 1853, called *Urbanidad y buenas maneras*. Carreños' handbook became a classic text about etiquette in Latin America. Carreño was Simón Rodríguez's nephew and Teresa Carreño's father.

[15] Philipe Francois Nazaire Fabre d'Eglantine (1750-1794) was a French actor, dramatist, poet, and politician. After the abolition of Gregorian calendar during the French Revolution, he sat on the committee entrusted with the creation of the French Republic's French Republican Calendar. The calendar was designed by the politician and agronomist Gilbert Romme, although it is usually attributed to Fabre d'Eglantine, who invented the names of the months.

[16] Jean-Jacques Rousseau (1712-1778) published *Émile: or, On Education*, (1782) a treatise on the nature of education based on a philosophy of man's innate goodness and the education of the whole citizen.

[17] Fanny de Villars was only the first of many amorous liaisons. Ramón Urdaneta's *Los amores de Simón Bolívar y sus hijos secretos* (2003), chronicles the "Liberator's many love lives." According to Urdaneta, there were at least eighteen women who had intimate relations with Bolívar, and Urdaneta dedicates a chapter to each woman. There is an additional chapter dedicated to other (supposedly undocumented) lovers, and another chapter titled "The Children of Simón Bolívar." If Urdaneta's data is correct, Bolívar sired over a dozen offspring in as many unions.

[18] De la Parra does not state what currency Bolívar inherited, but it was most likely Spanish reales. Bolívar came from a wealthy, established line of Creole aristocrats, and aside from the cash he inherited, was heir to a vast estate of sugar and cacao haciendas, indigo fields, cattle ranches and copper mines. (Murray 28). In 1811 the first coin in Venezuela was called el *peso venezolano.* Since 1879 Venezuela's currency has been called the *bolívar.*

[19] *Daphnis and Chloe*, is a second century AD pastoral tale by Longus that helped to initiate the European vogue for pastoral fiction. The characters, who are shepherds, lived in an idyllic, edenic setting.

[20] Eugene de Beauharnais (1781 - 1824) was born in Paris, and became Napoleon's adoptive son after his father's execution. In 1804 he was officially named a member of the imperial family as prince of France.

[21] Madame Récamier (1777-1849) held a salon in Paris that attracted leading writers and politicians of the early nineteenth century.

[22] Madame de Staël (1766-1817) also known as Germaine Necker, was a French writer. She held one of the most popular salons in Paris and influenced literary taste in Europe at the turn of the 19th century.

[23] Alexander von Humboldt (1769-1859) was a German naturalist and explorer who travelled extensively through Latin America and described it from a modern, scientific point of view. He published his travels in four volumes over twenty-one years, *Le voyage aux régions equinoxes du Nouveau Continent (*1799-1804).

[24] Charles Maurice de Talleyrand (1754- 1838) was a religious, a politician, and a French diplomat of extreme relevance during the events at the end of the 18th century and the beginning of the 19th century. During this time he achieved high position in politics under the reign of Luis XVI.

[25] François René de Chateaubriand, (1768-1848) was a French politician, writer, and pioneer of Romanticism. He is known for his autobiography and novel *René* (1802). He entered the French army in 1786 and was in Paris during the first years of the French Revolution.

[26] Paulina Bonaparte, also known as Paulina Borghese (1780-1825), was Napoleón Bonaparte's younger sister. Jacques-Louis David (1748-1825) was a French painter in the neoclassic style who painted a famous portrait of Paulina Borghese.

[27] During that time Simón Bolívar started to use a very wide top hat which became very famous in all Europe.

[28] An account in *The Acts of the Apostles* in the Bible that describes how the Apostle Paul became a follower of Jesus and stopped persecuting early Christians on his way from Jerusalem to Damascus, Syria. A term for a revelatory experience.

[29] José Celestino Mutis y Bosio (1732-1808) was a Spanish priest, botanist, mathematician and a professor at the University of el Rosario, Bogota. He proposed in two occasions (1763 and 1764) to the Crown of Spain an expedition to the New Kingdom of Granada.

[30] Francisco José de Caldas y Tenorio (1768-1816) was an eminent Colombian scientist, soldier, geographer, botanist, astronomer, naturalist, and journalist.

[31] De la Parra intended to write a book about Bolívar's life told from the point of view of the women who influenced him. She continued to study Latin American history and began a correspondence with Vicente Lecuna, the foremost scholar on Bolívar at the time, but this book was never written.

[32] Manuel Ricardo Palma Soriano (1833-1919) was a Peruvian writer and journalist. His *Tradiciones peruanas* (1893) was a collection of South American history and legends.

[33] Colonel José Bustamante ordered Venezuelan officers in Lima arrested, and the division returned to Colombia. Bolívar offered to resign the presidency of Colombia in February 1827, and Santander and his party demanded that he do so; the next month Bolívar renounced his friendship with Santander.

[34] Francisco José de Paula Santander (1792-1840) was a distinguished Colombian statesman, lawyer, revolutionary, politician and soldier of the Colombian Independence. Bolívar criticized Santander for his greed and dishonesty, and the Vice President reluctantly promised to institute reforms. Santander advocated New Granada becoming independent of Venezuela.

[35] Domingo Caicedo y Sanz de Santa María (1783-1843) was president of Colombia between 1830 and 1831.

[36] Giuseppe Garibaldi (1807-1882) was an Italian politician and military leader who supported the fight for South American Independence, participated in the Uruguayan Civil War, and fought for the unification of Italy.

[37] "Cast the first stone," is a reference to *John* 8:7. When a mob was ready to execute a woman caught in adultery, Jesus said to them, "Let he who is without sin cast the first stone.

CHAPTER TEN

THE SHORT STORIES

"Mama X"

The loss of innocence and the quest for identity are the main themes of de la Parra's most successful short story "Mama X," which was integrated into Chapter 6 of *Iphigenia*. This piece won first prize in a short story contest in 1922 sponsored by El Luchador, a newspaper out of Ciudad Bolívar. "Mama X" is the short story that forms the flashback scene in which María Eugenia reminisces about her friendship with Cristina. The contest rules specified that the story's theme had to represent "the national culture." The story of "Mama X" took place between two Spanish schoolgirls who were studying in a French Catholic school. The judges created a special prize for de la Parra's entry. "Mama X" was published in 1923 in *El Nuevo Diario*, in Caracas. De la Parra published *Iphigenia* in Paris in 1924.

The story of Cristina and the narrator's friendship reinforces the reason why the protagonist, María Eugenia, dedicates such a long letter, a loving piece of her own self, to her best friend. Cristina and the narrator's friendship is based on a secret: the fact that Cristina is a "natural child." Back in Caracas, living a confined life with her fussy and conservative relatives, Cristina represents María Eugenia's only lifeline to happier schooldays. Writing to Cristina affords her with an opportunity to describe her current restricted and bored condition. When, months later, María Eugenia receives Cristina's terse and abrupt reply to her own long outpouring of her feelings, she is disappointed and heartbroken. Cristina's life had taken a decidedly different turn: she was about to be married to a rich man. "This morning I received a letter from Cristina Iturbide. It is her grudging and late reply to my poor mammoth letter (*Iphigenia* 183)." Regretting that she poured out her soul to her friend, María Eugenia exclaims, "Oh! What a betrayal of oneself; what an irreparable indiscretion; what a feeling of shame before the nakedness of one's soul! (183)." Following these words María Eugenia recalls the secret that cemented the girls' friendship and segues into the story of "Mama X." The

touching story is the search for the secret of Cristina's illegitimate birth
and the identity of her unknown mother, who may be a famous opera
singer.

The unruly narrator was enrolled in the school after many frustrating
and failed attempts to be tutored. Cristina is sent to the school because she
is motherless and her father has to travel on business. The Spanish
language unites the girls, and the two of them investigate and finally get to
the bottom of Cristina's family secret: she is an illegitimate child, the
result of a liaison between her Spanish father and an Englishwoman who is
an opera diva.

Cristina overheard her aunt and uncle discussing "a woman who has no
shame, no heart..." assuming that her aunt and uncle were talking about
her mother. From that point on, the friends become opera enthusiasts. In a
kind of "religious fanaticism" they attend opera matinees. The story ends
with the friends attending a musical performance and Cristina wondering
if the soprano who is performing could be her mother. Part of the story's
charm lies in the girls' innocence as Cristina attempts to learn her birth
history. In Spanish, *hija natural* is one way to say "illegitimate." The girls
are puzzled by this new use of the word "natural" and wonder what it
could mean, as they logically associate "natural" with things that are good,
things as they should be, or things that have no defects. They look up
"natural" in the dictionary and learn that at the Battle of Lepanto, Juan of
Austria, the "natural" son of Charles V gained victory over the Turks. But
that definition does not solve the mystery. María Eugenia finally finds out
the alternative and denotative meaning of the word "natural" from her
father and then explains it to her friend. The short story foreshadows some
of the events that take place in *Mama Blanca's Memoirs*. In the novel the
young narrator has to eventually leave the paradise-like hacienda. In this
short story the narrator expresses her sadness at having to leave the
hacienda in Venezuela, where she was immensely happy, and where she
played for hours with her black friend and describes her unhappiness at
having to travel to Paris to be tutored. As in *Mama Blanca's Memoirs*,
"Mama X" is also about the loss of innocence and the author plays with
the alternative meanings of words, which have a powerful effect on the life
of a naïve young girl. Both the narrator and Cristina find themselves adrift
in a motherless world.

The following three short stories were written in 1915 and were first
published in *El Universal* in Caracas and other newspapers in Paris under
the pseudonym Fru-Fru[1]. In de la Parra's short stories lie the seeds for the
themes that will play out in her later prose, but they are very different from
the two longer novels she will later write. In the short stories we can see a

deliberate attempt to evade reality, and to introduce elements of the supernatural and the absurd. They are a precursor to the magical realism that is common in later Latin American literature. The short stories are playful exercises that do not take into account historical reminiscences and the *criollismo* touches that were a hallmark of Venezuelan literature at the time. Instead, the themes revolve around thwarted desires, self-deceit, the nature of art, the loss of love and beauty, and the perils of pride. These themes will be revisited in *Iphigenia*. The stories include descriptions of emotions, humor, love, melancholy, ecstasy, and the spirit of sacrifice. De la Parra was one of the first writers to include elements of the fantastic in her stories, a move away from romantic realism, naturalism and *costumbrismo*. This feature is evident in the short stories that all end tragically, a foretaste of the endings of later her novels. The narrator of *Iphigenia* eventually identifies with the Greek maiden who is sacrificed to society. The narrator of *Mama Blanca's Memoirs* recalls the unfortunate consequences of the family's move from the rural and paradise-like hacienda to Caracas.

The backgrounds of the tales contain elements found in fairy tales and folk-tales. At the time she was writing them, exotic themes in literature were much in vogue in Europe, but they were not present in Latin American literature. Going against the contemporary taste for Creole and rustic themes, these stories are deliberately playful, and show that de la Parra was experimenting and using new styles of narration. The stories represent a brief adventure in the realm of the fantastic and themes that would be later taken up at the time of the so-called "Boom" in Latin American literature.

José Martí's publication of *Ismaelillo* in 1882 influenced writing in the entire Latin American continent, and influenced both poetry and prose in America and in Spain. For the first time, a literary movement began in Latin America and spread from there to Spain, rather than the other way around. It is in this climate that de la Parra wrote her stories, with the newfound taste for adventure, mystery, the mystical, the sacred, and the exotic. Her stories invoke children's literature, fairy tales, the lives of mystics, and tales of the marvelous. The stories are lyrical, and take place in a realm where people and inanimate objects coexist, a world alive with cloth dolls, predatory insects, evil genies and wooden clocks. In these three stories, toys and inanimate objects come to life. De la Parra takes elements found in folklore and fairy tales, and poeticizes and transforms them. The reader is transported to a magical and fantastical world and the author explores an intuitive and imaginary world through the playful characters. These characters have intense experiences. Here the author gives free reign to her imagination. While the novels are set in a real place during a given time, the short stories allow de la Parra to deal with fantasy and open a window to a different world. The elements of irony, memory and nostalgia for which de la Parra is famous for, are also present in these stories.

De la Parra's later interest in Eastern disciplines and the mysticism of the Far East is evident in these early writings. In analyzing de la Parra's short stories, Douglas Bohórquez points out modernist characteristics along with romanticism and especially exoticism as reflected in her interest in Buddha, India, Japan and the fantastic[2]. She privileged Oriental culture and its mysticism and sacredness, as opposed to monotheism and Christianity. The reintroduction of the East with its gods, goddesses, and genies was being plumbed by a new continental literature that was trying to rid itself of romantic, criollo and costumbrismo subjects. The short stories "Lotus Flower"[3] and "Buddha and the Leper Woman" are early works set in exotic Eastern settings. In her later life this interest increased and she read about mysticism and the lives of the saints. In a letter to Zea-Uribe (December, 1930), she wrote, "I do not cease to think that the tropics, like the Far East, are lands where mysticism grows spontaneously." At the height of her interest in Simon Bolívar, she misguidedly began to think of him as an Eastern yogi.

Her stories have been overlooked by critics. While the stories were previously dismissed as literary exercises and looked on as the author's brief flirtation with the realm of the fantastic, she can be considered to be a forerunner of women's use of magical realism as a means to escape reality and create new worlds from which to examine the themes of nostalgia, solitude and loneliness. In her letters and her diary she meditated on the impermanence of life and often rebuked herself for her own materialism and ambition. In her more Zen or Buddhist moments, during her spiritual quest, coming to grips with her impending death, de la Parra wrote in her diary, on January 18, 1936, "Every time I'm faced with true misfortune, I ask myself, why undertake anything, why want anything? When we possess something, we are like children getting a new toy, playing "mine," thinking ourselves to be immortal. Everything is lent to us; everything is a plaything for us for a while"(*Obra* 462). Although de la Parra did not pursue the short story form, she later encouraged her friend the Cuban folklorist Lydia Cabrera to collect oral Afro-Cuban folk-tales that were in danger of being lost. Cabrera followed her friend's advice and collected and wrote the *Contes Negres de Cuba* (1936), and dedicated the work to her.

"Historia de la Señorita Grano de Polvo Bailarina del Sol" (Miss Dust Mote, Sun Dancer)[4]

The story is narrated by a writer who looks up from a dull task to contemplate a rag doll named Jimmy. On a fine April morning the writer notices that Jimmy's attention is focused on a sunbeam as the rays of the sun enter the room. He strikes up a conversation with the rag doll, who, when asked what is on his mind, replies that he is thinking about the past, as always. But on this particular warm spring morning the sunbeam reminds him of a tiny, beautiful dancer, Miss Dust Mote, who once danced in the slanting rays of the sunbeam. The dancer, who was born in a crack in the floor from the sole of a shoe, has been living in Jimmy's wallet for over a year. The narrator convinces Jimmy to take Miss Dust Mote out and let her dance in the sunbeam. He convinces Jimmy that although the dancer may not live more than two hours, it would be two ecstatic hours and well worth the risk. The doll fetches the dancer and releases her into the sunbeam. The narrator and Jimmy are transfixed as they marvel at the dancer's grace and beauty. Suddenly, a large and "stupid" insect swallows her up. As the two, shocked and speechless look on, the narrator notices a large tear falling from Jimmy's felt eye. In this story, the rag doll and the writer converse, and the outcome of the story is a sad revelation for both. The themes of memories of a blissful time, the contemplation of art and beauty, and the loss of happy memories are common themes which de la Parra will once again take up in *Mama Blanca's Memoirs*. The writer in the story is at a loss for words because the beauty of the dancer is indescribable. This story contains an element of longing and the desire to capture an ideal moment and hold on to it.

It was a morning near the end of April. The marvelous weather contrasted brutally with the mundane writing task at hand that day. After a while I picked up my head and noticed Jimmy, my rag doll propped up and sitting in front of me, leaning against the lamp base. The lampshade looked like it was his parasol. He didn't see me, and his eyes, with an expression I didn't recognize, were fixed with a strange intensity on a ray of sunshine which slanted across the room.

"What's wrong, Jimmy dear," I asked, "What are you thinking about?"

"Of the past," he answered simply, without looking at me, and then he was deep in contemplation once again.

And as if he was afraid he had hurt my feelings with his brusque response: "It's not that I'm trying to hide anything from you," he assured me. "It's just that there is nothing you can... er... do for me, "and he sighed in a way that broke my heart.

He waited a while. He adjusted the two patches of white felt which surrounded his black pupils and gave soul to his expression. His gaze turned inward, in a melancholic reverie. Then he said to me:

"Yes, I'm thinking about the past. I'm always thinking about the past. But especially today, this warm and insinuating spring rekindles my memory. Look at the sunbeam that falls on your feet, look closely, and see how it transforms the carpet: this sunbeam reminds me so much of the one in which I first met...oh! I'm afraid you'll have to forgive me for the inadequacy of my words! Imagine the fairest, shiniest, most madly ethereal creature who ever danced on this miserable earth. She appeared and immediately my fantasies came to life in her miraculous presence. She was enchanting! She drifted down along the sunbeam, the same sunbeam I was just recalling, outshining with her dazzling presence even that stream of light. Air currents imperceptible to our crude senses animated a community of similar beings around her, but these others lacked her supreme grace and shimmering seductiveness. For an instant she frolicked with them, weaving in and out of their circle, escaping skillfully through a gap, darting out of the clumsy embrace of a huge drunk mosquito... all the while a sweet and barely perceptible draft was bringing her closer to me. My God, how lovely she was!

"As for her face, she had none, properly speaking. I have to admit that in reality she had no precise form. But she took on from the sun all the faces I would have been able to dream of and which were exactly the ones I dreamed of when I thought of love. Her smile, instead of staying within the lines of her mouth, extended to all her movements. So that she appeared at the same time golden as a gleam of copper, pale and grey as twilight, and dark and mysterious as the night. She was as smooth as velvet, as wild as sand blown by the wind, treacherous as the foam at the edge of a breaking wave. She was thousands of things in so rapid a succession that my words can't keep up with their metamorphosis.

"I stood watching her a long time, invaded by a kind of holy stupor... Suddenly I cried out... The ethereal ballerina was about to touch the floor. All my being protested against the ignominy of such an encounter, and I shuddered violently.

"My brusque movement produced extreme agitation in the world of the sunbeam and lots of little genies reeled about, I think from vertigo. But my eyes never lost sight of my beloved. Immobile, holding my breath, I fixed my eyes on her with my hand outstretched. Ah, divine happiness! She had fallen into that outstretched hand. I won't go into detail about my spiritual state. My heart was beating so fast that in my trembling hand, my darling was still dancing. It was a slow, measured waltz of infinite coquettishness.

"Miss Dust Mote," I said.

"How did you know my name?"

"Through intuition," I answered, "through… I mean… love."

"Love," she exclaimed. "Ah" and she began to dance again, this time in an impertinent way. I thought I heard her laugh to herself.

"Don't laugh," I reproached her, "I really love you. I'm serious."

"But, I don't take anything seriously," she retorted. "I'm Miss Dust Mote, Sun Dancer. I'm well aware that my ancestry isn't illustrious. I was born in a crack in the floor and I never really knew my mother. When I'm told that she was a lowly shoe sole, I have to believe it, but it doesn't matter to me now because I'm the Sun Dancer. You can't love me. If you love me, you may also want to take me away with you, and then what would become of me? Try it, draw back your hand a while and look at me out of the sunlight."

"I obeyed. I could hardly believe my eyes when in my hand, drawn back into the shadows, I contemplated a pitifully unattractive little thing, dishwater grey in color, totally lifeless and flat. I felt like crying!

"You see!" she said. "The experiment proves it. I live only by my art. Quickly, put me back into the sunbeam!"

I obeyed. Grateful, she danced again an instant in the sun. "What's your hand made of?"

"Felt, I answered innocently."

"It's so coarse! "she exclaimed. "I much prefer my path of air." And she tried to fly away.

"I don't know what came over me. Furious at the insult, but even more afraid of losing my prize, I gambled my entire life on a bold decision. She would become opaque, but she would be mine, I thought. I grabbed her and imprisoned her in the wallet I carry over my heart.

"Here I am, a year later. But happiness evades me. This fairy that I'm hiding, I still haven't dared to look at her, so vivid is the vision that first awakened my love. I still would rather keep her like this than lose her all of a sudden by setting her free."

"You mean, you still have her in your wallet?" I asked him, burning with curiosity.

"Yes, would you like to see her?"

Without waiting for my answer and because he couldn't resist his own desire, he opened the wallet and took out what he referred to as "the mummy of Miss Dust Mote." Out of friendship, I pretended to see her, but to tell the truth, I saw absolutely nothing. There was a moment of painful silence between us.

"If you want some advice, "I finally said, "I'm telling you to set your friend free. Take advantage of this sunbeam. Even if it only lasts two hours, it will be two hours of ecstasy. Keeping her isn't worth the torture you are going through."

"You really think so?" he asked, looking at me anxiously."Two hours. Oh, how I'm tempted. Yes, let's get it over with: so be it!"

Saying this, he took out Miss Dust Mote from his wallet and placed her in the beam of light once again. It was a marvelous resurrection. Shaking off her mysterious lethargy, the little ballerina began to fly madly about, unpredictably, almost supernaturally, just as Jimmy had described to me enthusiastically. I understood his passion. What a sight he was, standing stock still, his mouth wide open, drunk with beauty. The bitter sense of sacrifice combined with the pure rapture of contemplation. And to tell the truth, his face seemed more beautiful to me than the little fairy's dance because it shone with a moral quality that was missing in the illusive ballerina.

At once we both shouted. An enormous, yawning insect, as big as a pinhead, had just swallowed Miss Dust Mote.

What more can be said?

My poor Jimmy stared blankly as he considered the extinction of his delight. We were silent a long time, incapable of finding any way to express either my remorse or his despair. He uttered no reproach against me, or even against fate, but I saw clearly how, under the pretext of adjusting one of the felt patches that gave expression to his face, he furtively wiped away a tear.

"El Genio del Pesacartas" (The Genie of the Letter Scale)

The story begins with the traditional "once upon a time," introduction that begins the standard fairy tale. The story's leading character is also a toy, this time a gnome constructed out of leather and wire. The proud gnome traces his ancestry to Ireland, a nod to Celtic lore. The gnome rules the letter scale on a poet's desk. He is loath to admit that he once belonged to a company of minstrels, occupying as he does a privileged position as the "spirit" of the letter scale. But he has a nasty disposition. He is ill-humored, arrogant, and looks down on the other "inhabitants" of the poet's desk: a gold watch, a nut shell, a bouquet of flowers, a lamp, a ruler, an inkwell, sticks of sealing wax and a seal. When the poet sits at his desk, the gnome smiles hypocritically as if to imply that as long as he is on his watch at the desk, all will be well. One evening, the gnome hears music and realizes that his fellow minstrels have come to join him. But his arrogance and pride will not allow him to acknowledge them. In his rage he falls into the inkwell, which he had previously taunted and spit into. The minstrels try to rescue him, but the inkwell, wanting to get even, shuts his lid and traps the gnome within. The poet retrieves the soiled gnome and tries to clean him. When this proves fruitless, yet he doesn't want to throw him away.The soiled gnome is relegated to drawer to live with a broken paper clip, a turtle shell and a roll of old bills. The gnome still has his pride, however, and thinks back on the days when he reigned on the poet's desk and was responsible for weighing the mail. Now the two minstrels occupy the privileged spot on the poet's desk.

The story, like the one about the Miss Dust Mote, the tiny dancer, is based on an inanimate object on a writer's desk that comes alive. The themes of this story include creativity, pride, self-importance, and the danger of forgetting the past and one's roots. Revenge also plays a part in the story.

Once upon a time there was a very clever and ingenious gnome made of barbed wire, cloth and glove leather. His body resembled a potato, his head a white truffle, and his feet two little spoons. Out of a piece of hat wire he fashioned himself a pair of arms and legs. His hands, enveloped by cream colored chamois didn't fail to lend him a certain British elegance, undone perhaps by the hat made out of a red pepper. As far as the eyes, which were especially mysterious, they gazed obstinately to the left, which gave him a very pronounced wall-eyed look.

He was proud of his Irish origins; that classic land of fairies, sylphs and little people, but he had never confessed to anyone that there in his country he had been part of a modest company of minstrels or traveling singers; that detail would never have interested anyone.

After goodness knows how many extraordinary travels and adventures, he managed to obtain one of the loftiest positions a leather gnome could aspire to. He was the genie in the letter scale on a poet's desk. That is to say that while installed in the shiny machine he helped to balance, he smiled maliciously the whole day long. At first he was undoubtedly aware the honor the trustworthy post gave him. But by dint of listening to the poet, his master, who always said, "Careful! Don't anyone touch him, don't pass the feather duster across him, look how clever he is… He's the one who controls which letters and notes get to come in and out." He became so pretentious that he totally lost his real sense of importance- so that whenever they took him from his place to weigh the letters he would fly into a rage and scream that no one had the right to bother him, that he was at home where he belonged and that he would double the price of the postage and would utter other ridiculous oaths.

So he passed his days sitting in the scale like a Merovingian prince on his throne. From there he disdainfully contemplated the diminutive world of the desk: a gold watch, a nutshell, a bunch of flowers, a lamp, an inkwell, a ruler, and bars of sealing wax lined up respectfully near a crystal seal.

"Yes," he told them from above, "I am the genie of the scale and you are all my humble subjects. The nutshell is my boat if I want to go back to Ireland. The clock is here to tell me when I want to go to sleep. The bunch of flowers is my garden, the lamp gives me light when I want to stay up, the ruler notes the progress of my growth (my shoe size in medieval footwear is one hundred and seventy centimeters). I don't know yet what I'll do with the sealing wax- --as far as the inkwell here, there's no doubt it's for when I want to blow saliva bubbles.

And so saying, he shamelessly began to spit into the inkwell.

"You have no manners," the inkwell protested. "If I could climb up there, I would put a big blot on your cheek and I would write "Evil Gnome" on your back with big letters."

"Yes, but since you weigh more than lead with your dirty sewer water you can't do anything to me. If I lean towards you, like it or not, you will have to reflect my image."

And in effect, his image appeared in the bottom of the black copper lid shining like a little devil.

When his master sat at the desk, the gnome took on a hypocritical air and laughed as if to say. "All is going well. You can go ahead and write lovely pages. I am here.

Then the poet, who was kind by nature and was easily fooled, looked complacently at the genie and placed a stick of green incense into its holder and lit it. The smoke rose in fine plumes towards the gnome and enveloped his head in its sweet blue caress. The diminutive character happily smelled the perfume and shook so that the scale registered fifteen grams instead of ten, which was his usual weight, and he concluded that incense was the only food worthy of him, since he was the only one who enjoyed it.

One night when he was sleeping soundly, he was awakened by sweet music. Two poor minstrels dressed more or less like him came to serenade him: one of them played a guitar and sang with a passionate expression; the other accompanied him with his hands folded over his heart as is to say, 'What divine music, I've never felt such pleasure.'

"What is this? What's going on?" asked the gnome rubbing his eyes with his fist. "Who dares to play and sing at night here on my table?"

"It's us," the guitar player sweetly replied. "It appears that you've been very lucky since the day you left our traveling company. Today you are a grand personage... and as you can see, we've made the trip here. We're very tired..."

"In the first place, I prohibit you from addressing me informally, and secondly, I don't know you. What a joke! Me in a minstrel show... Are you crazy? Get out of here, you vagabonds."

"But really, don't you recognize us, your lordship?" the disappointed musicians insisted. "There were three of us, remember, and we were very successful... I was in the middle, my partner was to the right, and you were on the left, squinting cross-eyed so the people laughed. You still have that look. Here, take this photo one of our fans of us took on the night before you escaped. And removing his guitar he offered a piece of paper. In effect, it showed the three wire and leather minstrels: the one on the right was indeed the genie of the letter scale. "Ah- this is too much, he shouted, exasperated. I don't like jokes. I am the genie of the letter scale and I don't have anything in common with beggars like you."

"But sir, "the guitar player replied," invaded by a profound sadness, "We're not asking you for much: only that you allow us to live here on your lovely property. Please know that we've used up all our money on our travels."

"Which doesn't concern me."

"We won't bother you at all—we'll play lovely ballads."

"I don't like music. Besides, I can see it coming. You'll ruin my reputation with your noise, thank you very much, and I have an enviable situation... I know a certain inkwell that would be happy to splatter you with his slander. You'll have to figure it out for yourselves. I don't know you..."

"Is that your last word?" the minstrels asked, defeated by such ingratitude.

"It's my last word," concluded the genie of the letter scale.

But the unfortunate musicians remained, desperate and not knowing what to do.

"Are you going to leave right now?" he shouted, rising to his feet, "or do I have to call the police?"

But in his over excitement he slipped, lost his footing, and cursing, fell to the bottom of the inkwell, which swallowed him up.

Without paying heed to his other sentiments which were ungenerous and unworthy, the minstrels tried to free their old friend. But as luck would have it, the inkwell, which had a score to settle, quickly pulled down his lid and the minstrels could not move it.

The following day when the poet witnessed the disaster, he understood what happened and felt repugnance for the genie's ingratitude. After extracting him from his black well and trying in vain to clean him up, not knowing what to do with him, and not wanting to throw him into the trash, he put him away in the bottom of a drawer. In his exile, the leather gnome didn't lose his pride. He continues to regale the members of his new social set, a broken paper weight, a turtle shell and a roll of old receipts with his fantastic tales.

"When I was in charge on the letter scale, it was I who allowed the telegrams to arrive. But one day, a crazy man threw me into the inkwell."
As for the two minstrels, the poet placed them on a branch of leaves. They look like two colorful birds in a virgin forest and there they sing all day long in an enchanting manner.

"El Ermitano del Reloj" ("The Hermit in the Clock")

With its standard fairy tale beginning, this story is about a carved wooden figure of a Capuchin monk named Brother Barnabé, who lives inside a wooden clock shaped like a chapel. It is the monk's duty to ring the bell to sound the hour on the hour. Neatly dressed in his tunic, thinking he is responsible for striking the hours, the self-satisfied monk has lived happily for fifty years, proud of his job. He claims the attention of the other objects surrounding him, and he delights the children who gather in front of the clock to wait for him to strike the noon hour because then they get to see him longer. But one day Brother Barnabé grew bored. He is reminded by the rule in his cell that it is his duty to strike the hours both day and night, but one night, at three in the morning, the ebony elephant who claims to be the Queen of Sheba's pet tempts the monk to visit his mistress between the times he has to strike the hours. The monk is conscious of his obligations and demurs, but eventually agrees to visit the Queen of Sheba, who is painted at the bottom of a Chinese porcelain soup tureen. The queen longs to meet the monk because she too, is bored. She regales the monk with her adventures, and he is distracted by her astonishing stories. He, in turn, tells her about his humble life, well aware that it is lacking in imagination. The monk's next day is filled with feverish anticipation that the elephant will once again take him to see the queen, and when the elephant doesn't appear, he sets out on his own, but it takes him two hours to reach the china closet that holds the tureen. The queen tells him never to return; his stories are boring. The disappointed monk now realizes that his true calling is to ring the hour. He returns home to his clock only to discover that in his absence the clock worked without him, and he was not needed all along. The veil has been lifted from his eyes, he is afraid to be exposed to the public scorn of the other household objects, and hangs himself.

The moral of this story with its unexpected and macabre ending seems to be a cautionary tale about leaving well-enough alone and taking pride in one's job, no matter how boring. The themes of carrying out one's duty, sticking to a daily schedule and not seeking adventure and change are virtues exhorted by María Eugenia's Aunt Clara and Grandmother in Iphigenia. Both the monk and the Queen of Sheba are bored, and boredom is the reason María Eugenia takes up writing. Like the monk, she will be reminded of her duty to society, and though she will try to elope and get away from her hum-drum world, she will not succeed and will give in to societal duty and marry a man for money. Although the heroine, unlike the monk, does not commit suicide, she sacrifices herself to keep the mechanism of her society running.

Once upon a time there was a Capuchin monk who lived in a wooden clock and whose job it was to ring in the hour. Twelve times a day and twelve times a night, bit by bit a clever mechanism opened the door of the chapel clock and the hermit could be seen outside pulling the rope ringing the bell as many times as the hour so the ding dong of its peals could be heard. Then suddenly the door would shut as though it wanted to squash the man. The Capuchin was in splendid health despite his age and his solitary lifestyle. A clean, well-brushed and spotless wool habit reached down to his bare feet which were shod in sandals. His long white beard contrasted with his fresh and rosy cheeks, inspiring respect. He had, so to speak, all he required to be happy. Not suspecting that the clock worked off a mechanism, he was sure it was he who rang the bells, which filled him with a lively sense of power and importance.

It never occurred to him to mix with the multitudes. The great service of announcing the hours to all was enough. As for the others, let them get along. If ever someone, attracted by his prestige, came to consult him about a difficult matter, be it an illness or some other thing, he wouldn't even open the door. Then he would answer through the keyhole, a thing which lent an imposing and occult air of mystery to his oracles.

During the course of many, many years, Brother Barnabé, (for this was his name), found his job as a bell ringer so attractive, it was all he needed in life. Just think about it a while, the entire population of the dining room fixed their eyes on the little chapel and had no other distraction other than to see the friar appear and pull on the rope to ring the bell. Among these was a fruit bowl that lived the unhappiest life in the world. Since its beginning it had been broken into two pieces, thanks to a maid's clumsiness, and it had been patched together with iron staples. The fruit which was placed into it before the bowl was set on the table hurled the most humiliating taunts at the bowl, thinking their precious persons to be unworthy of being contained by it.

Well, then, that fruit bowl which held a wound in its side that was continuously kept alive by the salt of its pride, was much consoled by the monk in the clock's mechanism.

"Look," it said to the mocking fruit, "look at that man in the brown habit. In a few minutes he's going to tell us the hour has come when you will all be gobbled up." And the fruit bowl, in anticipation, savored its vengeance. But the fruit, not believing a single word of it, answered back, "You're nothing but an envious cripple. It's not possible that such a sweet song could foretell such a fatal outcome."

And the fruit also treated the Capuchin complacently, as well as some old magazines that lived in a chest and spent their whole lives repeating to themselves things that had happened twenty years ago, and the tobacco tin, and the sugar tongs, and the pictures hanging on the wall, and the liquor decanters, all, all of them, fixed their gaze on the clock, and every time the door opened bit by bit, they experienced the same, sweet and innocent happiness.

When ten to twelve approached, the children arrived and sat around the fireplace in a circle and waited patiently for noon to arrive, a solemn moment for all of them, because then the monk, instead of hiding himself as quick as a thief once he finished his task like he did, for example, at one o'clock and two o'clock (when you doubted you saw him at all), no, on the contrary, then he stayed a while longer, so you could see him, that is, long enough to ring the bell twelve times. Ah! Then Brother Barnabé was not in a hurry. He was well aware that he was being admired. As though he had no care in the world, attentive to his task, he pulled the rope while he furtively spied the effect his presence produced. The children cried, "Look at how fat he's gotten." "No, he looks the same." "No, sir, he's younger." "It's not the same guy, it's his son." And so on, and so forth.

The tines of the forks of the silverware already set on the table laughed merrily, the sun shone brightly on the gold of the picture frames and the bright colors of the napkin fabrics encircled in their holders. The family portraits quizzically raised their eyebrows as if to say, "What, is the monk still here? Once, long ago when we were children he charmed us then."

It was a triumphant moment. The grownups arrived on the dot, everyone sat down at the table and Brother Barnabé, having finished his task, reentered the chapel, deeply satisfied in having performed his duty.

"But, oh, the day came when this feeling was no longer enough. He grew tired of always ringing the bell on the hour and above all, he got tired of never being able to leave. Pulling the rope to ring the bell is up to a point a public function everyone admires. But how long can that last? Hardly one minute out of sixty, and what do you do the rest of the time? You can walk around in circles in the narrow cell and recite the rosary, meditate, sleep, peek under the door or through the slits in the bell tower and catch a vague glimpse of a ray of sun or a bit of moon shine. These pastimes do little to stir the soul. Brother Barnabé grew bored.

One day, the idea of escaping came to him. But he rejected that temptation when he reread the rules posted inside the chapel. They stated: It is absolutely prohibited for Brother Barnabé, under any circumstance, to leave the chapel in the clock. He must always be ready day and night to ring the bell. He can never disobey. The hermit had complied. But how difficult it was to submit. And it happened one night when his door was open to ring in the morning, what to his surprise that before him he saw an elephant who stood tranquilly looking at him with his malicious little eyes, and of course Brother Barnabé recognized him at once; it was the ebony elephant who lived in the highest shelf of the china closet, over there on the opposite side of the dining room. But since he had never seen him off the shelf, he thought the animal had been sculpted into the wood cabinet. He was glued to the spot, surprised at seeing him in front of him, and he forgot to shut the door after ringing in the hour.

"Well, well," said the elephant." I see my visit here has produced a certain effect. Are you afraid of me?"

"No, it's not that I'm afraid of you," babbled the hermit. "But I confess that… A visit! You've come to visit me?"

"But of course! I came to see you. You've done so much for everybody here that it's only right for someone to offer to do something nice for you. Furthermore, I know how unhappy you are. I came to cheer you up and to console you."

"How did you know? How could you have known? I've never told anyone. Maybe you're the devil?"

"Calm down, "the smiling elephant replied. "I have nothing in common with that grand personage. I'm nothing more than an elephant… but of the first order. I'm the Queen of Sheba's elephant. When this great sovereign lived in Africa, it was I who took her on her travels. I saw Solomon, his clothes were much grander than yours, but he didn't have that beautiful beard. As far as knowing that you are unhappy, I just guessed. Given such an existence, you'd have to be bored to death."

"I have no right to leave," the monk affirmed.

"Yes, but you don't have to be bored on account of that." This reply and the questioning look the elephant accompanied it with took the hermit by surprise. He didn't answer. He didn't dare to answer. It was so true! He was bored to death. That was it! He had an obvious duty, an unquestionable unspoken charge to ring in the hours. The elephant silently looked at him for a long time as if to take in the slightest thought of his speaker. Finally he spoke, "But, "he said innocently, "Why don't you have the right to leave?"

"I promised the Reverend Father, my spiritual advisor, when he sent me to guard the chapel clock."

"Ah, and that was a long time ago?"

"Fifty years, more or less," Brother Barnabe replied after making a quick mental calculation.

"And after fifty years you haven't heard any further news from that Reverend Father?"

"No, never."

"How old was he then?"

"I suppose he was around eighty years old."

"So that today he would be around one hundred and fifty, if I'm not mistaken. So, my dear friend, (and here the elephant laughed mockingly, a thing painful to the ear), then that means that he's forgotten all about you. Unless he's trying to trick you. In any case, you are more than free of your commitment."

"But," the monk objected," What about the rule of the discipline?"

"What discipline?"

"This is the rule." And he showed him the sign with the rule written on it hanging in his cell. The elephant read it carefully and said, "Do you want my humble opinion? The first purpose of this part of the document serves only to frighten you. It essentially says, 'Ring in the hours day and night.' That is your basic duty. It's enough for you to be at your place when you need to be. The rest doesn't apply to you."

"But what would I do in my spare time?"

"Whatever you want," said the ebony animal quickly changing his tone, speaking clearly and authoritatively. "You can climb on my back and I'll take you to the other side of the world to marvelous countries you don't even know about. Do you know that there are priceless treasures in the secret cabinet of which you haven't the slightest idea: a tobacco tin Napoleon sneezed into, Roman medals with Caesar's bust, jade fish that know everything that happens on the bottom of the sea, a small, empty ginger jar still so aromatic that one can get inebriated just passing by it (and then you have some surprising dreams). But the loveliest of all is the

Chinese porcelain soup tureen, the last remaining piece of a rare, stupendous service. Its bottom is decorated with flowers, and guess who's there? The Queen of Sheba herself, standing under a parasol, holding her prophetic parrot. She's lovely. If only you knew, she's worthy of being worshipped. It makes you want to get on your knees! And she's waiting for you. I'm her faithful elephant and I've been with her for three thousand years. Today she said to me, "Go find me the hermit in the clock. I'm sure he's mad to see me."

"The Queen of Sheba, the Queen of Sheba," Brother Barnabé murmured to himself, deep in his heart of hearts, alive with emotion. I won't forgive myself. I have to go. And aloud he said, "Yes, I want to go. But the hour! The hour! Think about it, elephant. It's already a quarter to four."

"No one will notice it if you strike four o'clock now. That way, you'll have an hour and a quarter between this stroke and the next one. That's more than enough time to pay your respects to the Queen of Sheba.

Then, leaving everything behind, breaking his faithful and exact habit of the past fifty years, Friar Barnabe feverishly rang in four o'clock and jumped on the elephant's back, which carried him through space. In a few seconds they found themselves before the door of the cupboard. The elephant knocked three times with his tusk and the door magically opened. He marveled at the maze inside where the tobacco tin, medals, fans, jade fish and little statues were and soon he found himself before the celebrated soup tureen. He knocked the three magical taps, the lid opened and our monk beheld the Queen of Sheba in the flesh, who stood in a flowery path before a throne made of gold and gems, smiling with an enchanting expression, holding her prophetic parrot.

"I finally get to see you, my lovely hermit, "she said. "Oh, how happy your visit makes me; I confess I wished it madly, for how many times when I heard the bell ring I said to myself,' What a sweet, crystalline sound! It's heavenly music. I'd love to meet the bell ringer, he must be a very talented man. Come closer, my lovely hermit."

Brother Barnabé obeyed. He felt alive in this unknown, marvelous world. He didn't know what to think. A queen was talking to him as though she was his friend, a queen wanted to meet him!

And she continued, "Here, take this rose, a souvenir from me. If you only knew how bored I get here. I've tried to amuse myself with the people who surround me. All of them, all of them court me, some more than others, but I finally got tired of them. The tobacco tin is not without its charm, in a passable way he can tell war stories, recall adventures and intrigues, but I couldn't stand the smell of him. The ginger jar has a certain

grace and charm, but I find it impossible to stand beside it before an
irresistible urge to sleep overcomes me. The fish are knowledgeable about
science, but they never speak. Only the Caesar in the gold medal and I had
some fun for a while, but his pride became insupportable. Didn't he try to
capture me under the pretext that I was a barbarian queen? I made up my
mind to ditch him, what with his laurel crown and his big, pretentious
nose, and so I left him alone, thinking only of you, the faraway bell ringer
who played such lovely music for me at night. So I said to my elephant,

"Go get him and bring him to me. We'll entertain each other, I'll tell
him my adventures and he'll tell me his. Would you like, my dear hermit,
to tell you about my life?"

"Oh, yes!" Brother Barnabé sighed ecstatically. "It must be so lovely!"
And the Queen of Sheba began to tell about the magnificent adventures
she'd had from the night she left Solomon until more recent times when,
escorted by her slaves, with her parasol and her birds, she installed herself
inside the soup tureen. There was enough material there to fill several
volumes, and still she hadn't told all of it. At random she talked about her
dreams. She'd been to Africa and Asia and the islands of the two oceans.
A Chinese prince, a horseman who rode a jade dolphin, had come to ask
for her hand in marriage, but she rejected him, since at the time she was
planning a trip to Peru accompanied by a young swain painted on a fan
who was on his way to Cyprus, who, as soon as he saw her, changed his
plans.

In Arabia she lived with a court of magicians, who in order to entertain
her, made enchanted birds fly before her very eyes, unleashed frightening
storms that stirred up her skirts, made statues buried beneath the sands
sing to her, waylaid entire caravans, lit up gardens, palaces and fountains
with dancing waters. But among these, the most extraordinary adventure
was the one about the gold Caesar. It's true that she repeated, "I was
offended by his pride," but evidently she was satisfied, because that
Caesar was a man of consequence. Sometimes, in the middle of her telling
a story, the poor monk timidly interrupted, "I think it's time for me to ring
in the hour. Please let me leave."

But then the Queen of Sheba passed her hand over the hermit's lovely
beard, and smilingly answered him, "How wicked you are, my lovely
Barnabé. Thinking about the bell while a Queen of Africa is telling you
her secrets! And besides, it's still night time and no one will notice you are
gone." And she took up the thread of her astonishing tale. When she was
finished, she addressed her guest with her most charming expression,
"And now, my darling Barnabé, it's your turn. I've told you everything
there is to tell about me. Now it's your turn."

And having the poor bewildered monk sit beside her as she sat in her dazzling throne, the queen threw back her head as though preparing to savor something exquisite. So at this point Brother Barnabébegan to tell about his life. He recounted how Father Anselm, his superior, took him to his clock-chapel one day, how he was made its guardian, how he felt at first about being the principal bell ringer, he described his cell, recited from beginning to end the rule he found written there, he told her about the only stool he could sit on was a wobbly one, that the hardest part of it was not being able to sleep more than three-quarters of an hour at a time for fear of not being awake to pull the rope at the right time. Surely while he enumerated such trivialities, deep inside he knew these could not interest anyone, but once he got started, he couldn't stop. He guessed that what was expected of him wasn't the true story of his life, which lacked any meaning, but rather one about a beautiful existence full of adventures, so with a little art he tried to embellish his pathetic one. But, alas, he was lacking in imagination and like it or not, he had to limit himself strictly to the facts, and that is to say, hardly anything. During a certain part of his story, he lifted his eyes which from the beginning he had modestly kept glued to the floor and he noticed that the slaves, the parrot, all, all of them, even the queen herself, were fast asleep. Only the elephant was still awake.

"Bravo!" he shouted. "Now we all know what a first-rate narrator you are. The pot of ginger doesn't hold a candle to you."

"Oh! Good Lord!" Father Barnabé implored. "Is the queen angry with me?"

"It doesn't matter. What I do know is we have to get back. It's daytime already. There's just enough time to put you on my back and get you back to the chapel."

And so it was. Quick as lightening the ebony elephant went across the dining room and stopped in front of the chapel. The city's cathedral clock was just striking eight o'clock. The Capuchin monk anxiously ran to ring the bell eight times, and sleep having overtaken him, he collapsed without being able to do anything else. Fortunately, no one noticed he'd been gone. He spent the entire day feverishly and anxiously. He carried out his duties as bell ringer mechanically, but his thoughts would not leave him for even a moment and these led him to the enchanted tureen where the Queen of Sheba lived, and he said to himself, "What does it matter if I'm bored during the day if at night the ebony elephant comes for me to bring me there? Ah, what a wonderful life awaits me!"

He waited the whole afternoon for the elephant to arrive. But nothing happened! Midnight, one in the morning, two in the morning came and went without nary a sign of the royal messenger. Not being able to stand it, and telling himself the elephant must have forgotten, Brother Barnabé set out. It was a long and difficult journey. He had to climb down the chimney by grabbing the curtain that covered it, and since the cloth didn't reach the floor, he had to jump from a distance five or six times his height. He crossed the great distance of the dining room on foot, stumbling in the dark and tripping over the table leg, leaping from a spoon and then having to fight with a savage mouse who cruelly bit his leg; it took him about two hours to reach the china cabinet. Once there he meticulously went through the same procedure the elephant had so that without any difficulty first the door and then the lid of the soup tureen opened. Trembling with excitement and happiness he found himself before the queen. She was very surprised.

"What's going on?" she asked. "What do you want, Mr. Capuchin?"

"But, don't you remember me?" Brother Barnabe courteously asked. "I'm the hermit in the clock… I came here yesterday."

"Ah! You're the same monk who was here yesterday? To be perfectly honest with you, I'm going to give you this advice: don't ever come back here. Frankly, your stories aren't interesting."

In the depth of his misfortune poor brother Brother Barnabé remained glued to the spot.

"You wanna get going," the prophetic parrot squawked as he hurled himself on top and started pecking at him. "We told you never to come back. Out, out of here, now!"

With this blow to his spirit Brother Barnabé one again took the path back to the chimney. Walking along, walking along, he said to himself, "This is what comes of neglecting my duty. I should have known ahead of time that this was nothing but the devil's temptation to undo all the rewards of a life of penitence and solitude. How is it possible for a poor monk dressed in a habit to compete against the memory of a Roman emperor in the queen's heart? But how beautiful, how beautiful she was! But now I must forget all that. From this day forward I will only think about my job; my job is to ring in the hour. I will perform it faithfully, happily, until the day death overtakes me in my old age. I pray to God no one noticed my flight! I just hope I get back in time. It's seven thirty! If I don't get there at the stroke of eight o'clock, I'm done for. That's when the household gets up and everybody starts their day."

And the poor monk hurried along, his poor legs already exhausted. When he got to the point when he had to climb up the chimney by holding on to the molding, all the blood in his body was ringing in his ears. By the time he got up there he was half dead. But it was useless to try! He didn't get there on time. It was already chiming eight o'clock. I'm telling it to you straight, I'm saying that's right: It was striking eight. Ringing out by itself, without him! Bit by bit the door of the clock opened, the rope was going up and down, just like his own hands were pulling it, and eight crystalline bell peals were ringing out...

To his stunned surprise, the poor Capuchin got it. He understood that the bell tower worked without him, that is to say, he contributed nothing to the workings of the mechanism. He understood that his daily work and his sacrifice were things to be laughed at, a public joke. Everything came crashing down at once: the pleasure he'd hoped to get from meeting the Queen of Sheba and the duty he had resolved to perform in his cell in the future from this day forward. That duty served no purpose. A black desperation, immense and absolute penetrated to the depth of his soul. He understood that a life lived under these conditions was impossible.

He tore the rose the queen had given him into tiny pieces, he took apart the clockwork that hung in the wall of his cell, and grabbing the length of rope that usually stuck out from under the ceiling, the very one he had cheerfully pulled many, many times, put it around his neck, and leaping up, he hanged himself.

"An Indian Gospel: Buddha and the Leper Woman"[5]

The word gospel is usually associated with accounts concerning the life, death and resurrection of Jesus. Or, a gospel can refer to a belief or a body of beliefs proclaimed or accepted as true. De la Parra recounts the turning point in the life of Siddhartha Guatama, the "Sage of the Sakyas." In this parable, the prince Guatama leaves his palace and meets a diseased woman and learns one of the "Four Noble Truths," that suffering is part of human existence, and decides to live his life as a mendicant.

Guatama was born a prince in the Sakya tribe whose forests for many leagues skirted the Himalaya Mountains. Legions of soldiers guarded their treasure, thousands of white slaves shone like lilies in the delight of the harem. His wife Yasodada had given him a son and beneath the whiteness of his marble palace his life flowed majestically like slowly flowing rivers. On the day he was born all the astrologers of the kingdom read Guatama's horoscope and all of them, with awe and respect, announced that the prince would shine on the world like the sun shines on the face of the earth, and bowing reverently, they predicted the immortality of his kingdom, which would be great and eternal in the memories of men.

And Guatama, who owned all the blessings of the land, also knew all the secrets of human wisdom.

But in the midst of that abundance, Guatama was poorer than the miserable beggar that extended his hand every morning upon seeing him coming down the road, and in the great splendor of his power, Guatama was as unhappy as the last sudra who tilled his fields, because an unknown yearning was torturing him and because twisted into his heart he always carried the terrible serpent that is weariness.

Seeing him silent and taciturn, everyone, surprised, asked how could that silent prince who never smiled reign. And searching for the cause of his illness, Guatama read the holy scriptures of the Vedas, he read the glorious stories of the Ramayana, he read the sacred codex of Manu and always in books the shadow of his tedium would surface like the victorious night overtakes the day at dusk. And since he never found the secret of his distress, preceded by heralds and servants and escorted by the docile caravan of his camels, Guatama left his native city and crossed deserts, forests and rivers and set off to consult with all the wise men of Golconda and all the learned men of Bijapur.

But that mysterious sadness that always followed him along his journey travelled with him. Through the desolation of the desert, it clung to him at all hours, like his camel's shadow clung to the sand. It accompanied him and persevered under the melancholy palms, it accompanied him in the silence of the mango groves. And when he sailed the rivers, Guatama's deep sadness was reflected at all times upon the mysteries of the waters like the four lanterns on the funeral ships that descend at night in the sacred flowing of the Ganges. One day, upon once again approaching his homeland near the gates of a populous city, Guatama slowed down his camel's pace. In the shadow of a ruined tower he had seen a smiling beggar woman lying in the dust of the road.

She was a lowly Sudra slave who had been thrown out of the city. Whoever walked near her, upon seeing her close up fearfully distanced themselves because the slave's body was filthy carrion mercilessly being consumed by the rabid dog of leprosy.

Only Gautama on seeing her immediately halted his camel. He had seen a smile bloom in the horror of that deformed mouth, and wanting to unravel the enigma of that miracle, he spoke to the woman saying, "Who are you who smiles, trapped as you are in the net of your suffering?"

"My lord, "said the woman," I am a leprous slave who belongs to the cursed cast of the untouchables. Why are you, prince of the Sakyas, stopping to talk to a fatherless daughter of an unfortunate sudra?

But Guatama, who had drunk at the fountains of wisdom, disdained laws and human precepts, and remaining at the untouchable's side, repeated his question, asking," How can you smile?"

"I smiled, Lord, as I watched your caravan go by, thinking my hours go by one after the other like the tired walking of those camels. Like them, my hours pass by slowly and hunchbacked because they also carry on their shoulders the weight of my treasure, which is this great pain. The slow caravan that carried my riches leads me to the throne of Lord Vishnu, and I watched it happily go by and with no fear at all because I am sure that no thief will rob me of it along the road.

"Woman," said Gautama, you are great and you are powerful in the smallness of your humility because you have overcome your enemy, suffering, you have adorned yourself with the jewels of your pain, you are the queen of your reign of resignation and the horror of your wounds is holy because it blooms with hope. And Gautama returned to his native city and since in the night of his weariness the memory of the the poor untouchable shone like the sun, one day he assembled all his ministers, all the notables of his kingdom, all his senators and slaves and said to them "I have found the immense wealth l searched for in vain for many years. It is Hope. I will cast it in the crucible of memory, I will make it gold coins in my words, and with my great treasure on my shoulders I will henceforth go everywhere to redeem the wretched. From this day forward I will reign on the throne of tears, I will sit on the throne of compassion, pain will be my homeland, and I will reign in it forever more, because of all the great kingdoms that exist in the world, only this, pain, will live eternally on the face of the earth. And our lord Guatama Sakya Muni took leave of his wife and child; he distributed his belongings among the poor, he dressed as a mendicant, and taking up a beggar's bowl he walked to the desert and fasted for forty days...

Notes

[1] The short stories were published collectively in *Obra*. All translations are mine, taken from the Spanish version in this publication.

[2] *Teresa de la Parra: del diálago de géneros y la melancolía*, 14.

[3] I was unable to find any copy of the story "Lotus Flower". It was not included in *Obra* or *Obras completas*.

[4] "Historia de la Señorita Grano de Polvo Bailarina del Sol"-The Story of Miss Dust Grain, Dancer of the Sun-Dancer" also appears in *El cuento venezolano*. Caracas: 1985 Dirección de la Cultura de la UCV, Ed. José Balza, and in *Venezuelan Short Stories*, Caracas, Monte Avila, Lyda Zacklin, Trans. Bruce Morgan, 1997.

---

[5] Translated from *Teresa de la Parra. Obras Completas*. Ed. Carlos García Prada. Editorial Arte. Caracas, Venezuela, 1982. pp. 665-668. First published in *El Universal* in 1925 under the pseudonym Fru-Fru.

CHAPTER ELEVEN

TERESA DE LA PARRA'S INTERVIEW IN *DIARIO DE LA MARINA*
(LA HABANA, APRIL 1, 1928 SECTION 1 PP1 AND 16.)[1]

BY ARMANDO MARIBONA

Apendice "Teresa de la Parra nos habla con unción de su Venezuela y con entusiasmo de su progreso." (Teresa de la Parra speaks fervently about her Venezuela with enthusiasm for its progress)

De la Parra was obviously caught off guard in this interview. Maribona was a celebrated caricaturist who published a drawing of de la Parra. This interview, in which she atypically discussed politics, upset political exiles who lived in Colombia, and this provoked their unfavorable reaction to her lecture in Barranquilla. "Days later she wrote her regrettable letter to the dictator, on April 12, 1928" (*Obra* xxxiv).

Lydia Cabrera's study. Well appointed furnishings. We request matches from an unpretentious servant who gratefully accepts a cigarette.

In the anteroom for a few moments. The author of *Iphigenia* appears with her quiet gestures, her tranquil beauty, and her air of harmonious weariness.

De la Parra: It's almost like I'm in another world…I hardly ever manage to keep up, to be in the present, and I'm thinking of something else…
Maribona: That absent expression makes it difficult to draw you. Massaguer's[2], was it a successful caricature?
De la Parra: Very lovely… a very charming caricature.
Maribona: "It's charming of you to call it a "caricature". Would it be more like a portrait.

De la Parra: "Well, let's call it a fair portrait, without exaggerated praise."

Maribona: "Praises don't flatter you? Aren't you used to them yet?"

De la Parra: "It's nice to be flattered physically. On the other hand, when people offer me intellectual and moral praise, that's work. I don't make a lot of effort, it's the truth, and I fear they find me harmless, not very intellectual. So I remain silent, and am considered to be proud. Believe me, I'm not proud; lazy, nothing more."

Maribona: "Do you like to travel?"

De la Parra:"Very much, but the pleasure of change, of the new, and the unexpected doesn't at times make up for the elusive sadness of being far from beloved people and places, to be far from oneself. It's been four years since I've lived incessantly in that state of absence that at times becomes unconsciousness... But let's see, show me the drawing!"

Maribona: "What drawing?"

De la Parra:" "The one you are doing."

Maribona: "I don't draw, I write."

De la Parra:"So this is an interview, not a caricature?"

Maribona: "That's right. I hope it'll be easier to capture the soft and rhythmic lines of your spiritual self than to capture your physical self."

De la Parra: "But I'm afraid of all interviews! Generally they make me say things I've never thought about: and on many occasions the end result doesn't reflect the spirit of the interview."

Maribona: "We were thinking of asking you about the politics of your country."

De la Parra: "I don't understand politics,"

Maribona: "A lot of people don't understand it, and they are politicians."

De la Parra: "But I never get mixed up in it, ever. I think the current situation in my country is good[3]. There are magnificent highways, peace, individual safety, the Colombians travel across my country tranquilly to sail from La Guaira. I'm a friend of President Gómez and his current actions seem good. They accuse him of having been strict but that was when the country was in a permanent state of revolution. A powerful habit of progress, of prosperity, guides Venezuela today, ranking her first place among American republics. The network of magnificent highways constructed by President Gómez links all the important cities and that has lowered by fifty percent the cost of transportation, proving how effective that effort was. Venezuela's public debt is less than 100 million pesos; her currency is on par with the dollar; the government has accrued 125 million bolivars and its obligations are up-to-date. There has been a big push for public education; health services are at their peak efficiency. Relations between Venezuela and foreign nations are maintained under the strict, rigid principle of equality among nations. President Gómez has a special interest in maintaining close and brotherly ties in his relations with the other Spanish-speaking republics of the New World, always having given Cuba tokens of his affection and appreciation. General Gómez has finished leading, and now calls on the collaboration of his government, which is capable and better prepared to administer. He is, to sum up, truly a great statesman, so that the needs of our America lead him on occasion to carry out the highest destiny of our race.

"That's why it gave me great satisfaction that as a testament of his high esteem for

President Machado he awarded him the Grand Collar of the Order of the Liberator, the oldest and most valuable decoration, created in 1813 by Simon Bolivar, the Father of Latin America himself, and is the highest token of esteem the government of Venezuela can bestow. This, combined with the recent gift to Cuba of statues of the Liberator, is evidence of the close sympathies this enchanting country inspires. The modern Central Highway that unites Venezuela and Colombia is 1,212 kilometers long, climbs to 15,000 feet and spans ten Venezuelan states.

"The country is second in the world as oil producer and the *petrolera* law has covered every emergency for the protection of the land and the richness of its subsoil. The exploitation is set for a determined number of years.

"Venezuela is a nationalistic country, jealous of its integrity, and up till now, in no period of its history has it allowed foreign interference in its internal affairs. No Venezuelan will open that door, nor is there any Venezuelan who will not guard it.

"The news that some cable agencies transmit is absolutely exaggerated. In Caracas recently there was a student uprising, no more or no less than what happens anywhere. Today I read about student strikes in Spain, and no one is alarmed by that, and rightly so, because these aren't anything but demonstrations of youthful over-excitement, always anti-establishment and exacting. The fear I had about embarking disappeared under the assurances our minister gave me and there I go confidently."

Maribona: "And why didn't you give a lecture, like Dr. Vasconcelos did?[4]

De la Parra: "I'm not capable of such a thing. I'm not good at evangelizing; I was born to be evangelized. What I want now, after the very cordial, unerring Cuban hospitality is to gather myself in the beloved corners of my country, where I have not been for five years..."

We then talked about the Lesca and the noble labor they achieve with great economic sacrifices so that France gets to know our America. We discussed the possibility of celebrating a Congress of the Latin Press in Caracas so that foreign journalists can learn about the real political and economic state of the country.

Maribona: "Have you written much while you were in Cuba, Teresa?"
De la Parra: "Not even one line. The infinite kindnesses of the Cubans have left me with no free time. I'll write on board, and later, when I arrive at my country, I'll publish a series of articles, I've planned and thought out, about the trip from Paris to Havana, with the group of intellectuals I was a part of during the crossing. I'll write about Havana, about Cuba."
Maribona: "Where will you publish these articles?"
De la Parra: "In *El Universal* in Caracas."
Maribona: "Not in the *Diario de la Marina*?
De la Parra: "If you want me to, with great pleasure."
Maribona: "How long will you stay in Venezuela?"
De la Parra: A month. I'll go back to Europe, where my images and memories will be more precisely fixed, and distance will make it easier to convert them to paragraphs.

It was late. The study was smoky. We took leave of the lovely, interesting and strong woman, so gentle in her expression. So beautiful, sweet and harmonious inside and out. Lydia Cabrera only knows how to deal with people of the same intellectual and spiritual caliber.

Notes

1 *Las Grietas de la ternura*, Elizabeth Garrels. Caracas: Monte Avila Editores 1986, pp. 138-143.
2 Conrado Massaguer (1889-1965 or 56?) was an illustrator in Cuba for the magazine *Social* in the 1920's and 1930's. (Collection of Cuban journals at the University of Miami, 1990).
3 During Juan Vicente Gómez's regime, Caracas was swarming with popular and student demonstrations. Gómez's police shot at demonstrators with machine guns, closed the universities, and sentenced the young people to hard labor on the roads or to prison or exile. Teresa wrote to Gómez to express her sympathy (Bosch 133). For granting this interview to the *Diario de la Marina,* she was taken to task by Venezuelans who were bitterly opposed to the Gómez dictatorship. According to Palacios, this interview was given in innocence, it was untimely, and de la Parra really had no idea of the political climate in Venezuela, or the importance of the

student protests in February, which she downplayed in the interview. She was unaware of the seriousness of the situation and the increased state of repression.

[4] José Vasconcelos (1882-1959) was a Mexican writer, philosopher and politician who served as Secretary of Public Education. He lectured extensively in South and Central America and at Columbia and Princeton Universities. In his book, *La Raza Cósmica*, (1925), he argued for "the cosmic race" or the modern mestizo nation. De la Parra read his book and commented on it in her letters.

Translator's Note: Obviously, de la Parra was expecting to sit for a caricature or a drawing of her and was not prepared to give an interview. Furthermore, it seems strange that she would know exactly how many miles of road, to the mile, had been constructed in Venezuela.

CHAPTER TWELVE

FRANCIS DE MIOMANDRE:
A FEW WORDS ON *IPHIGENIA*[1]

In his introduction to *Ifigenia*, Teresa de la Parra's French translator Francis de Miomandre proposed a critical analysis of the novel. He understood the charms the novel worked on the reader and tried to explain that the novel was the work of an intelligent woman who was providing a woman's point of view in giving the reader a portrait of a woman.[2] This is what Miomandre had to say:

I am grateful from the bottom of my heart for the success of this book. All the more for having seen the manuscript and knowing ahead of time it was worthy of success. At first it was called *The Diary of a Young Girl who Was Bored*, a title which seemed too modest for me, since it described only the minor aspect of the work. I like the current title, with its mythological allusion as long as a smile, one of these charming smiles, furtive and confidential, that belonged to Teresa de la Parra both as a woman and as a writer, furthermore. I have the honor of knowing her personally and she is one of the most genuine writers whom I have met in this valley of tears and ink called literature.

Ingenuousness; this is Teresa de la Parra's most notable and precious gift. It's difficult to imagine such a lack of posing, a fresh and sincere naturalness. Others writers, even the best, seem to hide it all, or preach too much, are hypocritical or cynical, write lyrically as though drunk on words, or are realists charged with physiological precision. What is remarkable about the author of *Iphigenia* is her exquisite insight in expressing emotions, moderation, balance, and the familiar conversational tone.

Have you ever thought about the contradictory phrase" a salon confession"? Well, then, here you have the work of this novelist: a confession for a given society. Teresa de la Parra says everything that goes through her head, a head as beautiful within as without, and we are never shocked, because even when she allows herself to be carried away by flights of fancy, or by the logical conclusions of her liberal convictions, she continues to follow an inner rule that keeps her from saying so, and going further than she should. This surety of temperance, this subtle harmony, this secret rhythm, come from our author's special sensibility that I don't wish to analyze, because this pedantic task would do no more than to smother and disassociate the subtle elements that compose it. Nothing is equal to the reading. Ten pages of the novel say more about her than a long critical analysis.

From the point of view of composition, *Iphigenia* is a well-constructed work, despite the slow cadence and the abundance of digressions (exquisite digressions that should by no means be left out.) It's the story of a girl from Caracas: María Eugenia Alonso, who returns to her home after a long absence highlighted by a few weeks spent in Paris, where, unknown to her, she spends the last of her money. Upon arriving in Caracas she realizes that she doesn't have any money to spend. She becomes the designated victim of the familial Euminides, the modern Iphigenia.

All around her are a series of carefully drawn characters all with clear-cut characteristics, delicious and wise. The Grandmother (Abuelita) severe and affectionate, the pious and bourgeois Aunt Clara, the two uncles: Eduard, hypocritical and boring, the false well-meaning man, the man admired by all; Pancho, the delicious madman, paradoxical and likeable, the colonial counterpart of Monsieur Dick, the adorable hero of David Copperfield; Gregoria, the black servant, full of wisdom and the collector of beautiful tales, and Mercedes, exquisite and elegant, but who hides her wounded soul behind a smile. It's impossible to forget any of these characters so full of truth and life, so far from conventionality and false originality. And I won't say anything about how these characters are drawn as they parade by. Always depicted with subtle and allusive traits, they remain, precisely for this reason, firmly etched in the spirit.

But the real substance of this book transcends beyond this. As perfect as the novel is, the argument interests us less than the reflections on its development is slowly suggested by the author. That's not to say that loving story does not captivate us, no; what takes place we do not see through our own eyes, but rather through the eyes of the narrator. It is she whom we follow at all times and the occurrences do not move us, but it is rather the repercussions they have on her spirit. The true story is the heroine's, the story of he heart, now wounded, now enchanted by the malice or the goodness of others; it's the story of her spirit, the spectacle of a changing universe which is recorded as on a sensitive photographic plate. So dwells within us the sweet authority of María Eugenia Alonso, who from the first pages, without our even realizing it, we see through her eyes, we hear with her ears, and we feel with her. We don't want to escape, not even for a moment, from this captivity. The phenomenon of intellectual transmission that this represents, as mysterious as it may seem, functions in a very natural way. It's as though as children we listened passionately to a story told by someone who vehemently believed in it.

Not for a moment do we think we are reading literature (despite the subtle grace that absorbs all science and all force into a crystalline cleanness that is the highest achievement in art). We feel only the sensation that we have been admitted into the confidence of a personal journal; we look over it enchanted, moved by the person who wrote it. We find it clever and naïve, sincere and delicate, so modest as to hide nothing. And if it's well written it's because its author through her birth, her education and her dreams is as incapable of expressing herself without elegance as she is to thinking without dignity.

Because of her refinement, for her love of humanity, for her brand of sweet philosophy towards the subtle and the strange, and above all, for her gentle malice, her spirit is akin to Jorge Hoore, with that of Anatole France, and is akin even more so to the spirit of that delicious Mexican, Gutiérrez Nájera, so unjustly forgotten. But these three are men, and as exquisite as they are in their sensibilities, they lack that supreme vibration, that indefinite phosphorescence that embraces the work of Teresa de la Parra.

Iphigenia is, above all, the portrait of a woman. Simple and complex, natural and in love with all artifice, tender, coquettish and full of life; yes, infinite and marvelously full of life: A woman.

"A Few More Words on Ifigenia"[3]

I was among the first in France to read Teresa de la Parra's *Ifigenia*, that delicious novel that has so stirred public opinion in South America. I translated a few fragments and wrote a prologue that today I think was too brief and insufficient. It's that the essence of this exquisite book does not entirely offer itself up at first reading. There are so many elements to attract us. Even if it were no more than the exoticism that seduces French readers. An entire world is revealed before our eyes. It is a half-modern, half-colonial society, whose contrasts contain the strong flavor mixed of flowery and perfumed atmosphere that make us dream and think of our beloved "islands" of yesteryear. Oh, the enchantment of those patios filled with jasmine, planted with orange trees, beneath whose shade one slides sweetly into a languid siesta! Those tropical fields, with their forests mysteriously inhabited by butterflies ten times larger than ours, those perfumed intoxicating nights; that Eden!

Then there are the characters. All of them new and original. Teresa de la Parra is a born novelist. She knows how to create types. We can never forget Gregoria, Mercedes, or Uncle Pancho, César Leal, Grandma or Aunt Clara. What a rare gift this is. It seems effortless. The narration moves along at a languid pace, from time to time cut by sudden outbursts. It's like a river that peacefully flows in a sweet backwater of dreams and meditations then suddenly becomes a waterfall breaking up on the slopes of emotion and tragedy. And all of this with a charming naturalness.

The development of this artistic temperament absolutely ignores the artifices of false rhetoric, of impoverished formulas with which writers clothe themselves with importance. It's like a beautiful child playing in the sun. The grace and harmony of his movements recall the spirit of a wise and a simple heart. One observation is enough: having written a book of more than 500 pages without once stumbling or hesitating is the highest praise one can heap upon the author.

Even so, it's not this which seduces me most, that's not even the secret of the book.

What in my opinion assures Teresa de la Parra that indestructible freshness, a trait of books destined to be classics, what will keep this novel readable when others much more pretentious or with more facile effects have been lost to memory, is that she has created a kind of girl who is at the same time modern yet one of the most eternal we can meet, simply because she is so real and so true.

The only thing art cannot replace is the truth and the character of María Eugenia Alonso who is so psychologically real, so profoundly so, that it makes us look deeper. María Eugenia *is*. That is all. She *is* and nothing more. She presents us all at once with the absolute sincerity of her daily confession and she is there. She is complex, of course, but her superficial complexity quickly leads us to see the lively and fundamental simplicity of her temperament and character. That this creature is being shaped, that this tender and restless cocoon feels pain and has revelatory insight thrust upon it, and that her inner beauty emerges, is the splendid metamorphosis of her secret.

It's impossible to discuss even María Eugenia Alonso's real character. That undoubtedly would cast ignorance on the laws that govern true works of art and living beings. One would have to be blind or act in bad faith to say what Maria Eugenia Alonso professes as doctrines of her moral life, the mischievous paradoxes she plays with and delights in scandalizing her grandmother and aunt with at times. That's not to say that misunderstanding her would result in accusing her of perversity or egoism. On the contrary. For me, at least, what struck me, what stood out on the second reading, which was more attentive and focused, was the ingeniousness of the central character. For centuries literary critics have waxed enthusiastic about the delicious freshness of Shakespeare's maidens, the innocence of their displays of spirit, the uneasy flirting that agitates and entertains them until love strikes and leaves them forever serious. How can one fail to see that María Eugenia Alonso is like them? It's the same stirring of desires, dreams, madness, paradoxes, the same thrust and parry confronting the lovers, the fireworks set off by youth. But soon the terrible archangel visits and with one beat of his wings knocks down their pride and prostrates them forever in the sacred act of consent.

I would like to show up to what point María Eugenia Alonso's flirting distances itself in its essence from the unhealthy coquettishness that motivated the majority of her contemporaries. Hers is exempt from perversity. Of course she wears makeup, exaggerates the color of her lips with Guerlain Red, wears very short dresses, and wears her hair in a boyish cut, all that is understood, but the question is? What do these tricks do for her? What does she want them to do for her?

She means nothing by it. Here lies her superiority. If she always strives to be pretty it's for her own self, for her own taste for elegance. She loves perfection. She belongs to that type (and that type also exists among men) for whom like it or not, elegance is a must. They are horrified by disorder, negligence, and imperfection. And if the majority of people who don't understand these subtleties criticize and reproach her it's because of the lesson they learn from it.

Some wear the elegance of spirit under the elegance of their clothing. María Eugenia Alonso is doubly elegant. When at the end of her story she gives up happiness and true love forever, because of serious reasons and the absolute modesty of her great soul, but doesn't speak up, as she takes the path towards the common and bourgeois marriage her destiny bequeaths her, like Iphigenia to the altar, she seems to walk towards something a thousand times more painful than her own sacrifice: how vulgar souls will judge her decision. They will no doubt accuse her of being selfish, of acting in her own interest, but what does it matter? A supreme divinity calls and leads her. She walks without looking back. The truly elegant do not live for opinion. They live to fulfill the mystery of interior perfection, the outside being merely a mystery and a symbol. María Eugenia Alonso knows the cost of giving up one's right to happiness. If she's given it up it is to dress herself in the splendid garments of an ethical ideal. Iphigenia was also dressed in fine garments before she walked to her sacrifice.

Notes

[1] *Obra* p.3-5.

[2] "In the prologue to the novel in 1924 Miomandre sets the tone and becomes the model for other male critics. He is happy about the success of the book and praises de la Parra's talent for writing. This critic translated *Ifigenia* into French for a collection that included the works of Katherine Mansfield and Virginia Woolf ("The Male Critic and the Woman Writer: Reading Teresa de la Parra's Critics," Elsa Krieger Gamberini, 178).

[3] *Obra*, p.311-313

CHAPTER THIRTEEN

IN HER OWN VOICE:
SELECTIONS FROM THE LETTERS
OF TERESA DE LA PARRA

Teresa de la Parra was a prolific letter writer. Her novel *Iphigenia* (1924), begins with the protagonist, María Eugenia, writing a long letter to her friend, Cristina, "A Very Long Letter Wherein Things are Told As They Are in Novels." After de la Parra's death in 1936, many of her letters were in the possession of her family, and some of these were destroyed or censored. The letters that were made public appear in *Teresa de la Parra, Obra: Narrativa, Ensayos, Cartas (*Biblioteca Ayacucho, 1991) and *Cartas a Lydia Cabrera.* These letters shed light on many aspects of her life: her loves, travels, hopes and aspirations, her valiant fight with tuberculosis and search for a cure. Above all, they offer insights into the author's literary method, the defense of her work, especially her novel *Iphigenia,* and they serve as a valuable adjunct for literary criticism. The selected fragments translated from de la Parra's letters complement what we know of her life, what inspired her to write, especially as they pertain her novels and her life as an intellectual and public speaker. As her biographer, María Fernando Palaces, said, de la Parra's letters are an unbound book, available for the reader who wants to bind it.

Today, de la Parra is remembered chiefly as the writer of two novels and three published lectures, *The Influence of Women on the Formation of the American Spirit.* She also wrote articles for newspapers and several short stories. One of these, "Mama X" became incorporated into *Iphigenia.* After *Mama Blanca's Memoirs* was published in 1929 and before she became ill, de la Parra wanted to write a "sentimental" historical novel on the life of Simón Bolívar, and in her letters she mentions several other projects that never came to fruition. In her letters, she suggests establishing partnerships and writing collaborations with her correspondents: Zaldumbide, Zea, and Carías. We know that she corresponded with Gabriela Mistral and Lydia Cabrera, among others, though none of these letters appear in *Obra.*

It is through these letters that we can witness de la Parra's enthusiasm for various projects wax and wane. Several times she suffered crises of confidence. Some of these were partly due to her illness, tuberculosis, which was misdiagnosed for a while and whose lack of treatment left her weak, depressed and unproductive. The letters reflect periods of activity and periods of depression. In a letter to her mother and her sisters when she is on shipboard on her way to Havana, she is proud and self-assured and happy to be the "Princess on Board," the center of attention, much like her heroine María Eugenia was on the *Arnus*. She was stung by the reception *Iphigenia* received in Caracas; after all, she claimed that the Caracas readership was all that mattered to her and that she never meant for the novel to be read outside Venezuela. She reeled from unflattering book reviews, but she was quick to rise to her own defense and she delighted in parrying with her detractors. In some of the most interesting letters she elaborates on and defends *Iphigenia* and she discusses the heroine's motivations as well as her own. She shows how a shy young girl, just like María Eugenia, can be transformed into a chic mademoiselle in a matter of months and describes the steps necessary to achieving this end in a rebuttal to Eduardo Gómez Esponda. She describes how a "young girl in braids" should go about this process of transformation in Paris, spelling out what to wear and where to buy it, where to get a haircut, and where to be seen. In short, she offers advice for the equivalent of today's extreme makeover.

She felt slandered; the Caracas press misquoted her and she was convinced it was doing its best to show her in a bad light. She held grudges; she wrote to her friends about the incident with C.. E...(Concha Espina), complained about it and refused to pardon her attacker. Sometimes de la Parra could be unreasonable. "When, in December of 1926, Chilean critic Armando Labarca published an article in *El Universal* praising *Ifigenia* for its author's gift of observation of the ridiculous aspects of people and things, of gentle conventionalisms, Parra refuted that she had made anything or anyone in her novel look ridiculous. The exasperated columnist mollified her by writing yet another column in which he praised her for her charming and contradictory letters" (Lemaitre, *Between Flight and Longing,* 104).

She showed surprise that Unamuno took the time to read her novel (all 520 pages of it!) and wrote back to answer his questions about certain characters and her choice of words. He asked her why she didn't write poetry. She walked in while Unamuno was lecturing on *Ifigenia*, analyzing the novel "like a naturalist examines an insect," and it made her feel like being two people at once: both a writer and a member of the audience. She felt her formal education was insufficient and wished she could have studied longer. During de la Parra's lifetime, higher education for young women of her class in Venezuela was out of the question, but this did not stop her from becoming a lifelong learner. She continued to read widely throughout her life and attended lectures at the Sorbonne and the Paris School of Ethnology. She made reading lists for herself and read extensively while she was confined in the sanitarium. She traveled and read about the places she planned to visit. She wrote to experts such as Vicente Lecuna, the leading historian on Bolívar, to get his advice for a novel she wanted to write about the Liberator.

Her letters show that she was ambivalent about her stay at the sanitarium in Leysin.[1] On the one hand, she considered herself a "prisoner surrounded by snow." On the other hand, she described her confinement as living in a Buddhist paradise. Her convalescence offered her a respite from the outside world, and an opportunity to read about the saints and mystics and to work on her spiritual life. She wrote that life in the sanitarium was like living in a small town where everyone knew what was going on in each other's private lives. She was fascinated by her fellow patients and wrote about the poignant moments in their lives as she witnessed them. She could not finish reading Thomas Mann's *The Magic Mountain* and could not make the connection between the novel's content and her own situation and her life in the sanitarium. The day came when she realized that she had become "the woman who needs nothing." This insight also added to her ambivalence. She could not decide whether she had achieved the Buddhist detachment she sought, or whether this state of detachment was a foreshadowing of her imminent death.

In Leysin, she grew nostalgic for the tropics and realized that there was more to Venezuela than Caracas and Macuto, where she had written her first novel.[2] She wanted to regain her strength back in order to explore the parts of Venezuela she had not visited. In her eagerness to write a romantic novel about Bolívar, she amassed books and other information and sought out Bolivar's descendents to interview to the point that the project overwhelmed her, and she gave up on it, but not without first consulting the foremost Bolívar scholar and planning to soak up atmosphere through travel that she felt to be essential to her book. She held romantic (and at times misguided or misinformed) views of Bolívar and his lover, Manuelita Saenz, and wanted the novel about Bolivar to be told from Sáenz's point of view.[3]

De la Parra had a romantic relationship with Gonzalo Zaldumbide. According to Venezuelan critic and de la Parra scholar Laura Febres, this liaison was an embarrassment to her family, who destroyed most of the correspondence between the two. Febres believes that there were many letters to and from Zaldumbide that were destroyed by the author's family. She believes that the two were planning to marry, but that Zaldumbide's prior marriage and de la Parra's health stood in the way, though de la Parra did not become ill or did not realize that she was ill until 1932.[4]

In the diary that de la Parra kept from 1931-1936, beginning in Bellevue in June of 1931, she records on October 18, 1931 that she had started putting her papers in order. She began this task by sorting through all her correspondence since 1924, rereading, cataloguing, or destroying letters. "I began with my correspondence with G. (Gonzalo). I spent all day Sunday all alone, rereading his letters and mine, I ripped up many, I have saved and sorted others. I saw four intense years of my life fly before me. Despite periods of monotony, I'd forgotten many things valuable to my inner life, and how sad it is to see how we die through what we leave behind, what was given in one moment and now has faded in memory despite remembering it with love and tenderness (*Obra* 455)."

De la Parra and Zaldumbide were a romantic pair from 1924 to 1929. There is an apocryphal tale about Zaldumbide placing a phone call to de la Parra on the morning of his wedding day, supposedly offering to call off his impending marriage to Isabel Rosales Paseico on the spot if de la Parra accepted his proposal, but her friend Lydia Cabrera and de la Parra's sister María deny this story. "Perhaps their plans for marriage failed because, as Juan Liscano remembers, Zaldumbide never appreciated her subtlety." (Sommer, in *Critical Edition, Mama Blanca's Memoirs*, xvi.) Gloria Stolk, in the paper she delivered to the III Congreso Interamericano para el studio de la Obra de las Escritoras at the University of Ottawa, May 1978, stated, "Teresa seems to have fallen in love with a handsome diplomat from Quito: Gonzalo Zaldumbide. He was a tall, elegant man, with refined features, also a writer, the author of a famous novel, *The Tragic Elegy,* a worthy match for Teresa. They went out and they were seen together in all the embassies and athenaeums and she wrote to her friend in Caracas to send her a copy of her birth certificate. This letter, which I've held in my very hands, and was one of the letters that Carias did not publish, following my advice, proves that Teresa was thinking of getting married. Years after Teresa's death, one day Zaldumbide confided to me that it was her delicate health that stood in the way of this union."(*Obra* xxxiv). Aside from letters to her beloved Lillo or Lillito, as she addressed her lover, de la Parra sent him telegrams and notes in which she expressed her "abundant and luxurious" love.

De la Parra's letters to Rafael Carías, Vicente Lecuna, and Luis Zea Uribe are variations on several themes. The letters to Carías best express de la Parra's literary and personal trajectory. In addition, Carías handled her personal and financial affairs, which she curiously did not want to entrust to her brothers. These letters begin with de la Parra's journey to Paris and they document her activities, her struggles, her depression, her travels, her opinions, and her illness. Through her letters we learn of her interest in mysticism, her love for all things Creole, and her increasing fascination with writing a different kind of book on Bolívar other than the many biographies and historical novels that already existed. She writes to Carías, Lecuna, and Zea Uribe about the reception of her works, and shared with them her ideas for future work. She informs them of her illness, describes life in the sanatorium, and worries about her finances as the bolívar declined in value.

At the time, Lecuna was the leading expert on Bolívar. De la Parra corresponded with him and kept the idea for writing a book about Bolívar from a different focus alive for three years. Her letters to Lecuna reveal her interest in the Venezuelan hero and the "Father of La Gran Colombia" from her initial enthusiasm to her flagging interest. It is as though she had too much material. She realized that she was a novelist, and not a historian, and this led to her abandoning this project altogether. It was also a time when her interest shifted to more mystical topics and she began to read about Buddhism and Indian religions. Her interest in mysticism is evident in the metaphysical exchanges in the letters she wrote to Zea Uribe, the Colombian who wrote *Mirando al Misterio* and who shared her beliefs in visions, transports and telegraphic communication. The nature and the tone of these exchanges contrasts sharply with the letters de la Parra wrote to her critics and her other correspondents.

Teresa de la Parra enjoyed a long friendship with the Cuban anthropologist Lydia Cabrera, and it is this relationship, along with her correspondence with Gabriela Mistral, that leads some critics to label de la Parra a lesbian: "As in the case of Gabriela Mistral, Teresa de la Parra's sexual difference, I was to find out, was something critics did not speak about or else busily masked by manipulating the author's life into a socially acceptable script. Thus the biographical fictions-to whose fabrication the authors themselves not infrequently contributed-stressing the most salient aspects of conventional femininity: Gabriela Mistral, the mother teacher, Teresa de la Parra, the charming social butterfly" (Molloy xii in *Mama Blanca*).

According to Laura Febres, who interviewed Cabrera, the two never shared a sexual relationship, and Cabrera was concerned that some scholars insisted on "outing" her friend.[5] De la Parra inspired Cabrera to collect Afro-Cuban folktales, which were later published as the *Contes*

Negres de Cuba or *Cuentos Negros de Cuba*. The two traveled together and shared similar tastes, but Cabrera told Febres that de la Parra and she were not lovers. One reason that may lead critics to label de la Parra as a lesbian is that heterosexual marriage does not fare well in *Iphigenia*. The main theme of the novel is the sacrificial marriage of a young girl from an aristocratic, but not wealthy, Caracas family to an overbearing, but rich and politically connected older man. A pattern runs through the Alonso family: men marry women with money and then fritter away their inheritances. One letter to Zaldumbide hints at economic problems which is another factor that may have kept the two from getting married.

In his book on Teresa de la Parra: *Del diálogo de géneros y la melancolía*, (1997) Venezuelan critic Douglas Bohórquez insists that de la Parra deserves greater recognition and must be shared intellectually with the country that once hardly seemed to appreciate her. For most Venezuelans, Rómulo Gallegos, the author of *Doña Barbara, Canaima,* and other novels is the "official" author of the country. But thanks to Teresa de la Parra, Venezuelan literature reinvented itself, and was given a feminine aesthetic, this critic reminds us. Her writing explored daily life at the time, and the relationship between tragedy and comedy.

He wrote that as of 1995 de la Parra's letters were incomplete, since her family censured some and burned others. He wondered what had happened to the notes for the novel about Bolívar she planned to write. Her work expressed a rejection of conventional forms and stereotypes, and she was constantly searching for new ways to write, from the intimate and the personal, to the collective and the oral. Sadly, however, she has yet to be assimilated into a literary tradition, and that is the challenge for modern scholars, according to Bohórquez. He suggests that what remains to be done is to tie de la Parra's life to her work, and her text to her biography, since her narrative has been studied from the point of view of traditional criticism. He saw the need to link her photos, her letters, her inner world, and her personal relationships to her fiction.

Translating and tying de la Parra's letters to her fiction is a crucial first step in assimilating her work not just into the Venezuelan literary tradition, but to the greater and ever growing appreciation of women's writing. The following excerpts from the letters of Teresa de la Parra published in *Obra: Narrativa, ensayos, cartas,* (Velia Bosch, Ayacucho, 1991) and *Cartas a Lydia Cabrera* (Hiriart, Rosario, 1988) reveal some of the personality of this complex and groundbreaking writer who defies categorization and refuses to be placed within any literary movement.

Letters to Carlos García Prada

I began this book with a translation of Teresa de la Parra's brief biography she wrote in a letter to Carlos García Prada, a professor of Latin American literature and a writer. In a letter she wrote him from Paris, on May 5, 1931 she thanked him for his warm reception of both her books. In 1942 García Prada edited fifteen poems by Porfirio Barba Jacob, a pseudonym for the gay Colombian poet Miguel Angel Osorio. In 1946 García Prada edited and illustrated *Blanca Nieves y compañia* (D.C. Heath), based on *Las Memorias de Mama Blanca.* In 1959, Houghton Mifflin published his *Tres Cuentos,* a forward thinking elementary Spanish reader and in 1982 he compiled the author's *Obras Completas.*

De la Parra was honored that García Prada wanted to publish *Ifigenia* for North American publication. But she felt *Mama Blanca* would be more appropriate and she asked him to get in touch with Waldo Frank, who would need to edit the text and reduce it like the French edition. She agreed to send García Prada her biography and some reviews, and mailed him her biography, written in the third person. She wrote to him again from Beauliue, France, August 26, 1931. "I am here in the Côte d'Azure, where I am spending summer and planning to visit Italy for a few weeks. Thank you for sending your letter of August 5 and your three essays, which make me feel as though I've known you a long time. I received the letter from Waldo Frank, who hasn't had the time to read *Iphigenia* and does not think it is the right time for an English translation. We must first get a publisher before we translate it. I am not in a hurry for this translation. Perhaps I will go to Venezuela next year. In this case, I would come to the US and I could speak with you and with the translator. Thanks again for your essay on Gabriela Mistral, which I enjoyed very much."

Letters to Rafael Carias

Teresa de la Parra met Venezuelan anthropologist Rafael Carias in 1919. He was the first to read the manuscript for *Iphigenia.*

On May 2, 1924, she wrote: "I am on a literary fast, not reading or writing, but I wanted to send you news of your friend María Eugenia. I entered the novel in a literary contest in Caracas and ten finalists were chosen from three hundred entries. García Calderon, who was the director of the publishing house and was a judge last year said that if I would have submitted it last year, it would have won. He likes María Eugenia but has only followed her up to the corral with Gregoria and the chickens. Only you and Parra Pérez have seen the whole book. I'm going to give it to

García Calderon, Zerega, and Zaldumbide, who also love the bored young lady who obviously was not as urn-marriageable as she thought. I'll be in Paris until May, then I want to publish the book in Madrid, the contest notwithstanding, and you'll be the first to get a copy.

The story of "Mama X," translated by Mauclair (the cousin of a famous writer), will be published in a Parisian magazine. I've been dancing in seven centimeter heels, wearing tight clothing, all which takes up my valuable time, but on the other hand, I'm methodically and systematically visiting all the old museums and monuments in Paris.

I'm taking elocution lessons and lessons in French diction, attending lectures at the Sorbonne, I've heard Colette and other contemporary French writers lecture. Something will come of this some day. I think all Venezuelans should travel to Europe, not only to take in its visual culture but also to dispel our fear of the unknown..I have received no letters from Venezuela, so keep me posted. I take my "Mercedes Galindo" cigarette holder everywhere, and it has served me faithfully. Emilia sends you her regards."

From Jean-les-Pins on March 1, 1926 she wrote about one of the reviews a detractor had written concerning her novel: "I received your letter and Dr. Lisandro Alvarado's review, so erudite and philosophical as to be incomprehensible. He may as well have written in Greek. We could have understood each other better, what with him speaking in an old dead tongue and me in this poor live language we speak along with the daily bread we eat. And neither of us would have understood the other. I feel like a wandering Jew after three months in Paris. Now I am in the Cote d'Azure with my mother and María and I've come here to baptize my second godchild. I've abandoned literature to the point where I left the reviews of *Iphigenia* that I was going to mail you in Paris. They mention me in the *Crónica Literaria Hispanoamerica.* If they have not published it in Caracas, I'd appreciate it if you would send it to *El Universal."*

On March 5, 1927, she wrote: "I received your clippings and it shook me up and made me read the review of *Iphigenia* with renewed interest. It's all relative and it's only after we've heard the bitter voice of censure and reproach that we can appreciate, by contrast, the sweetness that comes of understanding.

"I can see that my novel was not well received in Caracas. This doesn't absolutely wound me and my self-esteem as a writer since as a touchstone I can turn to the rest of the Spanish-speaking readership, who have been overly kind and charming, not to mention the French readers. The case of the Caraqueños' reaction, far from hurting me, allows me to make some interesting observations. There exists in Caracas, like in every small town, the germ of envy that invades and infects even those not capable of envy. Another thing I discovered about *Iphigenia* is that its ironic intent was misunderstood or not grasped. In Venezuela, diatribe is nonexistent, since there is no opposition. Irony is deformed and exaggerated and reduced to the category of insult. True irony, like charity, begins at home and should smile benevolently and should be perfumed with indulgence. Irony is different than cruel and vulgar mockery. In some circles in Caracas, my book has been slandered. Wounded by their own patriotism, the book has been judged as cruel mockery rather than indulgent irony. A friend asked me to delete María Eugenia Alonso's impression of Caracas in the second edition, especially the section describing the low, squat houses, an unpatriotic description on my part; while a Spanish critic thought the description of houses with their patios and their windows facing the street delicious and liked seeing a charming, sentimental city through María Eugenia Alonso's eyes. I believe the hostility directed at *Iphigenia* in Caracas is due to a pandemic of envy, an exaggerated patriotism and strict moralist incomprehension. Despite the negative criticism, I love Caracas. Those who think they know their native land well because they have never traveled outside it are mistaken. Through travel we get to know our own native land better. These days I am inspired to write about Creole subjects and am inspired to write another book. Despite what is said about *Iphigenia* in Caracas, it has been such a great success in Paris that it leaves me frightened and anxious. The French love it best. There is no South American living in Paris who hasn't read it or wants to read it.

The Infanta Eulelia, the King of Spain's aunt, who is a writer and has a charming spirit, was amused by *Iphigenia* and invited me to tea and showered me with kindness and attention, and told me how she laughed out loud at some passages, such as the one about the cutwork tablecloth, so loudly, in fact, that her maid came running to see what the matter was.

I am going to write a monthly column for *El Universal* in Caracas."

From Havana, July 12, 1930, she reported her pride after delivering her lectures: "Colombia was a great success and it gave me the idea to write the intimate life of Bolívar. I want to get a sense of place, which I will do when I return to Venezuela. The visit to San Pedro Alejandrino and the Quinta Bolívar showed me how important it is to have a sense of place. Cuba has a more Creole color than we do and the blacks are especially colonial. I want to travel to Venezuela to see the Llanos, the Andes and to return to the hacienda life of my childhood: all this is necessary to get to know Bolívar. I ask for your help in sending books. I was about to return to Europe to take the waters with my mother, but my friend Lydia is ill."

Writing from Leysin on February 23, 1932: "You are going to be pained and surprised that I am writing from the Grand Hotel in Leysin, a tuberculosis sanitarium. I have recently discovered I have a lesion in my lung. All is white, light and silence, I have given myself up to this capricious and traitorous disease and am resigned to it. My life is spiritual and I am in a state of grace. I am in the best sanitarium, the most expensive one with the best food. I live a life of books, sun and snow. This disease brings all kinds of people here. I'm hiding the disease from my mother."

She looked to Carias for business advice. The bolívar had been devalued, and she was concerned about the expense of the sanitarium. Since she had been ill, a slave to the snow, as she describes herself, she had thought of Caracas with infinite sweetness. She remembered her friends and this comforted her. She explained how she had fallen ill in October and was given a wrong diagnosis and lost four months of time that could have been used to cure her.

From Vevey on October 3, 1932 she wrote that she had come down from the mountain a few days ago and was optimistic about her disease but concerned about her finances. After spending eight months in Leysin she knew more about the disease and it turned her philosophical. "I've reached the point where my soul is more mature and open to sacrifice and mysticism. I tried to read *The Magic Mountain,* the Nobel Prize winner, and could not get through even the first volume; there are pages and pages about common people, it is full of commonplaces and it is over six hundred pages of rambling,when there are times when one word or one silent glance can be filled with wit and beauty. I will spend the winter in Leysin but I may have to move out of the Grand Hotel because of the expense."

Letters to Gonzalo Zaldumbide

She wrote to her lover, Ecuadorian writer and diplomat Gonzalo Zaldumbide, from San Juan de Luz, France, August , 1924. She was still grieving for the death of Emilia Ibarra, her friend and patron. The line "the soul would suffice and I could do without the body," corroborates Lydia Cabrera's statement that de la Parra had a low sexual drive.

"I feel the greatest hate for that thing called love, as fierce and brutal as the Sunday bulls and the poor injured horses. I think about our story, which I still don't understand. Like María says (María is the heroine of Jorge Isaacs' eponymous novel) I fear you and hate other men. If only you could love me with a woman's soul. The soul would suffice and I could do without the body. Will other hands place rose water on your eyes? Who knows?"

She addresses Zaldumbide as "Mon Cheri," in a letter written in December, 1924, and confides that, "being alone in my bed feels like a desert without you in it." She explains her preference for writing with a pencil instead of with the gold Eversharp pen given to her by a suitor three years ago. "I feel as though you are about to kiss my eyes and I close them to a dream of you."

On Christmas Eve, 1924, she wrote to him from Maracay and remembers a time of "dolce far niente" when she was still in love with him. She waits for him the same way María Eugenia waits for Gabriel's letter, an incident in her novel, and just like in *Iphigenia,* she has a young suitor, a sixteen-year old young man who writes her verses and adores her and chats with her, much like Perucho, María Eugenia's smitten cousin. She thinks back to their time spent together in Paris and signs off saying it has been a painful year for her.

In 1926 she addresses him as Lillo, his nickname, and tells him, "You grow more beloved." His letters to her keep her from getting bored and free her from monotony. "I am rich. I adore you with a love that grows in spite of the barriers. Unfortunately, we don't have the money to break down these barriers and smooth our path." She compares his letters to his kisses, but the letters last longer than kisses and leave her cheeks redder than lips painted with Guerlain Red.

In 1927 she writes to him while she's in a bad mood, having received a letter by way of Barceló. She refers to this letter as a sort of anonymous letter or unpublished negative article about *Iphigenia.* "You can't imagine the insults and the insinuations. The cause of it is envy. I'll probably get over it by tomorrow, but it bothers me today and I had to tell you about it." In April,1928 she writes to her "beloved Lillo," who is in Quito. "I am sad and alone, my love, "she confesses her life is full of black moods. She is alone in her sister Elia's house, living with two servants. She never stops thinking about him and how she loves him, but in a different way than when he arrived in Caracas four years ago. She hasn't met anyone since then with whom she shares this special relationship. She's been as faithful to him as though she was a 75 year old woman. Caracas still doesn't attract her and she flees from praise. "Women adore me and are wildly enthusiastic about my work." She writes about her two brothers' good reputations and their marriages in France. "When will that day arrive when we can send the literati and the politicos to the devil so we may live sweetly and peacefully in a dual nationality that will be our marriage in France?" He keeps her going. "If I'm successful, I'll forget about my detractors (Zeballos, Calderón and all the rest) who've worked so hard to hurt me. They've harmed me but they don't matter. Say hello to Carías."

On January 6, 1928 she wrote to him from Caracas, telling him that it was a sad time for her; she's in bad spirits, complains of diminished income, and still misses Emilia. She sat in her bedroom and remembers their intimate moments in San Juan de Luz, which feels natural, like sunshine, and this adds to her feelings of desperation. His love no longer has the power to overcome her sadness. She compares her eleven-year friendship with Emilia to one month of their love. She wanted to return to France on the *Arnus* on the 25th of November, and was about to pack her things. To his question about her literary production, she responds she's written nothing. She considers writing a great happiness and a blessing. She is hoping that by the time they are reunited she will have written so much he will have to stem the torrent of her words. To help unloosen her tongue, she had embarked on a reading plan consisting of Creole and Spanish works. Perhaps some day they will write together. She tells him about her fascination with colonial life in the Americas.

Letters to Enrique Bernardo Nuñez

Enrique Bernardo Nuñez wrote a favorable review of *Iphigenia*. "Teresa de la Parra: Ifigenia y sus críticos" published in *El Universal*, Caracas, on April 6, 1927. De la Parra wrote to the Venezuelan writer and journalist about an unflattering review written by Carlos de Villena, "Estudio crítico de la novella "Ifigenia" published in Bogotá, Colombia.

Writing to Nuñez from Paris in 1928 she hopes he's seen the first chapter of her new little book in *El Nuevo Tiempo*. It is doing well in Bogotá. The critic Carlos de Villena was furious at María Eugenia and treated her as though she was a real person rather than a fictional character. But that makes her feel good. "The real María Eugenia can be found on the streets, and while Carlos de Villena is taken by her and attacks her morals, deep inside, he is desperately in love with this beautiful, coquettish woman who is inaccessible. Who is he? A priest? But beneath it all he is a satyr. If he was a respectable person and a less vulgar one he might get a response from María Eugenia. But she does not want to pick a fight. I am proud to finish writing *Las Memorias de Mama Blanca*. It was written with love and is true to my current tastes. Unlike *Iphigenia,* it is not a novel and is not subject to discussion. Let's see how long it takes for it to be published. It took me seven years to write it. If this book is successful, I'll continue the series."

She wrote from the Hotel Vernet, in Paris on June, 1928 to inform Nuñez that she had returned from her travels in Colón, La Havana, Washington, D.C. and New York. She heard diatribes against Venezuela and its government and heard the same criticism at the Press Congress she attended in Cuba. "Public conscience has been stirred up in Caracas, but it's a blind alley and it's business as usual. We must be stoic about the situation; it's a different kind of tyranny. I'll always remember the land, its landscape and its dead. Things went well for her in Cuba, but the intellectual climate there left much to be desired. They are charming, generous and hospitable people. It's like Caracas except the people are not so narrow-minded and they have less money." The second edition of *Iphigenia* was due out and she wanted to include Nunez's criticism since he had praised the book. Being recognized in Venezuela for his research in history and politics, along with his writing, also made his opinion important to her.

In September, 1928 she wrote again from Paris and told Núñez she had also been to Vevey spending the past month reading up on Bolívar. The gray skies and the rain made her claustrophobic. Like Simon Rodriquez, she longed to travel on foot through the tropics, with books and a hammock, taking in the air, trees, the blue sea, and meeting the Blacks, Indians, and the uneuropeanized white Creoles. She found these Creoles charming, without Parisian elegance and pretentiousness. She saw traces of "la colonia" in Colombia and now wanted to find it in Venezuela. She was inspired by her visit to Quinta Bolívar.

Letters to her Mother and her Sisters

On board the ship that was sailing to Havana in March of 1927, de la Parra wrote a chatty letter to her mother and her sisters to report on the conference she had been invited to attend. She writes about the members of the delegation describes their activities on board. She describes the makeup of the groups. Typical of the fashion-conscious de la Parra, she describes what the women wore. This letter is uncharacteristically boastful. She is very proud to be in such distinguished company, and she seems pleased with herself.

She reported on the members of the conference. She especially liked the French group, led by Maurice de Waleffe. There were twelve distinguished women, and seven she deemed to be "pseudo writers" who were accompanying their husbands. She reported on the women's dress and makeup. The men represent the French elite. She writes about the brilliance of evening life and their attire. Besides Waleffe, in attendance were Paul Reboux, Vaudoyer, the critic from the *Revue des Deux Mondes*, Fernando Greg, a French poet, the editor of *Figaro*, the editor of *Temps* and others. As it happens in these cases, cliques or groups formed. The first group was hand-picked by Waleffe and was made up of the most influential men and the best looking women: Madame Reboux, (very pretty), Mme. Canelle, Mme Lasca, Mme Bremat and me. She writes that she is without a rival and Waleffe lets everyone know that she was invited by the Cuban government. She sits at the table of honor between the ministers of Cuba and France. Waleffe and the captain asked her to make up an invitation list and she enjoyed doing that. She is called "The Princess on Board" and everyone was nice to her. Fragments of her writing were circulated among the guests and she was pleased that the French elite were enthusiastic about her work. Her dresses were a success, despite the fact that Mme. Reboux wore only Lanvins. They composed and recited clever quatrains about each other and she sat at the most brilliant and cleverest table. She admired the French members of the group for their generosity, talent and intelligence.

The cable that was sent to the President read: "There are fifty eight attendees, twelve of whom are women. Among them is the novelist Teresa de la Parra." She was pleased that of all those attending the conference, only her name was mentioned. She admitted, "But I see that I am worse that I… (María Eugenia Alonso, the protagonist of Iphigenia who is fond of describing how chic she had become) telling you about my success."

Letters to Vicente Lecuna

A project that captured Tesesa de la Parra's fancy but was never completed was the idea of writing a historical novel about Simón Bolívar. She began a correspondence with Vicente Lecuna, a Caracas native who was the foremost Bolivarian historian. He was also a well-known engineer, educator and historian in Venezuela who organized and curated the Archive of Simón Bolivar. The two exchanged a number of letters in which de la Parra asked him for guidance, a reading list and other resources. The project never came to fruition. Either she was ultimately overwhelmed by the material, did not trust herself as a historian, or she suffered a depression or simply lost her enthusiasm. De la Parra identified strongly with her Venezuelan roots. With the success of the publication of *Mama Blanca's Memoirs* in 1929, with its nostalgic take on life on the hacienda and her interest in colonial history, and with the positive reception of the author's lectures on Bolívar in Havana in 1927 and her later lectures in Bogotá and Barranquilla, de la Parra began to wax nostalgic about colonial life and the role of Símon Bolívar in the history of the Americas. She saw him as a romantic hero, and despite the many biographies that existed, she wanted to write a historical novel about the "Liberator." During his presidency Antonio Guzmán Blanco decreed that every plaza in Venezuela would be called "Plaza Bolívar" and that every public office should hang a portrait of Bolívar. De la Parra believed Bolívar's virtues should be emulated. She admired his, abnegation, spirit of sacrifice, rectitude, and purity of soul, and she felt they should be models for Venezuela. Previous biographies of Bolívar did not capture his spirit.

De la Parra wanted to focus on the "softer side" of the South American hero, especially since she was interested in how the many women in his life had influenced the father of "La Gran Colombia," or the countries which eventually became Venezuela, Colombia, and Ecuador. De la Parra also identified with the physical suffering of Bolívar, who died at the age of 47 in 1830. She kept the idea of writing about Bolívar's "other life" alive for about three years. Her letters to Lecuna reveal the progression of her thoughts from her initial enthusiasm to her flagging interest. She imagined Bolívar as an apostle and a prophet who had been sacrificed. She wanted to dwell on his noble sentiments and his virtues. By 1931 she had gathered so much information she thought she would have to write several volumes. As her interest in Buddhism and Indian religions increased, she came to see Bolívar as a "yogi." She also saw him as a writer and a would-be poet and she wondered what would have happened if in 1830, the ailing Bolívar would have been sent to a place like Leysin. Would it have unleashed his "inner poet?" Pleading that she needed to distance herself from the topic, she put Bolívar aside to read more about mysticism and religion.

De la Parra wrote to Lecuna, from Panama on May 18, 1930. She was in Panama for a month-long stay before returning to Europe by way of Venezuela. She wrote him of her plan to write an intimate biography of Bolívar, something light and pleasant, in the style of the historical biographies so popular in France. She was more interested in writing about the lover than the hero. There was so much written about Bolívar. She conceived the idea after the good reception of her lecture about Bolívar in Cuba. She loved the places, lives and times of the 17th century colony and its life in the city, on the hacienda, and in Napoleonic Paris. She realized that the project would be a daring undertaking. She wanted to write the book (in Spanish) and have it translated into French. She wanted to read all about Bolívar- both the good and the bad. She asked Lecuna to provide a reading list, since he knew so much about Bolívar. The idea was in its early stages and she needed his help. Although the talk went well in Cuba, she later realized that when the newspaper published a summary of the talk, that it was full of errors.

Back in Havana on July 12, 1930, she wrote to Lecuna that it took four days to get from Cartagena to Havana. She felt the need to return to Venezuela and experience country life there. She was still interested in Bolívar's life but wanted to write from a different perspective than his heroic life. She was full of self- doubt and saw only the defects in her writing, and she had little initiative and incentive. She needed to travel to Venezuela to fill in Bolívar's background, and experience the landscape and take in the atmosphere. She raved about the old Cuban Blacks she had met and claimed that a conversation with an old black was priceless.

She imagined colonial life to be gracious and noble in some circles but there was much she had to strip away and unlearn; she had to free herself from the "print circus' and distance herself from what had been written, sort out fact from fiction, and she needed more background information. She wanted to return to Venezuela to visit El Llano, el Tuy, the Andes, and the Valley of Aragua. She wanted Lecuna to point out the errors in Bolívar's biographies and she promised to write to Rafael Carías, who would pay for the expenses Lecuna would incur. She felt that that facts about Bolívar's life would prove more interesting than fiction: "I detest the historical novel." She saw the need to recover the past, and felt that Blacks were the guardians of culture and speech. The whites had become too Europeanized and had lost what the Blacks had preserved seemingly effortlessly. "They are Blasco Ibañez's Andalusians or Valencians beneath the Creole panorama filled with birds, butterflies and all the flora and fauna too miraculously beautiful to describe." She had not done much in Bogotá but she visited Quinta Bolívar and found it charming.

She was very warm despite the fact that she was living in a comfortable and cool house in El Vedado. She had postponed traveling to New York and Europe because her friend Lydia was ill. She described the devil dances, Chango, the goat's head sacrificed to Chango to a background of song and African drums and music. She noted that visitors to Cuba did not get see this; neither tourists or intellectuals paid any attention to it.

Writing from Paris on February 1, 1931, she thanked Lecuna for his letters, books and papers he sent her. Now she is wavering between enthusiasm and lack of faith. What could she write that would be new? She wanted to write a lively biography giving attention to details of place, using family letters, and colonial Caracas, but she needed to live it and hear it, read the family letters and discuss the project with Lecuna. She wanted to recreate Bolívar's travels through the five republics. She had spoken with Professor Privet, who was president of the Society of Americanists in Paris, and who studied Indians and colonial society, and he told her that in the mountains near Mérida, Indians still lived in colonial towns. She wanted to visit one of Bolívar's relatives, a French countess, a descendant of Mme. Dervieu de Villars. She was really concerned about faithfully recreating the background. Maybe one book would not be enough; she might need to plan a series. She would ask her friends to send her information on Venezuelan folklore and traditions; it was the townspeople who preserved tradition and passed it on with ease. The holidays had gone well in Caracas, but they had not been as good as the ones presided over by The King of Spain in Madrid and Mussolini in Rome. She lamented the fact that the French continued to ignore Bolívar.

She wrote again to Lecuna on June 4, 1931 from Paris. She told him she felt nostalgia for the old days, and wanted to travel through the tropics on foot, horse and canoe. She still had questions about Bolívar and was rereading Venezuelan history. Since Caracas was far from Europe, the city possesed a "mystic soul" and she saw this trait in some of the old families as well . She was more interested in the Caracas of the 17th century than in contemporary Caracas. A few days earlier she had put aside her reading of America and Bolívar to read about the Orient, Buddhism and other Indian religions. She needed to refresh and distance herself and put it all into perspective. In a postscript she told Lecuna that she had seen her Havana lecture about Bolívar reprinted in a Caracas newspaper and that it was full of errors and things she never said. She felt the press was prejudiced against her and published articles that presented her in a bad light. She had reached the point in her life where she was happy to be in the background, spending her time with good friends, reading books, and nourishing her spirit.

Writing from the sanatorium in Leysin, in April of 1932, she informed Lecuna of her illness. She was hopeful she would be cured. Her life consisted of bed rest, solitude and silence, and pure air in "this prison of snow." She had renounced all her desires and was living in a Buddhist paradise. In one of his letters, Lecuna had mentioned Macuto, and she wrote Lecuna she had happy memories of Macuto. "It was there I wrote almost all of *Iphigenia*. I locked myself up in a little house that belonged to the Guzmáns, and the parlor had no roof. It was a run-down house, overgrown with weeds, with rats and lizards. I had it swept and furnished it with a pine table and a folding chair. In the afternoons, I bathed in the river. "There's nothing like bathing in a river in a hot climate to bring back intimate contact with nature." She promised to send Lecuna some of her unpublished work as soon as she was released from this "prison." She compared life in a sanatorium to living in a prison or a convent and she thought back on "outside life" as infernal, with its noise, speed, struggles, feuds and conflicts, and she asked herself how different Bolívar's life would have been had he lived in Leysin- maybe it would have unleashed the great poet in him.

A Letter to Miguel de Unamuno

Miguel de Unamuno was born a baker's son in Bilbao, Spain in 1864. He studied philosophy and letters at the University of Madrid and later became rector of the school. Growing up during political strife and violence affected his political views, and later in his life he focussed his works on the themes of conflict of life and thought, death, the non-being and the ideas of Christianity vs. reason. An author, philosopher and educator, de Unamuno was a great intellectual in Spain who was exiled in 1924 by dictator General Antonio Primo de Rivera.

A letter written to Miguel de Unamuno by de la Parra in July, 1925 was published in *El Universal* on December 19, 1926. She responded to Unamuno's analysis of *Iphigenia*. She reminded him that they had met several weeks ago. She did not think he would read even one of the 520 pages of her novel; perhaps he did not read novels and found them trivial. She had walked in on one of his lectures, which was his analysis of *Iphigenia* he was delivering to a large audience. He read the novel and wrote notes and was analyzing it in detail, "as patiently as a naturalist dissects an insect." Her presence did not change his lecture; it was as though she was not there. This allowed her to see herself as both the author and member of the audience. Seeing herself as a writer made her feel noble.

Referring to the sonnet María Eugenia wrote to Gabriel, Unamuno asked why she hadn't published more poetry. De la Parra responded, "Because in my entire life I've written only, and only with great effort, two or three poems I judge to be mediocre. Lyric poetry bares the soul and needs great purity and modesty or it risks becoming comical."

In another of his comments (no page reference), he questioned why the author used the word "fastidio" and not "hastio" in *Iphigenia's* title, since "hastio" was more Castilian and energetic?"

De la Parra responded, "The original title of my novel was *Iphigenia* and the subtitle was *The Diary of a Young Lady Who is Bored*[6]. Before I finished the book, fragments of it were published under this subtitle. But by mistake the editors wrote "se fastidia" and I didn't correct it, partially through inertia and because substituting "fastidia" was more spontaneous and natural in Venezuelan speech. I never expected my novel to be read outside Venezuela. But I agree with you that in Castilian Spanish, "hastio" would be more precise, and I'm glad this is your only objection. My rebellious spirit keeps me from following too many academic rules and I will not bow to the Academy's (La Real Academia Española) dictatorship, since I am more interested in the sound of words, rather than in necessity, our mother, and usage, our brother."[7]

A Letter to Lisandro Alvarado

Lisandro Alvarado was born in Venezuela in 1858 and devoted his life to the study of medicine, history, anthropology and linguistics. He spent a portion of his life working with the rural population of Venezuela, studying their culture, interactions and language. He published papers on his findings and continued to write until his death in 1929. He reviewed *Iphigenia* for *Elite* and his article appeared on December 1925. De la Parra was not at all pleased with the review. Giving her own take on the idea that old newspapers can be used for lining birdcages or wrapping fish, she responded to her critic using María Eugenia Alonso's voice. The heroine of *Iphigenia* comes upon Alvarado's review as she unwraps her china, after returning from a trip from the hacienda. De la Parra wrote this letter from Caracas, in 1926. In this playful and witty response to the critic, "written" by María Eugenia Alonso and signed with the heroine's name, de la Parra cleverly builds an argument, using María Eugenia's style, and a self-deprecating tone in her self defense.

The reference to "Esta pobre lengua viva," Velia Bosch's title for her critical work on de la Parra, comes from a letter from de la Parra to Carías, March 1926 in which she refers to Lisandro Alvarado's use of pompous language and calls it unintelligible. She prefers to use "this poor live language with which we pray for and eat our daily bread."María Eugenia has returned from the hacienda and she is unpacking her china, which is wrapped in Alvarado's review in *Elite*. The article is difficult to read because the newsprint is wrinkled. She read the review several times and it left her with a smile on her face. But Alvarado totally ignored Teresa de la Parra, the author.

Writing in the persona of María Eugenia, de la Parra continues, "All your criticisms are directed to me and my ideas, especially those I expressed one morning to the speechless Abuelita and Aunt Clara. Despite your paternal gallantry, you are indignant at my ideas. You seem to base your opinions on my revolutionary ideas, but admit it, Don Lisandro: just like Aunt Clara and Abuelita you become charmingly indignant upon hearing my ideas. This may be hidden among the flowery meanderings of your Greek and Latin culture, but I have found you out! Your review is like a second banishment to San Nicolas; your words have the same effect as the easily scandalized poor Aunt Clara as she raises her hands to her wavy gray hair, and your opinions, admonishments and predictions, coupled with those of Aunt Clara and Abuelita would have delighted me in that long-ago morning when I was eighteen. I assume that you were distracted by the many pleonasms, barbarisms and solecisms that plague this diary and led you to the same trap as Abuelita and Aunt Clara and kept you captive. I wish to free you from this trap and I thank you from the bottom of my soul. Do not forget, my dear critic and prisoner Don Lisandro, that if, when we are eighteen years old we wear Guerlain Red, smoke Egyptian cigars and espouse Voltarian ideas it's not because we want to be admired, but because we want to be reproached and criticized. I've learned since then that praise and reproach amount to the same thing. I'd like to know what you think about the author. I myself feel compassion, disdain and sympathy for her. But I don't hate her. She committed the horrible indiscretion of publishing her book in Paris and it is destined for the moths and the yellowed hands of time. But I forgive her because I see her picture published in several magazines, dailies and weeklies. She's always dressed in unfashionable clothes, standing in an ungainly pose, her face is wrinkled and stained by the linotype ink- it's all so sad and pathetic! If fame has disfigured her just like smallpox would, I'm glad to be living here in the shadows, where my face, always cared for with lotions, creams and powders, will slowly age with time without suffering the indignities of doing so in public.

But there's another punishment: in some circles in Caracas, the characters in my diary or story have been viewed as an authentic portrait gallery. Names have been attached to the character sketches, and the work has been judged according to how realistic it is and the author has been judged to be incompetent in her brushwork, but since these characters do not exist, the author of *Iphigenia* has been accused of being a bad artist and instead of roses, she receives thorns for practicing a profession that is not hers.

I detect in Teresa de la Parra a sensitive and delicate soul. In the midst of my sadness, I'm grateful to her. She carefully polished my diary before launching it to be judged. She gently exaggerated my defects with a malevolence imbued with kindness and goodwill. She knew that in order to get half the readers to approve, the other half would have to disapprove. She realized that some readers would find me delicious and the rest would detest me. She had the foresight to know that some would praise the work and others would censure it. I would have to learn to overcome misfortunes, imperfections and errors, much as one has to jump over tree trunks and stones to cross a river. It's moving to see how you've distorted my qualities, spicing them here and there with defects, like those smiles that wrinkle one's cheeks, stretch one's eyes, widens one's mouth and contribute to the interesting and lovable features in some faces. She's made my intelligence more enjoyable by charging it with an insufferable pedantry; and if my natural beauty is tolerable in the eyes of some, it's due to my obstinacy and petulance that doesn't let up even for a moment. My defects run deeper than these, and I deplore them, Don Lisandro, but please don't repeat this to anyone else!

I think *Iphigenia's* writer has a loving knowledge of our pleasant city of Caracas. If she retouched my story it was because she intended it to be read here. Like me, Teresa de la Parra appreciated Caracas and she brought her love to my diary. If she spoke ill of Caracas, it was decorous, respectable and precious, like old filigree. We must by all means preserve this city and not led her die of inaction. It is our duty. She is our contented, chatty sister, who daily distracts us with fantastic stories of chivalry and Perrault's tales with their disdain for realism.

If, like in the judgment of Paris, she were to award an apple, she would not give it to her contemporaries, nor to the men who congregate in clubs or on street corners, but to the black-garbed, gray-haired collection of ladies who once adorned the unadorned walls of parties and balls, whose industrious hands embroidered the slippers the dancers' feet wore. These women knew about the tempos and the slow rhythms that captivate and charm us. Nowadays we watch the vulgar dancers, who are intent on having too much fun, while we yawn.

As you yourself noted, my reclusive life made me a revolutionary for a while, but I am now very traditional. I'd like to return to the old days! If my reclusive life would only allow it, just like in Paris, where they organize conferences and lectures to preserve the Old Trianon, I would do the same for the restoration of women's circles. But perhaps my voice would be drowned out by the jazz band, and I'd have to interrupt my conversation and be forced to dance the Charleston.

I've come to the conclusion, Don Lisandro, that the best restorations are those brought on by nostalgia and illuminated by sweet melancholy; these will live on eternally noble in the divine grace of memory.

Having come to the end of these thoughts in my long letter, I'll go back to my trunk after taking leave of you. I'm checking the dishes in the cupboard to see if any of others broke during the trip and need to be replaced.

María Eugenia Alonso

Letters to Luis Zea Uribe

The Colombian doctor Luis Zea Uribe and de la Parra conducted their friendship through their letters. Zea Uribe was a health inspector in Baranquilla. He conducted experiments in telepathy, astronomy and helium. She addressed him as "my dear and noble friend," and her "great friend." Zea Uribe was the first to learn of her T.B symptoms in the summer of 1931. In her correspondence with Zea Uribe, de la Parra gives us an insight into life in a T.B. sanitarium and its rest cure. She talks about her disease, its initial misdiagnosis, and touches on the lives of the fellow four thousand patients who were taking the cure along with her. Although she claimed she could not get past the first volume of Thomas Mann's *The Magic Mountain* de la Parra could have mined her mountaintop experience to write her own version. Another lost opportunity and another project that she failed to get off the ground was a suggestion to Zea that together they mount a campaign to dismiss the myths about tuberculosis and to combat tubercuphobia. Zea had written *Mirando al Misterio* and he and de la Parra shared an interest in the supernatural and mysticism. The letters reveal exchanges about metaphysical phenomena such as visions, transports, seeing the light, and telepathic communication between them. Throughout her life, de la Parra was intrigued by mysticism.

"Teresa began to focus some of her newfound energy on the "monstrously stupid" injustice of tuberculophobia, which caused wild fears of automatic contagion, adding insult to the already grievous injury of tuberculosis itself. She never complained of rejection of her own family and friends; one or the other would spend as long as three weeks with her at least twice a year. In Teresa's proposal to Zea that they "wage a war against tuberculophobia" in their countries by writing a book, he the scientific part and she the descriptive, lay the beginnings of a new attitude toward the illness itself (*Between Flight and Longing: The Journey of Teresa de la Parra*, 212)."

From Leysin on September 11, 1932, she described her months of illness and the monotony of her life. She didn't fear death. She described her rest cure and the misconceptions about TB and her fellow patients' relapses and the desperate cases she witnessed. She told Zea the touching story of an 18-year-old girl's death and how it troubled her. She hoped she would get better so she could travel to Bogotá.

She described the fraternal spirit in the sanitarium, with everyone sharing the same routine and the same fears and she had good friends there. Life in the sanitarium was like small town life in Latin America; there was no respect for privacy, since there were feuds, flirtations, and gossip. There was much to observe and learn from. It was not like living among the idle rich who led empty lives. Life among the rich was shallow. She lived in a quiet world with four thousand other patients and witnessed much pain. The Grand Hotel was like a fort. She was aware of the border war between Colombia and Peru, and called it a silly fight over a few kilometers of jungle, and she sided with Colombia. She wondered how much longer she must endure this life, which was like being incarcerated in Sing Sing.

On Good Friday, March 25, 1933 she wrote Zea that life in Leysin was different from life on the outside; the days flew by like the horses on a merry-go-round. She had been practicing Coué[8] for five months: autosuggestion and visualization, which she practiced every morning after getting dressed. She visualized her friend Emilia Ibarra. In Leysin, she was the happiest she had ever been. She had attained Nirvana, the absence of desire. Just before she began writing this letter to him, she had received a letter from a woman patient who had been ill for four years, but who was now well enough to get around. This was her friend, Clemencia Miro, who asked, "What do you need, Teresa, from Montreaux or Lausanne?" I kept repeating to myself, "What do I need?" I concluded I needed nothing. I wrote back that I had just discovered that, "I was the woman who needed nothing," and this had left me sad. "Do you think one should be happy or sad about such a lack of ambition? Could this be, Zea, a precursor to death? An awareness of life's detachment?"

On this day, the death of Our Lord, she "felt" the resurrection and looked forward to the day when she could return by ship to Latin America, like the heroine of *Iphigenia,* and recalled her journey through el Quindio and the Magdalena in 1930 when she delivered her lectures in Colombia. Her mother still did not know she was ill. She shared his love and faith for the Americas and wondered if one day they would become superior countries. Can this incredible mixture of races form one homogenous one with the real qualities of a superior race? She had read Gobineau's theories, who was pessimistic about mixed races and anything not Aryan.[9] She read the opposite point of view: the Mexican Vasconcellos and Keserling. She asked if he could recommend other authors who shared this philosophy. She recalled the good character of the humble country blacks, generous and full of love in the purest sense. "Our childhood and youth was filled with their presence. I think back on Vicente Cochocho who existed and whom I brought back to life in *Mama Blanca*. What would he have to say about Gobinau? He was ungovernable and bore no trace of the symmetrical and orderly Aryan race, to be sure, but what of his fairness, his immense charity and his lyricism?" She concluded Aryans were good at organizing sanitariums and armies and cities where progress reigned, but they did not know where they were going and had no zest for life. "I have a sad story about rejection, about tuberculophobia (against which we will wage a campaign), a patient N.N. who was abandoned by her parents, as though she were a leper. They never answered her letters and they never came to bury her."

Still in Leysin in September of 1933, having moved to the Hotel Mont Blanc for economic reasons. She missed speaking Spanish. She was working on her spiritual life, listening to the radio, and writing letters. She thought she had been cured in August 1932, but then she suffered a relapse. That was the cruelty of this disease, she wrote; just when you thought you were getting better, you got sick all over again. She realized she needed to stay in Leysin another twenty months.

On September 22, 1933, she decried the "black legend" of tuberculosis and the layman's misconceptions about the disease, and how many poets and artists were afflicted by it. The disease brought on a euphoric state. People were forced to hide the disease as though it brought dishonor, and some arrived here too late to be cured. There was denial and stigma attached to T.B. The disease was not hereditary, nor was it contagious, unless it was transmitted through sputum. She wanted to wage war against it; the lives here could offer many lessons. She suggested he start a social campaign and they collaborate on a book. She wanted to give advice to his nurse, who had contracted T.B. She regretted not having a longer formal education. Her own life lessons so far had taught her that life had to be taken in stages, and the importance of learning to adapt.

Wishing him a happy Christmas Day in 1933 and happy 1934, she reported a period of directed reading, intense joy, and good health, but she felt a longing to return to the tropics. She told him of her idyllic fantasy life, her hope to live in Los Teques, living in the open air, in a hammock, under the trees. In the future she hoped to write a book that would spread the happiness and hope she now felt and which expressed her love of the tropical criollo landscape. She believed false European and North American culture were poisoning Latin America. " *Iphigenia,* my novel, is imbued with this spirit. I would like to write the reverse of *Iphigenia*. But I lack the spirit, faith, and enthusiasm I had when I wrote *Iphigenia.* "

A Letter to Eduardo Guzmán Esponda

Eduardo Guzmán Esponda was the director of the Colombian Academy of Language until his death in 1988, at the age of 99. He worked in the Ministry of Foreign Affairs, but later dedicated his life to the cultivation of letters. He wrote a review of *Iphigenia* "La novela de una caraqueña" published in *Sante Fe de Bogotá*, Bogotá, in 1927. Teresa de la Parra thanked him:

"I received the magazine *Santa Fe de Bogotá* with your review of *Iphigenia* and your kind words. It took me one and one half years to write *Iphigenia* and its writing consumed me. I am glad the novel was successful in Bogotá. Because I was educated outside my country (in Spain), I feel patriotism for my country. They share a common language and history, as do Mexico, Lima, Quito, Bogotá, the golden repositories of the times of the viceroyalties and captaincies." He had understood María Eugenia's restlessness and resignation, her disagreements with her cultural education, and her metamorphosis. But she took issue with his criticism of María Eugenia and why she didn't behave like a convent school graduate. She insisted that it would take only three months for someone like this young woman to attain intellectual refinement: dresses from Patou and Lanvin, 140 gauge stockings, polished nails, Guerlain red lipstick, visits to hairdressers like Antoine or Calou and about ten or twenty visits to milliners and dressmakers near the Place Vendome or Rue de la Paix, taking tea at the Ritz, dining at Ciro's, dancing at Florida, taking walks in Deauville. All those changes could take place without ever attending a salon. She reminded Guzmán Esponda that María Eugenia Alonso was shy when she met Mercedes Galindo, she spoke little at table, and she was awkward when she met Cesar Leal.

She realized that there was more to Caracas than deep mourning, formal visits, and windows that were finally opened after the period of mourning was over. She realized that Caracas society was up to date and received royally, played golf, bridge and tennis and danced the Charleston. But describing these activities would not make an interesting novel. Snobs or professionals are everywhere, and for the novelist to write about them would amount to an artist painting a fashionably dressed woman: not hard to reproduce, commonplace and lacking character. On the other hand, one can find color in these ancient houses, temples of boredom, aged with the smell of ancestral traditions.

"Your other objections are more serious because they attack the whole point of the novel. I'll cite a few examples. You pointed out the inconsistency of the character. Just like a man, you believed what María

Eugenia said. She never would have practiced the piano for ten hours, nor could she ever flee with that self-centered seducer Gabriel Olmedo as much as she wanted to believe she would. But you would never have suspected that. At the moment of crisis, all her plans are dashed and she is disappointed and lacks faith. Had I made her less real, instead of being annoyed, you would have been disappointed, with that sweet smile that indulgence paints on skeptical faces. You misunderstood the character and her workmanlike approach. You see her as a geometric figure rather than seeing her outline and her curves. The real objective of my book was to show our mysterious duality and the terrible conflicts that surprise us- between what we are and what we think we are. And the final painful question posed to the reader- Who is the real me; the me who thinks or the me who acts? I tried to come between *Iphigenia* and the reader, letting the reader know that she doesn't know herself. The only well-written part of *Iphigenia* is the part not written, what is said without words, so that the reader's benevolence could read in a whisper what the critic would read in a shout. You only read what was printed, the part in black and white, and would like to know, at any cost, the logical and concrete reasons for the heroine's actions. But you'll never learn it because she is illogical, because despite her ultramodern mentality that makes her praise revolution, she is guided, and always will be guided by her ancestors.

Bear in mind that like María Eugenia Alonso the sensitive and the temperamental (women and artists) have two "I's" within our souls, different and contradictory and seldom in accord: the one that speaks through the mouth of reason and the one motivated by reasons reason doesn't know. The first is geometric, logical and ruled by the ego and leads to success and when it prevails, the world judges us to be intelligent. The other is mad, sublimely mad, with the madness of great sacrifice and outlandish generosities, the mysterious "unknown guest" who sows disorder, mocks our wise tutor the ego, and buries our lives, like a gray stone stuck to a large building of societies constantly undergoing construction.

The unconscious reason that leads María Eugenia, her own "unfamiliar guest" is without a doubt what an old wise writer told me, which is her future maternity. And with it, all the renunciations and sacrifices that have accompanied it through the centuries. That is what makes her fall from the very beginning, under man's yoke and dominates her in a way so absolute and typical in our countries. True woman: sensitive, praised but without will, she submits, for she sincerely believes in her love for Leal and his superiority. Remember she was unhappy when Uncle Pancho mocked him. Of course there is a place in her soul where things appear as they are, but she won't admit this to herself: Gabriel had to say it for her. In Gabriel's last latter, so full of commonplaces, I've tried to describe a very typical phenomenon: a woman who becomes indignant when she hears the man she belongs to being insulted, even though she herself hates him.

As far as fearing spinsterhood, as you put it, that's not the reason-that's not why María Eugenia marries Leal. Admit that this word deserves more tact and reverence. Admit it deserves a nicer word that evokes the charming attitude of love. Since the beginning of time it's been this fear, that secretly teaches maidens to smile, to silently make the arrangements for funerals and wakes, discreetly plan weddings, and with her blessing she gives the bride a deep peace that smoothes the past and colors the roses in the dark destinies that were accepted, rather than chosen.

As you can see, with the analysis and examples I've given, I could have written more forceful pages and more eloquent ones with philosophical pretensions. *Iphigenia* would have been even longer than it is. Readers would have the logical explanation for everything, and my story would be symmetrical and polished in the literary style that is typical in those novels deemed to be serious literature. But such an achievement would have weighted me down for the rest of my life. I always preferred the humble and cool woods, where I could run away from all that. My feet know how tiring that road can be, and my poor unskilled hands, though active, are tired with having to wring the necks of the squawking birds of eloquence. In *Iphegenia* I did not wring all their necks, and when I sometimes leaf through the book, they come back like a gaggle of geese to bite my hands. I quickly lock them back between the covers of the book and the worst is over.

"I thank you once again and send my greetings."

Letters to Clemencia Miró

Clemencia Miró was the daughter of Gabriel Miró Ferrer (1879-1930), an outstanding Spanish prose stylist, an impressionistic writer whose vignettes would appeal to de la Parra. Clemencia was a friend who had spent four years in Leysin. She left the sanitarium on March 25, 1933. In a letter to Clemencia, de la Parra compared the patients at Leysin to soldiers, or crusaders undertaking a spiritual conquest. She felt that Leysin had a sacred atmosphere comparable to that of an English cathedral's. The letters document the friendship of the two carried out through visits during which they listened to music on the gramophone, the exchange of flowers, letters and postcards. In some of the letters de la Parra tells her friend about the doctors she is seeing, and the various treatments she undergoes while at Leysin and later in Madrid. Other letters describe travels with Lydia Cabrera through Spain and their eventual settling down in Madrid months before de la Parra died. These are examples of her letters:

Thank you dear Clemencia for your greetings and for your father's books, you have no idea how much I appreciate them: I need to read good Spanish literature, I have little at hand and I've already told you how much I admire your father, depth and form, he's a great artist; he influences me personally, something that doesn't happen with many since despite the fact that I admire them, are strangers to me. I like poets and writers who stimulate my dreams, these are the true masters of the soul.

Monday
Dear Clemencia:
    Thank you for your very loving letter last night. I also fell under the spell of your visit for many hours. Since no one here has pleasant experiences they seem go on indefinitely until we drown ourselves in sleep and another day arrives.
    When I am alone I don't tend to put on the phonograph, I don't know why, it's just habit. So yesterday the records we listened to were an open window to the past, a past that came from far away, from many centuries ago. Come back soon before you leave and we will play the same records again and others although they are scratched, are very lovely.
    I don't need anything from Lausanne or from anywhere else. I am the woman who never needs anything. It's been a while since I discovered this with regret; it's very sad.
I embrace you affectionately.
Teresa

Letters to Lydia Cabrera

Lydia Cabrera was born in Havana in 1900 and came from a well-to-do Cuban family. By 1927 she wanted to become independent from her family and went to Paris to study art at L'Ecole du Louvre. There was an interest in African art at the time, and Cabrera had heard African folk-tales from her black nanny. She is known for her collection of stories based on African folk tales and her writings on Santeria and Afro-Cuban religions. She left Cuba after the revolution and lived in Miami until she died in 1991.
    According to Palacios, Cabrera and de la Parra never lived together. Each lived her separate and independent lives. De la Parra wrote that she

sometimes felt invaded by Lydia, and they had their disagreements, even months before de la Parra died. According to both Palacios and Cabrera, de la Parra was never a passionate woman. Her relationship with Zaldumbide took her by surprise. Her relationship to others was based on social ties, and she was never part of an inner circle, as some critics suggest. Palacios describes the relationship between Lydia and de la Parra like that of that of a mother or a sister. Perhaps de la Parra assumed the role Emilia played in her own life and transferring to her relationship with Lydia. When Lydia went to Cuba in October of 1935, for a month, de la Parra wrote how she missed her. This is also the beginning of her disease, she lost 13 kilos in six months, had fevers and started coughing, but she neglected the symptoms and continued to smoke.

On April 23, 1936 the morning of de la Parra's death, Lydia offered her a cup of coffee, to which she replied, "I will eat a little earth."

Cabrera and de la Parra first met in 1924 in Havana on board a ship while de la Parra was on her way to Venezuela. De la Parra was in mourning for her friend and patron Emilia at the time and Cabrera and her group spotted her sitting alone in the dining room. Cabrera recalls "I was introduced to her and told her I was working to become independent, to seek my fortune and go to Paris to paint and study. She gave me her card and told me to look her up in Paris. I gave her mine and gratefully wrote, "Please don't forget me." Teresa was kind enough to write to me but I never answered her. We met again in Paris at the Hotel Vernet in 1927.

I have sad thoughts since those who knew Teresa de la Parra-Ana Teresa-are no longer with us. They would have appreciated the value of the analysis of her work the Cuban critic Rosario Hiriart is doing, her understanding of the human qualities of the beautiful and sweet prisoner of misty Leysin.

I've read some opinions and reviews about the writer who is the pride of Venezuelan letters. Years ago, a highly regarded book by Díaz Sanchez is the one I recall and impressed me the most. I have to confess that for the most part, what has been written and fallen into my hands gives a false impression of *Iphigenia's* author as a *femme du monde* concerned with her beauty night and day, body and soul, always "ponche de leche" as they said in Cuba during colonial times when they never missed a social event. That is to say, a superficial, self-sufficient Teresa dressed in the latest fashion, a snob who was nothing at all like the woman we knew close up: elegant, of course; very feminine, who knew that she was beautiful; and there was the mirror who reassured her of that at all hours of the day; but simple, enchantingly modest, too intelligent to give in to vanity. I have to clarify that I haven't read everything written about her in Venezuela so I have to excuse myself if my ignorance makes me commit an unforgivable error.

I met Gabriela Mistral in Barcelona in 1935, and that year, in Madrid, we frequently met in the apartment on Mario Rosa de Luna Street, in the Rosales neighborhood, that I had the privilege to share with Teresa de la Parra, who was very ill.

Gabriela admired Teresa de la Parra and felt affection for her. The spirituality, the sweet resignation, not to mention the elegance with which Teresa endured her suffering, conscious – though she made us believe otherwise-that she was about to die, moved her profoundly; as I recall led her through her example to Christianity from which she had strayed from with her reading on Buddhism. Dear Gabriela! I don't think anyone who met her could forget her. (Introduction, *Cartas a Lydia Cabrera)*

Describing her lectures, she wrote from Bogotá, May 1930
Dear Cabrita:

I won't talk about my impressions of the trip. The arrival moved me; not here in Bogotá, but in the small towns before that where poor, pretentious and ugly girls scarcely had time to give me flowers through the car's window and would shout things at me. All the pain of the disinherited! How could I have reflected that in a book that I wrote almost unconsciously and now I find myself so indifferent to and so repented? The praise moved me and humbled me for its excess. Here in Bogotá it doesn't move me the same way.

Since it's so late and I need to mail you my letter tomorrow (the Minister told me about an air rate) I'll speak of practicalities.

Two days after I gave my first lecture I received one hundred and fifty dollars, after I deducted the cost of the venues, which I gave away. Tomorrow another one, on Friday the last one. Maybe I'll repeat one at the Lorca giving lectures in various cities until I get to Cartagena, Barranquilla where I'll embark for Cuba or Venezuela passing through La Guaira.

I'll bid you good night until I don't know when, for my life is without rest or a free, free minute. How I long to be mistress of myself!
Kisses

From the Pension Augusta, Bogotá, 1930
Cabrita dear:
I'm back and enchanted from my trip to Tunja. A city that has not emerged from the seventeenth century. The streets, the people, the churches, despite the inevitable light bulbs and new images moved me. Although I went incognito, I was found out, which took away the freedom

that I wanted. But the people's tribute moved me, they celebrated as though my arrival was a great event. They invited me to the movie theater, the only film you can see on screen for lack of other means of publicity and announced that here was "the illustrious author of *Iphigenia.*" I sat in the presidential box: you should have seen the applause and the "vivas." Then they took me to a ball organized in my honor. The women, who never come out into the street due to the cold and because the city is deserted, were partying, with the sadness of women who have not lived or suspect what life is; beautiful and sad. As luck would have it while I was out in the street, the lights went out, something that often happens, and I could see the full moon, enchanting and evocative. When I got to bed it was horribly cold, imagine the colonial houses with a winter temperature (On the tenth I'll be in Havana). Tunja has no sun. The trip to Tunja was expensive, and a newspaper error announced the repeat of my lecture for today, instead of yesterday, and the theater was nearly empty. Half of what is usual. I think the impresario took advantage and made off like a bandit, (Gran Capitan) now I'm going to change the system. In Medellin I'm going to raise the admission to 1.50 and take the largest theater. But do I have the strength to continue resisting popularity, banquets and introductions? I'm drowning.
T

She reported on her health in the following letter, written on Friday, August 23 (probably 1935)
Dear Cabrita,
    The doctor Bosviel recommended to me is Kindberg's assistant and he is one of the best T.B. doctors of the generation after Rist and Cía. Ask over there. Like Vilbert he works with him and sees him every day and showed him how to replace the injections one by one so that finally yesterday we began a curative treatment (until now they had tried to calm it with very strong narcotics). It appears that with this method one achieves a radical cure. We shall see. These are injections that immunize the organism to certain toxins that produce asthma.
    Cabrita, I've suffered so much. Until now I didn't know to what depths suffering could bring one. It's like returning from a trip full of unsuspected experiences. Later I'll tell you. But there is no reason to be alarmed and upset, as I can see from your letters: you know that no one dies from asthma. I feel my whole self like an unbound book whose pages have been rearranged: effects from such a new experience and from the narcotics. I had taken lots of morphine and opium. I've stopped taking them, and now,

as I said, apart from the remedies like the injections, I'm only taking curatives.

Aside from medical treatments, I've been well taken care of. María came here and between her and Isabelita they've taken good care of me. Don't worry about my diet in the future, I'm going to be very careful, for I need to regain my spent strength. María Luisa is, as you have seen, a zealot when it comes to patients. I've insisted, in agreement with her, that she design a separate regimen, whose bills she'll present to me from the money she administers. This allows more freedom, though Isabelita had started with red meat. I want, besides, to eat what I feel like. This should prove that I'm well in my appetite and my vitality.

My current state is one of convalescence. I don't leave my room, though I spend my day on the couch, not in bed, so I can breathe better. (Do you know I spent forty-eight hours sitting in a chair with my head on the table without moving?) I have a continuous nasty *rale*[10] but bearable and no suffocation. At certain times I cough and spit abundantly. Generally it's like I was before, when I was taking bromides. During late afternoon the *rale* goes away but then I'm fatigued, which is worse. One can't look for the causes of this cyclone in motives—x,y or z, like some people like to. Kindberg, when he saw me, declared that one should not look for a reason for my state, because it was what is was, asthma is like that. He also said he had not seen it so pronounced continually, only in very old people. When this nightmare is further away from me I'll tell you what I felt like. Now I feel I am being renewed. I'm a little like Lala and those who don't want to hear about suffering. I still feel physical terror. In general, I feel like I can bear it and it's diminishing. There is no danger and I'm not hiding anything from you. So that, Cabrita, when you get this letter write to me that you are untroubled and that you continue to take your waters and baths in peace and with God. I'll see that you get this letter express mail.

You have no idea how much I missed you during my bad spells, but at the same time I'm glad this cyclone did not descend on us in Madrid or Barcelona. I'll say goodbye because I'm tired. Greetings to Saida and don't forget that I love you.

T

To an Unknown Recipient

There are a number of letters from de la Parra addressed to unknown recipients.

From Leysin, December 29, 1932 she wrote to an unknown recipient, most likely García Prada. The letter is addressed "To the writer of the prologue and the illustrator of *Mama Blanca*."

"The illustrations brought tears to my eyes and I'm longing to return to the world of the hacienda where everything is full of life, its smells, colors, movement, and bathing in the river. I agree with what you say about *Iphigenia*: I strove for a musicality I now find false and displeasing. I would have been better off without the unnecessary lyricism, but it was a true reflection of my writing at the time and the excessive romanticism we fall prey to in the tropics. I made María Eugenia Alonso the antithesis of myself. I gave her qualities and defects I don't have, so no one would confuse me with her. María Eugenia Alonso is a synthesis, a living copy of several women I've seen close up, who suffer in silence and to whom I wanted to give a voice. Out of modesty, I would never have made my own case public. The success of *Iphigenia* is due to the fact that the public loves confessions. It was published two years after I finished writing it. Now I'm beginning to identify with María Eugenia Alonso. How that would have upset me while I was writing the novel. When I traveled to Colombia in 1930, the public wanted to hear more confessions and were disappointed when instead I chose to speak about historical characters, Fanny de Villars, Doña Marina, Doña Manuelita, and Inca Garcilaso's mother. I'm living in a kind of prison with books. It's fine that they've deleted some parts of Vicente Cochocho, it all looks good and it appears a great deal of care went into the edition."

Notes

[1] Leysin was the leading health resort in the late 19th century. TB patients were drawn by the dry mountain air, and the "cure" consisted of bed rest and heliotherapy, exposing patients to sunlight, as first prescribed in 1903 by Dr. August Rollier, who was known as the "Sun Doctor." The disease was first identified by the German physician Robert Koch. Tuberculosis was also called consumption and phthisis. Clinics for tubercular patients first opened in 1887. During the period in which de la Parra lived, TB was the leading cause of death worldwide, believed to be the fate of melancholic, artistic or maladjusted poets and artists. Leysin had a reputation for the longevity of its patients.

[2] Macuto was a popular beach community adjoining La Guiara and provided escaped for Caraqueños at the end of the 19th century.

[3] The sad story of Bolívar's poignant journey between Bogotá and Santa Marta would later be chronicled in Gabriel García Marquez's *The General in His Labyrinth* (1990).

[4] Personal interview with Laura Febres, October 30, 2003, in Caracas, during the XXIX Simposio de docentes e investigadores de la literatura venezolana.

[5] Febres, Laura "Mándale un Saludo a Venezuela (Retazos de una conversación con Lydia Cabrera." *Perspectivas críticas sobre la obra de Teresa de la Parra.* Fundación Consorcio Cordillera, 1989.

[6] De la Parra sent a chapter of *Iphigenia* to Pocaterra for *La lectura semanal* and that is when the accidental title change occurred. Her first choice was to use the word "aburre" which conveys the meaning of bored, annoyed, or disgusted. But "fastidia" was used instead. This is the more general term for boredom in Castilian, but without the connotations of disgust and loathing. (*Between Flight and Longing*, 64).

[7] Like her compatriot Andrés Bello, de la Parra accepted Spanish as the common language of Latin American, but refused to give up the freshness of Latin American Spanish as opposed to the formal Spanish spoken on the peninsula or to adhere to the rules of the Real Academia. "I don't pretend to write for the Castilians. My lessons are aimed at my brothers, the inhabitants of Hispanic America. I think it is important to preserve the language of our fathers in its pure form, as a providential means of communication and as a fraternal link between the various nations of Spanish origins between the two continents." (129). *Literatura Mexicana e Hispano-americana.* Ed. Josefina Phoren, et al. Publicaciones Cultural, Mexico, 2000.

[8] Emile Coué (1857-1926) was the French psychotherapist who preached the power of the imagination and promoted the power of positive thinking in curing illnesses. He was considered the "prophet of autosuggestion," and is remembered for telling patients to recite daily, "Every day, in every way, I am getting better and better." De la Parra began practicing Coué, repeating the words he suggested, trying to visualize her dead friend and patron Emilia Ibarra.

[9] Joseph Arthur Gobineau (1816-1882) was a French diplomat and man of letters. He was an early proponent of the theory of Nordic supremacy and wrote anti-Semitic literature. His works include *The Inequality of Human Races* (1915) and *Five Oriental Tales* (1925).

[10] "Rale" refers to the clicking, rattling, or cracking noises made by one or both lungs of a human with a respiratory disease. It comes from the French word "to rattle."

CHAPTER FOURTEEN

BELLEVUE-FUENFRÍA-MADRID DIARY (1931-1936)

The entries selected from de la Parra's diary provide an intimate glance into her life five years before her death in Madrid. When she began this diary, she was depressed and trying to find her way out of that state. She valued her friendship with Lydia Cabrera and knew even before Lydia left for her trips to Cuba that she would miss her friend and feel extremely lonely without her. Where should she live? Should she rent a villa, furnished or unfurnished, in the *midi* in France, what would it cost and would it be better than living in Paris? As her Venezuelan biographer María Fernanda Palacios noted, the writer really never had a home of her own, and always lived as a guest or in hotels. But by 1935 she had grown tired of this life, and did not want to live in a sanitarium any longer. The diary records what de la Parra read, her reactions to it, who she saw and had dinner and drinks with. Towards the end of her life, as her health continued to fail, she recorded when she woke up, her weight, and her temperature. Her diary also shows that until her last days she continued to study, read contemporary literature, and both ancient and modern philosophy and history.

To repeat a cliché, de la Parra was not religious; she was spiritual. She received a Catholic upbringing and a strict convent school education, but she was interested in Eastern religions. Her two early articles "Lotus Flower: A Japanese legend" and "Buddha and the Leper Woman" are both retellings of Buddhist "gospels". She was an avid reader of Latin American history; she read philosophy and was interested in Freud's theories. The diary contains inconsequential trivia at times, but it also reflects her opinions concerning current events and records her relationships with people who were an important part of her life. Upon arriving in Madrid, she sorted through her letters and wistfully recalled her relationship with Gonzalo Zaldumbide, deciding to destroy some letters and keeping others.

De la Parra spent several years in sanitariums hoping to find a cure for her T.B. and asthma. She wrote many letters to friends in which she described the routine of living in these places, and she wrote about the lives of others who suffered from the disease. Like her missed opportunity to write the novel about Bolívar, she did not write a novel based on her experiences during those years, which could have been a woman's version of Thomas Mann's *The Magic Mountain*. But we do get a good sense of medical treatments of the times and prescribed cures.

Known for her good taste, her fashion sense and her love of comfort, de la Parra sadly died while living in an uncomfortable, drafty house in Madrid. Frivolous people came and went daily and intruded on her inner life and interrupted the solitude she sought. In her last entries she waits for her mother and sister María to arrive as her illness worsens. Fortunately, they arrived just before she died. The unsuitable surroundings notwithstanding, de la Parra died surrounded by her mother, her sister, and her best friend Lydia Cabrera. The first entry in this diary attests to de la Parra's appreciation for good friends and lasting friendships. The last entry nineteen days before her death notes that she continued her quest for knowledge[1]. The following are translations of some of the diary fragments.

She began the diary on June 6, 1931, admitting to herself that she was undergoing a moral crisis, during a time when she was deploring her lack of initiative and lack of desire, and feeling paralyzed. She wondered if the solution would come from within or without. "Only a great friendship, the kind one so rarely encounters in this life, friendship, not love, perhaps might through its contagion generously lend me some enthusiasm. Would another solution to this dilemma be taking a trip, although I wonder if the constant wanting to flee may point to a sign that I'm afraid of losing my independence. Perhaps a more physical calling would have saved me from the apathetic state I find myself in. I just finished reading Rilke, who claimed that every beginning was a beautiful one. The interior life is a marvelous one, so long as things can be born and move within it or it reflects things on the outside. To what profound mystery is my life now found, that is so fleeting, so capricious, so opaque and so fast that I can't even express it in words?"

The entry written in Beaulieu, dated September 2, 1931, records that she was writing in the mornings and continuing to study philosophy, especially the Stoics and Epicureans. She was continuing to read history, and was reading about Miranda's trip to Russia. She was still trying to decide where to live and spent that afternoon looking at villas, and finding one that she especially liked. She regained her desire to write, and an idea had come to her. But she knew that she had to finish her book about

Bolivar before undertaking another project. "I thought about a new book project before undertaking the biography that unnerves me at times."

During the following weeks in September she continued to read about Miranda's journey to Russia and was studying Cicero and *Phaedo* and the Neo-Platonists and Plotinus. "Read a biographical essay about Victor Hugo and his writing method: he did not believe in inspiration and worked every morning from dawn until lunch, never in the afternoons. Re read *Claudine* by Colette for the second time-first read her in 1920." She happily recalled her own habit of writing from 1921-1922 in Caracas. One evening she and Lydia went out at 6:00 p.m. to sit near the beach by an old house with cypresses where they watched the approaching nightfall and listened to someone playing the piano in another house. This brought back childhood memories of her mother, and she and Lydia conversed pleasantly for a long time. There followed enjoyable days of reading, although Lydia had injured her arm and had left for a while, leaving de la Parra anticipating her loneliness and concerned for her friend's health.

De la Parra's habit of reading in the mornings included reading the biography of Peter the Great, the scholastic philosophers and Abelard, and *My Voyage to Lhasa* by Mme. David[2]. On June 10, after reading St. Thomas in the morning, she went to dinner at 10:00 p.m. with Lydia at "The Reserve." She wrote, "There was a dinner in honor of the mayor of New York[3], and the beautiful people of the moment, the Dolly Sisters and millionaires were there. The atmosphere was vulgar on all sides, over spending, deplorable manners, things that want to make one become a communist." A few days later, on Sunday 13, she spent the morning translating Miomandre's stories, (*Les Contes de Cristal*), and admitted that they lost a lot in translation She was concerned that after drinking only one and a half cocktails with M. Morley at La Reserve one afternoon, she felt like she was drunk and ill, a sign of her impending illness.

The entry of Wednesday 23 points to a new stage in her life. "Starting today, I feel tranquil and serene in spirit and handling solitude well. Yesterday, the day before and all of last week I've been anxious and tormented by fixed ideas. I've continued studying philosophy and retaining and understanding it well. I've been reading Freud on psychology with great interest, especially now that I'm more accepting of certain things I judged to be arbitrary at first. Tonight I'll try to repeat the experiment. The night before last I had an interesting experience. I tried to recollect my dream and analyze it according to Freud's method. The dream had to do with the worries of the evening of the day before, to opinions heard in conversations, all in a symbolic form that could be analyzed easily thanks to curious coincidences. I wrote about it to Lydia since she was in the dream. The weather's been bad, cold and rainy but it has not affected me morally. This afternoon I got a letter from a Polish gentleman requesting information about my books, I think for a work on Latin American literature. Lunch with M. Morlay. Conversation about his anguished situation and a business deal for which he needs ten thousand francs. Had I been in a better situation, I would have offered them to him. I believe that's what he was hinting at. I told him about my current situation and my fears."

The writer never stopped mourning for her patron and, as she had confided to Dr. Zea Uribe in her letters to him, she sometimes tried to communicate with her departed friend. The Sunday 27 entry recalls what she considered to be a "telepathic experience" she wrote about to Zea Uribe and Lydia. "Friday after writing and sleeping soundly I felt something strange as though it were trying to wake me. I turned on the light, got up for a drink of water, went back to bed and turned out the light, still experiencing that strange feeling. I closed my eyes to go to sleep and upon opening them in the dim light (there was moonlight and I had the window open) I saw a reflection on the chest of drawers. A moment later, a light (very bright and big) turned off on top of the chest and lit up in a corner of the wall where it did not seem possible to be a reflection from outside. It was like that for ten minutes. It was midnight. I was not frightened and I said to myself, 'Emilia, if it's you, show me a sign, turn off the light, for example.' And the light went off. I think this was an answer to my question that I had been pondering in the afternoon concerning my readings about the immortality of the soul and my doubts concerning this despite so many proofs. Yesterday I prayed in church but today, Sunday, I went to mass. I've resolved to do it in good faith in memory of Emilia's soul who for her sake has made me say 'let us pray' with so deep and sad a request. Yesterday I wrote to Lydia about this in detail, even though I had talked to her about this resolution to attend mass regularly. When I return to Paris I'll have thirty masses said somewhere nearby and I will attend them all."

On Monday, October 5, her birthday, she found herself on the hotel's terrace thinking again about whether to live in the midi for at least six months of the year. She was finished with reading the history of philosophy. She summed up what that study had taught her. "Despite knowing that I'm far from having studied it thoroughly the effort even fragmentary and superficial leaves me very satisfied. It's been methodical if superficial. In my current state, sometimes my attention and my interest waned. But I did achieve something important, an overview of the characteristics, different tendencies, oppositions and reactions: the conflict between intuition and positivism, the infinite "I" and the objective. I've put aside the faith in positivist and naturalist dogmas, as I did formally the Catholic ones. I believe in the absolute superiority of unconscious forces over intellectual ones. God is all the mystery we want to know and is only perceptible to feeling which is much more powerful than intelligence and its limited concepts witnessed by the senses. I understood Bergson's intuition theory and the reflection that the reaction against dogmatic positivism and naturalism actually produces in art. I do it effortlessly. Pragmatism comes easily because I've always believed that all truths are relative and respectable from the point of view of the one who appreciates them. I've always been a skeptic not so much as from denying but because I believe in all the possibilities. This tendency has given me the reputation of being good (not true) often for lack of sincerity or to give my opinions (which I don't have) because they are all the same to me. Only extremism in whatever sense is capable of producing an opinion which is the answer to what I judge to be a lack of measure, eccentricity and injustice." She had spoken with Lydia over the phone, and her friend seemed sad and detached. This made her sad, and she missed her friend.

She recalled her relationship with Gonzalo Zaldumbide when she settled down in Neuilly on October 18. "I've started to go through old letters (since 1924) that I wanted to reread, file or get rid of. I began with my correspondence with G. I spent all of Sunday alone, rereading his letters and mine; I've ripped up many, saved and sorted out others. These are four intense years of my life I saw passing before me. Despite some monotony, how much I've forgotten of what's worth saving of my inner life, and how sad to see how we are dying as far as what we leave behind that once was given in one moment and has now withered in spite of remembering it with love and tenderness.

In the part of her diary written in Fuenfría, and beginning on January 1, 1936, de la Parra begins to record her temperature, 38.5 C. (101.3 F.)
She noted that he year began badly. Although there was a holiday meal with music and dancing in the sanatorium, the air was one of desolation, and she thought about the patients who would die before the year was out. "I could not take my eyes off Margarita who puts on such a pleasant face despite her condition (wasted lungs). Looking at her made me think of the condemned. I had to go to my room before midnight because of the pain that has turned me into a martyr for the past two months and has aggravated my nerves and they don't put me on a regimen or treat me." She notes that she is taking atropol, which intoxicated her and left her feverish and paralyzed. "A real outrage to pretend that as sick as I am they

treat me with drugs. I felt horrible all day." The doctors insisted she continue to take atropol, and she interpreted this as a sign of their pride. "How can anyone trust doctors? Their personal point of view comes before their patient's health. That's when they're not exploitive thieves like Soulas in Paris. In view of my condition and the fact that they are completely starving us Lydia and I have made plans to go to Madrid. I don't think the mountain climate is necessary."

On January 2, waking up with a normal temperature, 37.2 (98.96), she felt well and was happy and she followed her morning routine, reading in bed and taking notes. She convinced her doctor Colanje to agree to let her take only bismuth which is what she was taking before she arrived and which the doctors in Fuenfría prohibited because they thought it to be harmful. "Observing doctors as I have for the past four years I've come to the conclusion that one must cure oneself according to your own observations, they should only act as counselors whose advice should be taken or not according to one's experience. Bad lunch, as usual. We eat little." She did not sleep at siesta time, and continued reading St. Theresa, and she began Ferrero's book *Espoirs,* Gil Fortou's *Historia de Venezuela,* which she wanted to read slowly and study. She discussed Lydia's impending trip to Cuba with her and recalled an argument they had." I see she's hurt by what I said on the 31. But I don't think she's right. She won't give in to what I believe to be a sentimental right to follow her capricious dislikes. It would be cowardice on my part and I would gain nothing from it, like other times in my life, only a diminishment of my personality, a horrible sensation of being disoriented, of having lost my "I" and with it all my dignity. One has to make concessions to maintain affection, but none that amounts to a giving in because then you feel like you are in a dependent state with its consequent moral dissolution."

Her good health continued on the following day, Friday, January 3, with a normal temperature. She practiced Coué and read an article in. *Nouvelles Littéraires.* She began reviewing her notes from a book about Spanish literature. Lydia arrived and Dr. Colanje examined her and noticed a difference and when he listened to her chest, there were no bronchial sounds. She and Lydia decided to go Madrid, despite the fact that Dr. Tapia had not granted his permission. The food in Fuenfría was bad, and de la Parra was losing weight. "We decided Lydia will go to Madrid on Saturday. After lunch, reading but did not write urgent letters I planned to write. Long conversation with Lydia about the 31st. I'm happy to have cleared things up, she has to concede that I am right and she says so although she contradicts me later. We went down to eat badly as usual.." After lunch she continued to read Gil Fortou's Venezuelan history. "It's about Páez's presidency and then Dr. Vargas. His personality. All honor and no combativeness, apolitical, the times of the demagogues begins."

Thursday's entry mentions an uncomfortable night following a pneumo the previous Tuesday. Needing to get ready for the trip, she felt very tired at the least exertion and defenseless. The priest came to say goodbye, saying "If I've been lacking or I've done something wrong, I beg you to forgive me." Dr. González arrived, studied her X-ray and affirmed that she could not hope for more for progress.

On Sunday January 12 she woke up early and in a good mood. She looked over Renan's *Life of Jesus,* went for a walk on a beautiful, sunny day." I return with same appetite and good mood of days before. Lunch with Lydia and Luz. Then I make the mistake of staying to chat. Discussion about my regimen, places where I should not live, the mistakes of last summer, etc. All the series of observations that get on my nerves. Deductions... Result: disagreeable loneliness, evocations, memories and proof of things that leave me in an unpleasant state all afternoon, that is, for six hours. I try to read, Renan, Morand, Cervantes' "La Gitanilla" and I can't follow the reading. The little maid who makes a good impression on me comes and I hire her for ten *duros.* Her name is Vicenta. I finish the afternoon feeling bored. A phone conversation with Reyes about news from Venezuela puts me in a good mood."

The following day, Monday 13, contemplating the news from Venezuela made her think of the events taking place in her homeland. "If the government of Venezuela establishes itself in a legal and proper way I would be enchanted even though it would personally hurt my pension. My lungs are better since yesterday and also my stomach. A livelier state makes it boring to stay in bed, furthermore the splendid sunny days call to me a more active life: thinking of travel and an infinite desire to return to Venezuela. I believe the circumstances make me remember in an irritating way (almost phobic) what they tell me is disagreeable and remove deductions that excite me and disturb my peace. I insist on doing Coué as a way to destroy those bad states of the soul. They damage me in every possible way. I must check, guard myself against influences that are bad for me, make a plan and follow through with firmness in order to forget; so that nothing intrudes not an iota of rancor to trouble my solitude and inner life like it did yesterday. Keep my mind clear for reading, dreaming, planning, writing, all inner actions so important as to not bore myself with immobility."

On Tuesday 14, she wrote from the rented house in Madrid, on Mario Roso de Luna, 28. She was continuing with her practice of Coué and reviewing her notes before on the history of Spanish Literature, including the Arcipreste de Hita, Ayala, and Don Juan Manuel Lydia had left on a trip and she was sad. "I think of the mutual relation that I wish for, of a profound and tender friendship: little disagreements come between each other's points of view."

Her friend returned on Saturday, January 18. "After I wake up, Coué, breakfast, etc. I begin taking notes as usual and the maid interrupts me about her bills and the idea of the disorder makes me impatient and it's not what Carmen offered after making arrangements for the furniture, and I am indignant. I don't write the urgent letters I need to write. I can't read even though I have two interesting books: *The Life of Jesus* and *Mazarino* by Bailly. The radio (that had nothing on it) distracted me after the meal. Lydia arrives and we listen to *Madame Butterfly*, and as usually happens when I listen to opera with interest, I can't fall asleep. I fall asleep at two after taking Nuvinase and barely reading a few pages. I feel stupefied…"

Her temperature was almost normal that Tuesday 21, but the living conditions in Madrid were taking their toll on her spirit and she was left wondering how she would live out the rest of her days in that house. "I get up to bathe and distract myself in the kitchen watching the preparation of lunch, which turns out to be excellent. Rain and strong winds continue. After lunch I remind myself to read the *Nouvelles Littéraires*. I'm receptive, especially to poetry, which is good for me spiritually. Until now I've been reading badly without attention, with my spirit filled with thoughts and preoccupations mired in the most regrettable reality. I understand to what point the winged part of the soul can atrophy when you have to fight with the people living with you; if in addition to concerns about meals and shopping one adds children, then it goes without saying! I think a while about the happiness of hedonism and the epicurean ideal that I can enjoy during the remainder of my life above all if circumstance permit: I feel bad among people and have a sense of well-being with independence and solitude. I spend the rest of the day conversing with Lydia and I sleep soundly after eating."

Two days later, Thursday 23, she was overcome with fatigue and sleepiness. She fell into bed wondering what would become of her if circumstances would let her lead a normal life. "This crisis of endless fatigue in which I can't carry myself around, or even lift my arms is alarming. " A bronchial asthma attack that lasted several hours the next morning. Her room is cold and damp and leaky. The work on her notes is interrupted when Lydia arrives and they chat. The bookshelves in the library are badly constructed, and she can't arrange her books. "I understand the informality and negligence of the workers here, it reminds me of Caracas." After a good lunch with Lydia and a siesta, she tidied up the house and arranged books. Lydia worked all afternoon writing her book on ethnology. "The Ballesteros arrive after seven. I 'm sorry I greet them with coldly and that's on account of Lydia's influence. They are, however, the kind of people I should deal with, I believe they can do me great spiritual good since besides the great historical knowledge they possess, especially his, and their corresponding serenity of judgment make them kindred spirits. It's been a while since I've lived with a healthy similar spirit more advanced that serves as a booster. This is the flower of friendship, the only way 'social' life can be agreeable."

She considered Saturday, 25 a morning well spent reviewing and studying her notes, and making a bibliography of what she read the last few months. The next day, however, she woke up sad and depressed. "Everything around me in this house seems strange and detached. I like to have the comfort of my furniture and objects. I'm sorry I didn't bring the mementos from Paris I like to look at, they were from Emilia, objects I was familiar with in her house, as though they were my own, that I've taken with me these past twelve years since her death, but the few things I brought are placed so I can't see them from my bed, nor the books. They went with me to Leysin. I also listened to the radio: the one here only lets me listen to the voice of the horrible speaker from Madrid. Banalities of every kind and infernal parasites![4] Fernando arrives at noon, after my bath. We go to Rosales and sit in a café. Splendid sunny day. It's fun to watch the people in their Sunday best, the gayness of the southern city, shoeshine boys, beggars, soldiers, nannies. We drink aperitifs and have our photos taken, memories of Jean-Les-Pins, car trips to Cannes with María, etc. That whole time overcomes me while Lydia and Fernando converse... I think about the past ten years, four of which I've been sick and that is to say living outside the world. Waleffe sent me a romantic postcard telling me that he'll never forget me. It's now the third time he's written to me in this tone. Was his passion of '28 a sure thing and is this a renewal of it he's yielding to? Reading newspapers and *Mazarino*."

Letters from her sister María arrive from Caracas on Monday 27. "She tells me things are falling apart. Every day confirms that the foremen tricked poor Emilia, who was aware of the excessive cost, more than she should have paid an expensive architect, but she died thinking she was leaving me well-built houses and rents for the rest of my life... Siesta. Lydia goes out with Fernando and returns with my books: *Gallegan Anthology* (I scan it and the harmonious and graceful language charms me); *The Chronicle of Peter the Cruel* by Canciller de Ayala; *Oraculo Manual* by Gracían, and a critical work about modern Spanish poetry. I continue to take however, since I have a headache and am afraid of catching a cold, colifedrina and take other precautions."

Tuesday 28: "I sleep late (until 8:00) and wake up without appetite. After taking notes I feel a terrible neurasthenia, bored with everything that surrounds me, and with strained eyesight. I go to Lydia's room and chat with her until Fernando arrives. He makes *picadillo criollo*. We lunch badly enough. Siesta. I hardly read. Luz arrives. Charming and loving, but lacking in character. Hispanic-American pseudo-intellectual. She is the founder of magazines, clubs, etc. full of sentimental initiatives that have nothing to do with culture. Nevertheless, I'm cordial, I want to be useful, be charming, etc. It's that kind exuberant pretentiousness so typical of America. Invitation to Gabriela.[5] After eating still feel neurasthenia, everything oppresses me, the bad weather, the ugly furniture, the lack of daily freedom, the presence of F. for the rest of the time we are in Madrid, conflict with arrival of mother and María, will they fit in the house, etc. etc. I'm back with the feeling of neurasthenia like this morning. Since I feel this way I decide to occupy myself with manual tasks rather than in simple readings: revising letters, for example. It's been a while since I was subconsciously motivated perhaps through auto suggestion I feel the need to carry out initiatives and steady emotions."

On Wednesday 29 she followed through with her suggestion to write letters to her to her mother and sister María. She read a Kipling short story and something from *Nouvelles Litteraires*. Lydia was writing a newspaper article about life in Leysin. "I'm astonished at the speed with which she writes. She could easily write for a newspaper." After dinner, she and Lydia chatted until late.

She read newspapers from Caracas on Friday, 31. There is news about the days following General Gómez's death. "They give me a sad impression of the press and of false public spirit. The onlymotivation for the writers was a spirit of association found in all professions and guilds to form a public opinion that opposed whatever tyranny and that interests me. Although tone of flattery continues for Lopez Contreras. Neither do I like those associated with the initiative, those "individuals" whose life is not at all clean, those who could never be "English liberals" like the first rulers of the Republic. They are either servile flatterers or instruments of tyranny. Like always. I spend the rest of the day chatting with Lydia, who has not gone out. Story in the *Journal*: waiting for a date in Paris in the spring and it brings me memories and nostalgia for my active life, the special spell of Paris in the lovely days of my youth which is moving further and further away like an ocean that is crossing this illness. In my conversations with Lydia I continue to dwell on the years past , we talk of fond memories and sharing similar things. She leaves my room late."

On February 1, she read the article Lydia wrote about Terwagne in *Social* from Havana. "Her treatment of Leysin makes a good impression on me. I feel the passing of those two years, above all the months at the Grand Hotel like a dream full of enchantment and poetic possibilities. I think about the possibility of a book I so much want to write and I suddenly feel as though it lives within me, a sensation that fills me with the pleasure I felt when I was living with the characters in *Ifigenia* and *M. de Mama Blanca*. How happy it would be to return to that atmosphere of the soul bursting with creativity like a tree in spring!

The books from the library arrive. I think about the bibliography I want to create about chroniclers and other Americanists. To search in Baudini and notes for a book, especially Ballesteros and Chacon. It's necessary to orient the reading towards a fixed end, specialize in something, really and truly possess it and then with initiative, activity, perseverance. All these conditions are wiped out if you don't have a fixed plan. This disorder undoes the plan, above all for slow and ordered spirits like mine. Between the ugly furniture, the stained mosaic, Raty the cat's piss that dirties everything, the kitchen smells, etc. this house is the opposite of what I like, what my spirit, so sensitive to order, to comfort, to the fixed and beautiful needs. Sleepless night. I take advantage of this to listen to the radio."

Sunday 2 was a sunny, breezy day and de la Parra found it impossible to go out on account of the wind and bad weather. The ephedrine she was taking made her sleepy, tired and she complains of neurasthenia. Luz is visiting. "I feel even more bored, detached from what they are talking about, hostile. I analyze this feeling and find its causes. I would never like to have these feelings of not fitting in that sours the spirit. I suffer from feeling hemmed in, claustrophobic. I think that if I lived in a pleasant house with no one to bother me I would feel like when I lived in Leysin: serenity and the gift of being able to write outside of time. I'm up until two and sleep after taking Neurinase. Readings: Funck on Luther. Brentano and Isabel the Catholic by M. Also the pamphlet "Criticism" by Chacón that I find interesting. The only thing pleasant that happened today was to catalog the books I received from Paris."

The last entry in the diary is on Tuesday 4."Morning as usual. Coué. Taking notes, etc. I write to Comptair, Bendelac[6], the bank in Madrid, arrange papers. I notice that working seated in front of the desk instead of lying in bed makes me feel better spiritually. I eat a good lunch. Siesta. Read magazines. Long boring afternoon. Neurasthenia. Carmen Peruse comes and distracts me with kitchen expenses. Lydia arrives. I feel better and take a walk. On the other hand I feel an extreme weakness (a feeling I often have). I don't know what to attribute it to: it's as though I am being made weak by a great illness. I think I'm living an unhealthy life due to being shut in and the lack of fresh air: maybe there is carbon monoxide gas escaping from the kitchen, since all of us have headaches in the afternoon. It would be funny if this repeats what happened on Atelier Junot, at the beginning of my illness."

Afterword

Teresa de la Parra died in Madrid a few months later on April 23, 1936. She was originally buried in the cemetery in Almudena, Madrid. In 1947 her remains were brought to Caracas, to the Cementerio General del Sur, in the Parra-Sanojo family crypt. More than forty years later, in 1989, her remains were brought to their final resting place at the National Pantheon in Caracas in celebration of the centennial of her birth.

Notes

[1] All translations of the diary entries are mine and are taken from *Obra: (Narrativa, ensayos, cartas)*. Ed.Velia Bosch. Caracas: Biblioteca Ayacucho, 1991. 447-471.
[2] Alexandra David Néel (1868-1969) was a Belgian-French explorer, anarchist, spiritualist and Buddhist writer who traveled to Tibet in 1924 and in 1927 published *Voyage d'un Parissiene à Lhasa.*
[3] James. J. Walker was the flamboyant and fun-loving mayor of New York (1926-1932).
[4] The situation she describes is the political turmoil leading up to the Spanish Civil War. The war started a few months later, in July of 1936 and lasted until April of 1939.
[5] De la Parra was friends with Chilean poet Gabriela Mistral. In 1945 Mistral's emotional and inspiring Latin American poetry won the Nobel Prize in Literature.
[6] I.H. Bendelac published the second edition of *Ifigenia* in 1928. This edition included revisions and corrections by de la Parra.

BIBLIOGRAPHY

Acker, Bertie." Ifigenia: Teresa de la Parra's Social Protest." *Letras Femeninas* 14.1-2 (1988): 73-74. Print.

Aizenburg, Edna. "El *Bildungsroman* fracasado en Latinoamérica: el caso de *Ifigenia* de Teresa de la Parra." *Revista Iberoamericana* 51. 132-33 (1985): 539-46. Print.

Alvarado, Lisandro. "Una opinión sobre Ifigenia." *Teresa de la Parra ante la crítica.* ed.Velia Bosch, Monte Ávila Editores, 1985. Print.

Arias, Augusto. *Tres Ensayos.* Quito: Publicaciones del Instituto Eucuatoriano-Venezolano de la Cultura, 1941. Print.

Balza, José. "Sequential Narrations." 151-161- *Mama Blanca's Memoirs.* Trans. Harriet de Onís. Pittsburgh: University of Pittsburgh Press, 1993. Print.

Beard, Laura J. *Acts of Narrative Resistance: Women's Autobiographical Writings in the Americas.* Charlottesville: University of Virginia Press, 2009. Print.

Bohórquez, Douglas. *Teresa de la Parra: Del diálago de géneros y la melancolía.* Caracas: Monte Ávila Editores, 1997. Print.

Bosch, Velia. "Mama Blanca's Memoirs and the Author Remembered." *Mama Blanca's Memoirs.* Trans. Harriet de Onís .Pittsburgh: University of Pittsburgh Press, 1993. 127-135. Print.

—. *Esta pobre lengua viva: relectura de la obra de Teresa de la Parra: a medio siglo de la Memorias de Mama Blanca.* Caracas: Ediciones de la Presidencia de la Republica, 1979. Print.

—. *Teresa de la Parra ante la critica.* Caracas: Monte Avila Editores. 1980.

—. *Iconografía. Teresa de la Parra. Investigación, recopilación, y cronología.* Caracas: Biblioteca Ayacucho, 1984,

Byron, Christine. "Books and Bad Company": Reading the Female Plot in Teresa de la Parra's *Ifigenia.*" *Modern Language Quarterly* 64:3, September 2003. 349-79. Print.

Ching, Erik, et al. *Reframing Latin America.* Austin: U of Texas Press, 2007. Print.

Caula, Ana María. "Teresa de la Parra." *Latin American Women Writers: An Encyclopedia.* Ed. André, María Claudia and Eva Paulina Bueno. New York: Routledge, 2007. Print.

Díaz Sánchez, Ramón. *Teresa de la Parra: Clave para una interpretación.* Caracas: Ediciones Garrido, 1954. Print.

—. *Tres conferencias inéditas.* Caracas: Ediciones Garrido. 1961.

Díaz Seijas, Pedro. "La Intimidad femenina en Ifigenia." *Teresa de la Parra ante la crítica.* Ed. Velia Bosch, Monte Ávila Editores, 1985. Print.

Dimo, Edith and Amarilis Hidalgo de Jesús, eds. *Escritura y desafío: narradoras venezolanas del siglo XX.* Caracas: Monte Avila Editores, 1995. Print.

Febres, Laura. *Cinco perspectivas críticas sobre la obra de Teresa de la Parra.* Caracas: Editorial Arte, 1984. Print.

—. *Perspectivas críticas sobre la obra de Teresa de la Parra. Fundación Consorcio Cordillera* -"El lenguaje secularizado en el final de Ifigenia" Eidos, Vol. 3, no 1 Caracas 1988, p. 81-84. Print.

Ferris, Suzanne and Mallory Young. *Chick Lit: The New Woman's Fiction.* New York, Routledge, 2006. Print.

Fombona, Julieta. "Teresa de la Parra: las voces de la palabra" *Teresa de la Parra, Obra.* Caracas: Biblioteca Ayacucho, 1982. Pp ix-xxvi. Print.

Fox-Lockert, Lucía. *Women Novelists in Spain and Spanish America.* Metuchen: The Scarecrow Press, Inc. 1979.

Fuenmayor Ruiz, Victor. *El Inmenso llamado: las voces en la escritura de Teresa de la Parra.* Caracas, Universidad Central, 1974. Print.

Galovic Norris, Nélida. *Valoración literaria y semblanza biográfica.* Westminster:Instituto Literario y Cultural Hispánico. 2004. Print.

García Prada, Carlos. *Obras Completas de Teresa de la Parra.* Caracas: Editorial Arte

Gamberini, Elsa Crier. "The Male Critic and the Woman Writer: Reading Teresa de la Parra's Critics." *The Feminine Mode: Essays on Hispanic Women Writers.* Ed. Noël Valis and Carol Maier. Lewisburg: Bucknell University Press, 1990. Print.

Garrels, Elizabeth. *Las Grietas de la ternura: nueva relectura de Teresa de la Parra.* Caracas: Monte Ávila, 1986. Print.

—. "Piedra Azul, or the Colonial Paradise of Women" *Mama Blanca's Memoirs.* Trans. Harriet de Onís. Pittsburgh: University of Pittsburgh Press, 1993. 136-150. Print.

—. *Ifigenia. Diario de una señorita que escribió porque se fastidiaba.* Doral: Stockcero, 2008. Print.

Gollnick, Brian. "Approaches to Latin American Literature." *A Companion to Latin American Studies.* Philip Swanson, Ed. Arnold Publishers. 105-21. 2003. Print.

González, Anibal. *Killer Books*. Austin: University of Texas Press, 2001. Print.

González, Patricia Elena y Eliana Ortega. *La sartén por el mango: encuentro de escritoras latinonamericas*. Rio Piedras, Ediciones Huracán, 1984. Print.

Gordon Stillman, Ronni. "Teresa de la Parra Venezuelan Novelist and Feminist" *Latin American Women Writers*. Ed. Yvette E. Miller and Charles M. Tatum. *Latin American Literary Review*, 1977.pp.42-48.

Hidalgo de Jesús, Amarilis. *La novela moderna en Venezuela*. New York: Peter Lang, 1995. Print.

Hiriart, Rosario. *Más cerca de Teresa de la Parra: Diálogos con Lydia Cabrera*. Monte Ávila Editores, 1983. Print.

—. *Cartas a Lydia Cabrera*. Madrid: Ediciones Torremozas. 1988. Print.

Horne, Luz. "La Interrupción de un banquete de hombres solos: una lectura de Teresa de la Parra como contracanon del ensayo latinoamericano." *Revista de Crítica Literaria Latinoamericana*. XXXI, no 6 Lima-Hanover, 2005 pp,7-23. Print.

Ibieta, Gabriela, "Teresa de la Parra." *Spanish American Women Writers*: *A Bio-Bibliographical Source Book.* Ed. Martig, Diane E. New York: Greenwood Press, 1990. 415-26. Print.

Jara, René, and Hernán Vidal, Eds. *Testimonio y Literatura*. Minneapolis: Institute for the Study of Ideologies and Literature, 1986. Print

Jehenson, Myriam Yvonne. *Latin American Women Writers: Class, Race, and Gender*. Albany: State University of New York Press, 1995. Print.

Jones Hampton. *" Iphigenia* (The Diary of a Young Lady Who Wrote Because She Was Bored." *Belles Lettres: A Review of Books by Women*. Fall 1994 v.10 no.1 p.79.

Krieger Gamberini, Elsa. "The Male Critic and the Woman Writer: Reading Teresa de la Parra's Critics." *In the Feminine Mode: Essays on Hispanic Women Writers*. Ed. Noël Valis and Carol Maeir. Lewisburg:Bucknell University Press, 1990. Print.

Lemaître, Louis Antoine. *Between Flight and Longing: The Journey of Teresa de la Parra*. New York: Vantage Press, 1986. Print.

—. *Mujer Ingeniosa: Vida de Teresa de la Parra*. Madrid: Editorial la Muralla, 1987. Print.

Llebot, Amaya. '*Ifigenia'*: *caso único en la literatura nacional*. Caracas: Colección Avance, 1974. Print.

Lindstrom, Naomi. "Woman between Paris and Caracas: *Iphigenia* by Teresa de la Parra." Ed. Anne Lambright and Elisabeth Guerrero. *Unfolding the City: Women Write the City in Latin America*. *Minneapolis*: U of Minneapolis Press, 2007. 231-50. Print.

—. *Twentieth Century Spanish American Fiction*. Austin: University of
Texas Press, 1994. Print.

Liscano, Juan. "Testimony." *Mama Blanca's Memoirs*. Trans. Harriet de
Onís. Pittsburgh: University of Pittsburgh Press. 1993. 119-126. Print.

Marinone, Mónica. "Notas sobre Teresa de la Parra y su lectura de la
Conquista." *Celehis revista del Centro de Letras Hispanoamericanas*.
vol. 2 no. 2. Mar de Plata, 1992. 75-83.Print.

Martig, Diane. *Spanish American Women Writers: A Bio-Bibliographical
Source Book*. New York: Greenwood Press, 1990. Print.

Martin, Emilie Claire. "*Ifigenia* y el language de la moda." *Escritoria y
desafió: narradoras venezolanas del siglo XX*. Ed. Dimo, Edith and
Amarilis Hidalgo de Jesús. Caracas: Monte Avila Editores, 1995. Print.

Masiello, Francine. "Texto, ley, transgresión: especulación sobre las
novela (feminista) de vanguardia." *Revista Iiberoamericana*. (July-Dec
1985) 807-822. Print.

Mattalía, Sonia. *Máscaras suele vestir: Pasíon y revuelta: escrituras de
mujeres en América Latina*. Madrid: Vervuet Iberoamerica, 2003.
Print.

Molloy, Sylvia. "Disappearing Acts: Reading Lesbian in Teresa de la
Parra." *¿Entiendes? Queer Readings, Hispanic Writings*. Ed.
Bergmann, Emile and Paul Smith. Durham: Duke University Press,
1995. 231-256. Print.

Moya-Raggio, Eliana. "El Sacrificio de Iphigenia: Teresa de la Parra y su
vision." LaTorre: Revista *de la Universidad de Puerto Rico*, 2:5 (1988)
161-171. Print.

Mueller, RoseAnna. "Ifigenia no soy yo: Teresa de la Parra y el discurso
femenino" *XXIX Simposio de docentes e investigadores de la literatura
venezolana*, Tomo II. pp. 453-460. Print.

—. "Iván Feo's *Ifigenia*: Adaptating Teresa de la Parra's *Ifigenia* for
Film," *Hispanet* , vol 3,2010.

—. "Tales from the House of Smiles: Teresa de la Parra's *Mama Blanca's
Memoirs*," *Acta Issyensia Comparationis* 7, 2010.

"María Eugenia Alonso: The Modern Iphigenia Sacrified to Society," The
Woman in Latin American and Spanish Literature:Essays on Iconic
Characters. pp. 60-73. McFarland .2012. Print.

"Casting About: Self-Fashioning and Parody in Teresa de la Parra's
Iphigenia," Cambridge Scholars. In press. Print.

Mullaney, Janet Palmer. *Belles Lettres: A Review of Books by Women*.
Vol. 10. Fall, 1994. Print.

Palacios, Maria Fernanda. *Ifigenia: Mitología de la Doncella Criolla*.
Caracas: Fondo Editorial Angria Ediciones, 2001. Print.

—. *Teresa de la Parra*. Caracas: Editorial Arte. 2005. Print.

Palma, Angélica. "La novela de una venezolana: *Ifigenia*, por Teresa de la Parra."*Epistolario íntimo*. Caracas: Ediciones Línea Aeropostal venezolana, 1953.pp. 202-206. Print.

Pantin, Yolanda and Ana Teresa Torres. *El hilo de la voz: antología crítica de escritoras venezolanas del siglo XX*. Caracas: Fundación Polar, 2003. Print.

Parra, Teresa de la. *Iphigenia: The diary of a young lady who wrote because she was bored*. trans. Bertie Acker. Austin: University of Texas Press, 1993. Print.

—. *Obra: (narrativa, ensayos, cartas)*. Ed. Velia Bosch. Caracas: Biblioteca Ayacucho, 1991. Print.

—. *Ifigenia*, ed. Sonia Mattalía. Madrid: Grupo Anaya, 1992. Print.

—. *Las Memorias de Mamá Blanca*. Ed. Carlos García Prada and Clotilde M. Wilson. New York: The Macmillan Company, 1932. Print.

—. *Mama Blanca's Memoirs*. Trans. Harriet de Onis. Pittsburgh: University of Pittsburgh Press, 1993. Print.

—. *Epistolario íntimo*. Caracas: Linea Aeropostal Venezuelan, 1953. Print.

—. *Ifigenia*. ed. Elizabeth Garrels. Doral: Stockcero, 2008. Print.

—. *Obras Completas*. Ed. Carlos García Prada. Editorial Arte. Caracas, Venezuela, 1982. Print.

Picón Salas, Mariano. *Estudios de literatura venezolana*. Madrid: Ediciones Edime, 1961. Print.

—. *Cartas a Lydia Cabrera*. Madrid: Editorial Cruz del Sur, 1988. Print.

—. *Formación y proceso de la literatura venezolana.*Caracas: Monte Avila Editores. 1984. Print.

Pietri, Arturo Uslar, Ed. *Tres conferencias inéditas*, Caracas, 1961. Print.

Pratt, Annis. *Archetypal Patterns in Women's Fiction*. Bloomington: Indiana University Press, 1981. Print.

Reynolds, Guy. *Twentieth Century American Women's Fiction: A Critical Introduction*. New York: St. Martin's Press, 1999. Print.

Rivera, Francisco. *Teresa de la Parra e Ifigenia*. 4th ed. Caracas, Monte Ávila Editores, 1996. Print.

Rodríguez, Ileana. *House/Garden/Nation: Space, Gender and Ethnicity in Postcolonial Latin American Literatures by Women*. Durham: Duke University Press, 1994. Print.

Rosa, Richard and Doris Meyer. "Teresa de la Parra: America's Womanly Soul." *Reinterpreting the Spanish American Essay: Woman Writers of the 19th and 20th Centuries*. Ed. Doris Meyer. Austin: U of Texas Press. 1995. 115-24. Print.

Russ, Elizabeth. "Intersections of Race and Romance in the Americas: Teresa de la Parra's *Ifigenia* and Ellen Glasgow's *The Sheltered Life*." *Mississippi Quarterly: The Journal of Southern Cultures* 58.3-4 (2005): 737-759. Print.

—. Disordering History, Denying Politics: Performative Strategies in Teresa de la Parra's Influencia de la mujer en la formación del alma americana. *Latin American Literary Review*. 34.67 pp.161-69. Print.

Salamone, Alicia N. and Natalia Cisternas. "Identidades femeninas y rescritura de la historia en los ensayos de Teresa de la Parra." Santiago: *Revista Universum*. No 17. Universidad de Talca, 2002. 219-232. Print.

Salamone, Alicia N., Gilda Luongo, Natalia Cisternas, Darcie Doll and Graciela Quierolo. *Modernidad en otro tono: Escritura de mujeres latinoamericanas: 1920-1950*. Santiago: Universidad de Chile, 2004. Print.

Soang Wang, Lih-Lirng. *Power, Language and Culture: Teresa de la Parra in Latin American Feminism*. Diss. Urbana. 1995. Print.

Sommer, Doris. *Foundational Fictions: The National Romances of Latin America*. Berkeley: University of California Press, 1991. Print.

—. "It's Wrong to be Right:" Mama Blanca on Writing Like a Woman." *Mama Blanca's Memoirs*. Trans. Harriet de Onís. Pittsburgh: University of Pittsburgh Press, 1993. xvi-xxvii Print.

Stillman, Ronni Gordon. "Teresa de la Parra, Venezuelan Novelist and Feminist." *Latin American Women Writers: Yesterday and Today*. Eds. Yvette E. Miller and Charles Tatum. Washington, D.C. *Latin American Literary Review,* 1977. 42-47. Print.

Swanson, Philip, Ed. *The Companion to Latin American Studies*. Ed. New York: Oxford U Press, 2003. Print.

Truneau Castillo, Valentina. "Confesión de rebeldía y sacrificio: Notas sobre *Ifigenia*, de Teresa de la Parra." *Anales de Literatura Hispanoamericana*, 2005, 34. pp 125-139.

Unruh, Vicky. *Performing Women and Literary Culture in Latin America*. Austin: University of Texas Press, 2006. Print.

Uslar Pietri, Arturo. "El testimonio de Teresa de la Parra."*Obras Selectas*. Madrid: Ediciones Edime, 1953.

Viezzer, Moema. *Si me permiten hablar... Testimonio de Domitila, una mujer de las minas de Bolivia*. Colombia: Siglo XXI, 1977. Print.

Williams, Raymond Leslie. *The Twentieth-Century Spanish American Novel*. Austin: U Texas Press, 2003. Print.